VIRGINIA
GLENCOE
MATH

AUTHORS
Carter • Cuevas • Day • Malloy
Kersaint • Reynosa • Silbey • Vielhaber

Mc
Graw
Hill
Education

mheducation.com/prek-12

Send all inquiries to:
McGraw-Hill Education
8787 Orion Place
Columbus, OH 43240

ISBN: 978-0-07-906616-9
MHID: 0-07-906616-X

Printed in the United States of America.

3 4 5 6 7 QVS 22 21 20 19 18

CONTENTS IN BRIEF

Units organized by domain

Glencoe Math is organized into units based on groups of related standards called domains.
MP Mathematical Process Goals are embedded throughout the course.

MATHEMATICAL
PROCESS GOALS
HANDBOOK

Tetra Images/Getty Images

MP Mathematical Process Goals

Mathematical Process Goals Handbook

Richard Drury/Photodisc/Getty Images

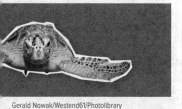

Gerald Nowak/Westend61/Photolibrary

Jill Braaten/McGraw-Hill Education

©Photo by Scott Bauer/USDA

Back in the Pack dog portraits/Flickr/Getty Images

Everything you need,

anytime, anywhere.

With ConnectED, you have instant access to all of your study materials—anytime, anywhere. From homework materials to study guides—it's all in one place and just a click away. ConnectED even allows you to collaborate with your classmates and use mobile apps to make studying easy.

Resources built for you—available 24/7:

- Your eBook available wherever you are
- Personal Tutors and Self-Check Quizzes to help your learning
- An Online Calendar with all of your due dates
- eFlashcard App to make studying easy
- A message center to stay in touch

Go Mobile!

Visit mheonline.com/apps to get entertainment, instruction, and education on the go with ConnectED Mobile and our other apps available for your device.

Go Online!

connectED.mcgraw-hill.com

your Username

your Password

Vocab

Learn about new vocabulary words.

Watch

Watch animations and videos.

Tutor

See and hear a teacher explain how to solve problems.

Tools

Explore concepts with virtual manipulatives.

Sketchpad

Discover concepts using The Geometer's Sketchpad®.

Check

Check your progress.

eHelp

Get targeted homework help.

Worksheets

Access practice worksheets.

Chapter 1
Ratios and Proportional Reasoning

Essential Question

HOW can you show that two objects are proportional?

p. 43

Chapter 2
Percents

Essential Question

HOW can percent help you understand situations involving money?

Real World
p. 119

Chapter 3
Rational Numbers

> **ℯ Essential Question**
>
> WHAT happens when you add, subtract, multiply, and divide fractions?

Real World
p. 251

Chapter 4
Expressions

Real World
p. 351

Essential Question

HOW can you use numbers and symbols to represent mathematical ideas?

Chapter 5
Equations and Inequalities

 Essential Question

WHAT does it mean to say two quantities are equal or that they have a linear relationship?

p. 389

x

Chapter 6
Measure Figures

Essential Question

HOW do measurements help you describe real-world objects?

Real World p. 503

xi

Chapter 7
Probability

Q **Essential Question**

HOW can you predict the outcome of future events?

Real World
p. 627

Chapter 8
Statistics

Essential Question

HOW do you know which type of graph to use when displaying data?

p. 697

Mathematical Process Goals Handbook

Essential Question

WHAT processes help me explore and explain mathematics?

Mathematical Process Goals

Mathematical Process Goals will help you become a successful problem solver and to use math effectively in your daily life.

MP Throughout this handbook, you will learn about each of these mathematical process goals and how they are integrated in the chapters and lessons of this book.

① **Focus on Mathematical Process Goals**
Mathematical Problem Solving

② **Focus on Mathematical Process Goals**
Mathematical Communication

③ **Focus on Mathematical Process Goals**
Mathematical Reasoning

④ **Focus on Mathematical Process Goals**
Mathematical Connections

⑤ **Focus on Mathematical Process Goals**
Mathematical Representations

Place a checkmark below the face that expresses how much you know about each Mathematical Process Goal. Then explain in your own words what it means to you.

☹ I have no clue.   😐 I've heard of it.   🙂 I know it!

Mathematical Process Goals

Mathematical Process Goal	☹	😐	🙂	What it Means to Me
①				
②				
③				
④				
⑤				

Persevere with Problems

What does it mean to persevere in solving problems?

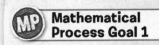

MP Mathematical Process Goal 1

Mathematical Problem Solving

Look up the word "persevere" in a dictionary. You might see "be persistent" or "follow something through to the end." When you persevere in solving math problems, you don't always stop at the first answer you get. You check if your solution is accurate, if it answers the problem, and if it makes sense!

Jared wants to paint his room. The dimensions of the room are 12 feet by 15 feet, and the walls are 9 feet tall. There are two windows, each with dimensions 6 feet by 5 feet. There are two doors, each with dimensions 30 inches by 6 feet. If a gallon of paint covers about 350 square feet, how many gallons of paint will he need to put two coats of paint on the wall?

1. **Understand** That's a lot of information! Go back and read the problem again. This time, circle the information given and underline what you are trying to find.

2. **Plan** Before you do ANY calculations, make a plan to solve the problem. List the steps you need to take.

   _____

   _____

   _____

3. **Solve** Apply your plan to solve the problem.

   Jared will need [ ] gallons of paint.

4. **Check** Is your solution accurate? Does it make sense? Explain.

   _____

   _____

   _____

5. Did you feel like giving up at any point while solving the problem? Explain.

   _____

   _____

It's Your Turn!

Solve each problem by using the four-step problem-solving model.

6. There are about 48,000 farms in Nebraska using approximately 45 million acres of land. This farmland covers about $\frac{9}{10}$ of the state. About how many acres are not made up of farmland?

Understand (Circle) the information you know and underline what you are trying to determine. Is there any information you will not use?

_____

Plan What strategy will you use to solve this problem?

_____

Solve Solve the problem. What is the solution?

_____

Check Does your answer make sense? Can you solve the problem another way to check your work?

_____

7. You and a friend went to the movies. You bought a student ticket and a drink. You split the cost of popcorn and a candy. You have $4.75 left. How much did you take with you? Show your steps below. Check your solution.

Student	$9	Popcorn	$6.50
Adult	$12	Candy	$5
Senior	$10	Drink	$4.50

_____

_____

_____

ⓕind it in Your Book!

MP **Persevere with Problems**

Look in Chapter 1. Provide an example of where Mathematical Process Goal 1 is used. Explain why your example represents this process.

_____

_____

_____

What does it mean to communicate precisely?

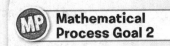

MP Mathematical Process Goal 2

Mathematical Communication

Communicating precisely is not just about giving the right answer. It also includes using terms, units, symbols, ideas, and procedures appropriately when discussing or solving problems.

Marlon drives his scooter to soccer practice every day. Each week, his scooter uses a quarter of a tank of gas. The practice field is 3 miles from his house and the gas tank holds 2.4 gallons of gas. He wants to find the unit rate per gallon of gas. Pair up with a classmate to discuss and answer the following.

1. In your own words, write the definitions for *ratio, equivalent ratio, bar diagram,* and *unit rate.*

_____

_____

_____

_____

2. How do the words from Exercise 1 relate to the problem?

_____

_____

_____

3. Discuss with your partner the steps you will use to solve this problem. Summarize your discussion, and then solve the problem.

_____

_____

_____

_____

4. What units of measure will describe the unit rate per gallon of gas?

_____

5. What is the unit rate per gallon for Marlon's scooter?

_____

Solve each problem.

The state of Colorado is shaped like a rectangle as shown in the map. The rate $\frac{1 \text{ cm}}{100 \text{ km}}$ can be used to find actual distances.

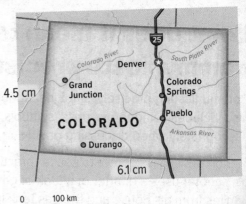

1 cm: 100 km

6. Use equivalent rates to find the actual distance x.

a. $\frac{4.5 \text{ cm}}{x}$

b. $\frac{6.1 \text{ cm}}{x}$

7. What is the perimeter of the state on the map? the actual perimeter?

8. Claire is in charge of the 7th grade picnic and needs to order the food for the 90 students attending. She surveys a sample population of 18 students. Ten students chose hamburgers, 7 chose hot dogs, and 1 chose a veggie burger.

a. Make a conjecture about how many students at the picnic will choose each type of food.

b. Discuss with a partner if these numbers are exact or estimates. Then determine what problems Claire may have by using those numbers.

Find it in Your Book!

MP **Attend to Precision**

Look in Chapter 1. Provide an example of where Mathematical Process Goal 2 is used. Explain why your example represents this process.

Reason Abstractly and Quantitatively

I need to double this recipe. How much flour do I need?

Suppose you want to double the ingredients from the recipe below. If you write an expression or an equation to figure out what you need, you are reasoning quantitatively. When you simplify the expression or solve the equation algebraically, you are reasoning abstractly.

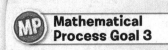

MP Mathematical Process Goal 3

Mathematical Reasoning

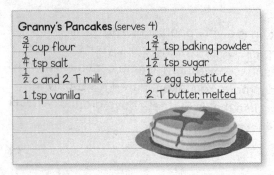

Granny's Pancakes (serves 4)

$\frac{3}{4}$ cup flour $1\frac{3}{4}$ tsp baking powder
$\frac{1}{4}$ tsp salt $1\frac{1}{2}$ tsp sugar
$\frac{1}{2}$ c and 2 T milk $\frac{1}{8}$ c egg substitute
1 tsp vanilla   2 T butter, melted

1. What skill(s) will you use to see how much of each ingredient you would use if you were to double the recipe?

_____

2. You planned for eight people to come for a pancake breakfast, but just found out that 10 people are coming! The recipe serves 4. Defne a variable and write an expression to determine the

   amount of each ingredient to serve 10 people. _____

_____

3. Use the expression from Exercise 2 to complete the recipe card so that it serves 10 people. Is it appropriate to round any of the ingredients? Explain.

_____

_____

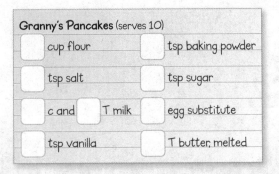

Granny's Pancakes (serves 10)

☐ cup flour   ☐ tsp baking powder

☐ tsp salt   ☐ tsp sugar

☐ c and ☐ T milk   ☐ egg substitute

☐ tsp vanilla   ☐ T butter, melted

It's Your Turn!

Reason abstractly or quantitatively to find a solution.

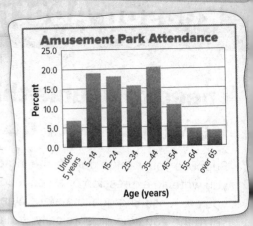

4. The graph shows the percent of people in different age groups that recently attended an amusement park. A total of 1.045 million people attended. How many of them were less than 25 years of age?

5. Cave exploration or spelunking is a very popular activity. Your family signs up for tours at a state park. On one of the tours, your brother is lowered 160 feet below the surface by rope. Then he continues another 70 feet below the surface to a room. You take the tree top tour where you climb to an adventure course that is 60 feet above ground. What is the difference between the elevations?

6. You and your family are traveling to a football game. You and your mother leave at 8:00 A.M. Your dad needs to wait for your sister to get home from dance practice, so he leaves at 9:30 A.M. If your mother drives at an average rate of 50 miles per hour, and your dad drives at an average rate of 65 miles per hour, when will he pass her? Suppose the game is 205 miles away. Who will get there first?

Find it in Your Book!

MP Reason Abstractly

Look in Chapter 1. Provide an example of where Process Goal 3 is used. Explain why your example represents this process.

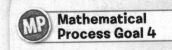
What is structure in mathematics?

Finding and making use of structure is important when solving problems. There is structure in writing and solving an equation or finding a pattern. We rely on being able to identify and use structure to sometimes find easier ways to solve problems.

MP Mathematical Process Goal 4

Mathematical Connections

At the Atlas Arcade, you can select a lunch combo from their new menu. First choose the type of sandwich. Then choose from a list of sides and a cookie.

Sandwich	Sides	Cookie
Chicken	Salad	Chocolate chip
Veggie	French fries	Oatmeal
Meatball	Onion rings	Raisin
	Soup	

1. Create a tree diagram or organized list that shows all of the possibilities for a veggie sandwich.

2. How many possible outcomes are there for a veggie sandwich?

3. How many total possibilities for all three types of sandwiches?

4. Can you think of another way to find the total number of outcomes?

5. Find a classmate that used a different method than you did and discuss the advantages and disadvantages of each method. Summarize your discussion.

Describe the method you would use to solve each of the following.
Then solve.

6. Haney's scores on his science tests were 76%, 93%, 87%, 91%, and 83%. Haney wants a 90% test average for the term. If all tests are weighted the same, is it possible for him to get a 90% test average if there is only one more test? Explain.

_____

_____

_____

7. You need to make a model of your bedroom for your art class. The scale is $\frac{3}{4}$-inch = 1 foot. What are the dimensions of your model?

_____

_____

_____

8. A rectangle has a length of 4 centimeters and a width of 3 centimeters. The length and width are each multiplied by a factor of 3. Is the ratio $\frac{\text{area of new rectangle}}{\text{area of original rectangle}}$ equivalent to the ratio $\frac{\text{side length of new rectangle}}{\text{side length of original rectangle}}$? If not, explain how they are related.

_____

_____

_____

Find it in Your Book!

MP **Make Use of Structure**

Look in Chapter 1. Provide an example of where Mathematical Process Goal 4 is used. Explain why your example represents this process.

_____

_____

_____

_____

Model with Mathematics

Are you a visual person or do you prefer to use words?

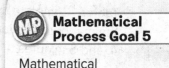

You might prefer to use diagrams or drawings when explaining ideas. Or you might prefer to use words. In math, we also use different ways to model the same idea. We can use words, graphs, tables, numbers, symbols, or diagrams.

1. Suppose you are selling T-shirts as a fundraiser for Key Club. The club makes a $6.30 profit for every T-shirt sold. Complete each model shown.

Words	Numbers	
_____ per T-shirt	**Profit ($)**	**Number of shirts**
	6.30	1
	12.60	
	18.90	

Symbols	Graph
Let p = profit t = number of T-shirts sold $p = \boxed{} \; t$	

All of these model the same relationship between profit and number of T-shirts sold, just in different ways.

2. Which relationship would you prefer to use to determine the profit if 100 T-shirts were sold? Explain.

_____

_____

_____

It's Your Turn!

Use the models shown to solve each problem.

3. A waterpark cycles about 24,000 gallons per minute through the local river.

a. Tables Complete the table to show the number of gallons used in 1, 2, 3, 4, and 5 minutes.

Time, x (minutes)	Gallons, y (thousand gallons)

b. Graph Graph the ordered pairs on the coordinate plane.

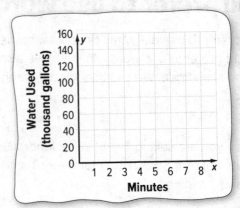

c. Symbols Write an equation to show the number of gallons of water y used in x minutes.

_____

4. Kitra is creating a treasure hunt for the school carnival. The scale on the map is 0.5 inch = 0.25 mile.

Map Length m (in.)	Distance d (mi)

a. Tables Complete the table to determine the actual distance for 0.5, 1, 1.5, 2, and 2.5 inches on the map.

b. Symbols Write an equation to determine the actual distance d for m inches on the map. _____

Find it in Your Book!

MP Model with Mathematics

Look in Chapter 5. Provide an example of where Mathematical Process Goal 5 is used. Explain why your example represents this process.

Use the Mathematical Process Goals

Solve.

The courtyard at Eastmoor Middle School is shaped like a rectangle that is 40.3 feet long. The width of the courtyard is 14.6 feet less than the length.

a. Draw and label a diagram of the school courtyard. What is the perimeter of the courtyard? _____

b. Student council wants to plant 14 trees so they are equally spaced around the courtyard. Draw a diagram showing where the trees should be planted. About how far apart are the trees? _____

Determine which mathematical process goals you used to determine the solution. Shade the circles that apply.

Which **Mathematical Process Goals** did you use? Shade the circle(s) that applies.

① Mathematical Problem Solving
② Mathematical Communication
③ Mathematical Reasoning
④ Mathematical Connections
⑤ Mathematical Representations

Reflect

Use what you learned about the mathematical process goals to complete the graphic organizer. Write two different processes that you use for each category. Then describe how each process helps you explore and explain mathematics.

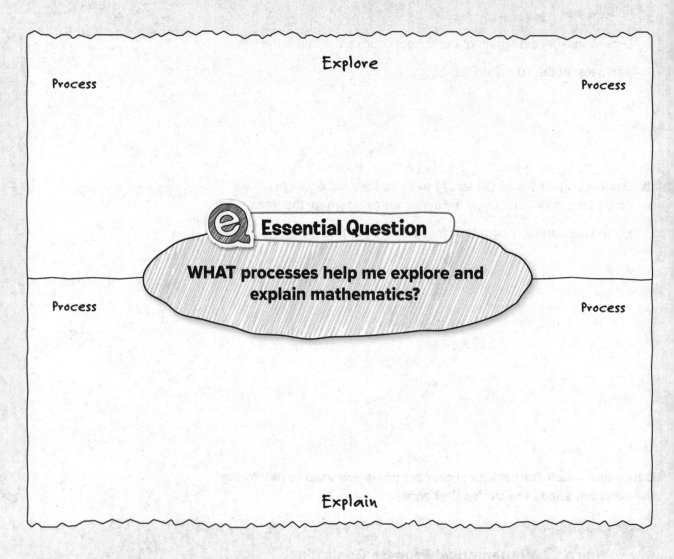

Explore

Process

Process

Essential Question

WHAT processes help me explore and explain mathematics?

Process

Process

Explain

Answer the Essential Question. WHAT processes help me explore and explain mathematics?

Chapter 1
Ratios and Proportional Reasoning

Essential Question

HOW can you show that two objects are proportional?

Virginia Standards
7.2, 7.3; 7.10a, e

Math in the Real World

Airplanes used for commercial flights travel at a speed of about 550 miles per hour.

Suppose an airplane travels 265 miles in one-half hour. Draw an arrow on the speedometer below to represent the speed of the airplane in miles per hour.

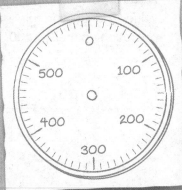

FOLDABLES®
Study Organizer

 Cut out the Foldable in the back of the book.

 Place your Foldable on page 90.

 Use the Foldable throughout this chapter as you learn about proportional reasoning.

Vocabulary

complex fraction	direct variation	rate of change
constant of proportionality	equivalent ratios	rise
constant rate of change	nonproportional	run
	proportion	slope
constant of variation	proportional	unit rate
coordinate plane	ordered pair	unit ratio
cross products	origin	*x*-axis
dimensional analysis	quadrants	*x*-coordinate
	rate	*y*-axis
		y-coordinate

Review Vocabulary

Functions A function is a relationship that assigns exactly one output value for each input value. The function rule is the operation performed on the input. Perform each indicated operation on the input 10. Then write each output in the organizer.

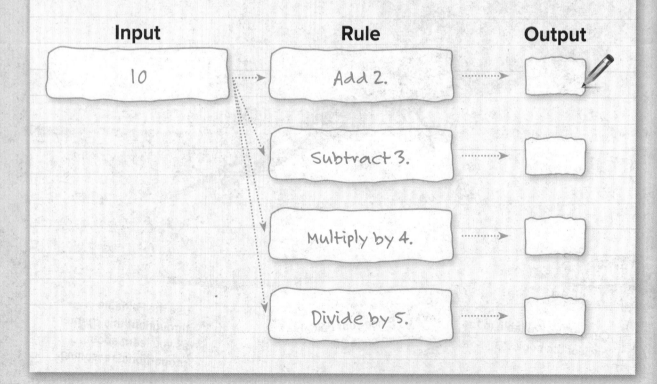

Input	Rule	Output
10	Add 2.	
	Subtract 3.	
	Multiply by 4.	
	Divide by 5.	

What Do You Already Know?

Read each statement. Decide whether you agree (A) or disagree (D). Place a checkmark in the appropriate column and then justify your reasoning.

Ratios and Proportional Reasoning			
Statement	A	D	Why?
A rate is a ratio that compares two quantities with different units.			
A relationship between two quantities is proportional.			
The cross products of the proportion $\frac{a}{b} = \frac{c}{d}$ are ac and bd.			
A linear relationship has a constant rate of change.			
Slope can be expressed as $\frac{rise}{run}$.			
The graph of a direct variation always passes through the origin.			

When Will You Use This?

Here are a few examples of how rates are used in the real world.

Activity 1 Professional race car drivers race in qualifying runs to compete for a good starting position. Do you think that they could predict their actual race time based on qualifying times? Explain your reasoning.

Activity 2 Go online at **connectED.mcgraw-hill.com** to read the graphic novel **The Go-Kart Race**. How long did it take Seth to complete 12 laps? How long is each lap?

Seth and Hannah in

The Go-Kart Race

That's ok. We can estimate the rest of the times based on your times so far.

Are You Ready?

Try the Quick Check below.
Or, take the Online Readiness Quiz.

 Check ✓

Quick Review

Example 1

Write the ratio of wins to losses as a fraction in simplest form.

Madison Mavericks	
Team Statistics	
Wins	10
Losses	12
Ties	8

wins ······▶ $\dfrac{10}{12} = \dfrac{5}{6}$
losses ·····▶

The ratio of wins to losses is $\dfrac{5}{6}$.

Example 2

Determine whether the ratios 250 miles in 4 hours and 500 miles in 8 hours are equivalent.

Compare the ratios by writing them in simplest form.

250 miles : 4 hours $= \dfrac{250}{4}$ or $\dfrac{125}{2}$

500 miles : 8 hours $= \dfrac{500}{8}$ or $\dfrac{125}{2}$

The ratios are equivalent because they simplify to the same fraction.

Quick Check

Ratios Write each ratio as a fraction in simplest form.

Seventh-Grade Field Trip	
Students	180
Adults	24
Buses	4

1. adults : students _____

2. students : buses _____

3. buses : people _____

Equivalent Ratios Determine whether the ratios are equivalent. Explain.

4. 20 nails for every 5 shingles
12 nails for every 3 shingles

_____

_____

5. 12 out of 20 doctors agree
15 out of 30 doctors agree

_____

_____

 **How Did You Do?**

Which problems did you answer correctly in the Quick Check?
Shade those exercise numbers below.

① ② ③ ④ ⑤

HOW can you use a bar diagram to solve a real-world problem involving ratios?

When Jeremy gets his allowance, he agrees to save part of it. His savings and expenses are in the ratio 7:5. If his daily allowance is $3, find how much he saves each day.

Hands-On Activity

You can use a bar diagram to represent the ratio 7:5.

Step 1   Complete the bar diagram below by writing *savings, expenses,* and *$3* in the correct boxes.

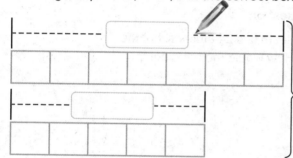

Total amount =

(Daily Allowance)

Step 2   Let *x* represent each part of a bar. Write and solve an equation to find the amount of money each bar represents.

$7x + \boxed{}x = 3$ Write the equation.

$12x = 3$ There are 12 parts in all.

$\dfrac{12x}{12} = \dfrac{3}{12}$ Division Property of Equality

$x = \dfrac{\boxed{}}{\boxed{}}$ or 0.25   Simplify.

Step 3   Determine the amount Jeremy saves each day. Since each part of the bar represents $0.25, Jeremy's savings are represented by

$7 \times \$\boxed{}$ or $1.75.

So, Jeremy saves $\boxed{}$ each day.

Investigate

Work with a partner to answer the following question.

1. The ratio of the number of boys to the number of girls on the swim team is 4:2. If there are 24 athletes on the swim team, how many more boys than girls are there? Use a bar diagram to solve. _____

Total athletes = [　　]

Analyze and Reflect

Work with a partner to answer the following question.

2. **MP Reason Inductively** Suppose the swim team has 24 athletes, but the ratio of boys to girls on the swim team is 3:5. How would the bar diagram

change? _____

_____

Create

On Your Own

3. **MP Model with Mathematics** Write a real-world problem that could be represented by the bar diagram shown below. Then solve your problem.

Total amount = 220

_____

_____

_____

4. **Inquiry** HOW can you use a bar diagram to solve a real-world problem involving ratios?

_____

_____

Real-World Link

 Watch ▶

Pulse Rate You can take a person's pulse by placing your middle and index finger on the underside of their wrist. Choose a partner and take their pulse for two minutes.

1. Record the results in the diagram below.

beats

minutes

2. Use the results from Exercise 1 to complete the bar diagram and determine the number of beats per minute for your partner.

|------ Beats in 2 minutes = [   ] ------|

Number of beats in 1 minute.	Number of beats in 1 minute.
|--- [ ] beats ---|	|--- [ ] beats ---|

So, your partner's heart beats [   ] times per minute.

3. Use the results from Exercise 1 to determine the number of beats for $\frac{1}{2}$ minute for your partner.

 Essential Question

HOW can you show that two objects are proportional?

 Vocab **Vocabulary**

rate

unit rate

 Which **Mathematical Process Goals** did you use? Shade the circle(s) that applies.

① Mathematical Problem Solving   ④ Mathematical Connections

② Mathematical Communication   ⑤ Mathematical Representations

③ Mathematical Reasoning

Find a Unit Rate

A ratio that compares two quantities with different kinds of units is called a **rate**. When you found each other's pulse, you were actually finding the heart *rate*.

$$\frac{160 \text{ beats}}{2 \text{ minutes}}$$

> The units *beats* and *minutes* are different.

When a rate is simplified so that it has a denominator of 1 unit, it is called a **unit rate**.

$$\frac{80 \text{ beats}}{1 \text{ minute}}$$

> The denominator is 1 unit.

The table below shows some common unit rates.

Rate	Unit Rate	Abbreviation	Name
$\frac{\text{number of miles}}{1 \text{ hour}}$	miles per hour	mi/h or mph	average speed
$\frac{\text{number of miles}}{1 \text{ gallon}}$	miles per gallon	mi/gal or mpg	gas mileage
$\frac{\text{number of dollars}}{1 \text{ pound}}$	price per pound	dollars/lb	unit price

Example

Tutor

1. Adrienne biked 24 miles in 4 hours. If she biked at a constant speed, how many miles did she ride in one hour?

$$24 \text{ miles in 4 hours} = \frac{24 \text{ mi}}{4 \text{ h}} \qquad \text{Write the rate as a fraction.}$$

$$= \frac{24 \text{ mi} \div 4}{4 \text{ h} \div 4} \qquad \text{Divide the numerator and the denominator by 4.}$$

$$= \frac{6 \text{ mi}}{1 \text{ h}} \qquad \text{Simplify.}$$

Adrienne biked 6 miles in one hour.

Got it? Do these problems to find out.

Find each unit rate. Round to the nearest hundredth if necessary.

a. $300 for 6 hours

b. 220 miles on 8 gallons

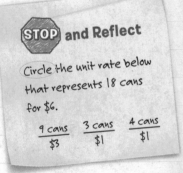

STOP and Reflect

Circle the unit rate below that represents 18 cans for $6.

$\frac{9 \text{ cans}}{\$3}$ $\frac{3 \text{ cans}}{\$1}$ $\frac{4 \text{ cans}}{\$1}$

> Show your work.

a. _____

b. _____

Example

Tutor

2. Find the unit price if it costs $2 for eight juice boxes.

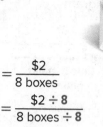

$$\$2 \text{ for eight boxes} = \frac{\$2}{8 \text{ boxes}}$$ Write the rate as a fraction.

$$= \frac{\$2 \div 8}{8 \text{ boxes} \div 8}$$ Divide the numerator and the denominator by 8.

$$= \frac{\$0.25}{1 \text{ box}}$$ Simplify.

The unit price is $0.25 per juice box.

Got it? Do this problem to find out.

c. Find the unit price if a 4-pack of mixed fruit sells for $2.12.

Show your work.

c. _____

Example

Tutor

3. The prices of 3 different bags of dog food are given in the table. Which size bag has the lowest price per pound rounded to the nearest cent?

Dog Food Prices	
Bag Size (lb)	**Price ($)**
40	49.00
20	23.44
8	9.88

- 40-pound bag
  $49.00 ÷ 40 pounds ≈ $1.23 per pound

- 20-pound bag
  $23.44 ÷ 20 pounds ≈ $1.17 per pound

- 8-pound bag
  $9.88 ÷ 8 pounds ≈ $1.24 per pound

The 20-pound bag sells for the lowest price per pound.

Alternative Method

One 40-lb bag is equivalent to two 20-lb bags or five 8-lb bags. The cost for one 40-lb bag is $49, the cost for two 20-lb bags is about 2 × $23 or $46, and the cost for five 8-lb bags is about 5 × $10 or $50. So, the 20-lb bag has the lowest price per pound.

Got it? Do this problem to find out.

d. Tito wants to buy some peanut butter to donate to the local food pantry. Tito wants to buy as much peanut butter as possible. Which brand should he buy?

Peanut Butter Sales	
Brand	**Sale Price**
Nutty	12 ounces for $2.19
Grandma's	18 ounces for $2.79
Bee's	28 ounces for $4.69
Save-A-Lot	40 ounces for $6.60

d. _____

Example

4. Lexi painted 2 faces in 8 minutes at the Crafts Fair. At this rate, how many faces can she paint in 40 minutes?

Method 1 Draw a Bar Diagram

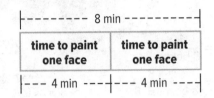

It takes 4 minutes to paint one face. In 40 minutes, Lexi can paint 40 ÷ 4 or 10 faces.

Method 2 Find a Unit Rate

$$2 \text{ faces in } 8 \text{ minutes} = \frac{2 \text{ faces} \div 8}{8 \text{ min} \div 8} = \frac{0.25 \text{ face}}{1 \text{ min}}$$ Find the unit rate.

Multiply the unit rate by 40 minutes.

$$\frac{0.25 \text{ face}}{1 \text{ min}} \cdot 40 \text{ min} = 10 \text{ faces}$$ Divide out the common units.

Using either method, Lexi can paint 10 faces in 40 minutes.

Guided Practice

1. CD Express offers 4 CDs for $60. Music Place offers 6 CDs for $75. Which store offers the better buy? (Examples 1–3)

2. After 3.5 hours, Pasha had traveled 217 miles. If she travels at a constant speed, how far will she have traveled after 4 hours? (Example 4) _____

3. Write 5 pounds for $2.49 as a unit rate. Round to the nearest hundredth. (Example 2)

4.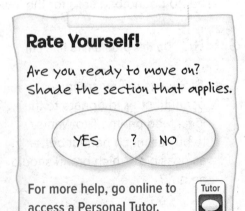

4. **Building on the Essential Question** Use an example to describe how a *rate* is a measure of one quantity per unit of another quantity.

Rate Yourself!

Are you ready to move on? Shade the section that applies.

YES ? NO

For more help, go online to access a Personal Tutor.

Independent Practice

Go online for Step-by-Step Solutions

Find each unit rate. Round to the nearest hundredth if necessary.
(Examples 1 and 2)

1. 360 miles in 6 hours _____

2. 6,840 customers in 45 days _____

 show your work.

3. 45.5 meters in 13 seconds _____

4. $7.40 for 5 pounds _____

5. Estimate the unit rate if 12 pairs of socks sell for $5.79. (Examples 1 and 2)

_____

6. **MP Justify Conclusions** The results of a swim meet are shown. Who swam the fastest? Explain your reasoning. (Example 3)

Name	Event	Time (s)
Tawni	50-m Freestyle	40.8
Pepita	100-m Butterfly	60.2
Susana	200-m Medley	112.4

7. Ben can type 153 words in 3 minutes. At this rate, how many words can he type in 10 minutes? (Example 4)

8. Kenji buys 3 yards of fabric for $7.47. Then he realizes that he needs 2 more yards. How much will the extra fabric cost? (Example 4)

9. The record for the Boston Marathon's wheelchair division is 1 hour, 18 minutes, and 27 seconds.

a. The Boston Marathon is 26.2 miles long. What was the average speed of the record winner of the wheelchair division?

Round to the nearest hundredth. _____

b. At this rate, about how long would it take this competitor to complete a 30-mile race? _____

10. At Tire Depot, a pair of new tires sells for $216. The manager's special advertises the same tires selling at a rate of $380 for 4 tires. How much do you save per tire if you purchase the manager's special? _____

H.O.T. Problems Higher Order Thinking

11. **MP Use Math Tools** Find examples of grocery item prices in a newspaper, on television, or on the Internet. Compare unit prices of two different brands of the same item. Explain which item is the better buy.

_____

_____

12. **MP Find the Error** Seth is trying to find the unit price for a package of blank compact discs on sale at 10 for $5.49. Find his mistake and correct it.

_____

_____

> 10 ÷ $5.49
> $1.82 each

MP Persevere with Problems Determine whether each statement is *sometimes, always,* or *never* true. Give an example or a counterexample.

13. A ratio is a rate.

_____

_____

14. A rate is a ratio.

_____

_____

15. **MP Justify Conclusions** A 96-ounce container of orange juice costs $4.80. At what price should a 128-ounce container be sold in order for the unit rate for both containers to be the same? Explain your reasoning.

_____

_____

Extra Practice

Find each unit rate. Round to the nearest hundredth if necessary.

16. 150 people for 5 classes

30 people per class

$$\frac{150\ people \div 5}{5\ classes \div 5} = \frac{30\ people}{1\ class}$$

30 people per class

17. 815 Calories in 4 servings

203.75 Calories per serving

$$\frac{815\ Calories \div 4}{4\ servings \div 4} = \frac{203.75\ Calories}{1\ serving}$$

203.75 Calories per serving

18. $1.12 for 8.2 ounces

19. 144 miles on 4.5 gallons

20. (MP) **Justify Conclusions** A grocery store sells a 6-pack of bottled water for $3.79, a 9-pack for $4.50, and a 12-pack for $6.89. Which package costs the least per bottle? Explain your reasoning.

21. (MP) **Justify Conclusions** Dalila earns $108.75 for working 15 hours as a holiday helper wrapping gifts. At this rate, how much money will she earn if she works 18 hours the next week? Explain.

22. (MP) **Use Math Tools** Use the graph that shows the average number of heartbeats for an active adult brown bear and a hibernating brown bear.

   a. What does the point (2, 120) represent on the graph?

   b. What does the ratio of the y-coordinate to the x-coordinate for each pair of points on the graph represent?

   c. Use the graph to find the bear's average heart rate when it is active and when it is hibernating.

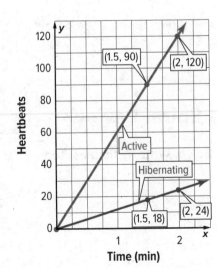

23. The table shows the number of hours a group of friends worked doing various jobs and the amount each earned. Select the correct hourly rate to complete the table. Then place a checkmark in the row for the person who had the greatest hourly rate.

$6.25	$7.90
$6.75	$8.00
$7.25	$8.70

	Hours Worked	Amount Earned ($)	Earnings per hour ($)	Greatest Hourly Rate?
Caleb	5	36.25		
Jeremy	7.5	65.25		
Maria	4.25	34.00		
Rosa	8	54.00		

24. Mrs. Ross needs to buy dish soap. There are four different sized containers. Sort the brands from least to greatest unit price. Round each unit price to the nearest thousandth.

Dish Soap Prices	
Brand	**Price**
Lots of Suds	$0.98 for 8 ounces
Bright Wash	$1.29 for 12 ounces
Spotless Soap	$3.14 for 30 ounces
Lemon Bright	$3.50 for 32 ounces

	Brand	Unit Price (per ounce)
Least		
Greatest		

Which brand is the best buy? _____

Spiral Review

Solve. Write in simplest form.

25. $\dfrac{1}{2} \times \dfrac{4}{7} = \dfrac{\Box}{\Box}$

26. $\dfrac{2}{3} \times \dfrac{1}{6} = \dfrac{\Box}{\Box}$

27. $\dfrac{1}{4} \div \dfrac{3}{8} = \dfrac{\Box}{\Box}$

Complex Fractions and Unit Rates

Real-World Link

Speed Skating Dana is skating laps to train for a speed skating competition. She can skate 1 lap in 40 seconds.

1. Write a ratio in simplest form comparing Dana's time to her number of laps.

Dana's time (s) ····▶ [ ]

Number of Laps ····▶ [ ]

2. Suppose Dana skates for 20 seconds. How many laps will she skate?

3. Write the ratio of Dana's time from Exercise 2 to her number of laps.

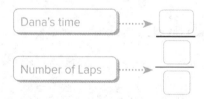

Dana's time ····▶ [ ]
                    ———
Number of Laps ····▶ [ ]

4. How could you simplify the ratio you wrote in Exercise 3?

Essential Question

HOW can you show that two objects are proportional?

Vocab

Vocabulary

complex fraction

Virginia Standards
7.3

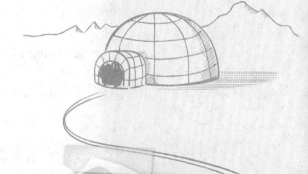

Which MP Mathematical Process Goals did you use? Shade the circle(s) that applies.

① Mathematical Problem Solving

② Mathematical Communication

③ Mathematical Reasoning

④ Mathematical Connections

⑤ Mathematical Representations

Simplify a Complex Fraction

Fractions like $\dfrac{20}{\frac{1}{2}}$ are called complex fractions. **Complex fractions** are

fractions with a numerator, denominator, or both that are also fractions. Complex fractions are simplified when both the numerator and denominator are integers.

 Examples

 Tutor

1. Simplify $\dfrac{\frac{1}{4}}{2}$.

Recall that a fraction can also be written as a division problem.

$\dfrac{\frac{1}{4}}{2} = \dfrac{1}{4} \div 2$ Write the complex fraction as a division problem.

$\quad = \dfrac{1}{4} \times \dfrac{1}{2}$ Multiply by the reciprocal of 2, which is $\frac{1}{2}$.

$\quad = \dfrac{1}{8}$ Simplify.

So, $\dfrac{\frac{1}{4}}{2}$ is equal to $\dfrac{1}{8}$.

2. Simplify $\dfrac{1}{\frac{1}{2}}$.

Write the fraction as a division problem.

$\dfrac{1}{\frac{1}{2}} = 1 \div \dfrac{1}{2}$ Write the complex fraction as a division problem.

$\quad = \dfrac{1}{1} \times \dfrac{2}{1}$ Multiply by the reciprocal of $\frac{1}{2}$, which is $\frac{2}{1}$.

$\quad = \dfrac{2}{1}$ or 2   Simplify.

So, $\dfrac{1}{\frac{1}{2}}$ is equal to 2.

> **Got it?** Do these problems to find out.
>
> **a.** $\dfrac{2}{\frac{2}{3}}$ **b.** $\dfrac{6}{\frac{1}{3}}$
>
> **c.** $\dfrac{\frac{2}{3}}{7}$ **d.** $\dfrac{\frac{2}{4}}{2}$

Divide Fractions

To divide by a whole number, first write it as a fraction with a denominator of 1. Then multiply by the reciprocal.

So, $\dfrac{\frac{1}{4}}{2}$ can be written as $\dfrac{1}{4} \div \dfrac{2}{1}$.

 Show your work.

a. _____

b. _____

c. _____

d. _____

Find Unit Rates

When the fractions of a complex fractions represent different units, you can find the unit rate.

 Examples

3. Josiah can jog $1\frac{1}{3}$ miles in $\frac{1}{4}$ hour. Find his average speed in miles per hour.

Write a rate that compares the number of miles to hours.

$$\frac{1\frac{1}{3} \text{ mi}}{\frac{1}{4} \text{ h}} = 1\frac{1}{3} \div \frac{1}{4} \qquad \text{Write the complex fraction as a division problem.}$$

$$= \frac{4}{3} \div \frac{1}{4} \qquad \text{Write the mixed number as an improper fraction.}$$

$$= \frac{4}{3} \times \frac{4}{1} \qquad \text{Multiply by the reciprocal of } \frac{1}{4}, \text{ which is } \frac{4}{1}.$$

$$= \frac{16}{3} \text{ or } 5\frac{1}{3} \qquad \text{Simplify.}$$

So, Josiah jogs at an average speed of $5\frac{1}{3}$ miles per hour.

4. Tia is painting her house. She paints $34\frac{1}{2}$ square feet in $\frac{3}{4}$ hour. At this rate, how many square feet can she paint each hour?

Write a ratio that compares the number of square feet to hours.

$$\frac{34\frac{1}{2} \text{ ft}^2}{\frac{3}{4} \text{ h}} = 34\frac{1}{2} \div \frac{3}{4} \qquad \text{Write the complex fraction as a division problem.}$$

$$= \frac{69}{2} \div \frac{3}{4} \qquad \text{Write the mixed number as an improper fraction.}$$

$$= \frac{69}{2} \times \frac{4}{3} \qquad \text{Multiply by the reciprocal of } \frac{3}{4}, \text{ which is } \frac{4}{3}.$$

$$= \frac{276}{6} \text{ or } 46 \qquad \text{Simplify.}$$

So, Tia can paint 46 square feet per hour.

Got it? Do these problems to find out.

e. Mr. Ito is spreading mulch in his yard. He spreads $4\frac{2}{3}$ square yards in 2 hours. How many square yards can he mulch per hour?

e. _____

f. Aubrey can walk $4\frac{1}{2}$ miles in $1\frac{1}{2}$ hours. Find her average speed in miles per hour.

f. _____

Example

5. On Javier's soccer team, about $33\frac{1}{3}\%$ of the players have scored a goal. Write $33\frac{1}{3}\%$ as a fraction in simplest form.

$$33\frac{1}{3}\% = \frac{33\frac{1}{3}}{100} \qquad \text{Definition of percent}$$

$$= 33\frac{1}{3} \div 100 \qquad \text{Write the complex fraction as a division problem.}$$

$$= \frac{100}{3} \div 100 \qquad \text{Write } 33\frac{1}{3} \text{ as an improper fraction.}$$

$$= \frac{\overset{1}{\cancel{100}}}{3} \times \frac{1}{\cancel{100}} \qquad \text{Multiply by the reciprocal of 100, which is } \frac{1}{100}.$$

$$= \frac{1}{3} \qquad \text{Simplify.}$$

So, about $\frac{1}{3}$ of Javier's team has scored a goal.

Guided Practice

Check ✓

Simplify. (Examples 1 and 2)

1. $\dfrac{18}{\frac{3}{4}} =$ _____

2. $\dfrac{\frac{3}{6}}{4} =$ _____

3. $\dfrac{\frac{1}{3}}{\frac{1}{4}} =$ _____

Show your work.

4. Pep Club members are making spirit buttons. They make 490 spirit buttons in $3\frac{1}{2}$ hours. Find the number of buttons the Pep Club makes

per hour. (Examples 3 and 4) _____

5. A county sales tax is $6\frac{2}{3}\%$. Write the percent as a fraction in

simplest form. (Example 5) _____

6. **Building on the Essential Question** What is a

complex fraction? _____

_____

_____

Rate Yourself!

How confident are you about simplifying complex fractions? Check the box that applies.

For more help, go online to access a Personal Tutor.

Independent Practice

Go online for Step-by-Step Solutions eHelp

Simplify. (Examples 1 and 2)

1. $\dfrac{\frac{1}{2}}{3} =$ _____

2. $\dfrac{\frac{2}{3}}{11} =$ _____

3. $\dfrac{\frac{8}{9}}{6} =$ _____

4. $\dfrac{\frac{2}{5}}{9} =$ _____

5. $\dfrac{\frac{4}{5}}{10} =$ _____

6. $\dfrac{\frac{1}{4}}{\frac{7}{10}} =$ _____

7. Mary is making pillows for her Life Skills class. She bought $2\frac{1}{2}$ yards of fabric. Her total cost was \$15. What was the cost per yard? (Examples 3 and 4)

_____

8. Doug entered a canoe race. He rowed $3\frac{1}{2}$ miles in $\frac{1}{2}$ hour. What is his average speed in miles per hour? (Examples 3 and 4)

_____

9. Monica reads $7\frac{1}{2}$ pages of a mystery book in 9 minutes. What is her average reading rate in pages per minute? (Examples 3 and 4) _____

Write each percent as a fraction in simplest form. (Example 5)

10. $56\frac{1}{4}\% =$ _____

11. $15\frac{3}{5}\% =$ _____

12. $13\frac{1}{3}\% =$ _____

13. A bank is offering home loans at an interest rate of $5\frac{1}{2}\%$. Write the percent as a fraction in simplest form. (Example 5) _____

14. **MP Be Precise** Karl measured the wingspan of the butterfly and the moth shown below. How many times larger is the moth than the butterfly?

$3\frac{1}{4}$ in.

Black Swallowtail Butterfly

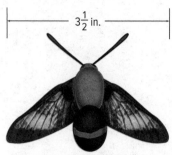

$3\frac{1}{2}$ in.

Hummingbird Moth

H.O.T. Problems Higher Order Thinking

15. **MP Construct an Argument** Explain how complex fractions can be used to solve problems involving ratios. _____

16. **MP Reason Inductively** Write three different complex fractions that simplify to $\frac{1}{4}$.

17. **MP Persevere with Problems** Use mental math to find the value of $\frac{15}{124} \cdot \frac{230}{30} \div \frac{230}{124}$.

18. **MP Justify Conclusions** The value of a mutual fund increased by $3\frac{1}{8}$%. Write $3\frac{1}{8}$% as a fraction in simplest form. Justify your answer.

19. **MP Persevere with Problems** The distance around the tire of a motorized scooter is 21.98 inches. The tires make one revolution every $\frac{1}{10}$ second. Find the speed of the scooter in miles per hour. Round to the nearest tenth. (*Hint:* The speed of an object spinning in a circle is equal to the distance around the circle divided by the time it takes to complete one revolution.)

Extra Practice

Simplify.

20. $\dfrac{\frac{1}{1}}{\frac{1}{4}} =$ 4

Homework Help ➡

$\dfrac{\frac{1}{1}}{\frac{1}{4}} = 1 \div \frac{1}{4}$

$= \frac{1}{1} \times \frac{4}{1}$

$= \frac{4}{1}$ or 4

21. $\dfrac{\frac{12}{1}}{\frac{3}{5}} =$ _____

22. $\dfrac{\frac{9}{10}}{9} =$ _____

23. $\dfrac{\frac{1}{2}}{\frac{1}{4}} =$ _____

24. $\dfrac{\frac{1}{12}}{\frac{5}{6}} =$ _____

25. $\dfrac{\frac{5}{6}}{\frac{5}{9}} =$ _____

26. Mrs. Frasier is making costumes for the school play. Each costume requires 0.75 yard of fabric. She bought 6 yards of fabric. How many costumes can Mrs. Frasier make?

_____

27. A lawn company advertises that they can spread 7,500 square feet of grass seed in $2\frac{1}{2}$ hours. Find the number of square feet of grass seed that can be spread per hour.

_____

Write each percent as a fraction in simplest form.

28. $2\frac{2}{5}\% =$ _____

29. $7\frac{3}{4}\% =$ _____

30. $8\frac{1}{3}\% =$ _____

31. **MP** **Justify Conclusions** The value of a certain stock increased by $1\frac{1}{4}\%$.

Explain how to write $1\frac{1}{4}\%$ as a fraction in simplest form. _____

_____

_____

32. Debra bought $3\frac{1}{4}$ yards of fabric at a remnant sale for $13. Determine if each of the following remnant deals have the same unit price as Debra's deal. Select yes or no.

a. $4\frac{2}{3}$ yards for $16   ☐ Yes   ☐ No

b. $2\frac{3}{4}$ yards for $11   ☐ Yes   ☐ No

c. $6\frac{1}{2}$ yards for $26   ☐ Yes   ☐ No

33. The table shows the distances traveled by 4 cyclists. Sort the speeds of the riders, in miles per hour, from slowest to fastest.

	Rider	Speed (mph)
Slowest		
Fastest		

Bicycle Rides		
Rider	Distance	Time
Elena	$20\frac{1}{2}$ mi	$2\frac{1}{4}$ h
Julio	$12\frac{1}{4}$ mi	$1\frac{1}{2}$ h
Kevin	$20\frac{2}{3}$ mi	$1\frac{2}{3}$ h
Lorena	$33\frac{1}{4}$ mi	$2\frac{1}{3}$ h

Which rider had the fastest rate of speed? ☐

Spiral Review

Fill in each box with the equivalent customary measurement.

34. 2 feet = ☐ inches

35. 5 tons = ☐ pounds

36. 8 gallons = ☐ quarts

Fill in each box with the equivalent metric measurement.

37. 1 meter = ☐ centimeters

38. 1 liter = ☐ milliliters

39. 1 kilogram = ☐ grams

Convert Unit Rates

 ## Real-World Link

Animals Squirrels, chipmunks, and rabbits are capable of running at fast speeds. The table shows the top running speeds of these animals.

Animal	Speed (mph)
Squirrel	10
Chipmunk	15
Cottontail Rabbit	30

 Essential Question

HOW can you show that two objects are proportional?

 Vocabulary

unit ratio
dimensional analysis

Virginia Standards
7.3

1. How many feet are in 1 mile? 10 miles?

   1 mile = _____ feet

   10 miles = _____ feet

2. How many seconds are in 1 minute? 1 hour?

   1 minute = _____ seconds

   1 hour = _____ seconds

3. How could you determine the number of feet per second a squirrel can run?

   _____

   _____

4. Complete the following statement. Round to the nearest tenth. 10 miles per hour ≈ [ ] feet per second

FINISH

Which **MP** Mathematical Process Goals did you use? Shade the circle(s) that applies.

① Mathematical Problem Solving   ④ Mathematical Connections

② Mathematical Communication   ⑤ Mathematical Representations

③ Mathematical Reasoning

Convert Rates

The relationships among some commonly used customary and metric units of measure are shown in the tables below.

Customary Units of Measure		Metric Units of Measure	
Smaller	Larger	Smaller	Larger
12 inches	1 foot	100 centimeters	1 meter
16 ounces	1 pound	1,000 grams	1 kilogram
8 pints	1 gallon	1,000 milliliters	1 liter
3 feet	1 yard	10 millimeters	1 centimeter
5,280 feet	1 mile	1,000 milligrams	1 gram

Each of the relationships in the tables can be written as a **unit ratio**. Like a unit rate, a unit ratio is one in which the denominator is 1 unit. Below are three examples of unit ratios.

$$\frac{\textbf{12 inches}}{\textbf{1 foot}} \qquad \frac{\textbf{16 ounces}}{\textbf{1 pound}} \qquad \frac{\textbf{100 centimeters}}{\textbf{1 meter}}$$

The numerator and denominator of each of the unit ratios shown are equal. So, the value of each ratio is 1.

You can convert one rate to an equivalent rate by multiplying by a unit ratio or its reciprocal. When you convert rates, you include the units in your computation.

The process of including units of measure as factors when you compute is called **dimensional analysis**.

$$\frac{10 \text{ ft}}{1 \text{ s}} = \frac{10 \cancel{\text{ft}}}{1 \text{ s}} \cdot \frac{12 \text{ in.}}{1 \cancel{\text{ft}}} = \frac{10 \cdot 12 \text{ in.}}{1 \text{ s} \cdot 1} = \frac{120 \text{ in.}}{1 \text{ s}}$$

 ## Example

1. A remote control car travels at a rate of 10 feet per second. How many inches per second is this?

$$\frac{10 \text{ ft}}{1 \text{ s}} = \frac{10 \text{ ft}}{1 \text{ s}} \cdot \frac{12 \text{ in.}}{1 \text{ ft}} \qquad \text{Use 1 foot} = 12 \text{ inches. Multiply by } \frac{12 \text{ in.}}{1 \text{ ft}}.$$

$$= \frac{10 \cancel{\text{ft}}}{1 \text{ s}} \cdot \frac{12 \text{ in.}}{1 \cancel{\text{ft}}} \qquad \text{Divide out common units.}$$

$$= \frac{10 \cdot 12 \text{ in.}}{1 \text{ s} \cdot 1} \qquad \text{Simplify.}$$

$$= \frac{120 \text{ in.}}{1 \text{ s}} \qquad \text{Simplify.}$$

So, 10 feet per second equals 120 inches per second.

Examples

Tutor

2. A swordfish can swim at a rate of **60 miles per hour. How many feet per hour is this?**

You can use 1 mile = 5,280 feet to convert the rates.

$$\frac{60 \text{ mi}}{1 \text{ h}} = \frac{60 \text{ mi}}{1 \text{ h}} \cdot \frac{5,280 \text{ ft}}{1 \text{ mi}}$$ Multiply by $\frac{5,280 \text{ ft}}{1 \text{ mi}}$.

$$= \frac{60 \text{ mi}}{1 \text{ h}} \cdot \frac{5,280 \text{ ft}}{1 \text{ mi}}$$ Divide out common units.

$$= \frac{60 \cdot 5,280 \text{ ft}}{1 \cdot 1 \text{ h}}$$ Simplify.

$$= \frac{316,800 \text{ ft}}{1 \text{ h}}$$ Simplify.

A swordfish can swim at a rate of 316,800 feet per hour.

3. Marvin walks at a speed of **7 feet per second. How many feet per hour is this?**

You can use 60 seconds = 1 minute and you can use 60 minutes = 1 hour to convert the rates.

$$\frac{7 \text{ ft}}{1 \text{ s}} = \frac{7 \text{ ft}}{1 \text{ s}} \cdot \frac{60 \text{ s}}{1 \text{ min}} \cdot \frac{60 \text{ min}}{1 \text{ h}}$$ Multiply by $\frac{60 \text{ s}}{1 \text{ min}}$ and $\frac{60 \text{ min}}{1 \text{ h}}$.

$$= \frac{7 \text{ ft}}{1 \text{ s}} \cdot \frac{60 \text{ s}}{1 \text{ min}} \cdot \frac{60 \text{ min}}{1 \text{ h}}$$ Divide out common units.

$$= \frac{7 \cdot 60 \cdot 60 \text{ ft}}{1 \cdot 1 \cdot 1 \text{ h}}$$ Simplify.

$$= \frac{25,200 \text{ ft}}{1 \text{ h}}$$ Simplify.

Marvin walks 25,200 feet in 1 hour.

Got it? Do these problems to find out.

a. A gull can fly at a speed of 22 miles per hour. About how many feet per hour can the gull fly?

b. An AMTRAK train travels at 125 miles per hour. Convert the speed to miles per minute. Round to the nearest tenth.

STOP and **Reflect**

To convert meters per hour to kilometers per hour, circle the relationship you need to know.

100 cm = 1 m

60 s = 1 min

1,000 m = 1 km

Show your work.

a. _____

b. _____

Example

4. The average speed of one team in a relay race is about 10 miles per hour. What is this speed in feet per second?

We can use 1 mile = 5,280 feet, 1 hour = 60 minutes, and 1 minute = 60 seconds to convert the rates.

$$\frac{10\text{ mi}}{1\text{ h}} = \frac{10\text{ mi}}{1\text{ h}} \cdot \frac{5{,}280\text{ ft}}{1\text{ mi}} \cdot \frac{1\text{ h}}{60\text{ min}} \cdot \frac{1\text{ min}}{60\text{ s}}$$

Multiply by distance and time unit ratios.

$$= \frac{10\text{ mi}}{1\text{ h}} \cdot \frac{5{,}280\text{ ft}}{1\text{ mi}} \cdot \frac{1\text{ h}}{60\text{ min}} \cdot \frac{1\text{ min}}{60\text{ s}}$$

Divide out common units.

$$= \frac{10 \cdot 5{,}280 \cdot 1 \cdot 1\text{ ft}}{1 \cdot 1 \cdot 60 \cdot 60\text{ s}}$$

Simplify.

$$= \frac{52{,}800\text{ ft}}{3{,}600\text{ s}}$$

Simplify.

$$\approx \frac{14.7\text{ ft}}{1\text{ s}}$$

Simplify.

The relay team runs at an average speed of about 14.7 feet per second.

Guided Practice

1. Water weighs about 8.34 pounds per gallon. About how many ounces per gallon is the weight of the water? (Examples 1 and 2)

_____

2. A skydiver is falling at about 176 feet per second. How many feet per minute is he falling? (Example 3)

_____

3. Lorenzo rides his bike at a rate of 5 yards per second. About how many miles per hour can Lorenzo ride his bike? (*Hint*: 1 mile = 1,760 yards) (Example 4)

_____

4. **Building on the Essential Question** Explain why the ratio $\frac{3\text{ feet}}{1\text{ yard}}$ has a value of one.

_____

_____

_____

Rate Yourself!

☐ I understand how to convert unit rates.

▶▶ Great! You're ready to move on!

☐ I still have questions about converting unit rates.

▯▯ No Problem! Go online to access a Personal Tutor.

Independent Practice

Go online for Step-by-Step Solutions

eHelp

1 A go-kart's top speed is 607,200 feet per hour. What is the speed in miles per hour? (Examples 1 and 2)

_____

_____

2. The fastest a human has ever run is 27 miles per hour. How many miles per minute did the human run? (Example 3)

_____

3 A peregrine falcon can fly 322 kilometers per hour. How many meters per hour can the falcon fly? (Example 3)

_____

4. A pipe is leaking at 1.5 cups per day. About how many gallons per week is the pipe leaking? (*Hint*: 1 gallon = 16 cups) (Example 4)

_____

5. Charlie runs at a speed of 3 yards per second. About how many miles per hour does Charlie run? (Example 4)

_____

6. **MP Model with Mathematics** Refer to the graphic novel frame below. Seth traveled 1 mile in 57.1 seconds. About how fast does Seth travel in miles per hour?

_____

I can't believe how fast I was going.

SKREEECH!

7. The speed at which a certain computer can access the Internet is 2 megabytes per second. How fast is this in megabytes per hour?

_____

8. MP **Use Math Tools** The approximate metric measurement of length is given for a U.S. customary unit of length. Use your estimation skills to complete the graphic organizer below. Fill in each blank with _foot_, _yard_, _inch_, or _mile_.

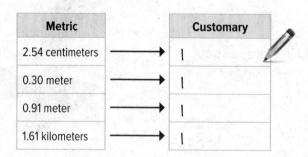

Metric		Customary
2.54 centimeters	→	|
0.30 meter	→	|
0.91 meter	→	|
1.61 kilometers	→	|

🔥 H.O.T. Problems Higher Order Thinking

9. MP **Which One Doesn't Belong?** Circle the rate that does not belong with the other three. Explain your reasoning.

| 60 mi/h | 88 ft/s | 500 ft/min | 1,440 mi/day |

_____

_____

10. MP **Reason Inductively** When you convert 100 feet per second to inches per second, will there be more or less than 100 inches. Explain.

_____

_____

_____

11. MP **Persevere with Problems** Use the information in Exercise 8 to convert 7 meters per minute to yards per hour. Round to the nearest tenth.

_____

_____

12. MP **Model with Mathematics** Write and solve a real-world problem in which a rate is converted.

_____

_____

Name _____ My Homework _____

Extra Practice

13. 20 mi/h = ⎡1,760⎤ ft/min

$$\frac{20 \text{ mi}}{1 \text{ h}} \cdot \frac{5,280 \text{ ft}}{1 \text{ mi}} \cdot \frac{1 \text{ h}}{60 \text{ min}} =$$

$$\frac{105,600 \text{ ft}}{60 \text{ min}} = 1,760 \text{ ft/min}$$

ework
elp

14. 16 cm/min = ⎡9.6⎤ m/h

$$\frac{16 \text{ cm}}{1 \text{ min}} \cdot \frac{1 \text{ m}}{100 \text{ cm}} \cdot \frac{60 \text{ min}}{1 \text{ h}} =$$

$$\frac{960 \text{ m}}{100 \text{ h}} = 9.6 \text{ m/h}$$

15. 45 mi/h = ⎡   ⎤ ft/s

16. 26 cm/s = ⎡   ⎤ m/min

17. 24 mi/h = ⎡   ⎤ ft/s

18. 105.6 L/h = ⎡   ⎤ L/min

19. The table shows the speed and number of wing beats per second for various flying insects.

   a. What is the speed of a housefly in feet per second? Round to the nearest hundredth.

_____

   b. How many times does a dragonfly's wing beat per minute?

_____

   c. About how many miles can a bumblebee travel in one minute?

_____

   d. How many times can a honeybee beat its wings in one hour?

_____

Flying Insects		
Insect	Speed (miles per hour)	Wing Beats per Second
Housefly	4.4	190
Honeybee	5.7	250
Dragonfly	15.6	38
Hornet	12.8	100
Bumblebee	6.4	130

20. A model airplane flew a distance of 330 feet in 15 seconds. Select all of the unit rates that are equivalent to the speed of the model airplane.

- ☐ 15 miles per hour
- ☐ 12 miles per hour
- ☐ 1320 feet per minute
- ☐ 1,056 feet per minute

21. The table shows how far some of the world's fastest animals can run in different lengths of time at their top speed.

Select the correct top speed to complete the table.

Animal	Top Speed (mph)
Cheetah	
Elk	
Lion	
Quarter Horse	

45	60
50	65
55	70

Fastest Animals on Land	
Animal	**Distance and Time**
Cheetah	3,080 feet in 30 seconds
Elk	2,970 feet in 45 seconds
Lion	4,400 feet in 60 seconds
Quarter Horse	6,050 feet in 75 seconds

Which animal had the fastest rate of speed? [   ]

Spiral Review

Determine if each pair of rates are equivalent. Explain your reasoning.

22. $36 for 4 baseball hats; $56 for 7 baseball hats

_____

_____

_____

23. 12 posters for 36 students; 21 posters for 63 students

_____

_____

_____

24. An employer pays $22 for 2 hours. Use the ratio table to determine how much she charges for 5 hours.

Payment	$22		
Hours	2		5

Proportional and Nonproportional Relationships

 Real-World Link

Pizza Party Ms. Cochran is planning a year-end pizza party for her students. Ace Pizza offers free delivery and charges $8 per medium pizza.

1. Complete the table to determine the cost for different numbers of pizzas ordered.

Cost ($)	8				
Pizza	1	2	3	4	5

2. For each number of pizzas, fill in the boxes to write the relationship of the cost and number of pizzas as a ratio in simplest form.

$$\frac{16}{2} = \frac{\boxed{}}{1} \qquad \frac{24}{3} = \frac{\boxed{}}{\boxed{}}$$

$$\frac{32}{\boxed{}} = \frac{\boxed{}}{\boxed{}} \qquad \frac{\boxed{}}{5} = \frac{\boxed{}}{\boxed{}}$$

3. What do you notice about the simplified ratios?

_____

_____

 Essential Question

HOW can you show that two objects are proportional?

 Vocabulary

proportional
nonproportional
equivalent ratios

 Virginia Standards
7.10e

Which **MP** **Mathematical Process Goals** did you use? Shade the circle(s) that applies.

① Mathematical Problem Solving
② Mathematical Communication
③ Mathematical Reasoning
④ Mathematical Connections
⑤ Mathematical Representations

Identify Proportional Relationships

Two quantities are **proportional** if they have a constant ratio or unit rate. For relationships in which this ratio is not constant, the two quantities are **nonproportional**.

In the pizza example on the previous page, the cost of an order is *proportional* to the number of pizzas ordered.

$$\frac{\text{cost of order}}{\text{pizzas ordered}} = \frac{8}{1} = \frac{16}{2} = \frac{24}{3} = \frac{32}{4} = \frac{40}{5} \text{ or } \$8 \text{ per pizza}$$

All of the ratios above are **equivalent ratios** because they all have the same value.

 ## Example

Tutor

1. **Andrew earns $18 per hour for mowing lawns. Is the amount of money he earns proportional to the number of hours he spends mowing? Explain.**

Find the amount of money he earns for working a different number of hours. Make a table to show these amounts.

Earnings ($)	18	36	54	72
Time (h)	1	2	3	4

For each number of hours worked, write the relationship of the amount he earned and hour as a ratio in simplest form.

$$\frac{\text{amount earned}}{\text{number of hours}} \longrightarrow \quad \frac{18}{1} \text{ or } 18 \quad \frac{36}{2} \text{ or } 18 \quad \frac{54}{3} \text{ or } 18 \quad \frac{72}{4} \text{ or } 18$$

All of the ratios between the two quantities can be simplified to 18.

The amount of money he earns is proportional to the number of hours he spends mowing.

> **Got it?** **Do this problem to find out.**

Show your work.

a. At Lakeview Middle School, there are 2 homeroom teachers assigned to every 48 students. Is the number of students at this school proportional to the number of teachers? Explain your reasoning.

a. _____

Examples

Watch ▷ Tutor 💬

2. Uptown Tickets charges $7 per baseball game ticket plus a $3 processing fee per order. Is the cost of an order proportional to the number of tickets ordered? Explain.

Cost ($)	10	17	24	31
Tickets Ordered	1	2	3	4

For each number of tickets, write the relationship of the cost and number of tickets as a ratio in simplest form.

$\dfrac{\text{cost of order}}{\text{tickets ordered}}$ → $\dfrac{10}{1}$ or 10 $\dfrac{17}{2}$ or 8.5 $\dfrac{24}{3}$ or 8 $\dfrac{31}{4}$ or 7.75

Since the ratios of the two quantities are not the same, the cost of an order is *not* proportional to the number of tickets ordered.

3. You can use the recipe shown to make a fruit punch. Is the amount of sugar used proportional to the amount of mix used? Explain.

Find the amount of sugar and mix needed for different numbers of batches. Make a table to help you solve.

Fruit Punch
$\frac{1}{2}$ cup sugar
1 envelope of mix
2 quarts of water

Cups of Sugar	$\frac{1}{2}$	1	$1\frac{1}{2}$	2
Envelopes of Mix	1	2	3	4

For each number of cups of sugar, write the relationship of the cups and number of envelopes of mix as a ratio in simplest form.

$\dfrac{\text{cups of sugar}}{\text{envelopes of mix}}$ → $\dfrac{\frac{1}{2}}{1}$ or 0.5 $\dfrac{1}{2}$ or 0.5 $\dfrac{1\frac{1}{2}}{3}$ or 0.5 $\dfrac{2}{4}$ or 0.5

All of the ratios between the two quantities can be simplified to 0.5. The amount of mix used is proportional to the amount of sugar used.

Got it? Do this problem to find out.

Show your work.

b. At the beginning of the year, Isabel had $120 in the bank. Each week, she deposits another $20. Is her account balance proportional to the number of weeks of deposits? Use the table below. Explain your reasoning.

b. _____

Time (wk)	1	2	3	
Balance ($)				

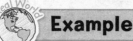

Example

4. The tables shown represent the number of pages Martin and Gabriel read over time. Which situation represents a proportional relationship between the time spent reading and the number of pages read? Explain.

Pages Martin Read	2	4	6
Time (min)	5	10	15

Pages Gabriel Read	3	4	7
Time (min)	5	10	15

Write the ratios for each time period in simplest form.

$$\frac{\text{pages}}{\text{minutes}} \longrightarrow \frac{2}{5}, \frac{4}{10} \text{ or } \frac{2}{5}, \frac{6}{15} \text{ or } \frac{2}{5} \qquad \frac{3}{5}, \frac{4}{10} \text{ or } \frac{2}{5}, \frac{7}{15}$$

All of the ratios between Martin's quantities are $\frac{2}{5}$. So, Martin's reading rate represents a proportional relationship.

Guided Practice

1. The Vista Marina rents boats for $25 per hour. In addition to the rental fee, there is a $12 charge for fuel. Use a table to determine if the number of hours you rent the boat is proportional to the total cost. Explain. (Examples 1–3)

Rental Time (h)			
Cost ($)			

2. Which situation represents a proportional relationship between the hours worked and amount earned for Matt and Jane? Explain. (Example 4)

Matt's Earnings ($)	12	20	31
Time (h)	1	2	3

Jane's Earnings ($)	12	24	36
Time (h)	1	2	3

3. **Building on the Essential Question** Explain what makes two quantities proportional.

Rate Yourself!

How confident are you about determining proportional relationships? Shade the ring on the target.

For more help, go online to access a Personal Tutor.

FOLDABLES Time to update your Foldable!

Independent Practice

Go online for Step-by-Step Solutions

For Exercises 1 and 2, use a table to solve. Then explain your reasoning.
(Examples 1 and 2)

1 An adult elephant drinks about 225 liters of water each day. Is the number of days the water supply lasts proportional to the number of liters of water the elephant drinks?

Time (days)	1	2	3	4
Water (L)				

2. An elevator *ascends*, or goes up, at a rate of 750 feet per minute. Is the height to which the elevator ascends proportional to the number of minutes it takes to get there? (Examples 1–3)

Time (min)	1	2	3	4
Height (ft)				

3. Which situation represents a proportional relationship between the number of laps run by each student and their time? (Example 4)

Desmond's Time (s)	146	292	584
Laps	2	4	8

Maria's Time (s)	150	320	580
Laps	2	4	6

Copy and Solve Use a table to help you solve. Then explain your reasoning. **Show your work on a separate piece of paper.**

4. Plant A is 18 inches tall after one week, 36 inches tall after two weeks, 56 inches tall after three weeks. Plant B is 18 inches tall after one week, 36 inches tall after two weeks, 54 inches tall after three weeks. Which situation represents a proportional relationship between the plants'

height and number of weeks? (Example 4) _____

5 Determine whether the measures for the figure shown are proportional.

a. the length of a side and the perimeter _____

b. the length of a side and the area _____

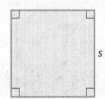

s

6. **(MP) Justify Conclusions** MegaMart collects a sales tax equal to $\frac{1}{16}$ of the retail price of each purchase. The tax is sent to the state government.

   a. Is the amount of tax collected proportional to the cost of an item before tax is added? Explain.

Retail Price ($)	16	32	48	64
Tax Collected ($)				

   b. Is the amount of tax collected proportional to the cost of an item after tax has been added? Explain.

Retail Price ($)	16	32	48	
Tax Collected ($)				
Cost Including Tax ($)				

H.O.T. Problems Higher Order Thinking

7. **(MP) Find the Error** Blake ran laps around the gym. His times are shown in the table. Blake is trying to decide whether the number of laps is proportional to the time. Find his mistake and correct it.

Time (min)	1	2	3	4
Laps	4	6	8	10

   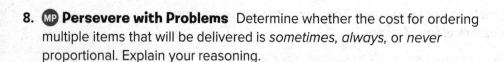

   It is proportional because the number of laps always increases by 2.

8. **(MP) Persevere with Problems** Determine whether the cost for ordering multiple items that will be delivered is *sometimes*, *always*, or *never* proportional. Explain your reasoning.

9. **(MP) Model with Mathematics** Give real-world examples of two similar situations in which one is a proportional relationship and the second one is nonproportional.

Extra Practice

For Exercises 10–12, use a table to solve. Then explain your reasoning.

10. A vine grows 7.5 feet every 5 days. Is the length of the vine on the last day proportional to the number of days of growth?

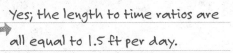

Yes; the length to time ratios are all equal to 1.5 ft per day.

Time (days)	5	10	15	20
Length (ft)	7.5	15	22.5	30

11. **STEM** To convert a temperature in degrees Celsius to degrees Fahrenheit, multiply the Celsius temperature by $\frac{9}{5}$ and then add 32°. Is a temperature in degrees Celsius proportional to its equivalent temperature in degrees Fahrenheit?

Degrees Celsius	0	10	20	30
Degrees Fahrenheit				

12. On Saturday, Querida gave away 416 coupons for a free appetizer at a local restaurant. The next day, she gave away about 52 coupons an hour.

a. Is the number of coupons Querida gave away on Sunday proportional to the number of hours she worked that day?

Hours Worked on Sunday	1	2	3	4
Coupons Given Away on Sunday				

b. Is the total number of coupons Querida gave away on Saturday and Sunday proportional to the number of hours she worked on Sunday?

Hours Worked on Sunday	1	2	3	4
Coupons Given Away on Weekend				

13. **MP Justify Conclusions** The fee for ride tickets at a carnival is shown in the table at the right.

a. Is the fee for ride tickets proportional to the number of tickets? Explain your reasoning.

Tickets	5	10	15	20
Fee ($)	5	9.50	13.50	16

b. Can you determine the fee for 30 ride tickets? Explain.

14. Mr. Martinez is comparing the prices of oranges from several different markets. Determine whether each market uses proportional or nonproportional pricing. Place a checkmark in the column for the correct type of relationship.

Number of Oranges	5	10	15	20
Total Cost ($)	3.50	6.50	9.00	10.25

Number of Oranges	5	10	15	20
Total Cost ($)	3.25	6.50	9.75	13.00

Number of Oranges	5	10	15	20
Total Cost ($)	3.75	7.50	11.25	15.00

Number of Oranges	5	10	15	20
Total Cost ($)	3.65	7.30	10.80	14.30

Proportional   **Nonproportional**

15. A grocery store sells a 2.5-pound bag of mixed nuts for $9.25. The prices of mixed nuts are proportional. Determine if each ofthe following bags of mixed nuts could have been sold by the grocery store. Select yes or no.

a. 4.4 pounds for $16.28 ☐ Yes ☐ No

b. 3.2 pounds for $12 ☐ Yes ☐ No

c. 2.8 pounds for $10.50 ☐ Yes ☐ No

Spiral Review

Find the value of each expression if $x = 12$.

16. $3x$ _____

17. $2x - 4$ _____

18. $5x + 30$ _____

19. $3x - 2x$ _____

20. $x - 12$ _____

21. $\frac{x}{4}$ _____

Make a table to solve the situation.

22. Brianna downloads 9 songs each month onto her MP3 player. Show the total number of songs downloaded after 1, 2, 3, and 4 months.

Month				
Number of Songs				

Case #1 'Round and 'Round

The Forte family visited the Mall of America in Minneapolis. The Ferris wheel in the mall's amusement park is about 22.5 meters tall.

What is the approximate height of the Mall of America Ferris wheel in feet if 1 foot is about 0.3 meter?

In mathematics, there is a *four-step problem-solving plan* you can use to help you solve any problem. The four steps are *Understand, Plan, Solve,* and *Check.*

Understand *What are the facts?*

- The Mall of America Ferris wheel is about 22.5 meters tall.
- You need to find the height of the Ferris wheel in feet.

Plan *What is your strategy to solve this problem?*

To solve the problem, write an expression that converts meters to feet. Then divide out common units.

Solve *How can you apply the strategy?*

One foot is about 0.3 meter. Convert 22.5 meters to feet.

$$22.5 \text{ meters} \cdot \frac{1 \text{ foot}}{0.3 \text{ meter}} \approx \frac{22.5}{0.3} \text{ or } \boxed{} \text{ feet}$$

So, the Ferris wheel is about 75 feet tall.

Check *Does the answer make sense?*

There is a little more than 3 feet in a meter.

Since $3 \cdot 22.5$ is 67.5 and 75 feet is a little more than 67.5 feet, the answer is reasonable.

Analyze the Strategy

MP Reason Inductively Explain in your own words how the four-step plan helps you solve real-world problems.

Case #2 Cool Treats

Mr. Martino's class learned the average American consumes about 23 quarts of ice cream every year. The class also learned the average American in the north-central United States consumes about 19 quarts more.

How much ice cream in gallons is consumed every year by the average American in the north-central United States?

Understand

Read the problem. What are you being asked to find?

I need to find _____

Fill in each box with the information you know.

The average American consumes about ☐ quarts of ice cream.

The average American in the north-central United States consumes about ☐ quarts more.

Plan

Choose two operations to solve the problem.

I will _____

Solve

How will you use the operations?

I will _____

Find total quarts.

☐ + ☐ = ☐

Convert to gallons.

☐ quarts · $\dfrac{1 \text{ gallon}}{☐ \text{ quarts}}$ = _____ gallons

The average American in the north-central United States consumes about ☐ gallons of ice cream each year.

Check

Use information from the problem to check your solution.

_____

Work with a small group to solve the following cases.
Show your work on a separate piece of paper.

Collaborate

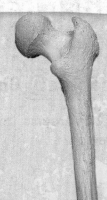

Case #3 Financial Literacy

Terry opened a savings account in December with $150 and deposited $30 each month beginning in January.

What is the value of Terry's account at the end of July?

_____

Case #4 STEM

About how many centimeters longer is the average femur than the average tibia? (Hint: 1 inch ≈ 2.54 centimeters)

_____

Bones in a Human Leg	
Bone	Length (in.)
Femur (upper leg)	19.88
Tibia (inner lower leg)	16.94
Fibula (outer lower leg)	15.94

Case #5 Patterns

Numbers that can be represented by a triangular arrangement of dots are called *triangular numbers*. The first four triangular numbers are shown.

Describe the pattern in the first four numbers. Then list the next three triangular numbers.

_____

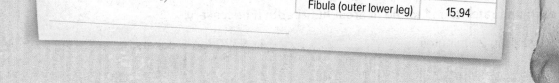

1   3   6   10

Case #6 Transportation

Mr. Norman has agreed to drive 4 students to their gymnastics practice.

If one student rides in the front seat and three students ride in the back, in how many ways can the 4 students be arranged in the car?

_____

Use any strategy!

Mid-Chapter Check

Vocabulary Check

1. **MP Be Precise** Define *complex fraction*. Give two examples of a complex fraction.

   _____

   _____

2. Fill in the blank in the sentence below with the correct term.

   When a rate is simplified so that it has a denominator of 1 unit, it is

   called a(n) _____ rate.

Skills Check and Problem Solving

Find each unit rate. Round to the nearest hundredth if necessary.

3. 750 yards in 25 minutes _____

4. $420 for 15 tickets _____

Simplify.

5. $\dfrac{9}{\frac{1}{3}} =$ _____

6. $\dfrac{\frac{1}{2}}{4} =$ _____

7. $\dfrac{\frac{1}{6}}{1\frac{3}{8}} =$ _____

8. A tourist information center charges $10 per hour to rent a bicycle. Is the rental charge proportional to the number of hours you rent the bicycle? Justify your response.

   _____

9. **MP Persevere with Problems** A cruise ship is traveling at a speed of 20 knots. A knot is approximately equal to 1.151 miles per hour. What is the approximate speed the ship is traveling in yards per second? Round to the nearest tenth. _____

Graph Proportional Relationships

Vocabulary Start-Up

Maps have grids to locate cities. The **coordinate plane** is a type of grid that is formed when two number lines intersect at their zero points. The number lines separate the coordinate plane into four regions called **quadrants**.

An **ordered pair** is a pair of numbers, such as (1, 2), used to locate or graph points on the coordinate plane.

| The *x*-coordinate corresponds to a number on the *x*-axis. | ···▶(1, 2)◀··· | The *y*-coordinate corresponds to a number on the *y*-axis. |

Label the coordinate plane with the terms *ordered pair*, *x*-coordinate, and *y*-coordinate.

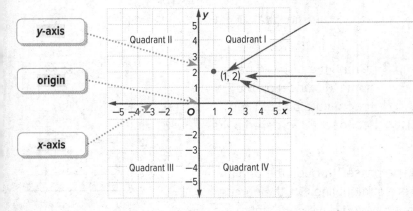

Graph points (2, 3) and (−3, −2) above. Connect the three points on the coordinate plane. Describe the graph.

_____

Which MP **Mathematical Process Goals** did you use? Shade the circle(s) that applies.

① Mathematical Problem Solving   ④ Mathematical Connections
② Mathematical Communication   ⑤ Mathematical Representations
③ Mathematical Reasoning

Essential Question

HOW can you show that two objects are proportional?

 Vocabulary

coordinate plane
quadrants
ordered pair
x-coordinate
y-coordinate
y-axis
origin
x-axis

Virginia Standards
7.10e

Identify Proportional Relationships

Another way to determine whether two quantities are proportional is to graph the quantities on the coordinate plane. If the graph of the two quantities is a straight line through the origin, then the two quantities are proportional.

Real World Example

Tutor

1. The slowest mammal on Earth is the tree sloth. It moves at a speed of 6 feet per minute. Determine whether the number of feet the sloth moves is proportional to the number of minutes it moves by graphing on the coordinate plane. Explain your reasoning.

Step 1 Make a table to find the number of feet walked for 0, 1, 2, 3, and 4 minutes.

Time (min)	0	1	2	3	4
Distance (ft)	0	6	12	18	24

Step 2 Graph the ordered pairs (time, distance) on the coordinate plane. Then connect the ordered pairs.

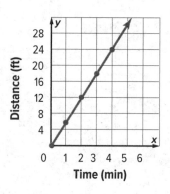

The line passes through the origin and is a straight line. So, the number of feet traveled is proportional to the number of minutes.

Got it? Do this problem to find out.

Show your work.

a. James earns $5 an hour babysitting. Determine whether the amount of money James earns babysitting is proportional to the number of hours he babysits by graphing on the coordinate plane. Explain your reasoning in the work zone.

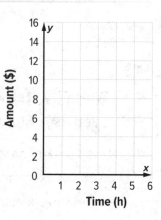

a. _____

Example

Tutor

2. The cost of renting video games from Games Inc. is shown in the table. Determine whether the cost is proportional to the number of games rented by graphing on the coordinate plane. Explain your reasoning.

Video Game Rental Rates	
Number of Games	Cost ($)
1	3
2	5
3	7
4	9

Step 1 Write the two quantities as ordered pairs (number of games, cost).

The ordered pairs are (1, 3), (2, 5), (3, 7), and (4, 9).

Step 2 Graph the ordered pairs on the coordinate plane. Then connect the ordered pairs and extend the line to the y-axis.

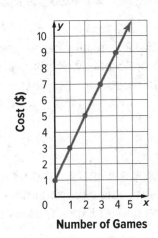

Number of Games

The line does not pass through the origin. So, the cost of the video games is not proportional to the number of games rented.

Check The ratios are not constant. $\frac{1}{3} \neq \frac{2}{5}$ ✔

> **Quick Review**
> Remember that the independent variable is the input and the dependent variable is the output. When drawing a graph, include the labels for both axes.

Got it? Do this problem to find out.

b. The table shows the number of Calories an athlete burned per minute of exercise. Determine whether the number of Calories burned is proportional to the number of minutes by graphing on the coordinate plane. Explain your reasoning in the Work Zone.

Calories Burned	
Number of Minutes	Number of Calories
0	0
1	4
2	8
3	13

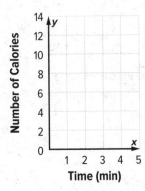

Time (min)

Show your work.

b. _____

Example

Tutor

3. Which batting cage represents a proportional relationship between the number of pitches thrown and the cost? Explain.

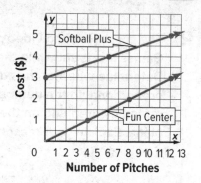

The graph for Softball Plus is a straight line, but it does not pass through the origin. So, the relationship is not proportional.

The graph for the Fun Center is a straight line through the origin. So, the relationship between the number of the pitches thrown and the cost is proportional.

Guided Practice

Check ✓

1. The cost of 3-D movie tickets is $12 for 1 ticket, $24 for 2 tickets, and $36 for 3 tickets. Determine whether the cost is proportional to the number of tickets by graphing on the coordinate plane. Explain your reasoning. (Examples 1 and 2)

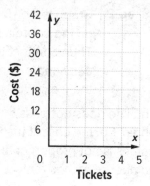

_____

_____

2. The number of books two stores sell after 1, 2, and 3 days is shown. Which book sale represents a proportional relationship between time and books? Explain. (Example 3)

_____

_____

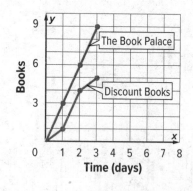

3. 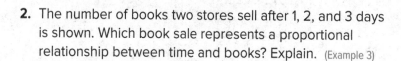 **Building on the Essential Question** How does graphing relationships help you determine whether the

relationship is proportional or not? _____

_____

_____

Rate Yourself!

How confident are you about identifying proportional relationships by graphing? Check the box that applies.

☹ 😐 🙂

For more help, go online to access a Personal Tutor.

Tutor

FOLDABLES Time to update your Foldable!

Independent Practice

Go online for Step-by-Step Solutions

MP **Model with Mathematics** Determine whether the relationship between the two quantities shown in each table are proportional by graphing on the coordinate plane. **Explain your reasoning.** (Examples 1 and 2)

 1

Savings Account	
Week	Account Balance ($)
1	125
2	150
3	175

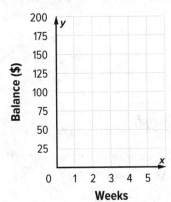

_____
_____

2.

Calories in Fruit Cups	
Servings	Calories
1	70
3	210
5	350

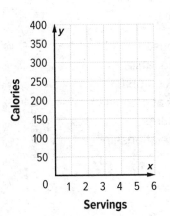

_____
_____

3 The height of two plants is recorded after 1, 2, and 3 weeks as shown in the graph at the right. Which plants' growth represents a proportional relationship between time and height? Explain. (Example 3)

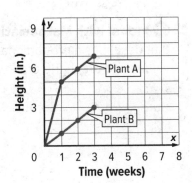

_____
_____

4. The perimeter of a square is 4 times as great as the length of any of its sides. Determine if the perimeter of a square is proportional to its side length. Explain.

_____

5. A health club charges $35 a month for membership fees. Determine whether the cost of membership is proportional to the number of months. Explain your reasoning.

_____

_____

🔥 H.O.T. Problems Higher Order Thinking

6. **MP Reason Abstractly** Describe some data that when graphed would represent a proportional relationship. Explain your reasoning.

_____

_____

_____

7. **MP Persevere with Problems** The greenhouse temperatures at certain times are shown in the table. The greenhouse maintains temperatures between 65°F and 85°F. Suppose the temperature increases at a constant rate. Create a graph of the time and temperatures at each hour from 1:00 P.M. to 8:00 P.M. Is the relationship proportional? Explain.

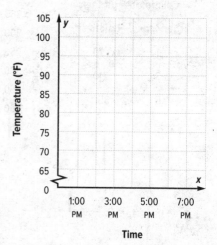

Time	Temperature (°F)
1:00 P.M.	66
6:00 P.M.	78.5
8:00 P.M.	83.5

_____

_____

_____

8. **MP Model with Mathematics** Write a real-world problem that describes a proportional relationship. Make a table of values and graph the ordered pairs on the coordinate plane.

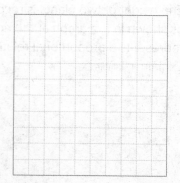

Extra Practice

Determine whether the relationship between the two quantities shown in each table are proportional by graphing on the coordinate plane. Explain your reasoning.

9.

Cooling Water	
Time (min)	Temperature (°F)
5	95
10	90
15	85

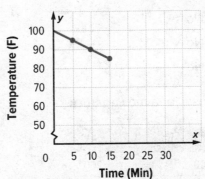

Homework Help

Not proportional; The graph does not pass through the origin.

10.

Pizza Recipe	
Number of Pizzas	Cheese (oz)
1	8
4	32
7	56

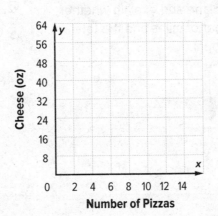

Copy and Solve Determine if each situation represents a proportional relationship. Graph on a separate piece of paper. Write an explanation for each situation.

11. **MP Justify Conclusions** An airplane is flying at an altitude of 4,000 feet and descends at a rate of 200 feet per minute. Determine whether the altitude is proportional to number of minutes. Explain your reasoning.

12. Frank and Allie purchased cell phone plans through different providers. Their costs for several minutes are shown. Graph each plan to determine whose plan is proportional to the number of minutes the phone is used. Explain your reasoning.

Cell Phone Plans		
Time (min)	Frank's Cost ($)	Allie's Cost ($)
0	0	4.00
3	1.50	4.50
6	3.00	5.00

13. The relationship between the number of heartbeats and the time shown in the graph is proportional. Determine if each ordered pair represents a point from this relationship. Select yes or no.

a. (5, 10) ☐ Yes   ☐ No

b. (14, 7) ☐ Yes   ☐ No

c. (8, 16) ☐ Yes   ☐ No

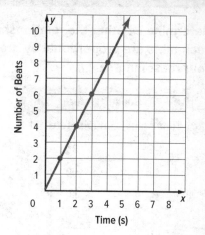

14. The table shows the rental costs for a moving truck.

Rental Costs				
Miles Driven	50	100	150	200
Total Cost ($)	40	60	80	100

Graph the data on the coordinate plane and explain whether the relationship between the number of miles and the total cost is proportional or nonproportional.

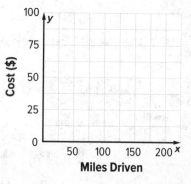

Spiral Review

Write each ratio as a fraction in simplest form.

15. A class has 10 boys and 15 girls. What is the ratio of boys to girls? _____

16. A car dealership has 55 cars and 11 vans. What is the ratio of cars to vans? _____

17. A drawer has 4 red shirts and 8 green shirts. What is the ratio of red shirts to the total number of shirts? _____

18. A store sells 13 coffees and 65 hot chocolates. What is the ratio of coffees to hot chocolates? _____

Inquiry HOW are proportional and nonproportional linear relationships alike? HOW are they different?

Albert and Bianca joined an online discussion group. Each student posted four comments. The number of replies to each of their comments is shown in the table. Determine if each data set represents a proportional relationship.

Hands-On Activity

Tools

Step 1 Arrange centimeter cubes to model the number of replies per comment as shown in the diagram below.

Student	Albert				Bianca			
Comment Number	1	2	3	4	1	2	3	4
Number of Replies								

Step 2 Complete each table. Then graph the data on the coordinate plane. You may wish to use a different color pencil for each data set.

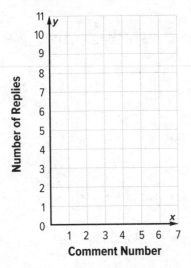

Albert's Comments

Comment Number (x)	Number of Replies (y)
1	2
2	4
3	
4	

Bianca's Comments

Comment Number (x)	Number of Replies (y)
1	1
2	4
3	
4	

Analyze and Reflect

Work with a partner to answer the following questions.

1. Describe any patterns in the data.

   _____

   _____

2. Connect the ordered pairs with a straight line for each graph. Then describe the graphs.

   _____

   _____

   _____

3. Predict the next three points on the graph for each data.

   _____

   _____

   _____

4. Compare and contrast the relationship shown in each graph. What do you notice?

   _____

   _____

   _____

Create

5. **MP Model with Mathematics** Use a table and graph to describe a real-world situation that represents a proportional relationship. Then explain how you could change your situation so that it represents a nonproportional relationship.

   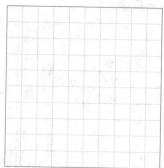

   _____

   _____

6. **inquiry** HOW are proportional and nonproportional linear relationships alike? HOW are they different?

   _____

   _____

Solve Proportional Relationships

Real-World Link

Watch

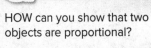

Fruit Smoothies Katie and some friends want to buy fruit smoothies. They go to a health food store that advertises a sale of 2 fruit smoothies for $5.

1. Fill in the boxes to write a ratio that compares the cost to the number of fruit smoothies.

$$\frac{\$\square}{\square \text{ smoothies}}$$

2. Suppose Katie and her friends buy 6 fruit smoothies. Complete the ratio that compares the cost to the number of fruit smoothies.

$$\frac{\$\square}{6 \text{ smoothies}}$$

3. Is the cost proportional to the number of fruit smoothies for two and six smoothies? Explain.

____

____

____

Essential Question

HOW can you show that two objects are proportional?

Vocabulary

proportion
cross product

Virginia Standards
7.3; 7.10e

Which MP **Mathematical Process Goals** did you use? Shade the circle(s) that applies.

① Mathematical Problem Solving
② Mathematical Communication
③ Mathematical Reasoning
④ Mathematical Connections
⑤ Mathematical Representations

Write and Solve Proportions

Work Zone

Words A **proportion** is an equation stating that two ratios or rates are equivalent.

Numbers	Algebra
$\dfrac{6}{8} = \dfrac{3}{4}$	$\dfrac{a}{b} = \dfrac{c}{d}, b \neq 0, d \neq 0$

Consider the following proportion.

$$\frac{a}{b} = \frac{c}{d}$$

$$\frac{a}{\overset{}{\underset{1}{b}}} \cdot \overset{1}{b}d = \frac{c}{\overset{}{\underset{1}{d}}} \cdot b\overset{1}{d} \qquad \text{Multiply each side by } bd \text{ and divide out common factors.}$$

$$ad = bc \qquad \text{Simplify.}$$

The products ad and bc are called the **cross products** of this proportion. The cross products of any proportion are equal.

$$\frac{6}{8} \times \frac{3}{4} \longrightarrow \begin{array}{c} 8 \cdot 3 \\ 6 \cdot 4 \end{array} = \frac{24}{24}$$

Example

1. **After 2 hours, the air temperature had risen 7°F. Write and solve a proportion to find the amount of time it will take at this rate for the temperature to rise an additional 13°F.**

   Write a proportion. Let t represent the time in hours.

   $$\begin{array}{ll} \text{temperature} \longrightarrow \\ \text{time} \longrightarrow \end{array} \frac{7}{2} = \frac{13}{t} \begin{array}{ll} \longleftarrow \text{temperature} \\ \longleftarrow \text{time} \end{array}$$

   $$7 \cdot t = 2 \cdot 13 \qquad \text{Find the cross products.}$$

   $$7t = 26 \qquad \text{Multiply}$$

   $$\frac{7t}{7} = \frac{26}{7} \qquad \text{Divide each side by 7.}$$

   $$t \approx 3.7 \qquad \text{Simplify.}$$

   It will take about 3.7 hours to rise an additional 13°F.

> **Got it?** Do these problems to find out.

Show your work.

Solve each proportion.

a. $\dfrac{x}{4} = \dfrac{9}{10}$

b. $\dfrac{2}{34} = \dfrac{5}{y}$

c. $\dfrac{7}{3} = \dfrac{n}{21}$

a. _____

b. _____

c. _____

Example

2. If the ratio of Type O to non-Type O donors at a blood drive was 37:43, how many donors would be Type O, out of 300 donors?

Type O donors ⟶ $\dfrac{37}{37 + 43}$ or $\dfrac{37}{80}$
total donors ⟶

Write a proportion. Let t represent the number of Type O donors.

Type O donors ⟶ $\dfrac{37}{80} = \dfrac{t}{300}$ ⟵ Type O donors
total donors ⟶   ⟵ total donors

$37 \cdot 300 = 80t$ Find the cross products.

$11{,}100 = 80t$ Multiply.

$\dfrac{11{,}100}{80} = \dfrac{80t}{80}$ Divide each side by 80.

$138.75 = t$ Simplify.

There would be about 139 Type O donors.

Got it? Do this problem to find out.

> **d.** The ratio of 7th grade students to 8th grade students in a soccer league is 17:23. If there are 200 students in all, how many are in the 7th grade?

Show your work.

d. _____

Use Unit Rate

You can also use the unit rate to write an equation expressing the relationship between two proportional quantities.

Examples

3. Olivia bought 6 containers of yogurt for $7.68. Write an equation relating the cost c to the number of yogurts y. How much would Olivia pay for 10 yogurts at this same rate?

Find the unit rate between cost and containers of yogurt.

$$\dfrac{\text{cost in dollars}}{\text{containers of yogurt}} = \dfrac{7.68}{6} \text{ or } \$1.28 \text{ per container}$$

The cost is $1.28 times the number of containers of yogurt.

$c = 1.28y$ Let c represent the cost. Let y represent the number of yogurts.

$= 1.28(10)$ Replace y with 10.

$= 12.80$ Multiply.

The cost for 10 containers of yogurt is $12.80.

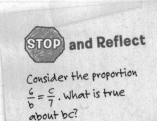
4. Jaycee bought 8 gallons of gas for $31.12. Write an equation relating the cost c to the number of gallons g of gas. How much would Jaycee pay for 11 gallons at this same rate?

Find the unit rate between cost and gallons.

$$\frac{\text{cost in dollars}}{\text{gasoline in gallons}} = \frac{31.12}{8} \text{ or } \$3.89 \text{ per gallon}$$

The cost is $3.89 times the number of gallons.

$$c = 3.89g \qquad \text{Let } c \text{ represent the cost. Let } g \text{ represent the number of gallons.}$$

$$= 3.89(11) \qquad \text{Replace } g \text{ with 11.}$$

$$= 42.79 \qquad \text{Multiply.}$$

The cost for 11 gallons of gas is $42.79.

Got it? Do this problem to find out.

 Show your work.

e. Olivia typed 2 pages in 15 minutes. Write an equation relating the number of minutes m to the number of pages p typed. How long will it take her to type 10 pages at this rate?

e. _____

Guided Practice

Solve each proportion. (Examples 1 and 2)

1. $\frac{k}{7} = \frac{32}{56}$ $k =$ _____

2. $\frac{3.2}{9} = \frac{n}{36}$ $n =$ _____

3. $\frac{41}{x} = \frac{5}{2}$ $x =$ _____

4. Trina earns $28.50 tutoring for 3 hours. Write an equation relating her earnings m to the number of hours h she tutors. Assuming the situation is proportional, how much would Trina earn tutoring for 2 hours? for 4.5 hours? (Examples 3 and 4)

_____

5. **Building on the Essential Question** How do you solve a proportion?

_____

_____

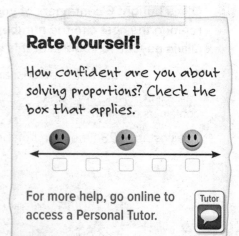

Rate Yourself!

How confident are you about solving proportions? Check the box that applies.

For more help, go online to access a Personal Tutor.

FOLDABLES Time to update your Foldable!

Name _____ My Homework _____

Solve each proportion. (Examples 1 and 2)

1. $\dfrac{1.5}{6} = \dfrac{10}{p}$ $p =$ _____

2. $\dfrac{44}{p} = \dfrac{11}{5}$ $p =$ _____

3. $\dfrac{2}{w} = \dfrac{0.4}{0.7}$ $w =$ _____

Assume the situations are proportional. Write and solve by using a proportion. (Examples 1 and 2)

4. Evarado paid $1.12 for a dozen eggs at his local grocery store. Determine the cost of 3 eggs.

5. Sheila mixed 3 ounces of blue paint with 2 ounces of yellow paint. She decided to create 20 ounces of the same mixture. How many ounces of yellow paint does Sheila need for the new mixture?

Assume the situations are proportional. Use the unit rate to write an equation, then solve. (Examples 3 and 4)

6. A car can travel 476 miles on 14 gallons of gas. Write an equation relating the distance d to the number of gallons g. How many gallons of gas does this car need to travel 578 miles.

7. Mrs. Baker paid $2.50 for 5 pounds of bananas. Write an equation relating the cost c to the number of pounds p of bananas. How much would Mrs. Baker pay for 8 pounds of bananas?

8. A woman who is 64 inches tall has a shoulder width of 16 inches. Write an equation relating the height h to the width w. Find the height of a woman who has a shoulder width of 18.5 inches.

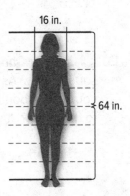

16 in.

64 in.

9. At an amusement park, 360 visitors rode the roller coaster in 3 hours. Write and solve a proportion to find the number of visitors at this rate who will ride the roller coaster in 7 hours. (Examples 3 and 4)

_____

10. **MP Reason Abstractly** Use the table to write a proportion relating the weights on two planets. Then find the missing weight. Round to the nearest tenth.

Weights on Different Planets Earth Weight = 120 pounds	
Mercury	45.6 pounds
Venus	109.2 pounds
Uranus	96 pounds
Jupiter	304.8 pounds

a. Earth: 90 pounds; Venus: [_____] pounds

b. Mercury: 55 pounds; Earth: [_____] pounds

c. Jupiter: 350 pounds; Uranus: [_____] pounds

d. Venus: 115 pounds; Mercury: [_____] pounds

H.O.T. Problems Higher Order Thinking

11. **MP Justify Conclusions** A powdered drink mix calls for a ratio of powder to water of 1:8. If there are 32 cups of powder, how many total cups of water are needed? Explain your reasoning. _____

_____

_____

_____

MP Persevere with Problems Solve each equation.

12. $\frac{2}{3} = \frac{18}{x+5}$ _____

13. $\frac{x-4}{10} = \frac{7}{5}$ _____

14. $\frac{4.5}{17-x} = \frac{3}{8}$ _____

15. **MP Justify Conclusions** A rectangle has an area of 36 square units. As the length and the width change, what do you know about their product? Is the length proportional to the width? Justify your reasoning.

Rectangle	Length	Width	Area (units^2)
A	3	12	36
B	6	6	36
C	9	4	36

_____

_____

Extra Practice

Solve each proportion.

16. $\dfrac{x}{13} = \dfrac{18}{39}$ $x = $ _6_____

$x \cdot 39 = 13 \cdot 18$

$39x = 234$

$\dfrac{39x}{39} = \dfrac{234}{39}$

$x = 6$

Homework Help

17. $\dfrac{6}{25} = \dfrac{d}{30}$ $d = $ _____

18. $\dfrac{2.5}{6} = \dfrac{h}{9}$ $h = $ _____

Assume the situations are proportional. Write and solve by using a proportion.

19. For every person who has the flu, there are 6 people who have only flu-like symptoms. If a doctor sees 40 patients, determine approximately how many patients you would expect to have only flu-like symptoms.

20. For every left-handed person, there are about 4 right-handed people. If there are 30 students in a class, predict the number of students who are right-handed.

_____

21. Jeremiah is saving money from a tutoring job. After the first three weeks, he saved $135. Assume the situation is proportional. Use the unit rate to write an equation relating the amount saved *s* to the number of weeks *w* worked. At this rate, how much will Jeremiah save after eight weeks?

_____

22. **MP** **Make a Prediction** A speed limit of 100 kilometers per hour (kph) is approximately equal to 62 miles per hour (mph). Write an equation relating kilometers per hour *k* to miles per hour *m*. Then predict the following measures. Round to the nearest tenth.

a. a speed limit in mph for a speed limit of 75 kph

_____

b. a speed limit in kph for a speed limit of 20 mph

_____

23. Part of Nicole's pumpkin muffin recipe is shown. How many cups of flour are needed to make

5 dozen muffins? [ ]

> Pumpkin Muffin Recipe
> Yield: 2 dozen muffins
> 4.5 cups flour
> 1.5 cups sugar
> 1 teaspoon nutmeg

24. An amusement park line for passengers waiting to ride a rollercoaster is moving about 16 feet every 10 minutes. Jason and his friends are standing 40 feet from the front of the line. Select values to set up a proportion to represents this situation.

16	40
10	x

$$\frac{\boxed{}}{\boxed{}} = \frac{\boxed{}}{\boxed{}}$$

Solve the proportion to determine how long it will take for Jason and his friends to reach the front of the line.

[ ]

Spiral Review

25. The table shows the cost to have various numbers of pizzas delivered from Papa's Slice of Italy pizzeria. Is the relationship between the cost and the number of pizzas proportional? Explain.

Number of Pizzas	Cost ($)
1	12.50
2	20
3	27.50
4	35

26. Brenna charges $15, $30, $45, and $60 for babysitting 1, 2, 3, and 4 hours, respectively. Is the relationship between the amount charged and the number of hours proportional? If so, find the unit rate. If not, explain why not.

Find each unit rate.

27. 50 miles on 2.5 gallons _____

28. 2,500 kilobytes in 5 minutes _____

inquiry **HOW** is unit rate related to rate of change?

Happy Hound is a doggie daycare where people drop off their dogs while they are at work. It costs $3 for 1 hour, $6 for 2 hours, and $9 for 3 hours of doggie daycare. Farah takes her dog to Happy Hound several days a week. Farah wants to determine if the number of hours of daycare is related to the cost.

Hands-On Activity

Step 1 Assume the pattern in the table continues. Complete the table shown.

Happy Hound Doggie Daycare	
Number of Hours	Cost ($)
1	3
2	6
3	9
4	
5	

Step 2 The cost depends on the number of hours. So, the cost is the output y, and the number of hours is the _____. Graph the data on the coordinate plane below.

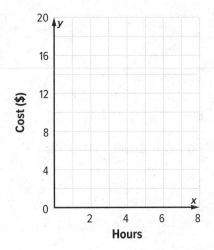

Investigate

Collaborate

Refer to the Investigation. Work with a partner.

1. **MP Justify Conclusions** Describe the graph.

   _____

2. What is the cost per hour, or unit rate, charged by Happy Hound?

   _____

3. Use the graph to examine any two consecutive points. By how much does y change? By how much does x change?

   _____

4. The first two ordered pairs on the graph are (1, 3) and (2, 6). You can find the _rate of change_ by writing the ratio of the change in y to the change in x.

   Find the rate of change shown in the graph. _____

Analyze and Reflect

Collaborate

Work with a partner to answer the following question.

5. Pampered Pooch charges $5 for 1 hour of doggie daycare, $10 for 2 hours, and $15 for 3 hours.

   a. What is the unit rate? _____

   b. What is the rate of change? _____

   c. **MP Reason Inductively** How do the rates of change for doggie daycare at Pampered Pooch and Happy Hound compare?

Create

On Your Own

6. **MP Model with Mathematics** Describe a doggie daycare situation that has a rate of change less than that of Happy Hound.

   _____

   _____

7. **Inquiry** HOW is unit rate related to rate of change?

   _____

   _____

Constant Rate of Change

Vocabulary Start-Up

A **rate of change** is a rate that describes how one quantity changes in relation to another. In a linear relationship, the rate of change between any two quantities is the same. A linear relationship has a **constant rate of change**.

 ### Real-World Link

A computer programmer charges customers per line of code written. Fill in the blanks with the amount of change between consecutive numbers.

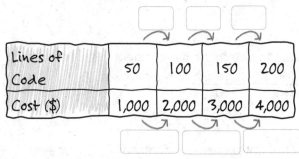

Lines of Code	50	100	150	200
Cost ($)	1,000	2,000	3,000	4,000

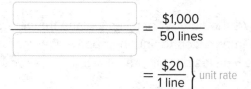

Label the diagram below with the terms *change in lines, change in dollars,* and *constant rate of change.*

$$\frac{\boxed{}}{\boxed{}} = \frac{\$1,000}{50 \text{ lines}}$$

$$= \frac{\$20}{1 \text{ line}} \Big\} \text{ unit rate}$$

The _____ is $20 per line of programming code.

  ### Essential Question

HOW can you show that two objects are proportional?

 Vocabulary

rate of change
constant rate of change

Virginia Standards
7.10a

Which **MP** Mathematical Process Goals did you use? Shade the circle(s) that applies.

① Mathematical Problem Solving
② Mathematical Communication
③ Mathematical Reasoning
④ Mathematical Connections
⑤ Mathematical Representations

Use a Table

You can use a table to find a constant rate of change.

 Example

1. The table shows the amount of money a booster club makes washing cars for a fundraiser. Use the information to find the constant rate of change in dollars per car.

Cars Washed

Number	Money ($)
5	40
10	80
15	120
20	160

+5 +40
+5 +40
+5 +40

Find the unit rate to determine the constant rate of change.

$$\frac{\text{change in money}}{\text{change in cars}} = \frac{40 \text{ dollars}}{5 \text{ cars}}$$ The money earned increases by $40 for every 5 cars.

$$= \frac{8 \text{ dollars}}{1 \text{ car}}$$ Write as a unit rate.

So, the number of dollars earned increases by $8 for every car washed.

> **Got it?** Do these problems to find out.

a. The table shows the number of miles a plane traveled while in flight. Use the information to find the approximate constant rate of change in miles per minute.

Time (min)	30	60	90	120
Distance (mi)	290	580	870	1,160

b. The table shows the number of students that buses can transport. Use the table to find the constant rate of change in students per school bus.

Number of Buses	2	3	4	5
Number of Students	144	216	288	360

Unit Rate
A rate of change is usually expressed as a unit rate.

 Show your work.

a. _____

b. _____

Use a Graph

You can also use a graph to find a constant rate of change and to analyze points on the graph.

Examples

Tutor

2. **The graph represents the distance traveled while driving on a highway. Find the constant rate of change.**

To find the rate of change, pick any two points on the line, such as (0, 0) and (1, 60).

$$\frac{\text{change in miles}}{\text{change in hours}} = \frac{(60 - 0) \text{ miles}}{(1 - 0) \text{ hours}}$$

$$= \frac{60 \text{ miles}}{1 \text{ hour}}$$

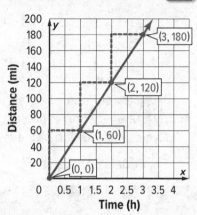

Ordered Pairs

The ordered pair (2, 120) represents traveling 120 miles in 2 hours.

3. **Explain what the points (0, 0) and (1, 60) represent.**

The point (0, 0) represents traveling zero miles in zero hours. The point (1, 60) represents traveling 60 miles in 1 hour. Notice that this is the constant rate of change.

Got it? Do these problems to find out.

c. Use the graph to find the constant rate of change in miles per hour while driving in the city.

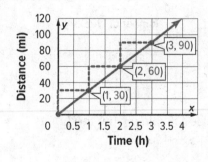

d. On the lines below, explain what the points (0, 0) and (1, 30) represent.

 Show your work.

C. _____

_____

_____

_____

Example

4. The table and graph below show the hourly charge to rent a bicycle at two different stores. Which store charges more per bicycle? Explain.

Pedals Rentals	
Time (hour)	Cost ($)
2	24
3	36
4	48

+1 +12
+1 +12

Super Cycles

Number of Hours

The cost at Pedals Rentals increases by $12 every hour. The cost at Super Cycles increases by $8 every hour.

So, Pedals Rentals charges more per hour to rent a bicycle.

Guided Practice

1. The table and graph below show the amount of money Mi-Ling and Daniel save each week. Who saves more each week? Explain. (Examples 1, 2, and 4)

Mi-Ling's Savings	
Time (weeks)	Savings ($)
2	$30
3	$45
4	$60

Daniel's Savings

Number of Weeks

2. Refer to the graph in Exercise 1. Explain what the points (0, 0) and (1, 10) represent. (Example 3)

3. **Building on the Essential Question** How can you find the unit rate on a graph that goes through the origin?

Rate Yourself!

Are you ready to move on? Shade the section that applies.

I have a few questions.

I'm ready to move on.

I have a lot of questions.

For more help, go online to access a Personal Tutor. Tutor

Independent Practice

Go online for Step-by-Step Solutions

eHelp

Find the constant rate of change for each table. (Example 1)

1

Time (s)	Distance (m)
1	6
2	12
3	18
4	24

2.

Items	Cost ($)
2	18
4	36
6	54
8	72

3 The graph shows the cost of purchasing T-shirts. Find the constant rate of change for the graph. Then explain what points (0, 0) and (1, 9) represent. (Examples 2 and 3)

_____

_____

_____

_____

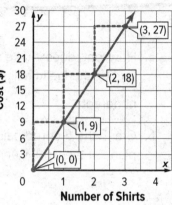

4. The Guzman and Hashimoto families each took a 4-hour road trip. The distances traveled by each family are shown in the table and graph below. Which family averaged fewer miles per hour? Explain. (Example 4)

Guzman's Road Trip	
Time (hours)	Distance (miles)
2	90
3	135
4	180

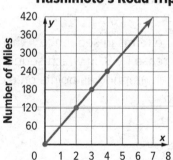

Hashimoto's Road Trip

_____

_____

_____

5. At 1:00 P.M., the water level in a pool is 13 inches. At 1:30 P.M., the water level is 18 inches. At 2:30 P.M., the water level is 28 inches. What is the constant rate of change?

_____

6  **MP Model with Mathematics** Refer to the lap times for Exercises **a** and **b**.

The race is 20 laps, which is 5 miles. Assuming your speed is constant...

Let's calculate Seth's times.

Lap	4	8	12	16	20
Distance(mi)	1	2	3	4	5
Time (s)	57.1	114.2	171.3		

a. How long does it take Seth to race 1 mile? Write the constant rate of change in miles per second. Round to the nearest hundredth. _____

b. Graph the ordered pairs (time, distance) on the coordinate plane at the right. Connect the points with a solid line.

Graph: Distance (miles) on y-axis from 0 to 5; Time (seconds) on x-axis labeled 50, 100, 150, 200, 250, 300.

🔥 H.O.T. Problems

7. **MP Model with Mathematics** Make a table where the constant rate of change is 6 inches for every foot.

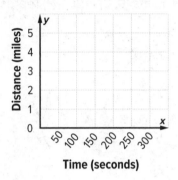

Feet	Inches

8. **MP Justify Conclusions** The terms in sequence A increase by 3. The terms in sequence B increase by 8. In which sequence do the terms form a steeper line when graphed as points on a coordinate plane? Justify your reasoning.

_____

_____

_____

9. **MP Persevere with Problems** The constant rate of change for the relationship shown in the table is $8 per hour. Find the missing values.

Time (h)	1	2	3
Earnings ($)	x	y	z

$x =$ _____ $y =$ _____ $z =$ _____

Extra Practice

Find the constant rate of change for each table.

10.

Time (h)	0	1	2	3
Wage ($)	0	9	18	27

$9 per hour

$$\frac{change\ in\ wages}{change\ in\ hours} = \frac{\$9}{1\ hour}$$

⬅ Homework Help

11.

Minutes	1,000	1,500	2,000	2,500
Cost ($)	38	53	68	83

12. Use the graph to find the constant rate of change. Then, explain what the points (0, 0) and (6, 72) represent.

_____

_____

_____

_____

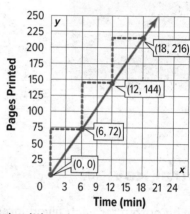

13. **MP Justify Conclusions** Ramona and Josh earn money by babysitting. The amounts earned for one evening are shown in the table and graph. Who charged more per hour? Explain.

Ramona's Earnings	
Time (hours)	Earnings ($)
2	18
3	27
4	36

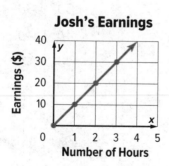

Josh's Earnings

_____

_____

14. The cost of 1 movie ticket is $7.50. The cost of 2 movie tickets is $15. Based on this constant rate of change, what is the cost of 4 movie tickets? _____

15. Reggie started a running program to prepare for track season. He ran a half hour each morning for 60 days. He averaged 6.5 miles per hour. What is the total number of miles Reggie ran over the 60-day period? [   ]

16. Select the correct constant rate of change for each table of data.

Number of Apples	3	7	11
Number of Seeds	30	70	110

☐ $\frac{1}{12}$ ☐ $\frac{1}{10}$ ☐ $\frac{12}{1}$ ☐ $\frac{10}{1}$

Number of Tables	4	6	9
Number of Chairs	48	72	108

☐ $\frac{1}{12}$ ☐ $\frac{1}{10}$ ☐ $\frac{12}{1}$ ☐ $\frac{10}{1}$

Number of Passengers	24	60	120
Number of Vans	2	5	10

☐ $\frac{1}{12}$ ☐ $\frac{1}{10}$ ☐ $\frac{12}{1}$ ☐ $\frac{10}{1}$

Number of Booklets	20	50	100
Number of Pages	2	5	10

☐ $\frac{1}{12}$ ☐ $\frac{1}{10}$ ☐ $\frac{12}{1}$ ☐ $\frac{10}{1}$

Spiral Review

Write the output for each given input in the tables below.

17.

Input	Add 4	Output
1	1 + 4	
2	2 + 4	
3	3 + 4	
4	4 + 4	

18.

Input	Subtract 5	Output
30	30 − 5	
40	40 − 5	
50	50 − 5	
60	60 − 5	

19.

Input	Multiply by 2	Output
1	1 × 2	
2	2 × 2	
3	3 × 2	
4	4 × 2	

20.

Input	Divide by 3	Output
3	3 ÷ 3	
6	6 ÷ 3	
9	9 ÷ 3	
12	12 ÷ 3	

Real-World Link

Recycling Hero Comics prints on recycled paper. The table shows the total number of pounds of recycled paper that has been used each day during the month.

Day of Month	Total Recycled (lbs)
3	36
5	60
6	72
7	84
12	144

 Essential Question

HOW can you show that two objects are proportional?

Vocab **Vocabulary**

slope
rise
run

 Virginia Standards
7.10a

1. Graph the ordered pairs on the coordinate plane.

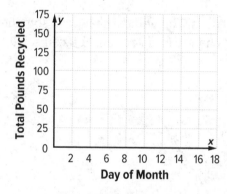

2. Explain why the graph is linear. _____

_____

3. Use two points to find the constant rate of change.

Point 1: _____   change in pounds ⟶ [   ] pounds
Point 2: _____   change in days ⟶ [   ] days

So, the constant rate of change is $\frac{24}{2}$ or [   ] pounds per day.

Which MP **Mathematical Process Goals did you use? Shade the circle(s) that applies.**

① Mathematical Problem Solving   ④ Mathematical Connections

② Mathematical Communication   ⑤ Mathematical Representations

③ Mathematical Reasoning

Slope is the rate of change between any two points on a line.

$$\text{slope} = \frac{\text{change in } y}{\text{change in } x} \quad \longleftarrow \text{ vertical change}$$
$$\longleftarrow \text{ horizontal change}$$

$$= \frac{2}{1} \text{ or } 2$$

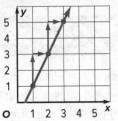

In a linear relationship, the vertical change (change in *y*-value) per unit of horizontal change (change in *x*-value) is always the same. This ratio is called the **slope** of the function. The constant rate of change, or unit rate, is the same as the slope of the related linear relationship.

The slope tells how steep the line is. The vertical change is sometimes called rise while the horizontal change is called run. You can say that slope $= \frac{\text{rise}}{\text{run}}$.

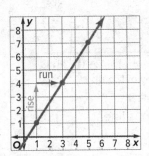

Count the number of units that make up the rise of the line in the graph shown above. Write this number for the numerator of the fraction below. Count the number of units that make up the run of the line. Write this number for the denominator of the fraction below.

$$\frac{\text{rise}}{\text{run}} = \frac{\square}{\square}$$

So, the slope of the line is $\frac{3}{2}$.

Real World

Example

Watch Tutor

1. The table below shows the relationship between the number of seconds *y* it takes to hear thunder after a lightning strike and the miles *x* you are from the lightning. Graph the data and find the slope. Explain what the slope represents.

Miles (*x*)	0	1	2	3	4	5
Seconds (*y*)	0	5	10	15	20	25

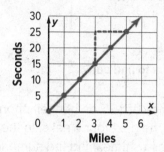

$$\text{slope} = \frac{\text{change in } y}{\text{change in } x} \quad \text{Definition of slope}$$

$$= \frac{25 - 15}{5 - 3} \quad \text{Use (3, 15) and (5, 25).}$$

$$= \frac{10}{2} \quad \begin{matrix}\longleftarrow \text{seconds} \\ \longleftarrow \text{miles}\end{matrix}$$

$$= \frac{5}{1} \quad \text{Simplify.}$$

So, for every 5 seconds between a lightning flash and the sound of thunder, there is 1 mile between you and the lightning strike.

> **Got it?** Do this problem to find out.

a. Graph the data about plant height for a science fair project. Then find the slope of the line. Explain what the slope represents in the work zone.

Week	Plant Height (cm)
1	1.5
2	3
3	4.5
4	6

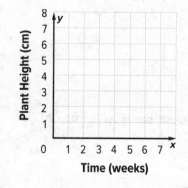

 Show your work.

a. _____

> **Slope** In everyday language, slope means inclination or slant.
>
> In math language, slope means the ratio of vertical change per unit of horizontal change; the steepness of a line.

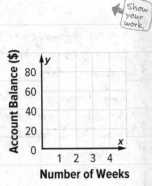

Account Balance ($)

Number of Weeks

Example

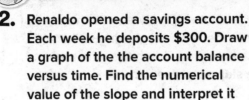
Tutor

2. Renaldo opened a savings account. Each week he deposits $300. Draw a graph of the the account balance versus time. Find the numerical value of the slope and interpret it in words.

The slope of the line is the rate at which the account balance rises, or $\frac{\$300}{1\ \text{week}}$.

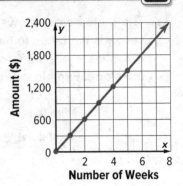

Amount ($)

Number of Weeks

Got it? Do this problem to find out.

b. _____

b. Jessica has a balance of $35 on her cell phone account. She adds $10 each week for the next four weeks. In the work zone, graph the account balance versus time. Find the numerical value of the slope and interpret it in words.

Guided Practice

Check ✓

1. The table at the right shows the number of small packs of fruit snacks y per box x. Graph the data. Then find the slope of the line. Explain what the slope represents. (Examples 1 and 2)

Boxes, x	3	5	7
Fruit Snacks, y	12	20	28

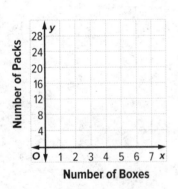

Number of Packs

Number of Boxes

2. **Building on the Essential Question** How is rate of change related to slope? _____

_____

_____

Rate Yourself!

How well do you understand slope? Circle the image.

Clear   Somewhat   Not So
          Clear   Clear

For more help, go online to access a Personal Tutor.

Tutor

Independent Practice

Go online for Step-by-Step Solutions

1 The table shows the number of pages Adriano read in *x* hours. Graph the data. Then find the slope of the line. Explain what the slope represents. (Example 1)

Time (h)	1	2	3	4
Number of pages	50	100	150	200

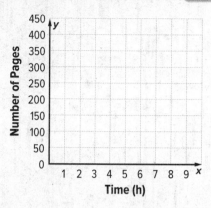

_____

_____

2. Graph the data. Find the numerical value of the slope and interpret it in words. (Example 2)

Number of Yards	1	2	3
Number of Feet	3	6	9

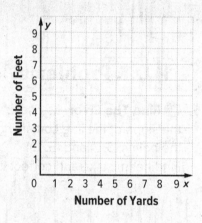

_____

_____

3 The graph shows the average speed of two cars on the highway.

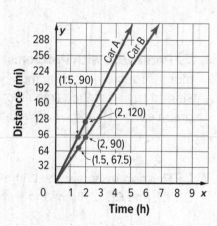

a. What does (2, 120) represent? _____

_____

b. What does (1.5, 67.5) represent? _____

_____

c. What does the ratio of the *y*-coordinate to the *x*-coordinate for each pair of points on the graph represent?

_____

d. What does the slope of each line represent?

_____

e. Which car is traveling faster? How can you tell from the graph?

_____

4. 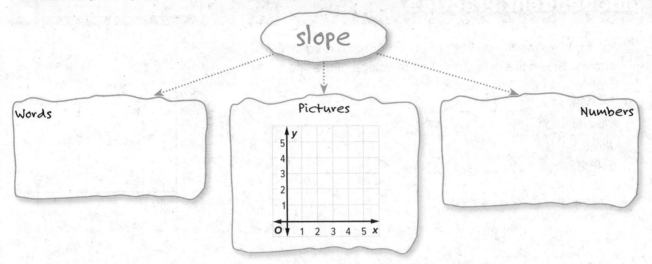 **MP Multiple Representations** Complete the graphic organizer on slope.

slope

Words

Pictures

Numbers

H.O.T. Problems Higher Order Thinking

5. **MP Find The Error** Marisol is finding the slope of the line containing the points (3, 7) and (5, 10). Find her mistake and correct it.

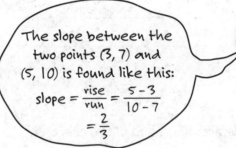

The slope between the two points (3, 7) and (5, 10) is found like this:

$$\text{slope} = \frac{rise}{run} = \frac{5-3}{10-7}$$
$$= \frac{2}{3}$$

6. **MP Persevere with Problems** Kaya is saving money at a rate of $30 per month. Eduardo is saving money at a rate of $35 per month. They both started saving at the same time. If you were to create a table of values and graph each function, what would be the slope of each graph?

7. **MP Reason Inductively** Without graphing, determine whether $A(5, 1)$, $B(1, 0)$, and $C(3, 3)$ lie on the same line. Explain your reasoning.

8. **MP Model with Mathematics** Name two points on a line that has a slope of $\frac{5}{8}$.

Extra Practice

9. **MP** **Justify Conclusions** The table to the right shows the number of markers per box. Graph the data. Then find the slope of the line. Explain what the slope represents.

Boxes	1	2	3	4
Markers	8	16	24	32

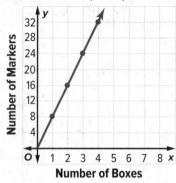

Use (1, 8) and (2, 16).

$$\text{slope} = \frac{\text{change in } y}{\text{change in } x}$$

$$= \frac{16 - 8}{2 - 1}$$

$$= \frac{8}{1}$$

So, there are 8 markers in every box.

10. The table shows the cost to rent a paddle boat from two businesses.

a. What does (1, 20) represent?

_____

_____

b. What does (2, 50) represent?

_____

_____

Paddle Boat Rentals		
Number of Hours	Water Wheels Cost ($)	Fun in the Sun Cost ($)
1	20	25
2	40	50
3	60	75
4	80	100

Copy and Solve **For Exercises 11–14, draw a graph on a separate sheet of grid paper to find each slope. Then record each slope and interpret its meaning.**

11. Joshua swims 25 meters in 1 minute. Draw a graph of meters swam versus time. Find the value of the slope and interpret it in words.

12. The table shows the amount Maggie earns for various numbers of hours she babysits. Graph the data. Then find the slope of the line. Explain what the slope represents.

Number of Hours	Earnings ($)
1	8
2	16
3	24
4	32

13. Zack completes 20 homework problems in 1 hour. Draw a graph of homework problems versus time. Find the value of the slope and interpret it in words.

14. The Jackson family rents 6 movies each month. Draw a graph of movies rented versus time. Find the value of the slope and interpret it in words.

15. Two weeks ago, Audrey earned $84 for 7 hours of work. This week, she earned $132 for 11 hours of work. Find the numerical value of the slope of the line

that represents Audrey's earnings. ☐

16. The ordered pairs (1, 4), (3, 12), and (5, 20) represent the distance y that Jairo walks after x seconds. Plot the ordered pairs on the coordinate plane and draw a line through the points.

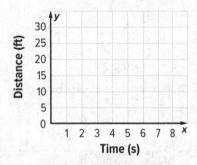

Find the slope of the line and explain what the slope represents.

☐

Spiral Review

Determine if each situation is proportional. Explain your reasoning.

17. Taxi cab passengers are charged $2.50 upon entering a cab. They are then charged $1.00 for every mile traveled.

_____

18. A restaurant charges $5 for one sandwich, $9.90 for two sandwiches, and $14.25 for three sandwiches.

_____

_____

19.

Tickets Purchased	1	2	3	4
Cost ($)	7.50	15	22.50	30

20.

Cups of Flour	3	6	9	12
Cups of Sugar	2	4	6	8

Direct Variation

Real-World Link

Speed The distance y a car travels after x hours can be represented by $y = 65x$. The table and graph also represent the situation.

Time (hours)	Distance (miles)
2	130
3	195
4	260

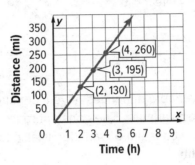

Essential Question

HOW can you show that two objects are proportional?

 Vocab

Vocabulary

direct variation
constant of variation
constant of proportionality

 Virginia Standards
7.10a, e

1. Fill in the blanks to find the constant ratio.

$$\frac{\text{distance traveled}}{\text{driving time}} = \frac{130}{2} = \frac{195}{\boxed{}} = \frac{\boxed{}}{4}$$

The constant ratio is $\boxed{}$ miles per hour.

2. The constant rate of change, or slope, of the line is $\frac{\text{change in miles}}{\text{change in time}}$, which is equal to $\frac{195 - 130}{3 - 2}$

or $\boxed{}$ miles per hour.

3. Write a sentence that compares the constant rate of change and the constant ratio.

zoom!

Which **MP** **Mathematical Process Goals** did you use? Shade the circle(s) that applies.

① Mathematical Problem Solving ④ Mathematical Connections

② Mathematical Communication ⑤ Mathematical Representations

③ Mathematical Reasoning

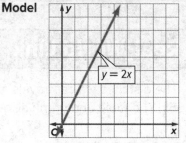

Words	A linear relationship is a direct variation when the ratio of y to x is a constant, k. We say y varies directly with x.	Model

Symbols	$\dfrac{y}{x} = k$ or $y = kx$, where $k \neq 0$

$y = 2x$

Example	$y = 2x$

Work Zone

When two variable quantities have a constant ratio, their relationship is called a **direct variation**. The constant ratio is called the **constant of variation**. The constant of variation is also known as the **constant of proportionality**.

In a direct variation equation, the constant rate of change, or slope, is assigned a special variable, k.

Example

1. **The height of the water as a pool is being filled is shown in the graph. Determine the rate in inches per minute.**

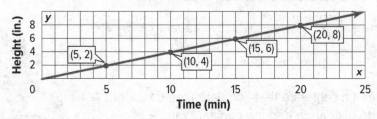

Since the graph of the data forms a line, the rate of change is constant. Use the graph to find the constant of proportionality.

$\dfrac{\text{height}}{\text{time}}$ ⟶ $\dfrac{2}{5}$ or $\dfrac{0.4}{1}$ $\dfrac{4}{10}$ or $\dfrac{0.4}{1}$ $\dfrac{6}{15}$ or $\dfrac{0.4}{1}$ $\dfrac{8}{20}$ or $\dfrac{0.4}{1}$

The pool fills at a rate of 0.4 inch every minute.

> **Direct Variation**
>
> When a relationship varies directly, the graph of the function will always go through the origin, (0, 0). Also, the unit rate r is located at (1, r).

Got it? Do this problem to find out.

Show your work.

a. Two minutes after a diver enters the water, he has descended 52 feet. After 5 minutes, he has descended 130 feet. At what rate is the scuba diver descending?

a. _____

Example

2. The equation $y = 10x$ represents the amount of money y Julio earns for x hours of work. Identify the constant of proportionality. Explain what it represents in this situation.

$$y = kx$$
↓
$$y = 10x$$

Compare the equation to $y = kx$, where k is the constant of proportionality.

The constant of proportionality is 10. So, Julio earns $10 for every hour that he works.

Got it? Do this problem to find out.

Show your work.

b. The distance y traveled in miles by the Chang family in x hours is represented by the equation $y = 55x$. Identify the constant of proportionality. Then explain what it represents.

b. _____

Determine Direct Variation

Not all situations with a constant rate of change are proportional relationships. Likewise, not all linear functions are direct variations.

Example

Weight (lb)	Cost ($)

3. Pizzas cost $8 each plus a $3 delivery charge. Show the cost of 1, 2, 3, and 4 pizzas. Is there a direct variation?

Number of Pizzas	1	2	3	4
Cost ($)	$11	$19	$27	$35

$\dfrac{\text{cost}}{\text{number of pizzas}}$ → $\dfrac{11}{1}, \dfrac{19}{2}$ or 9.5,

$\dfrac{27}{3}$ or 9, $\dfrac{35}{4}$ or 8.75

There is no constant ratio and the line does not go through the origin. So, there is no direct variation.

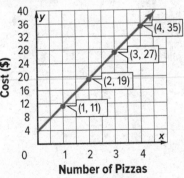

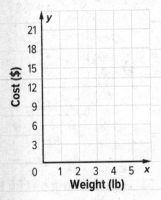

Got it? Do this problem to find out.

c. Two pounds of cheese cost $8.40. Show the cost of 1, 2, 3, and 4 pounds of cheese. Is there a direct variation? Explain.

c. _____

4. Determine whether the linear relationship is a direct variation. If so, state the constant of proportionality.

Time, *x*	1	2	3	4
Wages ($), *y*	12	24	36	48

Compare the ratios to check for a common ratio.

$\frac{\text{wages}}{\text{time}}$ → $\frac{12}{1}$ $\frac{24}{2}$ or $\frac{12}{1}$ $\frac{36}{3}$ or $\frac{12}{1}$ $\frac{48}{4}$ or $\frac{12}{1}$

Since the ratios are the same, the relationship is a direct variation. The constant of proportionality is $\frac{12}{1}$.

Guided Practice

1. The number of cakes baked varies directly with the number of hours the caterers work. What is the ratio of cakes baked to hours worked? (Examples 1 and 2) _____

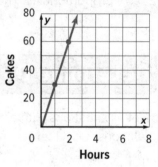

2. An airplane travels 780 miles in 4 hours. Make a table and graph to show the mileage for 2, 8, and 12 hours. Is there a direct variation? Explain.

(Examples 3 and 4) _____

_____

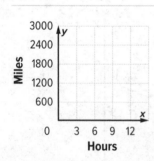

Hours			
Miles			

Rate Yourself!

How confident are you about direct variation? Check the box that applies.

3. **Building on the Essential Question** How can you determine if a linear relationship is a direct variation from an equation? a table? a graph? _____

_____

_____

For more help, go online to access a Personal Tutor.

Independent Practice

Go online for Step-by-Step Solutions

1 Veronica is mulching her front yard. The total weight of mulch varies directly with the number of bags of mulch.

What is the rate of change? (Example 1) _____

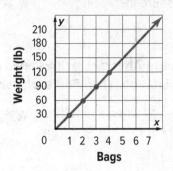

2. The Spanish club held a car wash to raise money. The equation $y = 5x$ represents the amount of money y club members made for washing x cars. Identify the constant of proportionality. Then explain

what it represents in this situation. (Example 2) _____

_____

_____

3. A technician charges $25 per hour plus $50 for a house call to repair home computers. Make a table and a graph to show the cost for 1, 2, 3, and 4 hours of home computer repair service. Is there a direct variation? (Example 3)

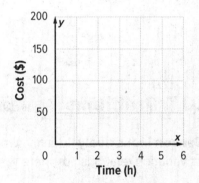

Time (h)				
Charge ($)				

_____

_____

Determine whether each linear relationship is a direct variation. If so, state the constant of proportionality. (Example 4)

4.

Pictures, x	3	4	5	6
Profit, y	24	32	40	48

_____

5

Minutes, x	185	235	285	335
Cost, y	60	100	140	180

_____

6.

Year, x	5	10	15	20
Height, y	12.5	25	37.5	50

_____

7.

Game, x	2	3	4	5
Points, y	4	5	6	7

_____

8. At a 33-foot depth underwater, the pressure is 29.55 pounds per square inch (psi). At a depth of 66 feet, the pressure reaches 44.4 psi. At what rate is the pressure increasing? _____

MP **Reason Abstractly** If y varies directly with x, write an equation for the direct variation. Then find each value.

9. If $y = 14$ when $x = 8$, find y when $x = 12$.

10. Find y when $x = 15$ if $y = 6$ when $x = 30$.

11. If $y = 6$ when $x = 24$, what is the value of x when $y = 7$?

12. Find x when $y = 14$, if $y = 7$ when $x = 8$.

🔥 H.O.T. Problems Higher Order Thinking

13. **MP** **Reason Inductively** Identify two additional values for x and y in a direct variation relationship where $y = 11$ when $x = 18$.

$x =$ _____ $y =$ _____ and $x =$ _____ $y =$ _____

14. **MP** **Persevere with Problems** Find y when $x = 14$ if y varies directly with x^2, and $y = 72$ when $x = 6$. _____

15. **MP** **Model with Mathematics** Tom is drawing rectangles in which the length varies directly with the width. One of his rectangles has a width of 2 centimeters and a length of 3.6 centimeters. Draw and label a rectangle with a width of 3.5 centimeters that could be one of Tom's rectangles. Then find the perimeter.

Show your work.

Extra Practice

16. The money Shelley earns varies directly with the number of dogs she walks. How much does Shelley earn for each dog she walks?

Since the points on the graph lie in a straight line, the rate of change is a constant. The constant ratio is what Shelley earns per dog.

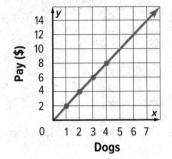

Homework Help ➡

$\dfrac{\text{pay } (\$) \longrightarrow}{\text{number of dogs} \longrightarrow}$ $\dfrac{2}{1}, \dfrac{4}{2}$ or $\dfrac{2}{1}, \dfrac{6}{3}$ or $\dfrac{2}{1}, \dfrac{8}{4}$ or $\dfrac{2}{1}$

Shelley earns $2.00 per dog.

17. A cake recipe requires $3\frac{1}{4}$ cups of flour for 13 servings and $4\frac{1}{2}$ cups of flour for 18 servings. How much flour is required to make a cake that serves 28? _____

Determine whether each linear relationship is a direct variation. If so, state the constant of variation.

18.

Age, x	11	13	15	19
Grade, y	5	7	9	11

_____

19.

Price, x	20	25	30	35
Tax, y	4	5	6	7

_____

20. (MP) **Multiple Representations** Robert is in charge of the community swimming pool. Each spring he drains it in order to clean it. Then he refills the pool, which holds 120,000 gallons of water. Robert fills the pool at a rate of 10 gallons each minute.

a. Words What is the rate at which Robert will fill the pool? Is it constant? _____

b. Graph Graph the relationship on the grid shown.

c. Algebra Write an equation for the direct variation.

_____

_____

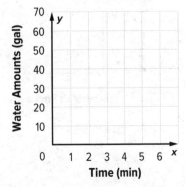

21. Determine if each equation represents a direct variation. Select yes or no.

    a. $y = 4x + 1$ ☐ Yes   ☐ No

    b. $y = 7.5x$ ☐ Yes   ☐ No

    c. $y = \frac{1}{15}x$ ☐ Yes   ☐ No

    d. $y = \frac{6}{x}$ ☐ Yes   ☐ No

22. Place a checkmark in the column below the correct direct variation equation, if possible.

					$y = 18x$	$y = 15x$	not a direct variation
Price, x	20	30	40	50	☐	☐	☐
Discount, y	2	4	6	8			

Seconds, x	2	6	7	11	☐	☐	☐
Feet, y	30	90	105	165			

Packages, x	3	5	7	9	☐	☐	☐
Crayons, y	54	90	126	162			

Hours, x	1	4	7	10	☐	☐	☐
Cost, y	15	30	45	60			

Spiral Review

23. The table below shows the number of sheets of paper in various numbers of packages. Graph the data.

Number of Packages	1	2	3	4
Number of Sheets	50	100	150	200

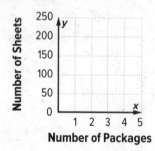

24. The cost of various numbers of tickets to a festival is shown in the table. Graph the data. Then find the slope of the line. Explain what the slope represents.

Number of Tickets	5	10	20	25
Cost ($)	40	80	160	200

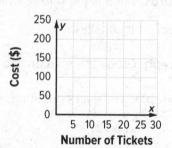

21ST CENTURY CAREER
in Engineering

Biomechanical Engineering

Did you know that more than 700 pounds of force are exerted on a 140-pound long-jumper during the landing? Biomechanical engineers understand how forces travel through the shoe to an athlete's foot and how the shoes can help reduce the impact of those forces on the legs. If you are curious about how engineering can be applied to the human body, a career in biomechanical engineering might be a great fit for you.

College & Career
READINESS

Is This the Career for You?

Are you interested in a career as a biomechanical engineer? Take some of the following courses in high school.

- ◆ Biology
- ◆ Calculus
- ◆ Physics
- ◆ Trigonometry

Find out how math relates to a career in Biomechanical Engineering.

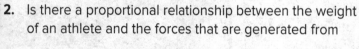

🅜🅟 Start Off on the Right Foot

Use the information in the graph to solve each problem.

1. Find the constant rate of change for the data shown in the graph below Exercise 2. Interpret its meaning.

    _____

    _____

    _____

2. Is there a proportional relationship between the weight of an athlete and the forces that are generated from

    running? Explain your reasoning. _____

    _____

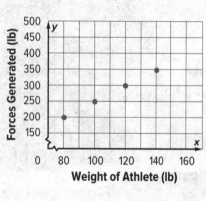

🅜🅟 Career Project

It's time to update your career portfolio! Use the Internet or another source to research the fields of biomechanical engineering, biomedical engineering, and mechanical engineering. Write a brief summary comparing and contrasting the fields. Describe how they are all related.

_____

_____

_____

_____

What subject in school is the most important to you? How would you use that subject in this career?

_____

_____

_____

_____

Vocabulary Check

Complete each sentence using the vocabulary list at the beginning of the chapter. Then circle the word that completes the sentence in the word search.

1. A _____ is a ratio that compares two quantities with different kinds of units.

2. A rate that has a denominator of 1 unit is called a _____ rate.

3. A pair of numbers used to locate a point in the coordinate plane is an _____ pair.

4. (0, 0) represents the _____.

5. A _____ fraction has a fraction in the numerator, denominator, or both.

6. A _____ variation is the relationship between two variable quantities with a constant ratio.

7. The _____ is the rate of change between any two points on a line.

8. One of the four regions into which a coordinate plane is separated is called a _____.

9. A _____ is an equation stating that two ratios or rates are equal.

10. The rate of _____ describes how one quantity changes in relation to another.

11. _____ analysis is the process of including units of measurement when you compute.

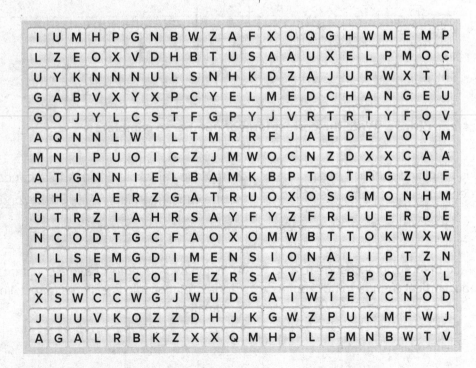

Use Your FOLDABLES

Use your Foldable to help review the chapter.

Tape here

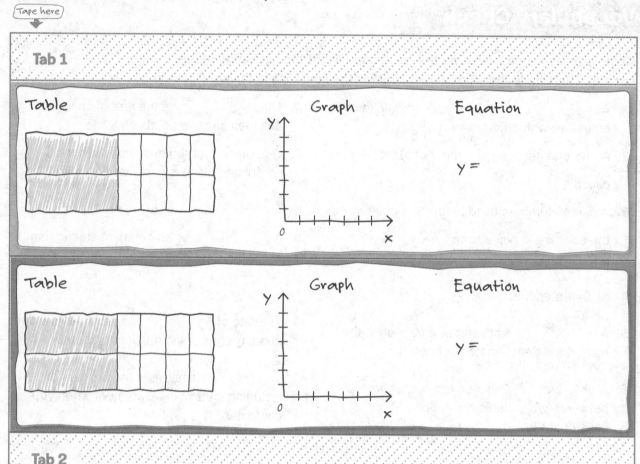

Tab 1

Table   Graph   Equation

y =

Table   Graph   Equation

y =

Tab 2

Tape here

Got it?

Identify the Correct Choice Write the correct term or number to complete each sentence.

1. When a rate is simplified so that it has a (numerator, denominator) of 1 unit, it is called a unit rate.

2. If Dinah can skate $\frac{1}{2}$ lap in 15 seconds, she can skate 1 lap in (7.5, 30) seconds.

3. Slope is the ratio of (horizontal change to vertical change, vertical change to horizontal change).

4. When two quantities have a constant ratio, their relationship is called a (direct, linear) variation.

Road Trip

The Jensen family took a trip in September. Sally is calculating the gas mileage in miles per gallon for her dad's SUV. When he fills the tank, her dad records the miles on the SUV as 24,033. Her dad pays $83.58 to fill up the empty gas tank of the SUV.

Write your answers on another piece of paper. Show all of your work to receive full credit.

Part A
What is the size of the SUV's tank in gallons? Round your answer to the nearest whole number.

Part B
At the destination, there was a quarter-tank of gas left in the vehicle and the miles were recorded as 24,297. Use a ratio equation to determine the gas mileage in miles per gallon for the trip. Round your answer to the nearest whole number.

Part C
Two months later, the Jensen family takes their mom's sedan on a different trip. When she fills the tank, Sally's mom records the miles on the sedan as 15,004. It takes $71.98 to fill up the vehicle's empty gas tank. What is the size of the sedan's tank in gallons? Round your answer to the nearest whole number.

Part D
At one point on the trip, the miles are recorded as 15,121 when the gas tank is 75% full. Use a ratio equation to determine the miles per gallon the sedan averages. Round your answer to the nearest whole number.

Part E
Which vehicle has the better gas mileage? Explain your reasoning.

Reflect

Answering the Essential Question

Use what you learned about ratios and proportional reasoning to complete the graphic organizer.

 Essential Question

HOW can you show that two objects are proportional...

... with a table?	... with a graph?	... with an equation?

Answer the Essential Question. HOW can you show that two objects are proportional?

Chapter 2
Percents

 Essential Question

HOW can percent help you understand situations involving money?

 Virginia Standards
7.2, 7.3

Math in the Real World

Biking The class goal for a biking fundraiser was to make $300 by the end of the pledge week. Halfway through the week, the students had made $210. Fill in the graph below to show the percent of the goal achieved.

Biking Fundraiser
Help Us Reach Our Goal

100%
90%
80%
70%
60%
50%
40%
30%
20%
10%
0%

FOLDABLES
Study Organizer

 Cut out the Foldable in the back of the book.

 Place your Foldable on page 178.

 Use the Foldable throughout this chapter to help you learn about percents.

Vocabulary

discount	percent equation	percent of increase	selling price
gratuity	percent error	percent proportion	simple interest
markdown	percent of change	principal	tip
markup	percent of decrease	sales tax	

Study Skill: Studying Math

Draw a Picture Drawing a picture can help you better understand numbers. For example, a *number map* shows how numbers are related to each other.

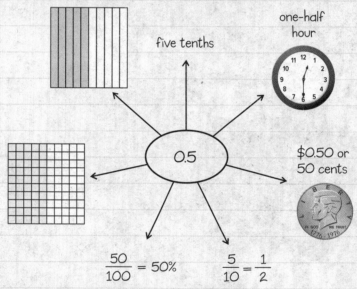

In the space below, make a number map for 0.75.

What Do You Already Know?

List three things you already know about percents in the first section. Then list three things you would like to learn about percents in the second section.

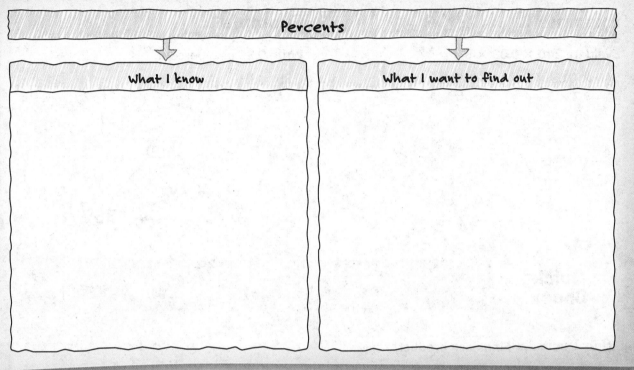

Percents

What I know

What I want to find out

When Will You Use This?

Here are a few examples of how percents are used in the real world.

Activity 1 Have you ever seen something offered at a discounted price? Look in a newspaper to find an advertisement for an item that is on sale for a certain percentage off its original price. Describe the ad and explain why you think it is or is not a good deal.

_____

_____

_____

Marisol, Blake, and Hiroshi in
Amusement Park Prices

Well, let's take a look...

There. Got it!

Activity 2 Go online at **connectED.mcgraw-hill.com** to read the graphic novel **Amusement Park Prices**. What is the full price of admission for each park?

_____

Are You Ready?

Try the Quick Check below.
Or, take the Online Readiness Quiz.

Check ✓

Quick Review

Example 1

Evaluate 240 × 0.03 × 5.

240 × 0.03 × 5

$= 7.2 × 5$ Multiply 240 by 0.03.

$= 36$ Simplify.

Example 2

Write 0.35 as a percent.

0.35 = 35%   Move the decimal point two places to the right and add the percent symbol.

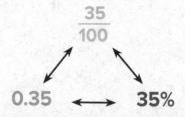

Quick Check

Multiply Decimals **Find each product.**

1. 300 × 0.02 × 8 = _____

2. 85 × 0.25 × 3 = _____

Show your work.

3. Suppose Nicole saves $2.50 every day. How much money will she have in 4 weeks? _____

Decimals and Percents **Write each decimal as a percent.**

4. 0.675 = _____

5. 0.725 = _____

6. 0.95 = _____

7. Approximately 0.92 of a watermelon is water. What percent represents this decimal? _____

How Did You Do?

Which problems did you answer correctly in the Quick Check?
Shade those exercise numbers below.

① ② ③ ④ ⑤ ⑥ ⑦

Inquiry HOW are percent diagrams used to solve real-world problems?

One fourth of the students in Mrs. Singh's music class chose a guitar as their favorite musical instrument. There are 24 students in Mrs. Singh's music class. How many students chose a guitar as their favorite musical instrument?

What do you know? _____

_____

_____

What do you need to find? _____

_____

Hands-On Activity 1

Bar diagrams can be used to represent a part of a whole as a fraction and as a percent.

Step 1 The bar diagram represents 100% of the class. Shade the bar diagram to show that $\frac{1}{4}$ or [ ]% of the class chose guitar as their favorite instrument.

| | | | 100% |

├--- [ ] % ---┤

Step 2 There are [ ] students in Mrs. Singh's music class. Divide the number of students equally into 4 sections. Fill in the number in each section.

├------------- 24 students -------------┤

| | | | 100% |

├--- [ ] % ---┤

So, [ ] students chose a guitar as their favorite musical instrument.

Hands-On Activity 2

There are 500 seventh-grade students at Heritage Middle School. Sixty percent of them play a musical instrument. How many seventh-grade students play a musical instrument?

Step 1 Supply the missing information for the second bar.

percent [   ] 100%

students [   ] [   ] total students

Step 2 Divide each bar into ten equal parts. Write 10% in each section of the first bar.

percent [**10%** |] 100%

students [|] [   ] total students

Step 3 Determine what number to write in each section of the second bar. Fill in that number.

percent [**10%** |] 100%

students [|] [   ] total students

Step 4 Shade 60% of the first bar and an equal amount on the second bar.

percent [**10%** |] 100%

students [|] [   ] total students

```
|------------      [    ]      ------------|
```

Since [   ] % corresponds to 6 sections, count the number of students in 6 sections. There are [   ] seventh-grade students who play a musical instrument.

Work with a partner. Use bar diagrams to solve each problem.

1. The seventh-grade class at Fort Couch Middle School has a goal of selling 300 tickets to the annual student versus teacher basketball game. The eighth-grade class has a goal of selling 400 tickets.

   a. By the end of the first week, the eighth-grade students sold 30% of their goal. How many tickets has the eighth grade sold? _____

      percent [   ] 100%

      tickets [   ] [   ]

   b. The seventh grade sold 60% of their goal. How many tickets do the students still need to sell? Explain. _____

      _____

      _____

      _____ [   ] 100%

      _____ [   ] [   ]

2. **MP** **Justify Conclusions** The graph shows the results of a survey asking 500 teens about their allowances. How many teens did *not* receive between $10 and $20? Explain.

   _____

   _____

   _____ [   ] [   ] %

   _____ [   ] [   ]

Weekly Allowance

10% more than $20

15% less than $10

75% $10–$20

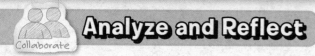
Analyze and Reflect

Work with a partner to complete the graphic organizer about percent and bar diagrams. The first one is done for you.

	Percent	Rate per 100	Whole	Part
	30%	$\frac{30}{100}$	150	45
3.	40%	$\frac{40}{100}$	150	
4.	50%	$\frac{50}{100}$	150	

5. Describe the pattern in the table above. Use the pattern to find 80% of 150.

_____

Create

On Your Own

MP **Model with Mathematics** Write a real-world problem for the bar diagrams shown. Then solve your problem.

6.

| 10% | 10% | 10% | 10% | 10% | 10% | 10% | 10% | 10% | 10% | 100% |

| 25 | 25 | 25 | 25 | 25 | 25 | 25 | 25 | 25 | 25 | 250 |

_____

_____

7.

| 25% | 25% | 25% | 25% | 100% |

| 15 | 15 | 15 | 15 | 60 |

_____

_____

_____

8. **Inquiry** HOW are percent diagrams used to solve real-world problems?

_____

_____

_____

Percent of a Number

Real-World Link

Pets Some students are collecting money for a local pet shelter. The model shows that they have raised 60% of their $2,000 goal or $1,200.

 Essential Question

HOW can percent help you understand situations involving money?

 Virginia Standards
7.3

	Percent	Decimal	Fractions
$2,000	100% ⇨	1 ⇨	$\frac{5}{5}$ or 1
$1,600	80% ⇨		
$1,200	60% ⇨		
$800	40% ⇨		
$400	20% ⇨		$\frac{1}{5}$
$0	0% ⇨	0 ⇨	0

FIDO

1. Fill in the decimal and fractional equivalents for each of the percents shown in the model.

2. Use the model to write two multiplication sentences that are equivalent to 60% of 2,000 = 1,200.

Which **MP** **Mathematical Process Goals** did you use? Shade the circle(s) that applies.

① Mathematical Problem Solving   ④ Mathematical Connections

② Mathematical Communication   ⑤ Mathematical Representations

③ Mathematical Reasoning

Find the Percent of a Number

To find the percent of a number such as 60% of 2,000, you can use either of the following methods.

- Write the percent as a fraction and then multiply.
- Write the percent as a decimal and then multiply.

Examples

Percent as a Rate

Find a percent of a quantity as a rate per 100.
For example, 5% of a quantity means $\frac{5}{100}$ times the quantity.

1. **Find 5% of 300 by writing the percent as a fraction.**

Write 5% as $\frac{5}{100}$ or $\frac{1}{20}$. Then find $\frac{1}{20}$ of 300.

$$\frac{1}{20} \text{ of } 300 = \frac{1}{20} \times 300 \qquad \text{Write a multiplication expression.}$$

$$= \frac{1}{\overset{}{\underset{1}{20}}} \times \frac{\overset{15}{\cancel{300}}}{1} \qquad \text{Write 300 as } \frac{300}{1}. \text{ Divide out common factors.}$$

$$= \frac{1 \times 15}{1 \times 1} \qquad \text{Multiply numerators and denominators.}$$

$$= \frac{15}{1} \text{ or } 15 \qquad \text{Simplify.}$$

So, 5% of 300 is 15.

2. **Find 25% of 180 by writing the percent as a decimal.**

Write 25% as 0.25. Then multiply 0.25 and 180.

$$
\begin{array}{r}
180 \\
\times\ 0.25 \quad \leftarrow \text{ two decimal places} \\
\hline
900 \\
+\ 360 \\
\hline
45.00 \quad \leftarrow \text{ two decimal places}
\end{array}
$$

So, 25% of 180 is 45.

Got it? **Do these problems to find out.**

Find the percent of each number.

- **a.** 40% of 70
- **b.** 15% of 100
- **c.** 55% of 160
- **d.** 75% of 280

Show your work.

a. _____

b. _____

c. _____

d. _____

Use Percents Greater Than 100%

Percents that are greater than 100% can be written as improper fractions, mixed numbers, or decimals greater than 1.

$$150\% = \frac{150}{100} = \frac{3}{2} = 1\frac{1}{2} = 1.5$$

Examples

3. **Find 120% of 75 by writing the percent as a fraction.**

Write 120% as $\frac{120}{100}$ or $\frac{6}{5}$. Then find $\frac{6}{5}$ of 75.

$$\frac{6}{5} \text{ of } 75 = \frac{6}{5} \times 75 \qquad \text{Write a multiplication expression.}$$

$$= \frac{6}{\cancel{5}} \times \frac{\cancel{75}^{15}}{1} \qquad \text{Write 75 as } \frac{75}{1}. \text{ Divide out common factors.}$$

$$= \frac{6 \times 15}{1 \times 1} \qquad \text{Multiply numerators and denominators.}$$

$$= \frac{90}{1} \text{ or } 90 \qquad \text{Simplify.}$$

So, 120% of 75 is 90.

> **Alternate Method**
> You can solve Example 3 using a decimal, and you can solve Example 4 using a fraction.

4. **Find 150% of 28 by writing the percent as a decimal.**

Write 150% as 1.5. Then find 1.5 of 28.

```
      28
    × 1.5   ← one decimal place
    ─────
     140
   + 28
   ──────
    42.0   ← one decimal place
```

So, 150% of 28 is 42.

Got it? Do these problems to find out.

Show your work.

Find each number.

e. 150% of 20

f. 160% of 35

e. _____

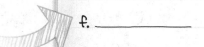

f. _____

Example

5. Refer to the graph. If 275 students took the survey, how many can be expected to have 3 televisions each in their houses?

Write the percent as a decimal. Then multiply.

23% of 275 = 23% × 275

= 0.23 × 275

= 63.25

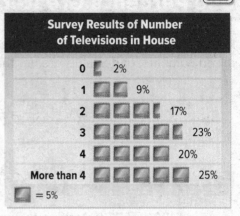

Survey Results of Number of Televisions in House

0	2%
1	9%
2	17%
3	23%
4	20%
More than 4	25%

= 5%

So, about 63 students can be expected to have 3 televisions each.

Commission

Refer to Exercise g. It is common for people who work in the sales industry to earn a commission on the products they sell.

Show your work.

Got it? Do this problem to find out.

g. _____

g. Mr. Sudimack earned a 4% commission on the sale of a hot tub that cost $3,755. How much did he earn?

Guided Practice

Find each number. Round to the nearest tenth if necessary. (Examples 1–4)

1. 8% of 50 = _____

2. 95% of 40 = _____

3. 110% of 70 = _____

Show your work.

4. Mackenzie wants to buy a backpack that costs $50. If the tax rate is 6.5%, how much tax will she pay? (Example 5)

_____

5. ⓔ **Building on the Essential Question** Give an example of a real-world situation in which you would find the percent of a number. _____

_____

_____

Rate Yourself!

Are you ready to move on? Shade the section that applies.

I have a few questions.

I'm ready to move on.

I have a lot of questions.

For more help, go online to access a Personal Tutor.

Tutor

Independent Practice

Go online for Step-by-Step Solutions eHelp

Find each number. Round to the nearest tenth if necessary. (Examples 1–4)

1. 65% of 186 = _____

2. 45% of $432 = _____

3. 23% of $640 = _____

Show your work.

4. 130% of 20 = _____

5 175% of 10 = _____

6. 150% of 128 = _____

7. 32% of 4 = _____

8. 5.4% of 65 = _____

9. 23.5% of 128 = _____

10. Suppose there are 20 questions on a multiple-choice test. If 25% of the answers are choice B, how many of the answers are *not* choice B?

(Example 5) _____

11. **MP Model with Mathematics** Refer to the graphic novel frame below. Find the dollar amount of the group discount each student would receive at each park.

_____

1. Pirate Bay $35.95
   20% discount
2. Funtopia $29.75
   15% discount
3. Zoomland $38.49
   25% discount

First, let's figure out what each student would be able to save off of their ticket at each park.

Marisol, Blake, and I want to get the best deal for our class.

12. In addition to her salary, Ms. Lopez earns a 3% *commission,* or fee paid based on a percent of her sales, on every vacation package that she sells. One day, she sold the three vacation packages shown. Fill in the table for each packages' commission. What was her total commission?

Package	Sale Price	Commission	
#1	$2,375		
#2	$3,950		
#3	$1,725		

_____

Copy and Solve For Exercises 13–21, find each number. Round to the nearest hundredth. Show your work on a separate piece of paper.

13. $\frac{4}{5}$% of 500

14. $5\frac{1}{2}$% of 60

15. $20\frac{1}{4}$% of 3

16. 1,000% of 99

17. 520% of 100

18. 0.15% of 250

19. 200% of 79

20. 0.3% of 80

21. 0.28% of 50

H.O.T. Problems Higher Order Thinking

22. **MP Persevere with Problems** Suppose you add 10% of a number to the number, and then you subtract 10% of the total. Is the result *greater than, less than,* or *equal to* the original number? Explain your reasoning.

_____

_____

23. **MP Reason Inductively** When is it easiest to find the percent of a number using a fraction? using a decimal? _____

_____

_____

24. **MP Reason Inductively** If you found the percent of a number and the product is greater than the number, what do you know about the percent?

Explain. _____

_____

_____

Extra Practice

Find each number. Round to the nearest tenth if necessary.

25. 54% of 85 = _45.9_

Homework Help

$0.54 \times 85 = 45.9$

26. 12% of $230 = _$27.60_

$$\frac{\cancel{12}^{3}}{\cancel{100}_{25}} \times 230 = \frac{3}{\cancel{25}_{5}} \times \cancel{230}^{46}$$

$$= \frac{3}{5} \times 46$$

$$= \frac{138}{5} \text{ or } 27.6$$

27. 98% of 15 = _____

28. 250% of 25 = _____

29. 108% of $50 = _____

30. 75.2% of 130 = _____

31. 0.5% of 60 = _____

32. 2.4% of 20 = _____

33. 7.5% of 30 = _____

34. In a recent year, 17.7% of households watched the finals of a popular reality series. There are 110.2 million households in the United States. How many households watched the finals?

_____

35. A family pays $19 each month for Internet access. Next month, the cost will increase by 5% because of an equipment fee. After this increase, what will be the cost for the Internet access?

_____

36. **MP** **Persevere with Problems** 250 people were asked to name their favorite fruit.
  a. Of those surveyed, how many people prefer peaches?

_____

  b. Which type of fruit did more than 100 people prefer?

_____

Favorite Fruit	
Berries	44%
Peaches	32%
Cherries	24%

37. The table shows the results of a survey of 200 movie rental customers. How many customers prefer horror movies?

Favorite Type of Movie	Percent of Customers
Comedy	15
Mystery	10
Horror	46
Science Fiction	29

38. The graph shows the Ramirez family budget. Their budget is based on a monthly income of $4,000.

Determine if each statement is true or false.

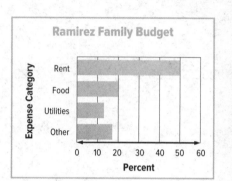

Ramirez Family Budget

a. The family budgeted $1,500 for rent. ☐ True ☐ False

b. The family budgeted $800 for food. ☐ True ☐ False

c. The family budgeted $200 more for utilities than for other expenses. ☐ True ☐ False

d. The family budgeted $1,200 more for rent than for food. ☐ True ☐ False

Spiral Review

Multiply.

39. $1.7 \times 54 =$ _____

40. $1.5 \times 3.65 =$ _____

41. $49.6 \times 2.7 =$ _____

42. Trent spent 50 minutes at the neighbor's house. He spent $\frac{2}{5}$ of the time swimming. How many minutes did Trent spend swimming? _____

Percent and Estimation

Real-World Link

Music Suppose 200 people are surveyed to find out how they learned to play an instrument. The results are shown in the table below.

Type of Teaching	Actual Percent	Estimated Percent	Fraction
Private Lessons	42%	40%	$\frac{2}{5}$
Lessons at School	32%		
Self-Taught	26%		

1. Estimate each percent. Choose an estimate that can be represented by a fraction that is easy to use. Then, write each estimated percent as a fraction in simplest form.

2. About how many people took lessons at school?

_____

3. Sarah estimates the percent of people who taught themselves to play an instrument as 25%, and then she found $\frac{1}{4}$ of 200. Would her answer be less than or greater than the actual number of people who were self taught? Explain. _____

_____

_____

Which **MP** **Mathematical Process Goals** did you use? Shade the circle(s) that applies.

① Mathematical Problem Solving

② Mathematical Communication

③ Mathematical Reasoning

④ Mathematical Connections

⑤ Mathematical Representations

Estimate the Percent of a Number

Sometimes an exact answer is not needed when using percents. One way to estimate the percent of a number is to use a fraction.

Another method for estimating the percent of a number is first to find 10% of the number and then multiply.

$$70\% = 7 \cdot 10\%$$

So, 70% equals 7 times 10% of a number.

Examples

1. **Jodi has paid 62% of the $500 she owes for her loan. Estimate 62% of 500.**

$$62\% \text{ of } 500 \approx 60\% \text{ of } 500 \qquad 62\% \approx 60\%$$
$$\approx \frac{3}{5} \cdot 500 \qquad\qquad 60\% = \frac{6}{10} \text{ or } \frac{3}{5}$$
$$\approx 300 \qquad\qquad\qquad \text{Multiply.}$$

So, 62% of 500 is about 300.

STOP and Reflect

What are two ways to estimate 22% of 130? Explain below.

2. **Marita and four of her friends ordered a pizza that cost $14.72. She is responsible for 20% of the bill. About how much money will she need to pay?**

Step 1 Find 10% of $15.00.

$$10\% \text{ of } \$15.00 = 0.1 \cdot \$15.00$$
$$= \$1.50$$

To multiply by 10%, move the decimal point one place to the left.

Step 2 Multiply.

20% of $15.00 is 2 times 10% of $15.00.

$$2 \cdot \$1.50 = \$3.00$$

So, Marita should pay about $3.00.

Show your work.

Got it? Do these problems to find out.

a. Estimate 42% of 120.

b. Dante plans to put 80% of his paycheck into a savings account and spend the other 20%. His paycheck this week was $295. About how much money will he put into his savings account?

a. _____

b. _____

Percents Greater Than 100 or Less Than 1

You can also estimate percents of numbers when the percent is greater than 100 or less than 1.

Check for Reasonableness

When the percent is greater than 100, the estimate will always be greater than the number.

Example

3. **Estimate 122% of 50.**

122% is about 120%.

120% of 50 = 100% of 50 + 20% of 50   120% = 100% + 20%

$= (1 \cdot 50) + \left(\dfrac{1}{5} \cdot 50\right)$ 100% = 1 and 20% = $\dfrac{1}{5}$

$= 50 + 10$ or 60   Simplify.

So, 122% of 50 is about 60.

> **Got it?** Do these problems to find out.

c. 174% of 200   **d.** 298% of 45   **e.** 347% of 80

Show your work.

c. _____

d. _____

e. _____

Example

4. There are 789 seventh grade students at Washington Middle School. About $\dfrac{1}{4}$% of the seventh grade students have traveled overseas. What is the approximate number of seventh grade students that have traveled overseas? Explain.

$\dfrac{1}{4}$% is one fourth of 1%. 789 is about 800.

1% of 800 = 0.01 · 800   Write 1% as 0.01.

$= 8$ To multiply by 1%, move the decimal point two places to the left.

One fourth of 8 is $\dfrac{1}{4} \cdot 8$ or 2.

So, about 2 seventh grade students have traveled overseas.

> **Got it?** Do this problem to find out.

f. A county receives $\dfrac{3}{4}$% of a state sales tax. About how much money would the county receive from the sale of a computer that costs $1,020?

f. _____

Example

Tutor

5. Last year, 639 students attended a summer camp. Of those who attended this year, 0.5% also attended summer camp last year. About how many students attended the summer camp two years in a row?

0.5% is half of 1%.

1% of 639 = 0.01 · 639

           ≈ 6

So, 0.5% of 639 is about $\frac{1}{2}$ of 6 or 3.

About 3 students attended summer camp 2 years in a row.

Guided Practice

Check ✓

Estimate. (Examples 1–4)

1. 52% of 10 ≈ _____

2. 79% of 489 ≈ _____

3. 151% of 70 ≈ _____

4. $\frac{1}{2}$% of 82 ≈ _____

5. Of the 78 teenagers at a youth camp, 63% have birthdays in the spring. About how many teenagers have birthdays in the spring? (Example 2)

_____

6. About 0.8% of the land in Maine is federally owned. If Maine has 19,847,680 acres, about how many acres are federally owned? (Example 5) _____

_____

7.  **Building on the Essential Question** How can you estimate the percent of a number? _____

_____

_____

Rate Yourself!

How confident are you about estimating percents? Shade the ring on the target.

I'm on target.

I need help.

For more help, go online to access a Personal Tutor.

Tutor

Independent Practice

Go online for Step-by-Step Solutions eHelp

Estimate. (Examples 1–4)

1. 47% of 70 ≈ _____

Show your work.

2. 39% of 120 ≈ _____

3 21% of 90 ≈ _____

4. 65% of 152 ≈ _____

5. 72% of 238 ≈ _____

6. 132% of 54 ≈ _____

7. 224% of 320 ≈ _____

8. $\frac{3}{4}$% of 168 ≈ _____

9. 0.4% of 510 ≈ _____

10. Financial Literacy Carlie spent $42 at the salon. Her mother loaned her the money. Carlie will pay her mother 15% of $42 each week until the loan is repaid. About how much will Carlie pay each week? (Example 2)

_____

11 The United States has 12,383 miles of coastline. If 0.8% of the coastline is located in Georgia, about how many miles of coastline are in Georgia? (Example 5)

_____

12. **MP** **Persevere with Problems** Use the graph shown.

a. About how many more hours does Avery spend sleeping than doing the activities in the "other" category? Justify your answer.

_____

b. What is the approximate number of minutes Avery spends each day on extracurricular activities?

_____

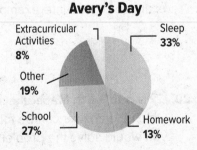

Avery's Day

Extracurricular Activities 8%

Sleep 33%

Other 19%

School 27%

Homework 13%

Estimate.

13. 67% of 8.7 ≈ _____

14. 54% of 76.8 ≈ _____

15. 10.5% of 238 ≈ _____

16. The average white rhinoceros gives birth to a single calf that weighs about 3.8% as much as its mother. If the mother rhinoceros weighs 3.75 tons, about how many pounds does its calf weigh? _____

17. The students at Monroe Junior High sponsored a canned food drive. The seventh-grade class collected 129% of its canned food goal.
   a. About how many canned foods did the seventh-graders collect if their goal was 200 cans? _____

   b. About how many canned foods did the seventh-graders collect if their goal was 595 cans? _____

H.O.T. Problems Higher Order Thinking

18. **MP** **Persevere with Problems** Explain how you could find $\frac{3}{8}$% of $800.

_____

19. **MP** **Use Math Tools** Is an estimate for the percent of a number *always*, *sometimes*, or *never* greater than the actual percent of the number? Give an example or a counterexample to support your answer.

_____

20. **MP** **Model with Mathematics** Write a multi-step real-world problem in which the answer can be found by estimating 18% of 30. Then explain how you would solve the problem.

_____

Extra Practice

Estimate.

21. 76% of 180 ≈ _135_

$$\frac{3}{4} \cdot 180 = 135 \text{ or}$$

$$0.1 \cdot 180 = 18$$

$$7.5 \cdot 18 = 135$$

22. 57% of 29 ≈ _18_

$$\frac{3}{5} \cdot 30 = 18 \text{ or}$$

$$0.1 \cdot 30 = 3$$

$$6 \cdot 3 = 18$$

23. 92% of 104 ≈ _____

24. $\frac{1}{2}$% of 412 ≈ _____

25. 0.9% of 74 ≈ _____

26. 32% of 89.9 ≈ _____

Homework Help

27. You use 43 muscles to frown. When you smile, you use 32% of these same muscles. About how many muscles do you use when you smile?

_____

28. **MP** **Justify Conclusions** The coastline of the Atlantic Coast is 2,069 miles long. Approximately $\frac{6}{10}$% of the coastline lies in New Hampshire. About how many miles of the coastline lie in New Hampshire? Explain how you estimated.

_____

_____

29. The table shows the number of passes attempted and the percent completed by the top quarterbacks in the NFL for a recent season.

a. Estimate the number of passes that Tom Brady completed.

_____

b. Is your estimate greater or less than the actual number of passes he completed? Explain. _____

_____

c. Without calculating, determine whether Tony Romo or David Garrard completed more passes. Justify your reasoning.

_____

_____

NFL Quarterbacks		
Player	Passes Attempted	Percent Completed
T. Brady	578	69
P. Manning	515	65
T. Romo	520	64
D. Garrard	325	64

30. The table shows the fundraising goals for three different activities and the percent of the goal that was actually raised.

Estimate the amount raised by each activity. Sort the estimates from least to greatest.

Activity	Goal	Percent of Goal Raised
Car Wash	$250	112%
Raffle	$200	143%
Magazine Sales	$240	102%

	Activity	Estimate
Least		
Greatest		

31. The graph shows the results of a survey of 510 students. Determine if each of the following are good estimates. Select yes or no.

a. about 125 students prefer cats ☐ Yes ☑ No

b. about 200 students prefer dogs ☐ Yes ☑ No

c. about 150 students prefer fish ☑ Yes ☐ No

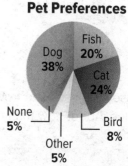

Pet Preferences

Dog 38%, Fish 20%, Cat 24%, Bird 8%, Other 5%, None 5%

Spiral Review

Solve each equation. Show your work.

32. $5n = 120$

33. $1{,}200 = 4a$

34. $6x = 39$

35. Marquita created the design at the right. She created the design from 8 equal-size rectangles. Write a fraction in simplest form that represents the yellow portion of the design.

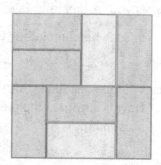

36. Write three fractions equivalent to $\frac{3}{5}$.

HOW is percent used to solve real-world problems?

The eighth grade had 300 tickets to sell to the school play and the seventh grade had 250 tickets to sell. One hour before the show, the eighth grade had sold 225 tickets and the seventh grade had sold 200 tickets. Complete the investigation below to find which grade sold the greater percent of tickets.

Hands-On Activity

Step 1 The bar diagrams below show 100% for each grade. Label the total tickets to be sold above each bar. Divide each bar into 10 equal sections. So, each section will represent 10%.

```
            |---------------------[     ] tickets -------------------|
eighth grade |   |                                                   |  100%
            |---------------------[     ] tickets -------------------|
seventh grade |  |                                                   |  100%
```

Step 2 Find the number that belongs in each section for both of the bars. Then write that number in the sections.

Eighth grade: Seventh grade:

$300 \div 10 = \boxed{}$ $250 \div 10 = \boxed{}$

Step 3 Find the number of sections to shade for each bar. Then shade the sections.

Eighth grade: Seventh grade:

$225 \div 30 = \boxed{}$ $200 \div 25 = \boxed{}$

The eighth grade sold $\boxed{}$ % of their tickets. The seventh grade

sold $\boxed{}$ % of their tickets.

The _____ grade sold the greater percent of their tickets.

Investigate

Work with a partner. Show your work using bar diagrams.

1. **MP** **Model with Mathematics** Vanlue Middle School has 600 students and Memorial Middle School has 450 students. Vanlue has 270 girls and Memorial has 225 girls. Which school has the greater percent of girls? Explain. _____

_____

_____

Vanlue ┊- - - - - - - - - - - - - - - [ ] students - - - - - - - - - - - - ┊

```
┌──────────────────────────────────────────────────┐
│                                                    │  100%
└──────────────────────────────────────────────────┘
```

Memorial ┊- - - - - - - - - - - [ ] students - - - - - - - - - - ┊

```
┌──────────────────────────────────────────────────┐
│                                                    │  100%
└──────────────────────────────────────────────────┘
```

Create

Work with a partner to answer the following question.

2. **MP** **Model with Mathematics** Seventy-five students were in the audience for a 3-D screening of a movie. Fifty students were in the audience for a 2-D screening of the same movie. Describe a situation in which the percent of students who went to the 2-D screening is greater than the percent of students who went to the 3-D screening. _____

_____

_____

3. **Inquiry** HOW is percent used to solve real-world problems? _____

_____

_____

_____

The Percent Proportion

Real-World Link

Monster Trucks The tires on a monster truck weigh approximately 2 tons. The entire truck weighs about 6 tons.

1. Write the ratio of tire weight to total weight as a fraction.

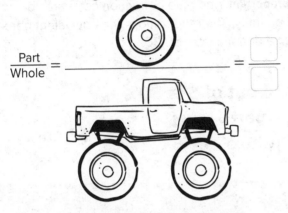

$$\frac{\text{Part}}{\text{Whole}} = \underline{\hspace{4cm}} = \frac{\square}{\square}$$

2. Represent the fraction above by shading in the model.

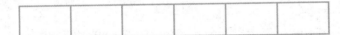

3. Write the fraction as a decimal to the nearest hundredth.

_____

4. About what percent of the monster truck's weight is the tires?

_____

Essential Question

HOW can percent help you understand situations involving money?

Vocabulary

percent proportion

Virginia Standards
7.3

Which **MP** **Mathematical Process Goals** did you use? Shade the circle(s) that applies.

① Mathematical Problem Solving
② Mathematical Communication
③ Mathematical Reasoning
④ Mathematical Connections
⑤ Mathematical Representations

Use the Percent Proportion

Type	Example		Proportion
Find the Percent	What percent of 5 is 4?		$\frac{4}{5} = \frac{n}{100}$
Find the Part	What number is 80% of 5?		$\frac{p}{5} = \frac{80}{100}$
Find the Whole	4 is 80% of what number?		$\frac{4}{w} = \frac{80}{100}$

In a **percent proportion**, one ratio or fraction compares part of a quantity to the whole quantity. The other ratio is the equivalent percent written as a fraction with a denominator of 100.

$$4 \text{ out of } 5 \text{ is } 80\%$$

$$\frac{\text{part}}{\text{whole}} \cdots\rightarrow \frac{4}{5} = \frac{80}{100} \Big\} \text{ percent}$$

Example

1. What percent of $15 is $9?

Words	What percent of $15 is $9?
Variable	Let n represent the percent.
Proportion	$\dfrac{\text{part}}{\text{whole}} \rightarrow \dfrac{9}{15} = \dfrac{n}{100} \Big\}$ percent

$\dfrac{9}{15} = \dfrac{n}{100}$ — Write the proportion.

$9 \cdot 100 = 15 \cdot n$ — Find the cross products.

$900 = 15n$ — Simplify.

$\dfrac{900}{15} = \dfrac{15n}{15}$ — Divide each side by 15.

$60 = n$

So, $9 is 60% of $15.

The Percent Proportion

The word of is usually followed by the whole.

Show your work.

a. _____

b. _____

Got it? Do these problems to find out.

a. What percent of 25 is 20?   b. $12.75 is what percent of $50?

Example

2. What number is 40% of 120?

> **Words**   What number is 40% of 120?
>
> **Variable**   Let p represent the part.
>
> **Proportion**   part $\longrightarrow$ $\dfrac{p}{120} = \dfrac{40}{100}$ } percent
>   whole $\longrightarrow$

$$\frac{p}{120} = \frac{40}{100}$$ Write the proportion.

$p \cdot 100 = 120 \cdot 40$ Find the cross products.

$100p = 4{,}800$ Simplify.

$\dfrac{100p}{100} = \dfrac{4{,}800}{100}$ Divide each side by 100.

$p = 48$ So, 48 is 40% of 120.

Got it? Do these problems to find out.

c. What number is 5% of 60?   **d.** 12% of 85 is what number?

Show your work.

c. _____

d. _____

Example

3. 18 is 25% of what number?

> **Words**   18 is 25% of what number?
>
> **Variable**   Let w represent the whole.
>
> **Proportion**   part $\longrightarrow$ $\dfrac{18}{w} = \dfrac{25}{100}$ } percent
>   whole $\longrightarrow$

$$\frac{18}{w} = \frac{25}{100}$$ Write the proportion.

$18 \cdot 100 = w \cdot 25$ Find the cross products.

$1{,}800 = 25w$ Simplify.

$\dfrac{1{,}800}{25} = \dfrac{25w}{25}$ Divide each side by 25.

$72 = w$ So, 18 is 25% of 72.

Got it? Do these problems to find out.

e. 40% of what number is 26?   **f.** 84 is 75% of what number?

e. _____

f. _____

STOP and Reflect

In the proportion $\dfrac{3}{20} = \dfrac{15}{100}$, identify the part, whole, and percent.

part = _____

whole = _____

percent = _____

Example

4. The average adult male Western Lowland gorilla eats about 33.5 pounds of fruit each day. How much food does the average adult male gorilla eat each day?

Western Lowland Gorilla's Diet	
Food	**Percent**
Fruit	67%
Seeds, leaves, stems, and pith	17%
Insects/insect larvae	16%

You know that 33.5 pounds is the part. You need to find the whole.

$$\frac{33.5}{w} = \frac{67}{100}$$ Write the proportion.

$$33.5 \cdot 100 = w \cdot 67$$ Find the cross products.

$$3{,}350 = 67w$$ Simplify.

$$\frac{3{,}350}{67} = \frac{67w}{67}$$ Divide each side by 67.

$$50 = w$$

The average adult male gorilla eats 50 pounds of food each day.

Guided Practice

 Check

Find each number. Round to the nearest tenth if necessary. (Examples 1–3)

1. What percent of $90 is $9?

2. What number is 2% of 35?

3. 62 is 90.5% of what number?

 Show your work.

4. Brand A cereal contains 10 cups of cereal. How many more cups of cereal are in Brand B cereal?
(Example 4)

 Brand A    Brand B 30% More Cereal

Rate Yourself!

How confident are you about using the percent proportion? Shade the ring on the target.

I'm on target.

I need help.

For more help, go online to access a Personal Tutor. Tutor

5. **Building on the Essential Question** How can you use the percent proportion to solve real-world problems?

FOLDABLES Time to update your Foldable!

Independent Practice

Go online for Step-by-Step Solutions

Find each number. Round to the nearest tenth if necessary. (Examples 1–3)

Show your work.

1. What percent of 60 is 15? _____

2. What number is 15% of 60? _____

3. 9 is 12% of which number? _____

4. 12% of 72 is what number? _____

5. What percent of 50 is 18? _____

6. 12 is 90% of what number? _____

7. A pair of sneakers is on sale as shown. This is 75% of the original price. What was the original price of the shoes? (Example 4) _____

Sale Price
$51

8. Of the 60 books on a bookshelf, 24 are nonfiction. What percent of the books are nonfiction? (Example 4) _____

Find each number. Round to the nearest hundredth if necessary.

9. 40 is 50% of what number? _____

10. 12.5% of what number is 24? _____

11. What percent of 300 is 0.6? _____

12. What number is 0.5% of 8? _____

Find each number. Round to the nearest hundredth if necessary.

13. **STEM** Use the table shown. Mercury's radius is 2,440 kilometers.

Planet	Radius (km)
Mercury	r
Mars	r + 957
Jupiter	29.3r

   a. Mercury's radius is what percent of Jupiter's radius?

   _____

   b. If the radius of Mars is about 13.7% of Neptune's radius, what is the radius of Neptune?

   _____

   c. Earth's radius is about 261.4% of Mercury's radius. What is the radius of Earth?

   _____

H.O.T. Problems Higher Order Thinking

14. **MP Reason Inductively** Seventy percent of the 100 students in a middle school cafeteria bought their lunch. Some of the students that bought their lunch leave the cafeteria to attend an assembly. Now only 60% of the remaining students bought their lunch. How many students are remaining in the cafeteria? Explain. _____

   _____

   _____

   _____

15. **MP Persevere with Problems** Without calculating, arrange the following from greatest to least value. Justify your reasoning.

   20% of 100, 20% of 500, 5% of 100

   _____

   _____

   _____

   _____

16. **MP Model with Mathematics** Write a real-world problem involving a percent that can be solved by using the proportion $\frac{3}{b} = \frac{60}{100}$. Then solve the proportion.

   _____

   _____

   _____

   _____

Extra Practice

Find each number. Round to the nearest tenth if necessary.

17. What number is 25% of 180? _45_

$$\frac{n}{180} = \frac{25}{100}$$

$$\frac{n}{180} = \frac{1}{4}$$

$$4n = 180$$

$$n = 45$$

Homework
Help

18. $3 is what percent of $40? _7.5%_

$$\frac{3}{40} = \frac{p}{100}$$

$$40p = 300$$

$$p = 7.5\%$$

19. 9 is 45% of what number? _____

20. 75 is 20% of what number? _____

21. What percent of 60 is 12? _____

22. What number is 5% of 46? _____

23. **MP Justify Conclusions** Roman has 2 red pencils in his backpack. If this is 25% of the total number of pencils, how many pencils are in his backpack? Explain.

24. **MP Justify Conclusions** Eileen and Michelle scored 48% of their team's points. If their team had a total of 50 points, how many points did they score? Explain.

Find each number. Round to the nearest hundredth if necessary.

25. What percent of 25 is 30? _____

26. What number is 8.2% of 50? _____

27. The types of flowers shown in the table make up an arrangement. What percent of the flowers in the arrangement are roses?

Flower Arrangement	
Lilies	4
Roses	15
Snapdragons	6

28. Select values to set up a percent proportion that represents each situation. Then solve each problem. Round to the nearest tenth if necessary.

100	80
60	x

Situation 1: A pair of shoes is on sale for 80% of the original price. The sale price is $60. What was the original price?

$$\frac{\square}{\square} = \frac{\square}{\square}$$

Situation 2: Maggie's goal was to collect 60 canned goods for a food drive. She actually collected 80. What percent of her goal did Maggie reach?

$$\frac{\square}{\square} = \frac{\square}{\square}$$

Situation 3: Craig has made 60% of 80 free throw attempts this season. How many free throws has he made?

$$\frac{\square}{\square} = \frac{\square}{\square}$$

Spiral Review

Multiply.

29. $\frac{1}{2} \times \frac{2}{3} =$ _____

30. $\frac{3}{5} \times \frac{1}{4} =$ _____

31. $\frac{2}{7} \times \frac{1}{6} =$ _____

Divide.

32. $\frac{2}{5} \div \frac{3}{4} =$ _____

33. $\frac{1}{3} \div \frac{5}{6} =$ _____

34. $\frac{1}{5} \div \frac{5}{7} =$ _____

The Percent Equation

Vocabulary Start-Up

You have used a percent proportion to find the missing part (*p*), percent (*n*), or whole (*w*). You can also use a **percent equation**. The percent equation is part = percent • whole.

Label the diagram that shows the relationship between the percent proportion and the percent equation with the terms *part, whole,* and *percent*. Use each term once.

$$\frac{\text{part}}{\text{whole}} = \underline{\hspace{3cm}}$$ Write the percent proportion.

$$\frac{\text{part}}{\text{whole}} \cdot \text{whole} = \text{percent} \cdot \underline{\hspace{2.5cm}}$$ Multiply each side by the whole.

$$\underline{\hspace{3cm}} = \text{percent} \cdot \text{whole}$$ Divide out common factors to obtain the percent equation.

Essential Question

HOW can percent help you understand situations involving money?

Vocabulary

percent equation

Virginia Standards
7.3

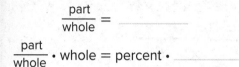 ### Real-World Link

A survey found that 16% of all seventh-graders at Lincoln Middle school think that tarantulas are the scariest creatures. There are 150 seventh-graders at the school. How would you write a percent equation to find how many seventh-graders said that tarantulas are the scariest creatures?

$$\boxed{} = 0.16 \cdot \boxed{}$$

BOO!

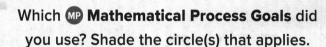

Which **MP** **Mathematical Process Goals** did you use? Shade the circle(s) that applies.

① Mathematical Problem Solving   ④ Mathematical Connections

② Mathematical Communication   ⑤ Mathematical Representations

③ Mathematical Reasoning

Use the Percent Equation

Type	Example	Equation
Find the Percent	3 is what percent of 6?	$3 = n \cdot 6$
Find the Part	What number is 50% of 6?	$p = 0.5 \cdot 6$
Find the Whole	3 is 50% of what number?	$3 = 0.5 \cdot w$

You can use the percent equation to solve problems that involve percent.

3 is 50% of 6

$$\underset{\text{part}}{\underline{3}} = \underset{\text{percent}}{\underline{0.5}} \times \underset{\text{whole}}{\underline{6}}$$

Note that the percent is written as a decimal.

Example

Tutor

Percent Equation

A percent must always be converted to a decimal or a fraction when it is used in an equation.

1. What number is 12% of 150?

Do you need to find the percent, part, or whole? _____

Estimate $0.10 \cdot 150 = 15$

$\underset{\text{part}}{\underline{\text{part}}} = \underset{\text{percent}}{\underline{\text{percent}}} \cdot \underset{\text{whole}}{\underline{\text{whole}}}$

$p = 0.12 \cdot 150$ Write the percent equation. 12% = 0.12

$p = 18$ Multiply.

So, 18 is 12% of 150.

18 is close to the estimate of 15. So, the answer is reasonable. You can also check your answer using the percent proportion.

Show your work.

Check $\dfrac{18}{150} \stackrel{?}{=} \dfrac{12}{100}$

$18 \cdot 100 \stackrel{?}{=} 150 \cdot 12$

$1{,}800 = 1{,}800 \checkmark$

a. _____

b. _____

c. _____

d. _____

Got it? Do these problems to find out.

Write an equation for each problem. Then solve.

  a. What is 6% of 200?

  b. Find 72% of 50.

  c. What is 14% of 150?

  d. Find 50% of 70.

Example

2. **21 is what percent of 40?**

Do you need to find the percent, part, or whole? _____

Estimate $\frac{21}{40} \approx \frac{1}{2}$ or 50%

part = percent · whole

21 =	n · 40	Write the percent equation.
$\frac{21}{40}$ =	$\frac{40n}{40}$	Divide each side by 40.
0.525 =	n	Simplify.

So, 21 is 52.5% of 40.

Check 52.5% ≈ 50% ✓

Got it? Do these problems to find out.

Percent
Remember to write the decimal as a percent in your final answer.

Write an equation for each problem. Then solve. Round to the nearest tenth if necessary.

e. What percent of 40 is 9?   **f.** 27 is what percent of 150?

Show your work.

e. _____

f. _____

Example

3. **13 is 26% of what number?**

Do you need to find the percent, part, or whole? _____

Estimate $\frac{1}{4}$ of 48 = 12

part = percent · whole

13 =	0.26 · w	Write the percent equation. 26% = 0.26
$\frac{13}{0.26}$ =	$\frac{0.26w}{0.26}$	Divide each side by 0.26.
50 =	w	Simplify.

So, 13 is 26% of 50.

Check 50 ≈ 48. ✓

Got it? Do these problems to find out.

Write an equation for each problem. Then solve. Round to the nearest tenth if necessary.

g. 39 is 84% of what number?   **h.** 26% of what number is 45?

g. _____

h. _____

Example

4. A survey found that 25% of people aged 18–24 gave up their home phone and only use a cell phone. If 3,264 people only use a cell phone, how many people were surveyed?

Words	3,264 people is 25% of what number of people?

Variable	Let w represent the number of people.

Equation	3,264 $=$ 0.25 $\cdot$ w

$3,264 = 0.25 \cdot w$ Write the percent equation. 25% = 0.25

$\dfrac{3,264}{0.25} = \dfrac{0.25w}{0.25}$ Divide each side by 0.25. Use a calculator.

$13,056 = w$ Simplify.

About 13,056 people were surveyed.

Guided Practice

 Check ✓

Write an equation for each problem. Then solve. Round to the nearest tenth if necessary. (Examples 1–3)

1. What number is 88% of 300?

2. 24 is what percent of 120?

3. 3 is 12% of what number?

4. A local bakery sold 60 loaves of bread in one day. If 65% of these were sold in the afternoon, how many loaves were sold in the afternoon? (Example 4) _____

5. Ⓠ **Building on the Essential Question** When might it be easier to use the percent equation rather than the percent proportion? _____

_____

Rate Yourself!

Are you ready to move on?
Shade the section that applies.

YES   ?   NO

For more help, go online to access a Personal Tutor. Tutor

FOLDABLES Time to update your Foldable!

Independent Practice

Go online for Step-by-Step Solutions

Write an equation for each problem. Then solve. Round to the nearest tenth if necessary. (Examples 1–3)

1. 75 is what percent of 150? _____

2. 84 is 60% of what number? _____

3. What number is 65% of 98? _____

4. Find 39% of 65. _____

5. Find 24% of 25. _____

6. What number is 53% of 470? _____

7. Ruben bought 6 new books for his collection. This increased his collection by 12%. How many books did he have before his purchases? (Example 4)

8. A store sold 550 video games during the month of December. If this made up 12.5% of its yearly video game sales, about how many video games did the store sell all year? (Example 4)

9. **MP Persevere with Problems** About 142 million people in the United States watch online videos. Use the graph that shows what type of videos they watch.

a. About what percent of viewers watch comedy, jokes, and bloopers? _____

b. About what percent watch news stories?

_____

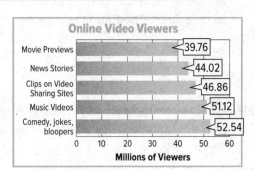

Write an equation for each problem. Then solve. Round to the nearest tenth if necessary.

10. Find 135% of 64. _____

11. What number is 0.4% of 82.1? _____

12. 450 is 75.2% of what number? _____

13. What percent of 200 is 230? _____

H.O.T. Problems Higher Order Thinking

14. **MP Model with Mathematics** Write a percent problem for which the percent is greater than 100 and the part is known. Use the percent equation to solve your problem to find the whole.

_____

15. **MP Persevere with Problems** If you need to find the percent of a number, explain how you can predict whether the part will be *less than*, *greater than*, or *equal* to the number.

_____

_____

_____

16. **MP Reason Abstractly** A museum has 50 pieces of art to display in an exhibit. Of these, 11 are photographs and 39 are color paintings. The manager wants to add more photographs so that they represent 25% of the pieces of art at the museum. Write and solve an equation to find the number of photos to be added. Then find the total number of pieces of art in the exhibit.

_____

17. **MP Reason Inductively** Explain when it might be more efficient to use the percent equation rather than the percent proportion.

_____

_____

_____

Extra Practice

Write an equation for each problem. Then solve. Round to the nearest tenth if necessary.

18. 9 is what percent of 45? _20%_

 Homework Help →

$$9 = n \times 45$$

$$\frac{9}{45} = \frac{45n}{45}$$

$$0.2 \text{ or } 20\% = n$$

19. What percent of 96 is 26? _27.1%_

$$26 = n \times 96$$

$$\frac{26}{96} = \frac{96n}{96}$$

$$0.271 \text{ or } 27.1\% = n$$

20. What percent of 392 is 98? _____

21. 30 is what percent of 64? _____

22. 33% of what number is 1.45? _____

23. 84 is 75% of what number? _____

24. 17 is 40% of what number? _____

25. 80% of what number is 64? _____

26. The length of Giselle's arm is 27 inches. The length of her lower arm is 17 inches. About what percent of Giselle's arm is her lower arm?

_____

27. Approximately 0.02% of North Atlantic lobsters are born bright blue in color. Out of 5,000 North Atlantic lobsters, how many would you expect to be blue in color?

_____

28. Financial Literacy Suppose you earn $6 per hour at your part-time job. What will your new hourly rate be after a 2.5% raise? Explain.

_____

_____

29. Taryn's grandmother took her family out to dinner. The receipt shows the total amount spent. Taryn's dinner was 20% of the total bill after tax and tip. How much was Taryn's dinner?

Le Bistro

Subtotal.............$58.38

Tax.....................$3.38

Tip...................$12.24

30. Model each situation below with a percent equation. Select the correct equation for each situation. Then solve each problem.

   a. Of the 300 students in a homeroom, 120 play a school sport. What percent of students play a school sport?

   Equation: [_____]   Solution: [_____]

$$x = 0.3 \cdot 120$$
$$x = 0.12 \cdot 300$$
$$120 = 300 \cdot x$$

   b. A survey of 120 middle schools showed that 30% have a foreign language program. How many schools have a foreign language program?

   Equation: [_____]   Solution: [_____]

   c. Katrina saved $300 last summer. Of that amount, 12% came from her allowance. How much came from her allowance?

   Equation: [_____]   Solution: [_____]

Spiral Review

Fill in each ◯ with <, >, or = to make a true statement.

31. 5.56 ◯ $5\frac{5}{7}$ **32.** 4.027 ◯ 4.0092 **33.** 88% ◯ 0.9

Use the graph to solve.

34. What number represents 100% of the fall student athletes?

Explain. _____

_____

Student Participation in Fall Sports

Determine Reasonable Answers

Case #1 Vacations

Wesley's family spent $1,400 on a trip to the Grand Canyon. They spent 30% of the total on a sightseeing helicopter flight. Wesley estimates that his family spent about $450 on the flight.

Determine whether Wesley's estimate is reasonable.

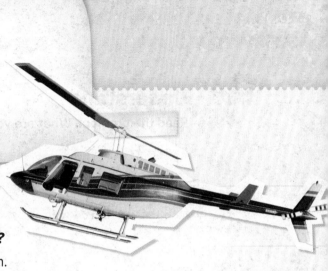

Understand *What are the facts?*

- Wesley's family spent $1,400 on vacation.
- Thirty percent of the total was spent on a helicopter flight.
- Wesley estimates that 30% is about $450.

Plan *What is your strategy to solve this problem?*

Make a bar diagram that represents 100%.

Solve *How can you apply the strategy?*

Fill in each section of the diagram with 10% of $1,400.

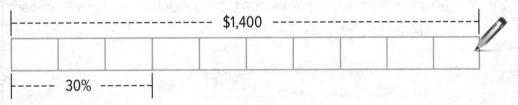

Add three sections to get a total of ☐.
So, the helicopter flight cost $420.

Check *Does the answer make sense?*

Wesley estimated the cost of the helicopter flight to be $450.
Since $450 is close to $420, his estimate was reasonable.

Analyze the Strategy

MP Make a Conjecture How can you use $\frac{1}{3}$ to determine if Wesley's estimate is reasonable? Explain.

_____

_____

Case #2 Don't forget the tip!

At a local Italian restaurant, Brett's bill was $17.50.
He decides to leave a 20% tip for the server.

Is $4 a reasonable tip?

Understand

Read the problem. What are you being asked to find?

I need to _____.

Is there any information that you do *not* need to know?

I do not need to know _____.

Plan

Choose a problem-solving strategy.

I will use the _____ strategy.

Solve

Use your problem-solving strategy to solve the problem.

Use a bar diagram to represent 100%. Divide it into [ ] parts. Each part

represents [ ] % or $ [ ] .

```
|--------------- $17.50 ---------------|
|   |   |   |   |   |   |   |   |   |   | 100%
|-- tip --|
```

Two parts, or [ ] %, equal $ [ ] + $ [ ] = $ [ ] .

Is $4 a reasonable tip? _____

Check

Use information from the problem to check your answer.

_____

_____

Collaborate

**Work with a small group to solve the following cases.
Show your work on a separate piece of paper.**

Favorite Vacation Spots

13% Other

15% California

48% Hawaii

24% Florida

Case #3 Travel

A travel agency surveyed 140 families about their favorite vacation spots.

Is it reasonable to say that 24 more families chose Hawaii over Florida? Explain.

Case #4 Exercise

A survey showed that 61% of middle school students do some kind of physical activity every day. Of those students, 9% play on the football team.

Suppose there are 828 middle school students in your school. About how many students would play on the football team?

Case #5 Clubs

Of the 36 students in the environmental club, 15 are boys and 21 are girls. The president of the club wants to add more boys so that the boys represent 50% of the students in the club.

Write and solve an equation to find the number of boys to be added. Then find the total number of students in the club.

Use any strategy!

Case #6 Bowling

In bowling, you get a spare when you knock down the ten pins in two throws.

How many possible ways are there to get a spare?

Mid-Chapter Check

Vocabulary Check

1. Fill in the blank in the sentence below with the correct term.

The _____ states that the part equals the percent multiplied by the whole.

Skills Check and Problem Solving

Find each number. Round to the nearest tenth if necessary.

2. What percent of 84 is 12? _____

Show your work

3. 15 is 25% of what number? _____

Estimate.

4. 20% of 392 _____

5. 78% of 112 _____

Write an equation for each problem. Then solve. Round to the nearest tenth if necessary.

6. **MP** **Use Math Tools** A computer costs $849.75 and the hard drive is 61.3% of the total cost. What is a reasonable estimate for the cost of the hard drive?

_____

7. What number is 35% of 72? _____

8. 16.1 is what percent of 70? _____

9. **MP** **Persevere with Problems** Ayana has 220 coins in her piggy bank. Of those, 40% are pennies. Out of the coins that are *not* pennies, 25% are quarters. How many of the coins are quarters?

_____

Inquiry **HOW can you use a bar diagram to show a percent of change?**

The admission price for the state fair has increased by 50% in the last five years. The admission price was $6 five years ago. What is the current admission price? Do the Activity below to find out.

Hands-On Activity

Use a bar diagram to solve.

Step 1 The bar diagram represents 100%.

price 5 years ago = $6	100%

Since 50% = $\frac{1}{2}$, divide the bar diagram in half. Fill in the missing information.

|------- price 5 years ago = [ ] -------|
| $3 | | 100% |

Step 2 The admission price increased by 50%. Complete the bar diagram that represents 150% of the price 5 years ago.

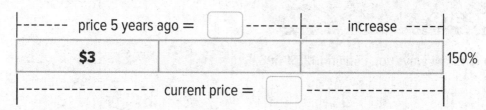

|------- price 5 years ago = [ ] ------|----- increase -----|
| $3 | | | 150% |
|------------------ current price = [ ] ------------------|

So, the current admission price is [ ] + [ ] or [ ].

 **Investigate**

Collaborate

Work with a partner to solve the following problems.

1. The height of a tree was 8 feet. After a year, the tree's height increased by

    25%. Draw a bar diagram to find the new height of the tree. _____

2.  **Model with Mathematics** The model below describes the following
   scenario: Ryan put $160 in a bank account. After 2 months, the total in his
   account decreased by 25%. Fill in the amount in Ryan's account after
   2 months.

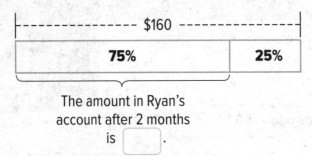

The amount in Ryan's
account after 2 months
is [   ].

 **Analyze and Reflect**

Collaborate

Work with a partner to answer the following question.

3. **Reason Inductively** Refer to Exercise 1. How can you find the new amount
   of a quantity that has increased over a period of time?

   _____

   _____

   _____

Create

On Your Own

4. Write two different ways you can find 125% of 8.

   _____

   _____

5. **Inquiry** HOW can you use a bar diagram to show a percent of change?

   _____

   _____

   _____

Percent of Change

Real-World Link

Speed Racer The Indy 500 is one of the world's great motor races. The table shows the average speed of the winning race cars for various years.

Year	Speed (mph)
1922	94
1955	128
2010	162

Essential Question

HOW can percent help you understand situations involving money?

Vocabulary

percent of change
percent of increase
percent of decrease
percent error

Virginia Standards
7.3

1. Write the ratio

   $$\dfrac{\text{speed increase from 1922 to 1955}}{\text{speed in 1922}}.$$

   Then write the ratio as a percent.

   Round to the nearest whole percent.

   $$\dfrac{\boxed{}}{94} = \boxed{}\%$$

2. Write the ratio

   $$\dfrac{\text{speed increase from 1955 to 2010}}{\text{speed in 1955}}.$$

   Then write the ratio as a percent.

   Round to the nearest whole percent.

   $$\dfrac{\boxed{}}{128} = \boxed{}\%$$

3. Why are the amounts of increase the same but the percents different?

Which MP **Mathematical Process Goals** did you use? Shade the circle(s) that applies.

① Mathematical Problem Solving
② Mathematical Communication
③ Mathematical Reasoning
④ Mathematical Connections
⑤ Mathematical Representations

Percent of Change

Words   A **percent of change** is a ratio that compares the change in quantity to the original amount.

Equation $\text{percent of change} = \dfrac{\text{amount of change}}{\text{original amount}}$

When you compare the amount of change to the original amount in a ratio, you are finding the percent of change. The percent of change is based on the original amount.

If the original quantity is increased, then it is called a **percent of increase**. If the original quantity is decreased, then it is called a **percent of decrease**.

$$\text{percent of increase} = \dfrac{\textbf{amount of increase}}{\textbf{original amount}}$$

$$\text{percent of decrease} = \dfrac{\textbf{amount of decrease}}{\textbf{original amount}}$$

Examples

 Watch Tutor

1. **Find the percent of change in the cost of gasoline from 1970 to 2010. Round to the nearest whole percent if necessary.**

Since the 2010 price is greater than the 1970 price, this is a percent of increase.

1970

2010

★ GAS ★

$1.30

★ GAS ★

$2.95

Step 1 Find the amount of increase.
$2.95 − $1.30 = $1.65

Step 2 Find the percent of increase.

$\text{percent of increase} = \dfrac{\textbf{amount of increase}}{\textbf{original amount}}$

$= \dfrac{\textbf{\$1.65}}{\textbf{\$1.30}}$ Substitution

≈ 1.27 Simplify.

$\approx 127\%$ Write 1.27 as a percent.

The cost of gasoline increased by about 127% from 1970 to 2010.

Percents

In the percent of change formula, the decimal repesenting the percent of change must be written as a percent.

2. Yusuf bought a DVD recorder for $280. Now, it is on sale for $220. Find the percent of change in the price. Round to the nearest whole percent if necessary.

Since the new price is less than the original price, this is a percent of decrease.

Step 1 Find the amount of decrease.
$280 − $220 = $60

Step 2 Find the percent of decrease.

$$\text{percent of decrease} = \frac{\text{amount of decrease}}{\text{original amount}}$$

$$= \frac{\$60}{\$280} \qquad \text{Substitution}$$

$$\approx 0.21 \qquad \text{Simplify.}$$

$$\approx 21\% \qquad \text{Write 0.21 as a percent.}$$

The price of the DVD recorder decreased by about 21%.

Percent of Change

Always use the original amount as the whole when finding percent of change.

Got it? Do these problems to find out.

a. Find the percent of change from 10 yards to 13 yards.

b. The price of a radio was $20. It is on sale for $15. What is the percent of change in the price of a radio?

Show your work.

a. _____

b. _____

Percent Error

Key Concept

Words	The **percent error** is a ratio that compares the inaccuracy of an estimate, or amount of error, to the actual amount.
Equation	$\text{percent error} = \dfrac{\text{amount of error}}{\text{actual amount}}$

Finding the percent error is similar to finding the percent of change. Instead of finding the amount of increase or decrease, you will find the amount an estimate is greater or less than the actual amount.

Suppose you guess there are 300 gum balls in a jar, but there are actually 400.

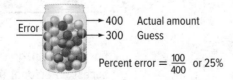

Error → 400 Actual amount
→ 300 Guess

Percent error = $\frac{100}{400}$ or 25%

Example

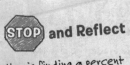
3. Ahmed wants to practice free-throws. He estimates the distance from the free-throw line to the hoop and marks it with chalk. Ahmed's estimate was 13.5 feet. The actual distance should be 15 feet. Find the percent error.

Step 1 Find the amount of error.
15 feet − 13.5 feet = 1.5 feet

Step 2 Find the percent error.

$$\text{percent error} = \frac{\text{amount of error}}{\text{actual amount}}$$

$$= \frac{1.5}{15} \qquad \text{Substitution.}$$

$$= 0.1 \text{ or } 10\% \qquad \text{Simplify.}$$

So, the percent error is 10%.

Got it? Do this problem to find out.

c. Find the percent error if the estimate is $230 and the actual amount is $245. Round to the nearest whole percent.

c. _____

Guided Practice

Find each percent of change. Round to the nearest whole percent if necessary. State whether the percent of change is an *increase* or a *decrease*. (Examples 1 and 2)

1. 30 inches to 24 inches _____

2. $126 to $150 _____

3. Jessie estimates the weight of her cat to be 10 pounds. The actual weight of the cat is 13.75 pounds. Find the

percent error. (Example 3) _____

4.  **Building on the Essential Question** Explain how two amounts of change can be the same but the percents of change can be different.

_____

_____

_____

Rate Yourself!

How confident are you about percent of change? Check the box that applies.

For more help, go online to access a Personal Tutor.

Independent Practice

Go online for Step-by-Step Solutions

Find each percent of change. Round to the nearest whole percent if necessary. State whether the percent of change is an *increase* or a *decrease*. (Examples 1 and 2)

1. 15 yards to 18 yards

2. 100 acres to 140 acres

3. $15.60 to $11.70

4. 125 centimeters to 87.5 centimeters

5. 1.6 hours to 0.95 hour

6. 132 days to 125.4 days

MP Be Precise Find the percent error. Round to the nearest whole percent if necessary. (Example 3)

7. Each week, Mr. Jones goes to the grocery store. Mr. Jones estimates that he will spend $120 when he goes to the grocery store this week. He actually spends $94.

8. Marcus estimates that 230 people will attend the choir concert. There was an actual total of 300 people who attended the choir concert.

For each situation, find each percent of change. Round to the nearest whole percent if necessary. State whether the percent of change is an *increase* or a *decrease*. (Examples 1 and 2)

9. Three months ago, Santos could walk 2 miles in 40 minutes. Today he can walk 2 miles in 25 minutes.

10. Last school year the enrollment of Genoa Middle School was 465 students. This year the enrollment is 525.

11. Refer to the rectangle at the right. Suppose the side lengths are doubled.

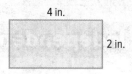
4 in.

2 in.

a. Find the percent of change in the perimeter. _____

b. Find the percent of change in the area. _____

12. 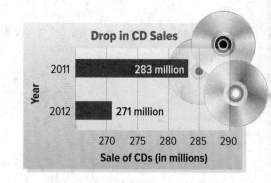 **Use Math Tools** Find examples of data reflecting change over a period of time in a newspaper or magazine, on television, or on the Internet. Determine the percent of change. Explain whether the data show a percent of increase or decrease.

13. Use the graph shown to find the percent of change in CD

sales from 2011 to 2012. _____

Drop in CD Sales

Year	Sale of CDs (in millions)
2011	283 million
2012	271 million

270 275 280 285 290
Sale of CDs (in millions)

H.O.T. Problems Higher Order Thinking

14. 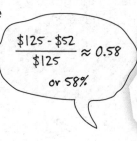 **Persevere with Problems** The costs of two sound systems were decreased by $10. The original costs of the systems were $90 and $60. Without calculating, which had a greater percent of decrease? Explain.

_____

_____

15. 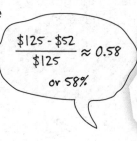 **Find the Error** Dario is finding the percent of change from $52 to $125. Find his mistake and correct it.

$$\frac{\$125 - \$52}{\$125} \approx 0.58$$

or 58%

_____

_____

_____

16. 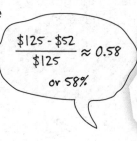 **Reason Inductively** If a quantity increases by 25% and then decreases by 25%, will the result be the original quantity? Explain.

_____

_____

_____

Extra Practice

Find each percent of change. Round to the nearest whole percent. State whether the percent of the change is an *increase* or *decrease*.

17. $12 to $6

50%; decrease

$12 - 6 = 6$

$\dfrac{6}{12} = 0.5$ or 50%

Homework Help ➤

18. 48 notebooks to 14 notebooks

_____

19. $240 to $320

_____

20. 624 feet to 702 feet

_____

21. The table shows the number of youth 7 years and older who played soccer from 2004 to 2012.

   a. Find the percent of change from 2008 to 2012. Round to the nearest tenth of a percent. Is it an increase or decrease?

   _____

   b. Find the percent of change from 2006 to 2008. Round to the nearest tenth of a percent. Is it an increase or decrease?

Playing Soccer	
Year	Number (millions)
2004	12.9
2006	13.7
2008	13.3
2010	14.0
2012	13.8

22. Shoe sales for a certain company were $25.9 billion. Sales are expected to increase by about 20% in the next year. Find the

projected amount of shoe sales next year. _____

23. **MP Be Precise** Eva estimates that 475 songs will fit on her MP3 player.

The actual amount of songs that fit is 380. Find the percent error. _____

24. The table shows Catalina's babysitting hours. She charges $6.50 per hour. Write a sentence that compares the percent of change in the amount of money earned from April to May to the percent of change in the amount of money earned from May to June. Round to the nearest percent if needed.

Month	Hours Worked
April	30
May	35
June	45

_____

_____

25. Dario increased his savings from $350 to $413, while Monica increased her savings from $225 to $270. Fill in each blank below to write a true statement.

[_____] had a higher percent of increase in savings. The difference in the percents of increase is [_____].

26. The line graph shows the level of the Elk River during a period of heavy rainfall.

Find the percent of increase in the river level from Monday to Tuesday, from Tuesday to Wednesday, from Wednesday to Thursday, and from Thursday to Friday. Round to the nearest tenth of a percent if necessary. Sort the percents of increase between consecutive days from least to greatest.

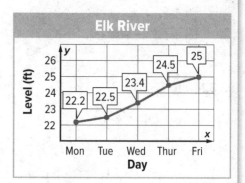

Elk River

	Consecutive Days	Percent of Increase
Least		
Greatest		

Spiral Review

Find each sum.

27. $1.5 + 2.25 =$ _____

28. $32.5 + 13.43 =$ _____

29. $66.99 + $8.15 =$ _____

30. The distances around Earth at the equator and through the North and South Poles are shown at the right. How many miles would you travel if you circled Earth along both routes?

_____

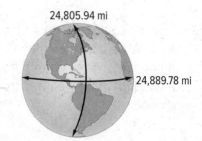

24,805.94 mi

24,889.78 mi

Sales Tax, Tips, and Markup

Real-World Link

Kayaks Alonso plans to buy a new kayak that costs $2,100. But when he buys the kayak, it actually costs more because he lives in a county where there is a 7% sales tax.

You can find the amount of tax on an item by multiplying the price by the tax percentage.

1. Circle the amount below that shows the amount of tax Alonso will pay for the kayak.

   $350 $235 $147

2. Use the amount of tax from Exercise 1 to fill in the receipt at the right. Then find the total cost Alonso will pay for the kayak.

3. Multiply 1.07 and $2,100. How does the result compare to your answer in Exercise 2?

   _____

4. On Alonso's kayaking trip, hiring a guide costs $50. Alonso wants to give the guide a 10% tip. Explain how to find the amount of the tip.

   _____

   _____

Jimmie's Kayaks

Kayak _____

Sales Tax + _____

_____

Total _____

Essential Question

HOW can percent help you understand situations involving money.

Vocabulary

sales tax
tip
gratuity
markup
selling price

Virginia Standards
7.3

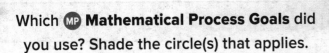

Which **MP** **Mathematical Process Goals** did you use? Shade the circle(s) that applies.

① Mathematical Problem Solving

② Mathematical Communication

③ Mathematical Reasoning

④ Mathematical Connections

⑤ Mathematical Representations

Sales Tax and Total Cost

Sales tax is an additional amount of money charged on items that people buy. The total cost of an item is the regular price plus the sales tax.

Example

1. **Drew wants to buy exercise equipment that costs $140 and the sales tax is 5.75%. What is the total cost of the equipment?**

Method 1 **Add sales tax to the regular price.**

First, find the sales tax.

Let t represent the sales tax.

part = percent × whole   Write the percent equation.

$t = 0.0575 × 140$ 5.75% = 0.0575

$t = 8.05$ Multiply.

Next, add the sales tax to the regular price.
$8.05 + $140 = 148.05

Method 2 **Add the percent of tax to 100%.**

$100\% + 5.75\% = 105.75\%$ Add the percent of tax to 100%.

Let t represent the total.

part = percent × whole   Write the percent equation.

$t = 1.0575 × 140$ 105.75% = 1.0575

$t = \$148.05$ Multiply.

The total cost of the exercise equipment is $148.05.

 Show your work.

Got it? **Do this problem to find out.**

a. _____

a. What is the total cost of a sweatshirt if the regular price is $42 and the sales tax is $5\frac{1}{2}\%$?

Tips and Markups

A **tip** or **gratuity** is a small amount of money in return for a service. The total price is the regular price of the service plus the tip.

A store sells items for more than it pays for those items. The amount of increase is called the **markup**. The **selling price** is the amount the customer pays for an item.

Examples

Tutor

2. A customer wants to tip 15% on a restaurant bill that is $35. What will be the total bill with tip?

Method 1 Add the tip to the regular price.

First, find the tip. Let t represent the tip.

$\underbrace{\text{part}} = \underbrace{\text{percent}} \times \underbrace{\text{whole}}$

$t = 0.15 \times 35$ 15% = 0.15

$t = 5.25$ Multiply.

Next, add the tip to the bill.

$\$5.25 + \$35 = \$40.25$ Add.

Method 2 Add the percent of tip to 100%.

$100\% + 15\% = 115\%$ Add the percent of tip to 100%.

The total cost is 115% of the bill. Let t represent the total.

$\underbrace{\text{part}} = \underbrace{\text{percent}} \times \underbrace{\text{whole}}$

$t = 1.15 \times 35$ 115% = 1.15

$t = 40.25$ Multiply.

Using either method, the total cost of the bill with tip is $40.25.

3. A haircut costs $20. Sales tax is 4.75%. Is $25 sufficient to cover the haircut with tax and a 15% tip?

Sales tax is 4.75% and the tip is 15%, so together they will be 19.75%. Let t represent the tax and tip.

$\underbrace{\text{part}} = \underbrace{\text{percent}} \times \underbrace{\text{whole}}$

$t = 0.1975 \times 20$ 0.15 + 0.0475 = 0.1975

$t = 3.95$ Multiply.

$\$20 + \$3.95 = \$23.95$ Add.

Since $\$23.95 < \$25$, $25 is sufficient to cover the total cost.

> **Got it?** Do these problems to find out.
>
> **b.** Scott wants to tip his taxicab driver 20%. If his commute costs $15, what is the total cost?
>
> **c.** Find the total cost of a spa treatment of $42 including 6% tax and 20% tip.

> **Mental Math**
>
> 10% of a number can be found by moving the decimal one place to the left. 10% of $20 is $2. So, 20% of $20 is $4.

Show your work.

b. _____

c. _____

Example

Markup

In Example 4, you could find the selling price by finding 125% of the amount the store pays.

4. **A store pays $56 for a GPS navigation system. The markup is 25%. Find the selling price.**

First, find the markup. Let *m* represent the markup.

$$\underbrace{\text{part}} = \underbrace{\text{percent}} \times \underbrace{\text{whole}} \qquad \text{Write the percent equation.}$$
$$m = 0.25 \times 56 \qquad 25\% = 0.25$$
$$m = 14 \qquad \text{Mulitply.}$$

Next, add the markup to the amount the store pays.

$$\$14 + \$56 = \$70 \qquad \text{Add.}$$

The selling price of the GPS navigation system is $70.

Got it? Do this problem to find out.

d. A store pays $150 for a portable basketball backboard and the markup is 40%. What is the selling price?

d. _____

Guided Practice

Find the total cost to the nearest cent. (Examples 1 and 2)

1. $2.95 notebook; 5% tax _____

2. $28 lunch; 15% tip _____

3. Jaimi went to have a manicure that cost $30. She wanted to tip the technician 20% and tax is 5.75%. How much did she spend total for the manicure? (Example 3)

_____

4. Find the selling price of a $62.25 karaoke machine with

a 60.5% markup. (Example 4) _____

5. **Building on the Essential Question** Describe two methods for finding the total price of a bill that includes a

20% tip. Which method do you prefer? _____

_____

_____

Rate Yourself!

How well do you understand finding sales tax, tips, and markups? Circle the image that applies.

Clear   Somewhat   Not So
          Clear   Clear

For more help, go online to access a Personal Tutor.

Independent Practice

Go online for Step-by-Step Solutions eHelp

Find the total cost to the nearest cent. (Examples 1 and 2)

1. $58 bill; 20% tip _____

 Show your work.

2. $43 dinner; 18% gratuity _____

 3 $1,500 computer; 7% tax _____

4. $46 shoes; 2.9% tax _____

5 **Financial Literacy** A restaurant bill comes to $28.35. Find the total cost if the tax is 6.25% and a 20% tip is left on the amount before tax.

(Example 3) _____

6. Toru takes his dog to be groomed. The fee to groom the dog is $75 plus 6.75% tax. Is $80 enough to pay for the service? Explain.

(Example 3) _____

_____

7. Find the selling price of a $270 bicycle with a 24% markup. (Example 4) _____

8. Find the selling price of a $450 painting with a 45% markup. (Example 4) _____

9. What is the sales tax on the chair shown if the tax rate is 5.75%? _____

$178.90

10. A store pays $10 for a bracelet, and the markup is 115%. A customer will also pay a $5\frac{1}{2}$% sales tax. What will be the total cost of the bracelet to the nearest cent? _____

11. **MP** **Persevere with Problems** The Leather Depot buys a coat from a supplier for $90 wholesale and marks up the price by 40%. If the retail price is $134.82, what is the sales tax? _____

12. **MP** **Model with Mathematics** Give an example of the regular price of an item and the total cost including sales tax if the tax rate is 5.75%.

_____

_____

13. **MP** **Which One Doesn't Belong?** In each pair, the first value is the regular price of an item and the second value is the price with gratuity. Identify the pair that does not belong with the other three. Explain your reasoning to a classmate.

| $30, $34.50 | | $54, $64.80 | | $16, $18.40 | | $90, $103.50 |

_____

_____

14. **MP** **Reason Abstractly** Prices for several cell phones are listed in the table. The table shows the regular price p and the price with tax t. The sales tax is 8%. Write a formula that could be used to calculate the price with tax.

Phone	Regular Price (p)	Price with Tax (t)
Flip phone	$80	$86.40
Slide phone	$110	$118.80
Video phone	$120	$129.60

_____

15. **MP** **Use a Counterexample** Is the following statement *true* or *false*? If *false*, provide a counterexample.

It is impossible to increase the cost of an item by more than 100%.

_____

_____

Extra Practice

Find the total cost to the nearest cent.

16. $99 CD player; 5% tax $103.95

 Homework Help

$0.05 \times 99 = 4.95$

$99.00
+ 4.95
$103.95

17. $13 haircut; 15% tip $14.95

$0.15 \times 13 = 1.95$

$13.00
+ 1.95
$14.95

18. $7.50 meal; 6.5% tax _____

19. $39 pizza order; 15% tip _____

20. $89.75 scooter; $7\frac{1}{4}$% tax _____

21. $8.50 yoga mat; 75% markup _____

22. (MP) **Reason Inductively** Diana and Sujit clean homes for a summer job. They charge $70 for the job plus 5% for supplies. A homeowner gave them a 15% tip. Did they receive more than $82 for their job? Explain.

_____

_____

23. (MP) **Find the Error** Jamar is finding the selling price of a pair of $40 skates with a 30% markup. Find his mistake and correct it.

$0.3 \times $40 = 12$
$40 - 12 = 28

_____

_____

_____

_____

24. The same pair of boots is sold at four stores in different counties. The costs and sales tax rates are shown in the table.

Sort the total costs after sales tax from least to greatest.

Store	Price	Tax Rate
Boot World	$54.90	5.5%
Shoes 'n More	$53.25	7%
Nos Zapatos	$52.20	6.25%
Frank's Footwear	$53.95	6.5%

	Store	Total Cost
Least		
Greatest		

Which store has the lowest price after sales tax? [ ]

25. An office supply store marks up their prices by 30%. Which of the following could be items sold by the store? Select all of that apply.

☐ office chair: cost: $72, selling price: $94.50

☐ printer paper: cost: $4.60, selling price: $5.98

☐ box of paper clips: cost: $1.20, selling price: $1.65

☐ file cabinet: cost: $60, selling price: $78

Spiral Review

Solve.

26. 45 − 4.5 = _____

27. 89 − 31.15 = _____

28. $102 − $25.75 = _____

29. Renata paid $35.99 for a dress. The dress was on sale for $14.01 off its regular price. What was the regular price of the dress?

30. Mr. Durant bought Console B for $20.99 off the advertised price. Find the total amount Mr. Durant paid.

Game Console	Advertised Price ($)
A	128.99
B	138.99
C	148.99

Real-World Link

Water Parks A pass at a water park is $58 dollars at the beginning of the season. The cost of the pass decreases each month.

1. Each month 10% is taken off the price of a season pass. Find the discounted price for August by completing the fill-ins below.

Season Pass

June: $58.00   July: $52.20

August: _____

Price in July   Write 10% as a decimal.   Amount of discount

_____   ×   _____   =   _____

Price in July   Amount of discount   Discounted price for August

_____   −   _____   =   _____

2. Multiply 0.9 and $52.20. How does the result compare to your answer in Exercise 1?

_____

_____

3. Write the definition of *discount* in your own words. _____

_____

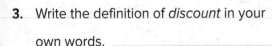 Which **MP** **Mathematical Process Goals** did you use? Shade the circle(s) that applies.

① Mathematical Problem Solving   ④ Mathematical Connections

② Mathematical Communication   ⑤ Mathematical Representations

③ Mathematical Reasoning

Find Sale Price and Original Price

Discount or **markdown** is the amount by which the regular price of an item is reduced. The sale price is the regular price minus the discount.

 Example Tutor

1. A DVD normally costs $22. This week it is on sale for 25% off the original price. What is the sale price of the DVD?

```
┌─────────── Original Price ──────────┐
            $22
├─────────────────────────┬───────────┤
│                         │           │
├─────── Sale Price ──────┼── 25% ──┤
```

Method 1 Subtract the discount from the regular price.

First, find the amount of the discount.

Let *d* represent the discount.

part = percent × whole   Write the percent equation.

$d = 0.25 \times 22$ 25% = 0.25.

$d = 5.50$ Multiply.

Next, subtract the discount from the regular price.

$22 - $5.50 = $16.50

Method 2 Subtract the percent of discount from 100%.

$100\% - 25\% = 75\%$ Subtract the discount from 100%.

The sale price is 75% of the regular price.

Let *s* represent the sale price.

part = percent × whole   Write the percent equation.

$s = 0.75 \times 22$ 75% = 0.75

$s = 16.50$ Multiply.

The sale price of the DVD is $16.50.

 Show your work.

Got it? Do this problem to find out.

a. _____

a. A shirt is regularly priced at $42. It is on sale for 15% off of the regular price. What is the sale price of the shirt?

Tutor

Example

2. A boogie board that has a regular price of $69 is on sale at a 35% discount. What is the sale price with 7% tax?

Step 1 Find the amount of the discount.

Let *d* represent the discount.

$$\underbrace{part} = \underbrace{percent} \times \underbrace{whole}$$ Write the percent equation.

d = 0.35 × 69   35% = 0.35

d = 24.15   Multiply.

Step 2 Subtract the discount from the regular price.

$69 − $24.15 = $44.85

Step 3 The percent of tax is applied after the discount is taken.

7% of $44.85 = 0.07 · 44.85   Write 7% as a decimal.

= 3.14   The tax is $3.14.

$44.85 + $3.14 = $47.99   Add the tax to the sale price.

The sale price of the boogie board including tax is $47.99.

Got it? Do this problem to find out.

b. A CD that has a regular price of $15.50 is on sale at a 25% discount. What is the sale price with 6.5% tax?

 Show your work.

b. _____

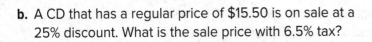

  Tutor

Example

3. A cell phone is on sale for 30% off. If the sale price is $239.89, what is the original price?

The sale price is 100% − 30% or 70% of the original price.

Let *p* represent the original price.

$$\underbrace{part} = \underbrace{percent} \times \underbrace{whole}$$

239.89 = 0.7 × p

$\dfrac{239.89}{0.7} = \dfrac{0.7p}{0.7}$ Divide each side by 0.7.

342.70 = p Simplify.

The original price is $342.70.

Percent Equation

Remember that in the percent equation, the percent must be written as a decimal. Since the sale price is 70% of the original price, use 0.7 to represent 70% in the percent equation.

Got it? Do this problem to find out.

c. Find the original price if the sale price of the cell phone is $205.50.

c. _____

Example

Tutor

4. Clothes Are Us and Ratcliffe's are having sales. At Clothes Are Us, a pair of sneakers is on sale for 40% off the regular price of $50. At Ratcliffe's, the same brand of sneakers is discounted by 30% off of the regular price of $40. Which store has the better sale price? Explain.

Find the sale price of the sneakers at each store.

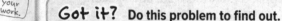

Clothes Are Us	**Ratcliffe's**
60% of $50 = 0.6 × $50	70% of $40 = 0.7 × $40
= $30	= $28

The sale price is $30.   The sale price is $28.

Since $28 < $30, the sale price at Ratcliffe's is the better buy.

Show your work.

Got it? Do this problem to find out.

d. If the sale at Clothes Are Us was 50% off, which store would have the better buy? Explain.

d. _____

Guided Practice

Check ✓

Show your work.

1. Mary and Roberto bought identical backpacks at different stores. Mary's backpack originally cost $65 and was discounted 25%. Roberto's backpack originally cost $75 and was on sale for 30% off of the original price. Which backpack was the better buy? Explain. (Examples 1, 2, and 4)

_____

2. A pair of in-line skates is on sale for $90. If this price represents a 9% discount from the original price, what is the original price to the nearest cent? (Example 3)

_____

3. **Building on the Essential Question** Describe two methods for finding the sale price of an item that is discounted 30%.

_____

_____

Rate Yourself!

Are you ready to move on? Shade the section that applies.

I have a few questions.

I'm ready to move on.

I have a lot of questions.

For more help, go online to access a Personal Tutor.

Tutor

Independent Practice

Go online for Step-by-Step Solutions

Find the sale price to the nearest cent. (Examples 1 and 2)

 show your work.

1. $64 jacket; 20% discount _____

2. $1,200 TV; 10% discount _____

3. $7.50 admission; 20% off;

5.75% tax _____

4. $4.30 makeup; 40% discount;

6% tax _____

5. A bottle of hand lotion is on sale for $2.25. If this price represents a 50% discount from the original price, what is the original price to the nearest cent? (Example 3)

_____

6. A tennis racket at Sport City costs $180 and is discounted 15%. The same model racket costs $200 at Tennis World and is on sale for 20% off. Which store is offering the better deal? Explain. (Example 4)

_____

_____

7. **MP** **Model with Mathematics** Refer to the graphic novel frame below.

a. Find the price that a student would pay including the group discount for

each amusement park. _____

_____

b. Which is the best deal? _____

8. The Wares want to buy a new computer. The regular price is $1,049. The store is offering a 20% discount and a sales tax of 5.25% is added after the discount. What is the total cost? _____

Find the original price to the nearest cent.

9. calendar: discount, 75%; sale price, $2.25 _____

10. telescope: discount, 30%; sale price, $126 _____

11. 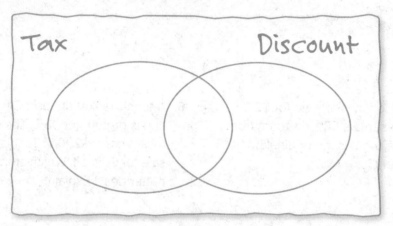 **Use Math Tools** Compare and contrast tax and discount.

Tax   Discount

H.O.T. Problems Higher Order Thinking

12. **Model with Mathematics** Give an example of the sale price of an item and the total cost including sales tax if the tax rate is 5.75% and the item is 25% off. _____

13. **Persevere with Problems** A store is having a sale in which all items are discounted 20%. Including tax, Colin paid $21 for a picture. If the sales tax rate is 5%, what was the original price of the picture? _____

14. **Reason Abstractly** Describe two methods for finding the sale price of an item that is discounted 30%. Which method do you prefer? Explain.

_____

_____

_____

_____

Extra Practice

Find the sale price to the nearest cent.

15. $119.50 skateboard;
20% off; 7% tax   *$102.29*

$0.20 \times \$119.50 = \$23.90$
$\$119.50 - \$23.90 = \$95.60$
$0.07 \times \$95.60 = \$6.69$
$\$95.60 + \$6.69 = \$102.29$

16. $40 sweater; 33% discount _____

17. $199 MP3 player; 15% discount _____

18. $12.25 pen set; 60% discount _____

19. Mrs. Robinson bought a novel at a bookstore on sale for 20% off its regular price of $29.99. Mr. Chang bought the same novel at a different bookstore for 10% off its regular price of $25. Which person received the better

discount? Explain. _____

_____

20. **MP Multiple Representations** An online store is having a sale on digital cameras. The table shows the regular price and the sale price for the cameras.

a. **Words** Write a rule that can be used to find the percent of decrease for any of the cameras.

_____

_____

_____

Camera Model	Regular Price	Sale Price	Discount
A	$97.99	$83.30	
B	$102.50	$82.00	
C	$75.99	$65.35	
D	$150.50	$135.45	

b. **Table** Complete the table for the discount.

c. **Numbers** Which model has the greatest percent discount?

_____

21. An appliance store is having a 15% off sale during a holiday weekend. Which of the following could be deals offered by the store during the sale? Select all that apply.

☐ washing machine: regular price: $680, sale price: $578

☐ refrigerator: regular price: $1,120, sale price: $896

☐ dryer: regular price: $340, sale price: $289

☐ chest freezer: regular price: $250, sale price: $212.50

22. The table shows the regular prices and sale prices of items at 4 different stores. Select the correct percent of discount offered by each store.

Store	Price	Sale Price	Percent of Discount
A	$68.20	$51.15	
B	$125.40	$100.32	
C	$269.75	$215.80	
D	$38.60	$32.81	

15%	25%
20%	30%

Spiral Review

Find the percent of change. Round to the nearest whole percent if necessary. State whether the percent of change is an *increase* or *decrease*.

23. 35 birds to 45 birds

24. 60 inches to 38 inches

25. $2.75 to $1.80

26. Complete the table to express each number of months in years. Write in simplest form. The first one is done for you.

Number of Months	1	2	3	4	6
Time in Years	$\frac{1}{12}$				

Financial Literacy: Simple Interest

Vocabulary Start-Up

Principal is the amount of money deposited or borrowed. **Simple interest** is the amount paid or earned for the use of money.

The simple interest formula is shown below. Fill in the diagram using the correct words from the word bank.

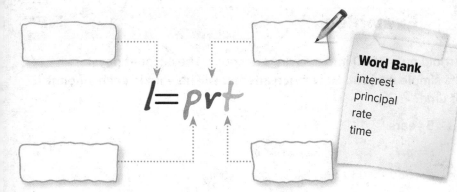

$$I = prt$$

Word Bank
interest
principal
rate
time

Essential Question

HOW can percent help you understand situations involving money?

Vocabulary

principal
simple interest

Virginia Standards
7.3

Real-World Link

Mrs. Ramirez is investing $400 in a savings account at a simple interest rate of 2% to purchase a laptop computer. She plans on investing the money for 18 months.

Based on this real-world situation, fill in the blanks with the correct numbers. Write the rate as a decimal. Time is expressed in years.

principal = [ ]   rate = [ ]   time = [ ] years

Which MP **Mathematical Process Goals** did you use? Shade the circle(s) that applies.

① Mathematical Problem Solving
② Mathematical Communication
③ Mathematical Reasoning

④ Mathematical Connections
⑤ Mathematical Representations

Simple Interest Formula

Words	Simple interest *I* is the product of the principal *p*, the annual interest rate *r*, and the time *t*, expressed in years.
Symbols	$I = prt$

If you have a savings account, the bank pays you interest for the use of your money. Use the formula $I = prt$ to find the amount of interest that will be earned.

Examples

Tutor

Arnold puts $580 into a savings account. The account pays 3% simple interest. How much interest will he earn in each amount of time?

1. **5 years**

$I = prt$	Formula for simple interest
$I = 580 \cdot 0.03 \cdot 5$	Replace *p* with $580, *r* with 0.03, and *t* with 5.
$I = 87$	Simplify.

So, Arnold will earn $87 in interest in 5 years.

2. **6 months**

6 months $= \dfrac{6}{12}$ or 0.5 year	Write the time as years.
$I = prt$	Formula for simple interest
$I = 580 \cdot 0.03 \cdot 0.5$	$p = \$580, r = 0.03, t = 0.5$
$I = 8.7$	Simplify.

So, Arnold will earn $8.70 in interest in 6 months.

Show your work.

Got it? Do these problems to find out.

a. _____

b. _____

a. Jenny puts $1,560 into a savings account. The account pays 2.5% simple interest. How much interest will she earn in 3 years?

b. Marcos invests $760 into a savings account. The account pays 4% simple interest. How much interest will he earn after 5 years?

Interest on Loans and Credit Cards

If you borrow money from a bank, you pay the bank interest for the use of their money. You also pay interest to a credit card company if you have an unpaid balance. Use the formula $I = prt$ to find the amount of interest owed.

  Examples

Tutor

3. Rondell's parents borrow $6,300 from the bank for a new car. The interest rate is 6% per year. How much simple interest will they pay if they take 2 years to repay the loan?

$I = prt$ Formula for simple interest

$I = 6,300 \cdot 0.06 \cdot 2$ Replace p with $6,300, r with 0.06, and t with 2.

$I = 756$ Simplify.

Rondell's parents will pay $756 in interest in 2 years.

STOP and Reflect

Explain in the space below how you would find the simple interest on a $500 loan at a 6% interest rate for 18 months.

4. Derrick's dad bought new tires for $900 using a credit card. His card has an interest rate of 19%. If he has no other charges on his card and does not make a payment, how much money will he owe after one month?

$I = prt$ Formula for simple interest

$I = 900 \cdot 0.19 \cdot \frac{1}{12}$ Replace p with $900, r with 0.19, and t with $\frac{1}{12}$.

$I = 14.25$ Simplify.

The interest owed after one month is $14.25.

So, the total amount owed would be $900 + $14.25 or $914.25.

Got it? Do these problems to find out.

Show your work.

c. Mrs. Hanover borrows $1,400 at a rate of 5.5% per year. How much simple interest will she pay if it takes 8 months to repay the loan?

c. _____

d. An office manager charged $425 worth of office supplies on a credit card. The credit card has an interest rate of 9.9%. How much money will he owe at the end of one month if he makes no other charges on the card and does not make a payment?

d. _____

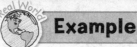

Example

5. Luis is taking out a car loan for $5,000. He plans on paying off the car loan in 2 years. At the end of 2 years, Luis will have paid $300 in interest. What is the simple interest rate on the car loan?

$I = prt$ — Formula for simple interest

$300 = 5{,}000 \cdot r \cdot 2$ — Replace *I* with 300, *p* with 5,000, and *t* with 2.

$300 = 10{,}000r$ — Simplify.

$\dfrac{300}{10{,}000} = \dfrac{10{,}000r}{10{,}000}$ — Divide each side by 10,000.

$0.03 = r$

The simple interest rate is 0.03 or 3%.

 Show your work.

Got it? Do this problem to find out.

e. _____

e. Maggie is taking out a student loan for $2,600. She plans on paying off the loan in 3 years. At the end of 3 years, Maggie will have paid $390 in interest. What is the simple interest rate on the student loan?

Guided Practice

 Check ✓

1. The Masters family financed a computer that cost $1,200. If the interest rate is 19%, how much will the family owe for the computer after one month if no payments are made? (Examples 1–4) _____

Show your work.

2. Samantha received a loan from the bank for $4,500. She plans on paying off the loan in 4 years. At the end of 4 years, Samantha will have paid $900 in interest. What is the simple interest rate on the bank loan? (Example 5)

_____

_____

3. **Building on the Essential Question** How can you use a formula to find simple interest?

_____

_____

_____

_____

Rate Yourself!

How confident are you about using the simple interest formula? Check the box that applies.

For more help, go online to access a Personal Tutor. Tutor

Independent Practice

Go online for Step-by-Step Solutions

Find the simple interest earned to the nearest cent for each principal, interest rate, and time. (Examples 1 and 2)

1. $640, 3%, 2 years _____

2. $1,500, 4.25%, 4 years _____

show your work.

3. $580, 2%, 6 months _____

4. $1,200, 3.9%, 8 months _____

Find the simple interest paid to the nearest cent for each loan amount, interest rate, and time. (Example 3)

5 $4,500, 9%, 3.5 years _____

6. $290, 12.5%, 6 months _____

7. Leon charged $75 at an interest rate of 12.5%. How much will Leon have to pay after one month if he makes no payments? (Example 4)

8. Jamerra received a $3,000 car loan. She plans on paying off the loan in 2 years. At the end of 2 years, Jamerra will have paid $450 in interest. What is the simple interest rate on the car loan? (Example 5)

9 **MP Justify Conclusions** Pablo has $4,200 to invest for college.

a. If Pablo invests $4,200 for 3 years and earns $630, what is the simple

interest rate? _____

b. Pablo's goal is to have $5,000 after 4 years. Is this possible if he

invests with a rate of return of 6%? Explain. _____

_____

10. Financial Literacy The table shows interest owed for a home improvement loan based on how long it takes to pay off the loan.

a. How much more interest is owed on $900 for 9 months than for 6 months?

_____

_____

b. Does the interest rate increase at a constant

rate? _____

_____

Time	Rate
6 months	2.4%
9 months	2.9%
12 months	3.0%
18 months	3.1%

 H.O.T. Problems Higher Order Thinking

11. MP Justify Conclusions Suppose you earn 3% on a $1,200 deposit for 5 years. Explain how the simple interest is affected if the rate is increased by 1%. What happens if the time is increased by 1 year?

_____

_____

_____

12. MP Persevere with Problems Dustin bought a $2,000 computer with a credit card. The minimum payment each month is $35. Each month 1% of the unpaid balance is added to the amount he owes.

a. If Dustin pays only $35 the first month, what will he owe the second

month? _____

b. If Dustin makes the minimum payment, what will he owe the third

month? _____

13. MP Reason Inductively Compare the two investments below. Which will have a greater account balance in the given time periods? Explain.

Investment A
Principal: $1,500
Interest Rate: 3%
Time: 30 years

Investment B
Principal: $1,500
Interest Rate: 4.5%
Time: 15 years

_____

_____

Extra Practice

Find the simple interest earned to the nearest cent for each principal, interest rate, and time.

14. $1,050, 4.6%, 2 years $96.60

Homework Help

$I = prt$

$I = \$1,050 \cdot 0.046 \cdot 2$

$I = 96.60$

15. $500, 3.75%, 4 months _____

16. $250, 2.85%, 3 years _____

17. $3,000, 5.5%, 9 months _____

Find the simple interest paid to the nearest cent for each loan amount, interest rate, and time.

18. $1,000, 7%, 2 years _____

19. $725, 6.25%, 1 year _____

20. $2,700, 8.2%, 3 months _____

21. $175.80, 12%, 8 months _____

22. Jake received a student loan for $12,000. He plans on paying off the loan in 5 years. At the end of 5 years, Jake will have paid $3,600 in interest. What is the simple interest rate on the student loan?

_____

23. Amy invests $3000 in a savings account that pays 2.35% simple annual interest. She makes no other deposits or withdrawals for 3.5 years. Determine if each statement is true or false.

   a. Amy's account will earn $246.75 in interest.   ☐ True   ☐ False

   b. Amy's account will be worth $2753.25 after 3.5 years.   ☐ True   ☐ False

   c. Amy's account would earn $15.75 more in interest if the annual interest rate were raised to 2.5%.   ☐ True   ☐ False

24. Mr. Chen needs to borrow $12,000 to buy a car. The table shows the terms of 3 different loan options.

Select the correct amounts for the interest paid and the monthly payments to complete the table.

Loan Option	Annual Interest Rate	Time (years)
A	5.35%	5
B	4.75%	3
C	5.1%	4

Interest Paid	Loan Option	Monthly Payment
	A	
	B	
	C	

$253.50	$380.83	$2,448.00
$301.00	$1,710.00	$3,210.00

Which loan option would you recommend for Mr. Chen? Explain your reasoning.

Spiral Review

Label the number line below from 0 to 10. Then graph each number.

25. 2.5

26. $8\frac{1}{4}$

27. 5.9

28. $\frac{1}{1}$

Inquiry **HOW is compound interest different from simple interest?**

Jin Li's parents deposit $2,000 in a college savings account. The account pays an interest rate of 4% compounded annually. Complete the Activity to find how much money will be in the account after 9 years.

Hands-On Activity

Compound interest is interest earned on the original principal and on interest earned in the past. At the end of each time period, the interest earned is added to the principal, which becomes the new principal for the next time period.

A computer spreadsheet is a useful tool for quickly performing calculations involving compound interest. To perform a calculation in a spreadsheet cell, first enter the equals sign. For example, enter =A4+B4 to find the sum of Cells A4 and B4.

Create a spreadsheet like the one shown.

Compound Interest ⬜ ⬛ ☒

	A	B	C	D
1	Rate	0.04		
2				
3	Principal	Interest	New Principal	Time (YR)
4	$2000.00	$80.00	$2080.00	1
5	$2080.00	$83.20	$2163.20	2
6	$2163.20	$86.53	$2249.73	3
7	$2249.73	$89.99	$2339.72	4
8	$2339.72	$93.59	$2433.31	5
9	$2433.31	$97.33	$2530.64	6
10	$2530.64	$101.23	$2631.86	7
11	$2631.86	$105.27	$2737.14	8
12				

Sheet 1 / Sheet 2 / Sheet 3 /

> The interest rate is entered as a decimal.

> The spreadsheet evaluates the formula A4×B1.

> The interest is added to the principal every year. The spreadsheet evaluates the formula A4 + B4.

What formula would the spreadsheet use to find the new principal at the end

of Year 9? _____

So, the account will have a balance of _____ after 9 years.

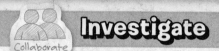

Investigate

Work with a partner. Create spreadsheets for the situations below.

1. Lakeesha deposits $1,500 into a Young Savers account. The account receives 4% interest compounded annually. What is the balance in Lakeesha's account after 2 years? after 3 years?

   2 Years: _____   3 Years: _____

2. Michael deposits $2,650 into an account. The interest rate on the account is 6% compounded annually. What is the balance in Michael's account after 2 years? after 3 years?

   2 Years: _____   3 Years: _____

Analyze and Reflect

3. **MP** **Reason Inductively** Suppose Elijah deposited $1,000 into a bank account paying 4.75% interest compounded annually. At the same time, Lily deposits $1,000 in a separate account that pays 5% simple interest. Elijah and Lily withdraw the money from their accounts after 6 years. Predict who made more money. Explain.

   _____

   _____

   _____

Create

4. **MP** **Model with Mathematics** Write a real-world problem that involves compound interest. Then create a spreadsheet and solve your problem.

   _____

   _____

   _____

5. **inquiry** HOW is compound interest different from simple interest?

   _____

   _____

   _____

   _____

21ST CENTURY CAREER
in Video Game Design

Video Game Designer

Are you passionate about computer gaming? You might want to explore a career in video game design. A video game designer is responsible for a game's concept, layout, character development, and game-play. Game designers use math and logic to compute how different parts of a game will work.

Is This the Career for You?

Are you interested in a career as a video game designer? Take some of the following courses in high school.

◆ 3-D Digital Animation
◆ Introduction to Computer Literacy
◆ Introduction to Game Development

Find out how math relates to a career in Video Game Design.

MP All Fun and Games

Use the information in the circle graph and the table to solve the problems below.

1. How many of the top 20 video games sold were sports games? _____

2. Out of the top 20 video games sold, how many more music games were there than racer games? _____

3. In Week 1, the total sales for a video game were $2,374,136. What percent of the total sales was from the United States?

   Round to the nearest whole percent. _____

4. Find the percent of change in sales of the video game from Week 1 to Week 3 in Japan. Round to the nearest whole

   percent. _____

5. Which country had a greater percent decrease in sales from Week 1 to Week 2: Japan or the United States? Explain.

   _____

   _____

   _____

   _____

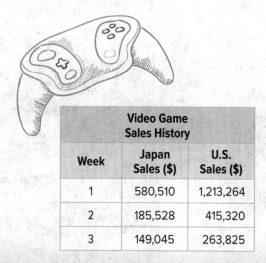

Video Game Sales History		
Week	Japan Sales ($)	U.S. Sales ($)
1	580,510	1,213,264
2	185,528	415,320
3	149,045	263,825

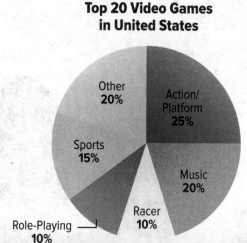

Top 20 Video Games in United States

- Other 20%
- Action/Platform 25%
- Sports 15%
- Music 20%
- Racer 10%
- Role-Playing 10%

MP Career Project

It's time to update your career portfolio! Choose one of your favorite video games. Make a list of what you think are the best features of the game. Then describe any changes that you, as a video game designer, would make to the game.

_____

_____

_____

_____

_____

List the strengths you have that would help you succeed in this career.

- _____
- _____
- _____
- _____
- _____

Vocabulary Check

Complete the crossword puzzle using the vocabulary list at the beginning of the chapter.

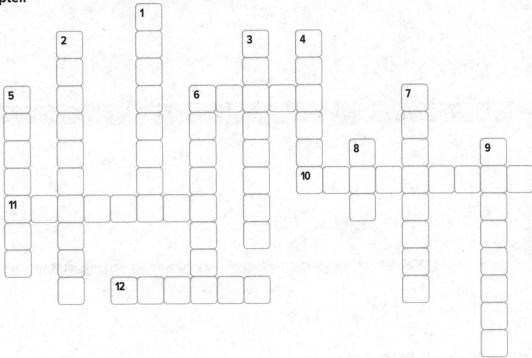

Down

1. type of percent when the final amount is greater than the original amount

2. statement that two ratios are equal

3. amount that the regular price is reduced

4. difference between what a store pays for an item and what a customer pays

5. price that a customer pays for an item

6. mathematical sentence stating that two expressions are equal

7. another term for the term in 3 down

8. gratuity

9. additional amount of money charged to items that people buy

Across

6. type of percent that compares the inaccuracy of an estimate to the actual amount

10. amount of money deposited or borrowed

11. amount paid or earned for the use of money

12. type of percent that compares the final and original amounts

Key Concept Check

Use Your FOLDABLES

Use your Foldable to help review the chapter.

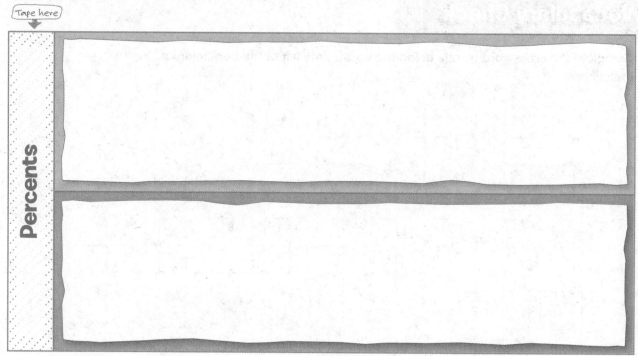

Got it?

Match each sentence with its solution.

1. 15% of what number is 45?

a. 125%

2. What percent of 20 is 15?

b. 12

3. What number is 30% of 60?

c. 300

4. What percent of 600 is 750?

d. 18

5. What number is 15% of 80?

e. 75%

6. 80% of what number is 20?

f. 25

DVD Deals

Anthony and Miguel go to the store to purchase some new DVDs. An advertisement in the window catches their attention.

Write your answers on another piece of paper. Show all of your work to receive full credit.

Part A
Does the information on the sign represent a proportional relationship? Explain how you know.

Part B
Miguel selects five DVDs to purchase. A few of the DVD cases appear to be damaged, so the manager gives Miguel a 20% discount on his entire purchase. Miguel tries to guess how much money will be deducted from the total cost. What is a reasonable estimate of the cost of the DVDs before tax is added? What is the actual cost before tax?

Part C
There is an 8% sales tax in the town where the store is located. What is Miguel's total cost after sales tax has been added?

Part D
Anthony decided to buy two DVDs that were not included in the deal. His price after tax was $21.60. What was the cost of the two DVDs before the sales tax was added?

Reflect

Answering the Essential Question

Use what you learned about percent to complete the graphic organizer. For each situation, circle an arrow to show if the final amount would be greater or less than the original amount. Then write a real-world percent problem and an equation that models it.

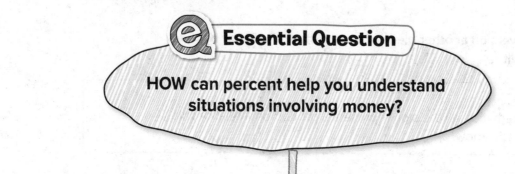

Essential Question

HOW can percent help you understand situations involving money?

Sales Tax	Simple Interest	Discount
⬆ ⬇	⬆ ⬇	⬆ ⬇
Equation:	Equation:	Equation:

Answer the Essential Question. HOW can percent help you understand situations involving money?

_____

_____

Chapter 3
Rational Numbers

 Essential Question

WHAT happens when you add, subtract, multiply, and divide fractions?

 Virginia Standards
7.1c; 7.1e; 7.2; 7.3

 Math in the Real World

Tennis About 70,000 tennis balls are used at the U.S. Open tennis tournament each year. This is only a small fraction of the 300,000,000 tennis balls produced each year. Write a fraction in simplest form that compares the number of tennis balls used at the U.S. Open to the number produced per year.

 FOLDABLES
Study Organizer

1 Cut out the Foldable in the back of the book.

2 Place your Foldable on page 270.

3 Use the Foldable throughout this chapter to help you learn about fractions, decimals, and percents.

Vocabulary

absolute value	graph	like fractions	rational numbers
bar notation	integer	negative integer	repeating decimal
common denominator	least common denominator	positive integer	terminating decimal
			unlike fractions

Review Vocabulary

An *improper fraction* is a fraction in which the numerator is greater than or equal to the denominator, such as $\frac{21}{4}$. A *mixed number* is a number composed of a whole number and a fraction, such as $5\frac{1}{4}$.

In the organizer below, write each mixed number as an improper fraction and each improper fraction as a mixed number. The first one in each column is done for you.

Mixed Numbers and Improper Fractions

Change Mixed Numbers

$3\frac{1}{2} = \frac{7}{2}$

$5\frac{1}{3} =$

$8\frac{2}{5} =$

$6\frac{4}{9} =$

$10\frac{3}{8} =$

$7\frac{3}{4} =$

$15\frac{5}{6} =$

Change Improper Fractions

$\frac{41}{4} = 10\frac{1}{4}$

$\frac{16}{3} =$

$\frac{23}{5} =$

$\frac{90}{11} =$

$\frac{66}{7} =$

$\frac{101}{2} =$

$\frac{87}{20} =$

What Do You Already Know?

List three things you already know about rational numbers in the first section. Then list three things you would like to learn about rational numbers in the second section.

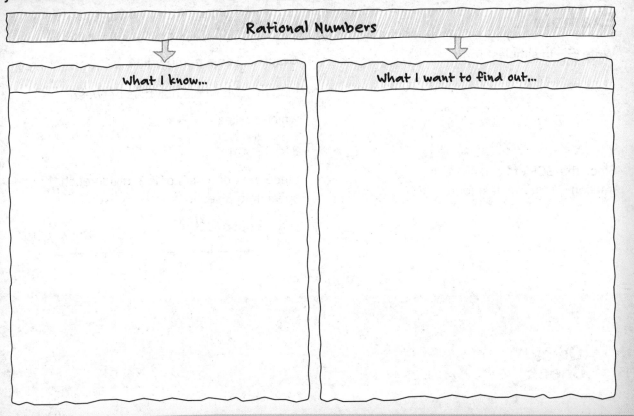

Rational Numbers

What I know...

What I want to find out...

When Will You Use This?

Here are a few examples of how rational numbers are used in the real world.

Activity 1 Use a tape measure to find the width of a closet in your home. Do you think that a shelf that is $28\frac{3}{4}$ inches long would fit in the space that you measured? Is it too long or too short? What would you need to do to make the new shelf fit?

_____

_____

Activity 2 Go online at **connectED.mcgraw-hill.com** to read the graphic novel *Get Organized*. What are the dimensions of each storage cube?

Are You Ready?

Try the Quick Check below.
Or, take the Online Readiness Quiz.

Check ✓

Quick Review

Example 1

Write $\frac{25}{100}$ in simplest form.

$$\frac{25}{100} = \frac{1}{4}$$

$\div 25$ (top)
$\div 25$ (bottom)

Divide the numerator and denominator by the GCF, 25.

Since the GCF of 1 and 4 is 1, the fraction $\frac{1}{4}$ is in simplest form.

Example 2

Graph $3\frac{2}{3}$ on a number line.

Find the two whole numbers between which $3\frac{2}{3}$ lies.

$$3 < 3\frac{2}{3} < 4$$

Since the denominator is 3, divide each space into 3 sections.

Draw a dot at $3\frac{2}{3}$.

0 1 2 3 4 5 6

Quick Check

Fractions Write each fraction in simplest form.

1. $\frac{24}{36} =$ _____

2. $\frac{45}{50} =$ _____

3. $\frac{88}{121} =$ _____

Show your work.

Graphing Graph each fraction or mixed number on the number line below.

4. $\frac{1}{2}$

5. $\frac{3}{4}$

6. $1\frac{1}{4}$

7. $2\frac{1}{2}$

How Did You Do?

Which problems did you answer correctly in the Quick Check?
Shade those exercise numbers below.

① ② ③ ④ ⑤ ⑥ ⑦

Integers and Absolute Value

Vocabulary Start-Up

Numbers like 5 and −8 are called integers. An **integer** is any number from the set {..., −4, −3, −2, −1, 0, 1, 2, 3, 4, ...}, where ... means *continues without end*.

Complete the graphic organizer.

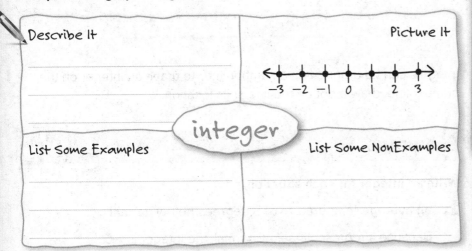

Describe It

Picture It

integer

List Some Examples

List Some NonExamples

Essential Question

WHAT happens when you add, subtract, multiply, and divide fractions?

Vocabulary

integer
negative integer
positive integer
graph
absolute value

Virginia Standards
7.1e

Real-World Link

- The bottom of a snowboarding halfpipe is 5 meters below the top. Circle the integer you would you use to represent this position?

  5   or   −5

- Describe another situation that uses negative integers. _____

_____

Awesome halfpipe!

Which **MP** **Mathematical Process Goals** did you use? Shade the circle(s) that applies.

① Mathematical Problem Solving

② Mathematical Communication

③ Mathematical Reasoning

④ Mathematical Connections

⑤ Mathematical Representations

Identify and Graph Integers

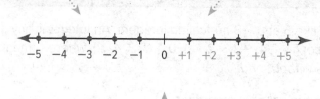

Negative integers are integers less than zero. They are written with a − sign.

Positive integers are integers greater than zero. They can be written with a + sign.

$$-5 \quad -4 \quad -3 \quad -2 \quad -1 \quad 0 \quad +1 \quad +2 \quad +3 \quad +4 \quad +5$$

Zero is neither negative nor positive.

Integers can be graphed on a number line. To **graph** an integer on the number line, draw a dot on the line at its location.

Examples

Write an integer for each situation.

1. **an average temperature of 5 degrees below normal**

Because it represents *below* normal, the integer is −5.

2. **an average rainfall of 5 inches above normal**

Because it represents *above* normal, the integer is +5 or 5.

Got it? Do these problems to find out.

Write an integer for each situation.

    a. 6 degrees above normal   **b.** 2 inches below normal

a. _____

b. _____

Example

3. **Graph the set of integers {4, −6, 0} on a number line.**

Draw a number line. Then draw a dot at the location of each integer.

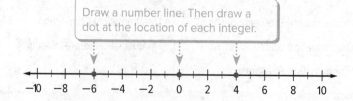

$$-10 \quad -8 \quad -6 \quad -4 \quad -2 \quad 0 \quad 2 \quad 4 \quad 6 \quad 8 \quad 10$$

Got it? Do these problems to find out.

Graph each set of integers on a number line.

c. $\{-2, 8, -7\}$　　　　　d. $\{-4, 10, -3, 7\}$

Absolute Value

Key Concept

Words	The absolute value of a number is the distance between the number and zero on a number line.

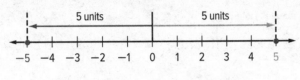
5 units　　　　5 units

$-5\ -4\ -3\ -2\ -1\ \ 0\ \ 1\ \ 2\ \ 3\ \ 4\ \ 5$

Examples	$|-5| = 5$	$|5| = 5$

On the number line in the Key Concept box, notice that -5 and 5 are each 5 units from 0, even though they are on opposite sides of 0. Numbers that are the same distance from zero on a number line have the same **absolute value**.

Examples

Tutor

Evaluate each expression.

4. $|-4|$

The graph of -4 is 4 units from 0.

So, $|-4| = 4$.

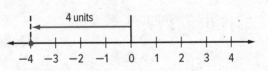
4 units

$-4\ -3\ -2\ -1\ \ 0\ \ 1\ \ 2\ \ 3\ \ 4$

> **Order of Operations**
> The absolute value bars are considered to be a grouping symbol. When evaluating $|-5| - |2|$, evaluate the absolute values before subtracting.

5. $|-5| - |2|$

$|-5| - |2| = 5 - 2$　　$|-5| = 5, |2| = 2$

So, $|-5| - |2| = 3$.

Got it? Do these problems to find out.

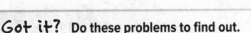

e. $|8|$　　　　f. $2 + |-3|$　　　　g. $|-6| - 5$

Example

6. Nick climbs 30 feet up a rock wall and then climbs 22 feet down to a landing area. The number of feet Nick climbs can be represented using the expression $|30| + |-22|$. How many feet does Nick climb?

$|30| + |-22| = 30 + |-22|$ The absolute value of 30 is 30.

$\qquad\qquad\quad = 30 + 22$ or 52 The absolute value of -22 is 22. Simplify.

So, Nick climbs 52 feet.

Guided Practice

Check ✓

Write an integer for each situation. (Examples 1 and 2)

1. a deposit of $16 _____

2. a loss of 11 yards _____

3. 6°F below zero _____

Show your work.

Evaluate each expression. (Examples 4–6)

4. $|-9| =$ _____

5. $|18| - |-10| =$ _____

6. $|-11| - |-6| =$ _____

7. Graph the set of integers {11, −5, −8} on a number line. (Example 3)

−8 −6 −4 −2   0   2   4   6   8   10   12

8. ⓔ **Building on the Essential Question** Why is the absolute value of a nonzero number positive? Explain your reasoning. _____

_____

_____

Rate Yourself!

☐   I understand integers and absolute value.

▶▶ Great! You're ready to move on!

☐   I still have some questions about integers and absolute value.

▯▮ No Problem! Go online to access a Personal Tutor.
Tutor

Name _____ My Homework _____

Write an integer for each situation. (Examples 1 and 2)

1. a profit of $9 _____

 show your work.

2. a bank withdrawal of $50 _____

3. 53°C below zero _____

4. 7 inches more than normal _____

Graph each set of integers on a number line. (Example 3)

 5. {0, 1, −3}

−3 −2 −1 0 1

6. {−5, −1, 10, −9}

−10 −8 −6 −4 −2 0 2 4 6 8 10

Evaluate each expression. (Examples 4 and 5)

7. |10| = _____

8. |−7| − 5 = _____

9. 1 + |7| = _____

10. The number of yards a football team moves on the field can be represented using the expression |8| + |−4|. How many yards does the football team move? (Example 6)

_____

11. In golf, scores are often written in relationship to *par*, the average score for a round at a certain course. Write an integer to represent a score that is 7 under par. (Examples 1 and 2)

_____

_____

12. A scuba diver descended 10 feet, 8 feet, and 11 feet. The total number of feet can be represented using the expression $|-10| + |-8| + |-11|$. What is the total number of feet the scuba diver descended?

13. **MP Use Math Tools** Mr. Chavez spent $199.99 for a new smart phone, $39.99 on a carrying case, and $59.99 on accessories. The expression $|-199.99| + |-39.99| + |-59.99|$ represents the total amount that Mr. Chavez spent. How much did Mr. Chavez spend altogether? Check your answer using estimation.

H.O.T. Problems Higher Order Thinking

14. **MP Reason Inductively** If $|x| = 3$, what is the value of x?

15. **MP Persevere with Problems** Two numbers A and B are graphed on a number line. Is it *always*, *sometimes*, or *never* true that $A - |B| \leq A + B$ and $A > |B|$? Explain.

16. **MP Which One Doesn't Belong?** Identify the expression that is not equal to the other three. Explain your reasoning.

| $15 - |-5|$ | $|-4| + 6$ | $-|7 + 3|$ | $|-10|$ |

17. **MP Persevere with Problems** Determine whether each statement is *always*, *sometimes*, or *never* true. Explain your reasoning.

a. $|x| = |-x|$

b. $|x| = -|x|$

c. $|-x| = -|x|$

Extra Practice

Write an integer for each situation.

18. 2 feet below flood level -2 _____

 Because it represents below flood level, the integer is -2.

19. an elevator goes up 12 floors _____

MP Model with Mathematics Graph each set of integers on a number line.

20. {3, −7, 6}

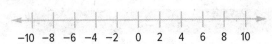

21. {−2, −4, −6, −8}

Evaluate each expression.

22. $|-12| =$ _____

23. $7 + |4| =$ _____

24. $|-9| + |-5| =$ _____

25. $|-10| \div 2 \times |5| =$ _____

26. $12 - |-8| + 7 =$ _____

27. $|27| \div 3 - |-4| =$ _____

28. Jasmine's pet guinea pig gained 8 ounces in one month. Write an integer to describe the amount of weight her pet gained.

_____

29. Determine if each statement is true or false.

  a. A $100 check deposited in a bank can be represented by +100.   ☐ True   ☐ False

  b. A loss of 15 yards in a football game can be represented by −15.   ☐ True   ☐ False

  c. A temperature of 20 below zero can be represented by −20.   ☐ True   ☐ False

  d. A submarine diving 300 feet below the surface can be represented by +300.   ☐ True   ☐ False

30. Rachel recorded the overnight low temperatures for one week in a table.

Low Temperatures							
Day	Sunday	Monday	Tuesday	Wednesday	Thursday	Friday	Saturday
Temperature (°F)	2	−6	4	−8	2	0	−1

Plot a point on the number line for each recorded temperature.

What is the distance on the number line between the points that represent the warmest and coldest temperatures? ☐

Spiral Review

Write the ordered pair corresponding to each point graphed at the right. Then state the quadrant or axis location of each point.

31. J _____

32. K _____

33. L _____

34. M _____

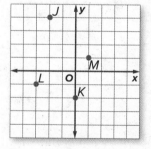

Graph and label each point on the coordinate plane.

35. A(2, 4)

36. B(−3, 1)

37. C(2, 0)

38. D(−3, −3)

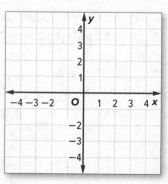

Inquiry HOW can you graph negative fractions on the number line?

Water evaporates from Earth at an average of about $-\frac{3}{4}$ inch per week.

Hands-On Activity

Graph $-\frac{3}{4}$ on a number line.

Step 1 Use the fraction strip below that is divided in fourths above a number line.

Mark a 0 on the right side and a −1 on the left side.

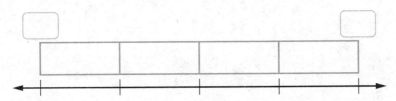

Step 2 Starting from the right, shade three fourths. Label the number line with $-\frac{1}{4}$, $-\frac{2}{4}$, and $-\frac{3}{4}$.

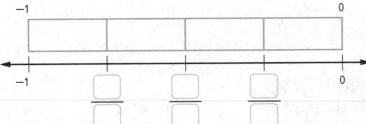

Step 3 Draw the number line portion of the model in Step 2.

Place a dot on the number line to represent $-\frac{3}{4}$.

So, on a number line, $-\frac{3}{4}$ is between ☐ and $\frac{☐}{☐}$ or $\frac{☐}{☐}$.

Investigate

MP Model with Mathematics Work with a partner. Graph each fraction on a number line. Use a fraction strip if needed.

1. $-\dfrac{3}{8}$

Show your work.

2. $-1\dfrac{2}{5}$

Analyze and Reflect

Work with a partner to complete each table. Use a number line if needed.

	< or >	
$\dfrac{7}{8}$	>	$\dfrac{3}{8}$
3. $\dfrac{9}{8}$		$\dfrac{5}{8}$
4. $\dfrac{13}{8}$		$\dfrac{3}{8}$
5. $\dfrac{15}{8}$		$\dfrac{13}{8}$

	< or >	
$-\dfrac{7}{8}$	<	$-\dfrac{3}{8}$
6. $-\dfrac{9}{8}$		$-\dfrac{5}{8}$
7. $-\dfrac{13}{8}$		$-\dfrac{3}{8}$
8. $-\dfrac{15}{8}$		$-\dfrac{13}{8}$

9. **MP Identify Repeated Reasoning** Compare and contrast the information in the tables.

_____

_____

Create

10. **MP Use Math Tools** Graph $-\dfrac{3}{4}$ and $\dfrac{3}{4}$ on a number line. Then use the graph to explain how the representations of the two fractions differ.

_____

_____

11. **Inquiry** HOW can you graph negative fractions on the number line?

_____

_____

Terminating and Repeating Decimals

Vocabulary Start-Up

Any fraction can be expressed as a decimal by dividing the numerator by the denominator.

The decimal form of a fraction is called a **repeating decimal**. Repeating decimals can be represented using **bar notation**. In bar notation, a bar is drawn only over the digit(s) that repeat.

$$0.3333... = 0.\overline{3} \qquad 0.1212... = 0.\overline{12} \qquad 11.38585... = 11.3\overline{85}$$

If the repeating digit is zero, the decimal is a **terminating decimal**. The terminating decimal $0.25\overline{0}$ is typically written as 0.25.

Match each repeating decimal to the correct bar notation.

0.1111...	0.6$\overline{1}$
0.61111...	0.$\overline{1}$
0.616161...	0.$\overline{61}$

Essential Question

WHAT happens when you add, subtract, multiply, and divide fractions?

Vocabulary

repeating decimal
bar notation
terminating decimal

Real-World Link

Jamie had two hits on her first nine times at bat. To find her batting "average," she divided 2 by 9.

$$2 \div 9 = 0.2222...$$

Write 0.2222... using bar notation. ☐

Round 0.2222... to the nearest thousandth. ☐

Which **Mathematical Process Goals** did you use? Shade the circle(s) that applies.

① Mathematical Problem Solving   ④ Mathematical Connections

② Mathematical Communication   ⑤ Mathematical Representations

③ Mathematical Reasoning

Write Fractions as Decimals

Our decimal system is based on powers of 10 such as 10, 100, and 1,000. If the denominator of a fraction is a power of 10, you can use place value to write the fraction as a decimal.

Complete the table below. Write fractions in simplest form.

Words	Fraction	Decimal
seven tenths	$\frac{7}{10}$	0.7
nineteen hundredths		
one-hundred five thousandths		

If the denominator of a fraction is a *factor* of 10, 100, 1,000, or any greater power of ten, you can use mental math and place value.

Examples

Tutor

Write each fraction or mixed number as a decimal.

1. $\frac{74}{100}$

Use place value to write the equivalent decimal.

$\frac{74}{100} = 0.74$ Read $\frac{74}{100}$ as *seventy-four hundredths*.

So, $\frac{74}{100} = 0.74$.

2. $\frac{7}{20}$

Think $\frac{7}{20} = \frac{35}{100}$ $\times 5$

So, $\frac{7}{20} = 0.35$.

3. $5\frac{3}{4}$

$5\frac{3}{4} = 5 + \frac{3}{4}$ Think of it as a sum.

$= 5 + 0.75$ You know that $\frac{3}{4} = 0.75$.

$= 5.75$ Add mentally.

So, $5\frac{3}{4} = 5.75$.

Got it? **Do these problems to find out.**

a. $\frac{3}{10}$

b. $\frac{3}{25}$

c. $-6\frac{1}{2}$

a. _____

b. _____

c. _____

Examples

Tutor

4. Write $\frac{3}{8}$ as a decimal.

$$
\begin{array}{r}
0.375 \\
8\overline{)3.000} \\
-24 \\
\hline
60 \\
-56 \\
\hline
40 \\
-40 \\
\hline
0
\end{array}
$$

Divide 3 by 8.

Division ends when the remainder is 0.

So, $\frac{3}{8} = 0.375$.

---

5. Write $-\frac{1}{40}$ as a decimal.

$$
\begin{array}{r}
0.025 \\
40\overline{)1.000} \\
-80 \\
\hline
200 \\
-200 \\
\hline
0
\end{array}
$$

Divide 1 by 40.

So, $-\frac{1}{40} = -0.025$.

---

6. Write $\frac{7}{9}$ as a decimal.

$$
\begin{array}{r}
0.777... \\
9\overline{)7.000} \\
-63 \\
\hline
70 \\
-63 \\
\hline
70 \\
-63 \\
\hline
7
\end{array}
$$

Divide 7 by 9.

Notice that the division will never terminate in zero.

So, $\frac{7}{9} = 0.777...$ or $0.\overline{7}$.

Bar Notation

Remember that you can use bar notation to indicate a number pattern that repeats indefinitely. $0.333... = 0.\overline{3}$.

Got it? Do these problems to find out.

Write each fraction or mixed number as a decimal. Use bar notation if needed.

d. $-\frac{7}{8}$

e. $2\frac{1}{8}$

f. $-\frac{3}{11}$

g. $8\frac{1}{3}$

Show your work.

d. _____

e. _____

f. _____

g. _____

Write Decimals as Fractions

Every terminating decimal can be written as a fraction with a denominator of 10, 100, 1,000, or a greater power of ten. Use the place value of the final digit as the denominator.

 Example

Watch | Tutor

7. **Find the fraction of the fish in the aquarium that are goldfish. Write in simplest form.**

$$0.15 = \frac{15}{100}$$ The digit 5 is in the hundredths place.

$$= \frac{3}{20}$$ Simplify.

So, $\frac{3}{20}$ of the fish are goldfish.

Fish	Amount
Angelfish	0.4
Goldfish	0.15
Guppy	0.25
Molly	0.2

Show your work.

Got it? Do these problems to find out.

Determine the fraction of the aquarium made up by each fish. Write the answer in simplest form.

h. molly   **i.** guppy   **j.** angelfish

h. _____

i. _____

j. _____

Guided Practice

Check ✓

Write each fraction or mixed number as a decimal. Use bar notation if needed. (Examples 1–6)

1. $\frac{2}{5} =$ _____

Show your work.

2. $-\frac{9}{10} =$ _____

3. $\frac{5}{9} =$ _____

4. During a hockey game, an ice resurfacer travels 0.75 mile. What fraction represents this distance? (Example 7)

_____

5. **Building on the Essential Question** How can you write a fraction as a decimal?

_____

_____

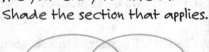

Name _____ My Homework _____

Independent Practice

Go online for Step-by-Step Solutions eHelp

Write each fraction or mixed number as a decimal. Use bar notation if needed. (Examples 1–6)

1. $\frac{1}{2} =$ _____

 Show your work.

2. $-4\frac{4}{25} =$ _____

3. $\frac{1}{8} =$ _____

4. $\frac{3}{16} =$ _____

5. $-\frac{33}{50} =$ _____

6. $-\frac{17}{40} =$ _____

7. $5\frac{7}{8} =$ _____

8. $9\frac{3}{8} =$ _____

9. $-\frac{8}{9} =$ _____

10. $-\frac{1}{6} =$ _____

11. $-\frac{8}{11} =$ _____

12. $2\frac{6}{11} =$ _____

Write each decimal as a fraction or mixed number in simplest form. (Example 7)

13. $-0.2 =$ _____

14. $0.55 =$ _____

15. $5.96 =$ _____

16. The screen on Brianna's new phone is 2.85 centimeters long. What mixed number represents the length of the phone screen? (Example 7)

_____

17 **STEM** A praying mantis is an interesting insect that can rotate its head 180 degrees. Suppose the praying mantis at the right is 10.5 centimeters long. What mixed number represents this length? (Example 7)

_____

18. **MP Persevere with Problems** Suppose you buy a 1.25-pound package of ham at $5.20 per pound.

    a. What fraction of a pound did you buy?

    _____

    b. How much money did you spend?

    _____

H.O.T. Problems Higher Order Thinking

19. **MP Identify Structure** Write a fraction that is equivalent to a terminating decimal between 0.5 and 0.75.

    _____

20. **MP Identify Structure** The distance between each of the two different numbers and zero on the number line is $2\frac{1}{4}$ units.

    a. What are the two numbers?

    b. What must be true of these numbers?

    _____

    _____

    _____

21. **MP Persevere with Problems** The value of pi (π) is 3.1415926... . The mathematician Archimedes believed that π was between $3\frac{1}{7}$ and $3\frac{10}{71}$. Was Archimedes correct? Explain your reasoning.

    _____

    _____

    _____

22. **MP Reason Inductively** A *unit fraction* is a fraction that has 1 as its numerator. Write the four greatest unit fractions that are repeating decimals. Then write each fraction as a decimal.

    _____

    _____

23. **MP Model with Mathematics** Write a real-world scenario in which it would be appropriate to write a value in fractional form.

    _____

    _____

Extra Practice

Write each fraction or mixed number as a decimal. Use bar notation if needed.

24. $\frac{4}{5} =$ ___0.8___

$$\overset{\times 2}{\overset{\curvearrowright}{\frac{4}{5}}} = \overset{}{\frac{8}{10}}$$
$$\underset{\times 2}{\underset{\curvearrowright}{}}$$

So, $\frac{4}{5} = 0.8$.

25. $-7\frac{1}{20} =$ _____

26. $-\frac{4}{9} =$ _____

27. $5\frac{1}{3} =$ _____

28. The fraction of a dime that is made up of copper is $\frac{12}{16}$. Write this fraction as a decimal.

_____

Write each decimal as a fraction or mixed number in simplest form.

29. $-0.9 =$ _____

30. $0.34 =$ _____

31. $2.66 =$ _____

Write each of the following as an improper fraction.

32. $-13 =$ _____

33. $7\frac{1}{3} =$ _____

34. $-3.2 =$ _____

35. **MP** **Be Precise** Nicolás practiced playing the cello for 2 hours and 18 minutes. Write the time Nicolás spent practicing as a decimal.

_____

Lesson 2 Terminating and Repeating Decimals **201**

36. The table shows the lengths of four hiking trails. Select the appropriate decimal equivalent of each trail length.

1.2	1.25	1.3	1.$\overline{3}$

1.6	1.$\overline{6}$	1.75

Hiking Trail	Trail Length	Decimal Equivalents
Lakeview	$1\frac{1}{4}$	
Forest Lane	$1\frac{1}{3}$	
Sparrow Stroll	$1\frac{3}{10}$	
Mountain Climb	$1\frac{2}{3}$	

37. Zoe went to lunch with a friend. After tax, her bill was $12.05. Which of the following rational numbers is equivalent to this amount? Select all that apply.

☐ $12\frac{1}{20}$ ☐ $\frac{25}{2}$ ☐ $\frac{241}{20}$ ☐ $12\frac{5}{100}$

Spiral Review

Round each decimal to the tenths place.

38. $5.69 \approx$ _____

39. $0.05 \approx$ _____

40. $98.99 \approx$ _____

Graph and label each fraction on the number line below.

41. $\frac{1}{2}$

42. $\frac{3}{4}$

43. $\frac{2}{3}$

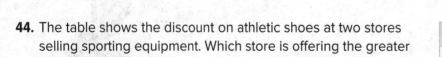

44. The table shows the discount on athletic shoes at two stores selling sporting equipment. Which store is offering the greater discount? Explain.

Store	Discount
Good Sports	$\frac{1}{5}$
Go Time	25%

_____

_____

Compare and Order Rational Numbers

Vocabulary Start-Up

A **rational number** is a number that can be expressed as a ratio of two integers written as a fraction, in which the denominator is not zero. The Venn diagram below shows that the number 2 can be called many things. It is a whole number, integer, and rational number. The number −1.4444... is only a rational number.

Common fractions, terminating and repeating decimals, percents, and integers are all rational numbers.

Write the numbers from the number bank on the diagram.

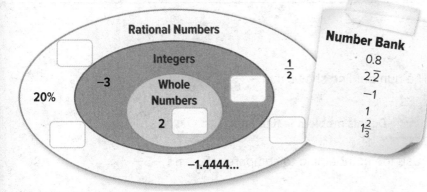

Number Bank
0.8
2.$\overline{2}$
−1
1
1$\frac{2}{3}$

Essential Question

WHAT happens when you add, subtract, multiply, and divide fractions?

Vocabulary

rational number
common denominator
least common denominator

Virginia Standards
7.1c

 Yum, pi!

Real-World Link

Not all numbers are rational numbers. The Greek letter π (pi) represents the nonterminating and nonrepeating number whose first few digits are 3.14... . This number is an *irrational number*.

Use the Internet to search for the digits of pi. Describe

what you find. _____

_____

Which MP **Mathematical Process Goals** did you use? Shade the circle(s) that applies.

① Mathematical Problem Solving   ④ Mathematical Connections

② Mathematical Communication   ⑤ Mathematical Representations

③ Mathematical Reasoning

Compare Rational Numbers

A **common denominator** is a common multiple of the denominators of two or more fractions. The **least common denominator** or **LCD** is the LCM or least common multiple of the denominators. You can use the LCD to compare fractions. You can also use a number line.

Example

1. Fill in the $\bigcirc$ with <, >, or = to make $-1\frac{5}{6}$ $\bigcirc$ $-1\frac{1}{6}$ a true sentence.

Graph each rational number on a number line.
Mark off equal-size increments of $\frac{1}{6}$ between -2 and -1.

$$\begin{array}{cccccccc} & & & & & & & \\ \hline -2 & -1\frac{5}{6} & -1\frac{4}{6} & -1\frac{3}{6} & -1\frac{2}{6} & -1\frac{1}{6} & -1 \end{array}$$

The number line shows that $-1\frac{5}{6} < -1\frac{1}{6}$.

> **Got it?** Do this problem to find out.

Show your work.

a. Use the number line to compare $-5\frac{5}{9}$ and $-5\frac{1}{9}$.

$$\begin{array}{cc} & \\ \hline -6 & -5 \end{array}$$

a. _____

LCD

To find the least common denominator for $\frac{7}{12}$ and $\frac{8}{18}$, find the LCM of 12 and 18.

$12 = 2 \times 2 \times 3$

$18 = 2 \times 3 \times 3$

$LCM = 2 \times 2 \times 3 \times 3$

$\quad = 36$

Example

2. Fill in the $\bigcirc$ with <, >, or = to make $\frac{7}{12}$ $\bigcirc$ $\frac{8}{18}$ a true sentence.

The LCD of the denominators 12 and 18 is 36.

$$\frac{7}{12} = \frac{7 \times 3}{12 \times 3} \qquad\qquad \frac{8}{18} = \frac{8 \times 2}{18 \times 2}$$

$$= \frac{21}{36} \qquad\qquad\qquad = \frac{16}{36}$$

Since $\frac{21}{36} > \frac{16}{36}, \frac{7}{12} > \frac{8}{18}$.

> **Got it?** Do these problems to find out.

b. $\frac{5}{6} \bigcirc \frac{7}{9}$ **c.** $\frac{1}{5} \bigcirc \frac{7}{50}$ **d.** $-\frac{9}{16} \bigcirc -\frac{7}{10}$

Example

3. In Mr. Huang's class, 20% of students own roller shoes. In Mrs. Trevino's class, 5 out of 29 students own roller shoes. In which class does a greater fraction of students own roller shoes?

Express each number as a decimal and then compare.

$20\% = 0.2$ $\frac{5}{29} = 5 \div 29$ or about 0.1724

Since $0.2 > 0.1724$, $20\% > \frac{5}{29}$.

More students in Mr. Huang's class own roller shoes.

> **Got it?** Do this problem to find out.

e. In a second period class, 37.5% of students like to bowl. In a fifth period class, 12 out of 29 students like to bowl. In which class does a greater fraction of the students like to bowl?

Percents as Decimals

To write a percent as a decimal, remove the percent sign and then move the decimal point two places to the left. Add zeros if necessary.

$20\% = 0.20$

Show your work.

e. _____

Order Rational Numbers

You can order rational numbers using place value.

Example

 Tutor

4. Order the set $\{3.44, \pi, 3.14, 3.\overline{4}\}$ from least to greatest.

Line up the decimal points and compare using place value.

3.140	Annex a zero.	3.440	Annex a zero.
3.1415926...	$\pi \approx 3.1415926...$	3.444...	$3.\overline{4} = 3.444...$
Since $0 < 1$, $3.14 < \pi$.		Since $0 < 4$, $3.44 < 3.\overline{4}$.	

So, the order of the numbers from least to greatest is $3.14, \pi, 3.44$, and $3.\overline{4}$.

> **Got it?** Do this problem to find out.

f. Order the set $\{23\%, 0.21, \frac{1}{4}, \frac{1}{5}\}$ from least to greatest.

Show your work.

f. _____

Example

Tutor

5. Nolan is the quarterback on the football team. He completed 67% of his passes in the first game. He completed 0.64, $\frac{3}{5}$, and 69% of his passes in the next three games. List Nolan's completed passing numbers from least to greatest.

Express each number as a decimal and then compare.

$67\% = 0.67$ $\quad\quad$ 0.64 $\quad\quad$ $\frac{3}{5} = 0.6$ $\quad\quad$ $69\% = 0.69$

Nolan's completed passing numbers from least to greatest are $\frac{3}{5}$, 0.64, 67%, and 69%.

Guided Practice

Check ✓

Fill in each ◯ with <, >, or = to make a true sentence. Use a number line if necessary. (Examples 1 and 2)

1. $-\frac{4}{5}$ ◯ $-\frac{1}{5}$

−1 $\quad\quad\quad\quad\quad\quad\quad\quad\quad\quad\quad\quad$ 0

2. $1\frac{3}{4}$ ◯ $1\frac{5}{8}$

1 $\quad\quad\quad\quad\quad\quad\quad\quad\quad\quad\quad\quad$ 2

3. Elliot and Shanna are both soccer goalies. Elliot saves 3 goals out of 4. Shanna saves 7 goals out of 11. Who has the better average, Elliot or Shanna? Explain. (Example 3)

_____

_____

4. The lengths of four insects are 0.02 inch, $\frac{1}{8}$ inch, 0.1 inch, and $\frac{2}{3}$ inch. List the lengths in inches from least to greatest. (Examples 4 and 5)

_____

5. **Building on the Essential Question** How can you

compare two fractions? _____

_____

_____

_____

Rate Yourself!

☐ I understand how to compare and order rational numbers.

 Great! You're ready to move on!

☐ I still have some questions about comparing and ordering rational numbers.

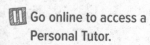 Go online to access a Personal Tutor.

Tutor

Independent Practice

Go online for Step-by-Step Solutions   eHelp

Fill in each ◯ with <, >, or = to make a true sentence. Use a number line if necessary. (Examples 1 and 2)

1. $-\dfrac{3}{5}$ ◯ $-\dfrac{4}{5}$

2. $-7\dfrac{5}{8}$ ◯ $-7\dfrac{1}{8}$

3. $6\dfrac{2}{3}$ ◯ $6\dfrac{1}{2}$

4. $-\dfrac{17}{24}$ ◯ $-\dfrac{11}{12}$

5 On her first quiz in social studies, Meg answered 92% of the questions correctly. On her second quiz, she answered 27 out of 30 questions correctly. On which quiz did Meg have the better score? (Example 3)

_____

Order each set of numbers from least to greatest. (Example 4)

6. $\{0.23, 19\%, \dfrac{1}{5}\}$

7. $\{-0.615, -\dfrac{5}{8}, -0.62\}$

8. Liberty Middle School is holding a fundraiser. The sixth-graders have raised 52% of their goal amount. The seventh- and eighth-graders have raised 0.57 and $\dfrac{2}{5}$ of their goal amounts, respectively. List the classes in order from least to greatest of their goal amounts. (Example 5)

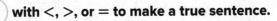

Fill in each ◯ with <, >, or = to make a true sentence.

9 $1\dfrac{7}{12}$ gallons ◯ $1\dfrac{5}{8}$ gallons

10. $2\dfrac{5}{6}$ hours ◯ 2.8 hours

11. **MP** **Model with Mathematics** Refer to the graphic novel frame below. If the closet organizer has a total width of $69\frac{1}{8}$ inches and the closet is $69\frac{3}{4}$ inches wide, will the organizer fit? Explain.

🔥 H.O.T. Problems Higher Order Thinking

12. **MP** **Justify Conclusions** Identify the ratio that does not have the same value as the other three. Explain your reasoning.

| 12 out of 15 | 0.08 | 80% | $\frac{4}{5}$ |

13. **MP** **Persevere with Problems** Explain how you know which number, $1\frac{15}{16}$, $\frac{17}{8}$, or $\frac{63}{32}$, is closest to 2.

14. **MP** **Reason Inductively** Are the fractions $\frac{5}{6}$, $\frac{5}{7}$, $\frac{5}{8}$, and $\frac{5}{9}$ arranged in order from least to greatest or from greatest to least? Explain.

15. **MP** **Model with Mathematics** Write a real-world problem in which you would compare and order rational numbers. Then solve the problem.

Extra Practice

Fill in each ◯ with <, >, or = to make a true sentence. Use a number line if necessary.

16. $-\dfrac{5}{7}$ ⬤< $-\dfrac{2}{7}$

Homework Help → Mark off equal-size increments of $\dfrac{1}{7}$ between −1 and 0.

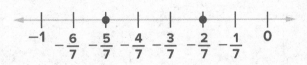

17. $-3\dfrac{2}{3}$ ◯ $-3\dfrac{4}{6}$

18. $\dfrac{4}{7}$ ⬤< $\dfrac{5}{8}$

The LCD of the denominators 7 and 8 is 56.

$\dfrac{4}{7} = \dfrac{4 \times 8}{7 \times 8} = \dfrac{32}{56}$ and $\dfrac{5}{8} = \dfrac{5 \times 7}{8 \times 7} = \dfrac{35}{56}$

Since $\dfrac{32}{56} < \dfrac{35}{56}$, $\dfrac{4}{7} < \dfrac{5}{8}$.

19. $2\dfrac{3}{4}$ ◯ $2\dfrac{2}{3}$

20. Gracia and Jim were shooting free throws. Gracia made 4 out of 15 free throws. Jim *missed* 6 out of 16 free throws. Who made the free throw a greater fraction of the time? _____

Order each set of numbers from least to greatest.

21. $\{7.49, 7\dfrac{49}{50}, 7.5\%\}$

_____

22. $\{-1.4, -1\dfrac{1}{25}, -1.25\}$

_____

23. **STEM** Use the table that shows the lengths of small mammals.

a. Which animal is the smallest mammal?

_____

b. Which animal is smaller than the European Mole but larger than the Spiny Pocket Mouse?

_____

c. Order the animals from greatest to least size.

_____

_____

Animal	Length (ft)
Eastern Chipmunk	$\dfrac{1}{3}$
European Mole	$\dfrac{5}{12}$
Masked Shrew	$\dfrac{1}{6}$
Spiny Pocket Mouse	0.25

24. The sales tax rates from 4 different counties are shown in the table. Convert each sales tax rate to a decimal. Then sort the counties from least to greatest tax rates.

County	Sales Tax Rate
Hamilton	$\frac{9}{160}$
Oakland	5.75%
Green	$5\frac{7}{8}\%$
Campbell	$\frac{11}{200}$

	County	Sales Tax Rate (as a decimal)
Least		
Greatest		

Which county has the lowest sales tax rate?

25. The daily price changes for a stock are shown in the table. Determine if each statement is true or false.

Day	Price Change
Monday	−0.21
Tuesday	−1.05
Wednesday	−0.23
Thursday	+0.42
Friday	−1.15

a. The price increased by the greatest amount on Thursday. ☐ True ☐ False

b. The price decreased by the greatest amount on Tuesday. ☐ True ☐ False

c. The price decreased by the least amount on Monday. ☐ True ☐ False

Spiral Review

Fill in each ◯ **with < or > to make a true sentence.**

26. −2 ◯ 2

27. −4 ◯ −5

28. −20 ◯ 20

29. −7 ◯ −8

30. −10 ◯ −1

31. 50 ◯ −100

32. Victoria, Cooper, and Diego are reading the same book for their language arts class. The table shows the fraction of the book each student has read. Which student has read the least amount? Explain your reasoning.

Student	Amount Read
Victoria	$\frac{2}{5}$
Cooper	$\frac{1}{5}$
Diego	$\frac{3}{5}$

_____

_____

Inquiry HOW can you use a number line to add and subtract like fractions?

In eight times at bat, Max hit 2 doubles, 5 singles, and struck out 1 time. Find the fraction of the times that Max hit either a single or a double.

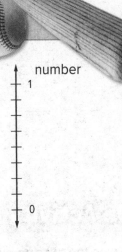

Hands-On Activity 1

Step 1 Since there were 8 times at bat, create a vertical line that is divided into eighths.

number

Step 2 Graph the fraction of doubles, $\frac{2}{8}$, on the number line.

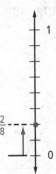

Step 3 From the $\frac{2}{8}$ point, count $\frac{5}{8}$ more on the number line.

So, $\frac{2}{8} + \frac{5}{8} = \dfrac{\boxed{}}{\boxed{}}$.

Max got a hit $\dfrac{\boxed{}}{\boxed{}}$ of the times he was at bat.

Hands-On Activity 2

Find $\frac{3}{6} - \frac{4}{6}$.

Step 1   Divide a number line into sixths. Since we do not know if our answer is negative or positive, include fractions to the left and to the right of zero.

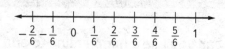

Step 2   Graph $\frac{3}{6}$ on the number line.

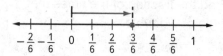

Step 3   Move 4 units to the _____ to show taking away $\frac{4}{6}$.

So, $\frac{3}{6} - \frac{4}{6} = \dfrac{\boxed{}}{\boxed{}}$.

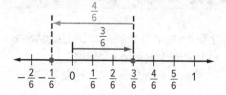

Hands-On Activity 3

Find $-\frac{4}{7} - \frac{2}{7}$. Fill in the missing numbers in the diagram below.

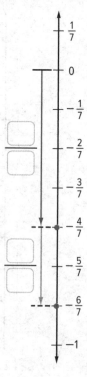

So, $-\frac{4}{7} - \frac{2}{7} = \dfrac{\boxed{}}{\boxed{}}$.

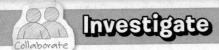
Work with a partner. Use a number line to add or subtract. Write in simplest form.

1. $\dfrac{1}{5} + \dfrac{2}{5} =$ _____

2. $-\dfrac{3}{7} + \left(-\dfrac{1}{7}\right) =$ _____

3. $-\dfrac{3}{8} + \dfrac{5}{8} =$ _____

4. $\dfrac{8}{12} - \dfrac{4}{12} =$ _____

5. $-\dfrac{4}{9} + \dfrac{5}{9} =$ _____

6. $\dfrac{4}{7} - \dfrac{6}{7} =$ _____

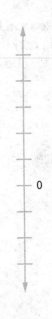

Analyze and Reflect

MP Use Math Tools Work with a partner to complete the table. The first one is done for you.

Expression	Use only the Numerators	Use a number line to add or subtract the fractions.
$-\dfrac{5}{6} - \left(-\dfrac{1}{6}\right)$	$-5 - (-1) = -4$	
7. $-\dfrac{5}{6} - \dfrac{1}{6}$	$-5 - 1 = -6$	
8. $\dfrac{5}{6} - \dfrac{1}{6}$	$5 - 1 = 4$	
9. $-\dfrac{5}{6} + \dfrac{1}{6}$	$-5 + 1 = -4$	

Create

On Your Own

10. **MP Reason Inductively** Refer to the table above. Compare your results for using only the numerators with your results for using a number line. Write a rule for adding and subtracting like fractions.

_____

_____

11. **Inquiry** HOW can you use a number line to add and subtract like fractions?

_____

_____

_____

Add and Subtract Like Fractions

 Real-World Link

Shoes Sean surveyed ten classmates to find which type of tennis shoe they like to wear.

Shoe Type	Number
Cross Trainer	5
Running	3
High Top	2

1. What fraction of students liked to wear cross trainers?

   Number of students that wear cross trainers. ⟶ ☐

   Total number of students surveyed. ⟶ ☐

2. What fraction of students liked to wear high tops?

   Number of students that wear high tops. ⟶ ☐

   Total number of students surveyed. ⟶ ☐

3. What fraction of students liked to wear either cross trainers or high tops?

   Fraction of students that wear cross trainers.   Fraction of students that wear high tops.

   $\dfrac{\boxed{}}{\boxed{}}$ + $\dfrac{\boxed{}}{\boxed{}}$ = $\dfrac{\boxed{}}{\boxed{}}$

   So, _____ of the students liked to wear either cross trainers or high tops.

4. Explain how to find $\frac{3}{10} + \frac{2}{10}$. Then find the sum.

   _____

   _____

 Essential Question

WHAT happens when you add, subtract, multiply, and divide fractions?

 Vocabulary

like fractions

 Virginia Standards
7.2

Which MP Mathematical Process Goals did you use? Shade the circle(s) that applies.

① Mathematical Problem Solving   ④ Mathematical Connections

② Mathematical Communication   ⑤ Mathematical Representations

③ Mathematical Reasoning

Add and Subtract Like Fractions

Words To add or subtract like fractions, add or subtract the numerators and write the result over the denominator.

Examples

Numbers	Algebra

$$\frac{5}{10} + \frac{2}{10} = \frac{5+2}{10} \text{ or } \frac{7}{10} \qquad \frac{a}{c} + \frac{b}{c} = \frac{a+b}{c}, \text{ where } c \neq 0$$

$$\frac{11}{12} - \frac{4}{12} = \frac{11-4}{12} \text{ or } \frac{7}{12} \qquad \frac{a}{c} - \frac{b}{c} = \frac{a-b}{c}, \text{ where } c \neq 0$$

Fractions that have the same denominators are called **like fractions**.

Examples

Tutor

Add. Write in simplest form.

1. $\dfrac{5}{9} + \dfrac{2}{9}$

$$\frac{5}{9} + \frac{2}{9} = \frac{5+2}{9} \qquad \text{Add the numerators.}$$

$$= \frac{7}{9} \qquad \text{Simplify.}$$

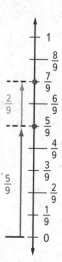

Work Zone

Negative Fractions

Remember $-\dfrac{1}{2} = \dfrac{-1}{2} = \dfrac{1}{-2}$.

Typically, the form $\dfrac{-1}{2}$ is used when performing computations.

Show your work.

2. $-\dfrac{3}{5} + \left(-\dfrac{1}{5}\right)$

$$-\frac{3}{5} + \left(-\frac{1}{5}\right) = -\frac{3}{5} + \left(\frac{-1}{5}\right)$$

$$= \frac{-3 + (-1)}{5} \qquad \text{Add the numerators.}$$

$$= \frac{-4}{5} \text{ or } -\frac{4}{5} \qquad \text{Use the rules for adding integers.}$$

Got it? Do these problems to find out.

a. $\dfrac{1}{3} + \dfrac{2}{3}$ b. $-\dfrac{3}{7} + \dfrac{1}{7}$

c. $-\dfrac{2}{5} + \left(-\dfrac{2}{5}\right)$ d. $-\dfrac{1}{4} + \dfrac{1}{4}$

a. _____

b. _____

c. _____

d. _____

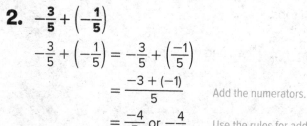

Example

Tutor

3. Sofia ate $\frac{3}{5}$ of a cheese pizza. Jack ate $\frac{1}{5}$ of a cheese pizza and $\frac{2}{5}$ of a pepperoni pizza. How much pizza did Sofia and Jack eat altogether?

$$\frac{3}{5} + \left(\frac{1}{5} + \frac{2}{5}\right) = \frac{3}{5} + \left(\frac{2}{5} + \frac{1}{5}\right)$$ Commutative Property of Addition

$$= \left(\frac{3}{5} + \frac{2}{5}\right) + \frac{1}{5}$$ Associative Property of Addition

$$= 1 + \frac{1}{5} \text{ or } 1\frac{1}{5}$$ Simplify.

So, Sofia and Jack ate $1\frac{1}{5}$ pizzas altogether.

Got it? Do this problem to find out.

e. Eduardo used fabric to make three costumes. He used $\frac{1}{4}$ yard for the first, $\frac{2}{4}$ yard for the second, and $\frac{3}{4}$ yard for the third costume. How much fabric did Eduardo use altogether?

Show your work.

e. _____

Examples

Tutor

4. Find $-\frac{5}{8} - \frac{3}{8}$.

$$-\frac{5}{8} - \frac{3}{8} = -\frac{5}{8} + \left(-\frac{3}{8}\right)$$ Add $-\frac{3}{8}$.

$$= \frac{-5 + (-3)}{8}$$ Add the numerators.

$$= -\frac{8}{8} \text{ or } -1$$ Simplify.

Subtracting Integers

To subtract an integer, add its opposite.

$-9 - (-4) = -9 + 4$
$\qquad\qquad = -5$

5. Find $\frac{5}{8} - \frac{7}{8}$.

$$\frac{5}{8} - \frac{7}{8} = \frac{5 - 7}{8}$$ Subtract the numerators.

$$= -\frac{2}{8} \text{ or } -\frac{1}{4}$$ Simplify.

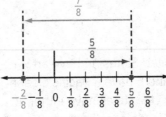

Got it? Do these problems to find out.

f. $\frac{5}{9} - \frac{2}{9}$ **g.** $-\frac{5}{9} - \frac{2}{9}$ **h.** $-\frac{11}{12} - \left(-\frac{5}{12}\right)$

f. _____

g. _____

h. _____

Choose an Operation

You can add or subtract like fractions to solve real-world problems.

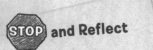 **STOP** and Reflect

In Example 6, what word or words indicate that you should subtract to solve the problem? Write your answer below.

 Example

 Tutor

6. About $\frac{6}{100}$ of the population of the United States lives in Florida. Another $\frac{4}{100}$ lives in Ohio. About what fraction more of the U.S. population lives in Florida than in Ohio?

$$\frac{6}{100} - \frac{4}{100} = \frac{6-4}{100}$$ Subtract the numerators.

$$= \frac{2}{100} \text{ or } \frac{1}{50}$$ Simplify.

About $\frac{1}{50}$ more of the U.S. population lives in Florida than in Ohio.

Guided Practice

 Check

Add or subtract. Write in simplest form. (Examples 1–5)

1. $\frac{3}{5} + \frac{1}{5} =$ _____

2. $\frac{2}{7} + \frac{1}{7} =$ _____

3. $\left(\frac{5}{8} + \frac{1}{8}\right) + \frac{3}{8} =$ _____

4. $-\frac{4}{5} - \left(-\frac{1}{5}\right) =$ _____

5. $\frac{5}{14} - \left(-\frac{1}{14}\right) =$ _____

6. $\frac{2}{7} - \frac{6}{7} =$ _____

7. Of the 50 states in the United States, 14 have an Atlantic Ocean coastline and 5 have a Pacific Ocean coastline. What fraction of U.S. states have either an Atlantic Ocean or Pacific Ocean coastline? (Example 6)

_____

8. **Building on the Essential Question** What is a simple rule for adding and subtracting like fractions?

_____

_____

Rate Yourself!

How confident are you about adding and subtracting like fractions? Check the box that applies.

For more help, go online to access a Personal Tutor. Tutor

FOLDABLES Time to update your Foldable!

Independent Practice

Go online for Step-by-Step Solutions eHelp

Add or subtract. Write in simplest form. (Examples 1, 2, 4, and 5)

1. $\dfrac{5}{7} + \dfrac{6}{7} =$ _____

2. $\dfrac{3}{8} + \left(-\dfrac{7}{8}\right) =$ _____

3. $-\dfrac{1}{9} + \left(-\dfrac{5}{9}\right) =$ _____

 Show your work.

4. $\dfrac{9}{10} - \dfrac{3}{10} =$ _____

5. $-\dfrac{3}{4} + \left(-\dfrac{3}{4}\right) =$ _____

6. $-\dfrac{5}{9} - \dfrac{2}{9} =$ _____

7. In Mr. Navarro's first period class, $\dfrac{17}{28}$ of the students got an A on their math test. In his second period class, $\dfrac{11}{28}$ of the students got an A. What fraction more of the students got an A in Mr. Navarro's first period class than in his second period class? Write in simplest form. (Example 6)

_____

8. To make a greeting card, Bryce used $\dfrac{1}{8}$ sheet of red paper, $\dfrac{3}{8}$ sheet of green paper, and $\dfrac{7}{8}$ sheet of white paper. How many sheets of paper did Bryce use? (Example 3)

_____

9. The table shows the Instant Messenger abbreviations students at Hillside Middle School use the most.

   a. What fraction of these students uses LOL or CUL8R when using Instant Messenger? _____

   b. What fraction of these students uses L8R or BRB when using Instant Messenger? _____

   c. What fraction more of these students write L8R than CUL8R when using Instant Messenger? _____

Instant Messenger Abbreviations	
L8R (Later)	$\dfrac{48}{100}$
LOL (Laughing out loud)	$\dfrac{26}{100}$
BRB (Be right back)	$\dfrac{19}{100}$
CUL8R (See you later)	$\dfrac{7}{100}$

10. **MP Model with Mathematics** Cross out the expression that does not belong. Explain your reasoning.

_____

_____

_____

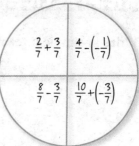

🔥 H.O.T. Problems Higher Order Thinking

11. **MP Justify Conclusions** Select two like fractions with a difference of $\frac{1}{3}$ and with denominators that are *not* 3. Justify your selection.

_____

_____

12. **MP Persevere with Problems** Simplify the following expression.

$$\frac{14}{15} + \frac{13}{15} - \frac{12}{15} + \frac{11}{15} - \frac{10}{15} + \cdots - \frac{4}{15} + \frac{3}{15} - \frac{2}{15} + \frac{1}{15}$$

13. **MP Justify Conclusions** Is the difference between a positive like fraction and a negative like fraction *always*, *sometimes*, or *never* positive? Justify your answer with an example.

14. **MP Use Math Tools** Explain how you could use mental math to find the following sum. Then find the sum. Support your answer with a model.

$$1\frac{1}{4} + 2\frac{1}{3} + 3\frac{2}{3} + 4\frac{1}{2} + 5\frac{1}{2} + 6\frac{3}{4}$$

_____

_____

_____

15. **MP Persevere with Problems** A construction company is replacing a window in a house. The window is currently 3 feet wide by 4 feet tall. The homeowner wants to add $4\frac{1}{2}$ inches to each side of the window. What is the new perimeter of the window in feet? Justify your reasoning.

_____

_____

Extra Practice

Add or subtract. Write in simplest form.

16. $\frac{4}{5} + \frac{3}{5} = 1\frac{2}{5}$

$$\frac{4}{5} + \frac{3}{5} = \frac{4+3}{5}$$

$$= \frac{7}{5} \text{ or } 1\frac{2}{5}$$

ework help

17. $-\frac{5}{6} + \left(-\frac{5}{6}\right) =$ _____

18. $-\frac{15}{16} + \left(-\frac{7}{16}\right) =$ _____

19. $\frac{5}{8} - \frac{3}{8} =$ _____

20. $\frac{7}{12} - \frac{2}{12} =$ _____

21. $\frac{15}{18} - \frac{13}{18} =$ _____

22. Two nails are $\frac{5}{16}$ inch and $\frac{13}{16}$ inch long. How much shorter is the $\frac{5}{16}$-inch nail? _____

MP Identify Structure Add. Write in simplest form.

23. $\left(\frac{81}{100} + \frac{47}{100}\right) + \frac{19}{100} =$ _____

24. $\frac{\frac{1}{3}}{6} + \frac{\frac{2}{3}}{6} =$ _____

25. A recipe for Michigan blueberry pancakes calls for $\frac{3}{4}$ cup flour, $\frac{1}{4}$ cup milk, and $\frac{1}{4}$ cup blueberries. How much more flour is needed than milk? Write in simplest form.

_____

26. The graph shows the location of volcanic eruptions.

a. What fraction represents the volcanic eruptions for both North and South America?

_____

b. How much larger is the section for Asia and South Pacific than for Europe? Write in simplest form.

_____

Worldwide Volcano Eruptions

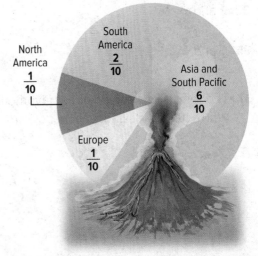

North America $\frac{1}{10}$

South America $\frac{2}{10}$

Asia and South Pacific $\frac{6}{10}$

Europe $\frac{1}{10}$

27. A group of friends bought two large pizzas and ate only part of each pizza. The picture shows how much was left. How many pizzas did they eat?

First Pizza   Second Pizza

[ ]

28. The table shows the results of a survey on students' favorite kind of movie. Select the appropriate values to complete the model to find the fraction of students that prefer comedy or action movies.

$$\frac{\Box}{\Box} + \frac{\Box}{\Box} = \frac{\Box}{\Box}$$

Type of Movie	Number of Students
Action	29
Comedy	42
Drama	14
Horror	15

14	50
15	60
29	71
42	100

What fraction of the students who were surveyed prefers comedy or action movies?

[ ]

Spiral Review

Fill in each ◯ with <, >, or = to make a true sentence.

29. $\frac{7}{8}$ ◯ $\frac{3}{4}$

30. $\frac{1}{3}$ ◯ $\frac{7}{9}$

31. $\frac{5}{7}$ ◯ $\frac{4}{5}$

32. $\frac{6}{11}$ ◯ $\frac{9}{14}$

Find the least common denominator for each pair of fractions.

33. $\frac{1}{2}$ and $\frac{1}{3}$ _____

34. $\frac{4}{7}$ and $\frac{3}{28}$ _____

35. $\frac{1}{5}$ and $\frac{7}{6}$ _____

36. $\frac{13}{15}$ and $\frac{7}{12}$ _____

37. The results of a survey about favorite lunch choices are shown. Which lunch was chosen most often?

_____

Favorite Lunch	
Food	Fraction of Students
Pizza	$\frac{39}{50}$
Hot Dogs	$\frac{3}{25}$
Grilled Cheese	$\frac{1}{10}$

Add and Subtract Unlike Fractions

 Real-World Link

 Essential Question

WHAT happens when you add, subtract, multiply, and divide fractions?

Time The table shows the fractions of one hour for certain minutes.

1. What fraction of one hour is equal to the sum of 15 minutes and 20 minutes?

15 minutes   20 minutes

$$\boxed{} + \boxed{} = \boxed{}$$

Number of Minutes	Fraction of One Hour	Simplified Fraction
5	$\frac{5}{60}$	
10	$\frac{10}{60}$	
15	$\frac{15}{60}$	
20	$\frac{20}{60}$	
30	$\frac{30}{60}$	

 Vocabulary

unlike fractions

✏ **Virginia Standards**
7.2

2. Write each fraction of an hour in simplest form in the third column of the table.

3. Explain why $\frac{1}{6}$ hour + $\frac{1}{3}$ hour = $\frac{1}{2}$ hour.

_____

_____

_____

_____

4. Explain why $\frac{1}{12}$ hour + $\frac{1}{2}$ hour = $\frac{7}{12}$ hour.

_____

_____

Which **MP** **Mathematical Process Goals** did you use? Shade the circle(s) that applies.

① Mathematical Problem Solving
② Mathematical Communication
③ Mathematical Reasoning
④ Mathematical Connections
⑤ Mathematical Representations

Add or Subtract Unlike Fractions

To add or subtract fractions with different denominators,

- Rename the fractions using the least common denominator (LCD).
- Add or subtract as with like fractions.
- If necessary, simplify the sum or difference.

Before you can add two **unlike fractions**, or fractions with different denominators, rename one or both of the fractions so that they have a common denominator.

Example

1. Find $\frac{1}{2} + \frac{1}{4}$.

Method 1 Use a number line.

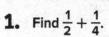

Divide the number line into fourths since the LCD is 4.

Method 2 Use the LCD.

The least common denominator of $\frac{1}{2}$ and $\frac{1}{4}$ is 4.

$$\frac{1}{2} + \frac{1}{4} = \frac{1 \times 2}{2 \times 2} + \frac{1 \times 1}{4 \times 1} \quad \text{Rename using the LCD, 4.}$$

$$= \frac{2}{4} + \frac{1}{4} \quad \text{Add the fractions.}$$

$$= \frac{3}{4} \quad \text{Simplify.}$$

Using either method, $\frac{1}{2} + \frac{1}{4} = \frac{3}{4}$.

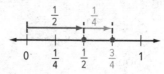 **Got it?** Do these problems to find out.

Add. Write in simplest form.

a. $\frac{1}{6} + \frac{2}{3}$

b. $\frac{9}{10} + \left(-\frac{1}{2}\right)$

c. $\frac{1}{4} + \frac{3}{8}$

d. $-\frac{1}{3} + \left(-\frac{1}{4}\right)$

Work Zone

STOP and Reflect

Circle the pairs of fractions that are unlike fractions.

$\frac{1}{3}$ and $\frac{5}{3}$ $\frac{1}{7}$ and $\frac{1}{5}$ $\frac{5}{9}$ and $\frac{4}{11}$

Show your work.

a. _____

b. _____

c. _____

d. _____

Example

2. Find $\left(-\dfrac{3}{4} + \dfrac{5}{9}\right) + \dfrac{7}{4}$.

$$\left(-\dfrac{3}{4} + \dfrac{5}{9}\right) + \dfrac{7}{4} = \left(\dfrac{5}{9} + \left(-\dfrac{3}{4}\right)\right) + \dfrac{7}{4} \qquad \text{Commutative Property of Addition}$$

$$= \dfrac{5}{9} + \left(-\dfrac{3}{4} + \dfrac{7}{4}\right) \qquad \text{Associative Property of Addition}$$

$$= \dfrac{5}{9} + 1 \text{ or } 1\dfrac{5}{9} \qquad \text{Simplify.}$$

Show your work.

> **Got it?** Do these problems to find out.

e. $\dfrac{2}{5} + \left(\dfrac{4}{7} + \dfrac{3}{5}\right)$

f. $\left(-\dfrac{3}{10} + \dfrac{5}{8}\right) + \dfrac{23}{10}$

e. _____

f. _____

Example

3. Find $-\dfrac{2}{3} - \dfrac{1}{2}$.

Method 1 Use a number line.

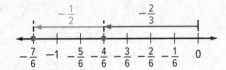

Divide the number line into sixths since the LCD is 6.

Method 2 Use the LCD.

$$-\dfrac{2}{3} - \dfrac{1}{2} = -\dfrac{2 \times 2}{3 \times 2} - \dfrac{1 \times 3}{2 \times 3} \qquad \text{Rename using the LCD, 6.}$$

$$= -\dfrac{4}{6} - \dfrac{3}{6} \qquad \text{Simplify.}$$

$$= \dfrac{-4}{6} - \dfrac{3}{6} \qquad \text{Rewrite } -\dfrac{4}{6} \text{ as } \dfrac{-4}{6}.$$

$$= \dfrac{-4 - 3}{6} \text{ or } \dfrac{-7}{6} \qquad \text{Subtract the numerators. Simplify.}$$

Check by adding $-\dfrac{7}{6} + \dfrac{1}{2} = -\dfrac{7}{6} + \dfrac{3}{6} = -\dfrac{4}{6}$ or $-\dfrac{2}{3}$ ✔

Using either method, $-\dfrac{2}{3} - \dfrac{1}{2} = -\dfrac{7}{6}$ or $-1\dfrac{1}{6}$.

Check for Reasonableness

Estimate the difference.

$-\dfrac{2}{3} - \dfrac{1}{2} \approx -\dfrac{1}{2} - \dfrac{1}{2}$ or -1

Compare $-\dfrac{7}{6}$ to the estimate.

$-\dfrac{7}{6} \approx -1$. So, the answer is reasonable.

> **Got it?** Do these problems to find out.

Subtract. Write in simplest form.

g. $\dfrac{5}{8} - \dfrac{1}{4}$

h. $\dfrac{3}{4} - \dfrac{1}{3}$

i. $\dfrac{1}{2} - \left(-\dfrac{2}{5}\right)$

g. _____

h. _____

i. _____

Choose an Operation

Add or subtract unlike fractions to solve real-world problems.

 Example

4. **STEM** Use the table to find the fraction of the total population that has type A or type B blood.

Blood Type Frequencies				
ABO Type	O	A	B	AB
Fraction	$\frac{11}{25}$	$\frac{21}{50}$	$\frac{1}{10}$	$\frac{1}{25}$

To find the fraction of the total population, add $\frac{21}{50}$ and $\frac{1}{10}$.

$$\frac{21}{50} + \frac{1}{10} = \frac{21 \times 1}{50 \times 1} + \frac{1 \times 5}{10 \times 5}$$ Rename using the LCD, 50.

$$= \frac{21}{50} + \frac{5}{50}$$ Add the fractions.

$$= \frac{26}{50} \text{ or } \frac{13}{25}$$ Simplify.

So, $\frac{13}{25}$ of the population has type A or type B blood.

Guided Practice

Add or subtract. Write in simplest form. (Examples 1–3)

1. $\frac{3}{5} + \frac{1}{10} =$ _____

2. $-\frac{5}{6} + \left(-\frac{4}{9}\right) =$ _____

3. $\left(\frac{7}{8} + \frac{3}{11}\right) + \frac{1}{8} =$ _____

Show your work.

4. $\frac{4}{5} - \frac{3}{10} =$ _____

5. $\frac{3}{8} - \left(-\frac{1}{4}\right) =$ _____

6. $\frac{3}{4} - \frac{1}{3} =$ _____

7. Cassandra cuts $\frac{5}{16}$ inch off the top of a photo and $\frac{3}{8}$ inch off the bottom. How much shorter is the total height of the photo now? Explain. (Example 4)

_____

_____

8. **Building on the Essential Question** Compare adding unlike fractions and adding like fractions.

_____

_____

_____

Rate Yourself!

Are you ready to move on?
Shade the section that applies.

YES   ?   NO

For more help, go online to access a Personal Tutor.

FOLDABLES Time to update your Foldable!

Independent Practice

Go online for Step-by-Step Solutions eHelp

Add or subtract. Write in simplest form. (Examples 1–3)

1. $\frac{1}{6} + \frac{3}{8} =$ _____

2. $-\frac{1}{15} + \left(-\frac{3}{5}\right) =$ _____

3. $\left(\frac{15}{8} + \frac{2}{5}\right) + \left(-\frac{7}{8}\right) =$

_____

4. $\left(-\frac{7}{10}\right) - \frac{2}{5} =$ _____

5. $\frac{7}{9} - \frac{1}{3} =$ _____

6. $-\frac{7}{12} + \frac{7}{10} =$ _____

7. $-\frac{4}{9} - \frac{2}{15} =$ _____

8. $\frac{5}{8} + \frac{11}{12} =$ _____

9. $\frac{7}{9} + \frac{5}{6} =$ _____

MP Justify Conclusions Choose an operation to solve each problem. Explain your reasoning. Then solve the problem. Write in simplest form. (Example 4)

10. Mrs. Escalante was riding a bicycle on a bike path. After riding $\frac{2}{3}$ of a mile, she discovered that she still needed to travel $\frac{3}{4}$ of a mile to reach the end of the path. How long is the bike path?

_____

_____

11 Four students were scheduled to give book reports in 1 hour. After the first report, $\frac{2}{3}$ hour remained. The next two reports took $\frac{1}{6}$ hour and $\frac{1}{4}$ hour. What fraction of the hour remained?

_____

_____

12. One hundred sixty cell phone owners were surveyed.

a. What fraction of owners prefers using their cell phone for text messaging or playing games? Explain.

_____

b. What fraction of owners prefers using their phone to take pictures or text message?

_____

How do you use a cell phone?

Taking pictures $\frac{3}{8}$

Playing games $\frac{1}{4}$

$\frac{3}{8}$ Text messaging

13. Pepita and Francisco each spend an equal amount of time on homework. The table shows the fraction of time they spend on each subject. Complete the table by determining the missing fraction for each student.

Homework	Fraction of Time	
	Pepita	Francisco
Math		$\frac{1}{2}$
English	$\frac{2}{3}$	
Science	$\frac{1}{6}$	$\frac{3}{8}$

14. Chelsie saves $\frac{1}{5}$ of her allowance and spends $\frac{2}{3}$ of her allowance at the mall. What fraction of her allowance remains? Explain.

 H.O.T. Problems Higher Order Thinking

15. ⓂⓅ **Persevere with Problems** Fractions whose numerators are 1, such as $\frac{1}{2}$ or $\frac{1}{3}$, are called *unit fractions*. Describe a method you can use to add two unit fractions mentally.

16. ⓂⓅ **Use a Counterexample** Provide a counterexample to the following statement.

The sum of three fractions with odd numerators is never $\frac{1}{2}$.

17. ⓂⓅ **Reason Inductively** Suppose a bucket is placed under two faucets. If one faucet is turned on alone, the bucket will be filled in 6 minutes. If the other faucet is turned on alone, the bucket will be filled in 4 minutes. What fraction of the bucket will be filled in 1 minute if both faucets are turned on at the same time? Explain.

Extra Practice

Add or subtract. Write in simplest form.

18. $\dfrac{5}{8} + \dfrac{1}{4} = \dfrac{7}{8}$ _____

Homework Help →

$$\dfrac{5}{8} + \dfrac{1}{4} = \dfrac{5}{8} + \dfrac{1 \times 2}{4 \times 2}$$
$$= \dfrac{5}{8} + \dfrac{2}{8}$$
$$= \dfrac{7}{8}$$

19. $\dfrac{4}{5} - \dfrac{1}{6} =$ _____

20. $\dfrac{5}{6} - \left(-\dfrac{2}{3}\right) =$ _____

21. $\dfrac{3}{10} - \left(-\dfrac{1}{4}\right) =$ _____

22. $-\dfrac{2}{3} + \left(\dfrac{3}{4} + \dfrac{5}{3}\right) =$ _____

23. $-\dfrac{7}{8} + \dfrac{1}{3} =$ _____

Choose an operation to solve each problem. Explain your reasoning. Then solve the problem. Write in simplest form.

24. Ebony is building a shelf to hold the two boxes shown. What is the least width she should make the shelf?

_____

_____

$\dfrac{4}{5}$ ft $\dfrac{3}{4}$ ft

25. Makayla bought $\dfrac{1}{4}$ pound of ham and $\dfrac{5}{8}$ pound of turkey. How much more turkey did she buy? _____

_____

26. **MP Persevere with Problems** Find the sum of $\dfrac{3}{4}{8}$ and $\dfrac{1}{3}{4}$. Write in simplest form.

_____

27. **MP Find the Error** Theresa is finding $\dfrac{1}{4} + \dfrac{3}{5}$. Find her mistake and correct it. Explain your answer.

_____

_____

_____

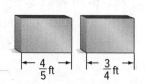

$$\dfrac{1}{4} + \dfrac{3}{5} = \dfrac{1+3}{4+5}$$

28. The table shows the number of hours Orlando spent at football practice last week. Select the appropriate numbers below to complete the model to find the number of hours Orlando spent practicing on Tuesday and Friday.

Day	Time (h)
Monday	$\frac{1}{2}$
Tuesday	$\frac{3}{4}$
Thursday	$\frac{1}{3}$
Friday	$\frac{5}{6}$

$$\frac{\square}{\square} + \frac{\square}{\square} = \frac{\square}{\square} + \frac{\square}{\square} = \frac{\square}{\square}$$

1	9
3	10
4	12
5	16
6	19

How many hours did Orlando spend practicing on Tuesday and Friday?

29. Brett has $\frac{5}{6}$ of his monthly income left to spend. He has budgeted $\frac{1}{8}$ of his income for a new video game and $\frac{1}{3}$ of his income for savings. Determine if each statement is true or false.

a. Brett will have $\frac{7}{8}$ of his income left if he only buys the video game. ☐ True ☐ False

b. Brett will have $\frac{1}{2}$ of his income left if he only puts money in savings. ☐ True ☐ False

c. Brett will have $\frac{3}{8}$ of his income left after buying the video game and putting money in savings. ☐ True ☐ False

Spiral Review

Write each improper fraction as a mixed number.

30. $\frac{7}{5} =$ _____

31. $\frac{14}{3} =$ _____

32. $\frac{101}{100} =$ _____

33. $\frac{22}{9} =$ _____

34. $\frac{77}{10} =$ _____

35. $\frac{23}{8} =$ _____

Add and Subtract Mixed Numbers

Real-World Link

Hockey Junior and adult hockey sticks are shown below.

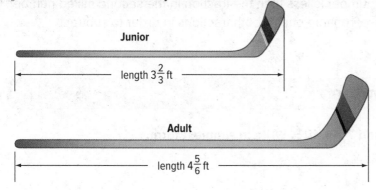

Junior

length $3\frac{2}{3}$ ft

Adult

length $4\frac{5}{6}$ ft

Essential Question

WHAT happens when you add, subtract, multiply, and divide fractions?

Virginia Standards
7.2

1. Use the expression $4\frac{5}{6} - 3\frac{2}{3}$ to find how much longer the adult hockey stick is than the junior hockey stick.

    Rename the fractions using the LCD, 6.

    Subtract the fractions. Then subtract the whole numbers.

    $4\frac{5}{6} - \boxed{}\frac{\boxed{}}{\boxed{}} = \boxed{}\frac{\boxed{}}{\boxed{}}$

2. Explain how to find $3\frac{7}{10} - 2\frac{2}{5}$. Then use your conjecture to find the difference.

    _____

    _____

    _____

Which ㎿ Mathematical Process Goals did you use? Shade the circle(s) that applies.

① Mathematical Problem Solving   ④ Mathematical Connections

② Mathematical Communication   ⑤ Mathematical Representations

③ Mathematical Reasoning

Add and Subtract Mixed Numbers

To add or subtract mixed numbers, first add or subtract the fractions. If necessary, rename them using the LCD. Then add or subtract the whole numbers and simplify if necessary.

Sometimes when you subtract mixed numbers, the fraction in the first mixed number is less than the fraction in the second mixed number. In this case, rename one or both fractions in order to subtract.

Examples

Tutor

1. Find $7\frac{4}{9} + 10\frac{2}{9}$. Write in simplest form.

Estimate $7 + 10 = 17$

$$7\frac{4}{9}$$
$$+ \ 10\frac{2}{9}$$

Add the whole numbers and fractions separately.

$$17\frac{6}{9} \text{ or } 17\frac{2}{3}$$ Simplify.

Check for Reasonableness $17\frac{2}{3} \approx 17$ ✔

---

2. Find $8\frac{5}{6} - 2\frac{1}{3}$. Write in simplest form.

Estimate $9 - 2 = 7$

$$8\frac{5}{6} \qquad \rightarrow \qquad 8\frac{5}{6}$$
$$-2\frac{1}{3} \qquad \rightarrow \qquad -2\frac{2}{6}$$

Rename the fraction using the LCD. Then subtract.

$$6\frac{3}{6} \text{ or } 6\frac{1}{2} \quad \text{Simplify.}$$

Check for Reasonableness $6\frac{1}{2} \approx 7$ ✔

> **Got it?** Do these problems to find out.

Add or subtract. Write in simplest form.

a. $6\frac{1}{8} + 2\frac{5}{8}$ b. $5\frac{1}{5} + 2\frac{3}{10}$ c. $1\frac{5}{9} + 4\frac{1}{6}$

d. $5\frac{4}{5} - 1\frac{3}{10}$ e. $13\frac{7}{8} - 9\frac{3}{4}$ f. $8\frac{2}{3} - 2\frac{1}{2}$

Properties

$120\frac{1}{2} + 40\frac{1}{3}$ can be written as $(120 + \frac{1}{2}) + (40 + \frac{1}{3})$. Then the Commutative and Associative Properties can be used to reorder and regroup the numbers to find the sum.

Show your work.

a. _____

b. _____

c. _____

d. _____

e. _____

f. _____

Example

3. Find $2\frac{1}{3} - 1\frac{2}{3}$.

Method 1 **Rename Mixed Numbers**

Estimate $2 - 1\frac{1}{2} = \frac{1}{2}$

Since $\frac{1}{3}$ is less than $\frac{2}{3}$, rename $2\frac{1}{3}$ before subtracting.

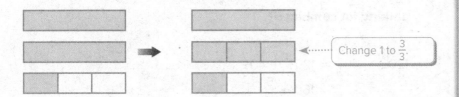

Change 1 to $\frac{3}{3}$.

$$2\frac{1}{3} \qquad = \qquad 1\frac{3}{3} + \frac{1}{3} \text{ or } 1\frac{4}{3}$$

$$
\begin{array}{ll}
2\frac{1}{3} \rightarrow & 1\frac{4}{3} \qquad \text{Rename } 2\frac{1}{3} \text{ as } 1\frac{4}{3}. \\
-1\frac{2}{3} \rightarrow & -1\frac{2}{3} \qquad \text{Subtract the whole numbers and then the fractions.} \\
\hline
& \frac{2}{3}
\end{array}
$$

Check for Reasonableness $\frac{2}{3} \approx \frac{1}{2}$ ✓

Method 2 **Write as Improper Fractions**

$$
\begin{array}{ll}
2\frac{1}{3} \rightarrow & \frac{7}{3} \qquad \text{Write } 2\frac{1}{3} \text{ as } \frac{7}{3}. \\
-1\frac{2}{3} \rightarrow & -\frac{5}{3} \qquad \text{Write } 1\frac{2}{3} \text{ as } \frac{5}{3}. \\
\hline
& \frac{2}{3} \qquad \text{Simplify.}
\end{array}
$$

So, $2\frac{1}{3} - 1\frac{2}{3} = \frac{2}{3}$.

Using either method, the answer is $\frac{2}{3}$.

Got it? Do these problems to find out.

Subtract. Write in simplest form.

g. $7 - 1\frac{1}{2}$ **h.** $5\frac{3}{8} - 4\frac{11}{12}$ **i.** $11\frac{2}{5} - 2\frac{3}{5}$

j. $8 - 3\frac{3}{4}$ **k.** $3\frac{1}{4} - 1\frac{3}{4}$ **l.** $16 - 5\frac{5}{6}$

Fractions Greater Than One

An improper fraction has a numerator that is greater than or equal to the denominator. Examples of improper fractions are $\frac{5}{4}$ and $2\frac{6}{5}$.

Show your work.

g. _____

h. _____

i. _____

j. _____

k. _____

l. _____

Choose an Operation

Add or subtract unlike fractions to solve real-world problems.

 Example

4. An urban planner is designing a skateboard park. The length of the skateboard park is $120\frac{1}{2}$ feet. The length of the parking lot is $40\frac{1}{3}$ feet. What will be the length of the park and the parking lot combined?

$$120\frac{1}{2} + 40\frac{1}{3} = 120\frac{3}{6} + 40\frac{2}{6}$$ Rename $\frac{1}{2}$ as $\frac{3}{6}$ and $\frac{1}{3}$ as $\frac{2}{6}$.

$$= 160 + \frac{5}{6}$$ Add the whole numbers and fractions separately.

$$= 160\frac{5}{6}$$ Simplify.

The total length is $160\frac{5}{6}$ feet.

Guided Practice

Add or subtract. Write in simplest form. (Examples 1–3)

1. $8\frac{1}{2} + 3\frac{4}{5} =$ _____

2. $7\frac{5}{6} - 3\frac{1}{6} =$ _____

3. $11 - 6\frac{3}{8} =$ _____

4. A hybrid car's gas tank can hold $11\frac{9}{10}$ gallons of gasoline. It contains $8\frac{3}{4}$ gallons of gasoline. How much more gasoline is needed to fill the tank? (Example 4) _____

5. **Building on the Essential Question** How can you subtract mixed numbers when the fraction in the first mixed number is less than the fraction in the second mixed number? _____

_____

_____

Rate Yourself!

How confident are you about adding and subtracting mixed numbers? Shade the ring on the target.

For more help, go online to access a Personal Tutor.

Independent Practice

Go online for Step-by-Step Solutions

Add or subtract. Write in simplest form. (Examples 1–3)

1. $2\frac{1}{9} + 7\frac{4}{9} =$ _____

2. $8\frac{5}{12} + 11\frac{1}{4} =$ _____

3. $10\frac{4}{5} - 2\frac{1}{5} =$ _____

4. $9\frac{4}{5} - 2\frac{3}{10} =$ _____

5. $11\frac{3}{4} - 4\frac{1}{3} =$ _____

6. $9\frac{1}{5} - 2\frac{3}{5} =$ _____

7. $6\frac{3}{5} - 1\frac{2}{3} =$ _____

8. $14\frac{1}{6} - 7\frac{1}{3} =$ _____

9. $8 - 3\frac{2}{3} =$ _____

MP Justify Conclusions For Exercises 10 and 11, choose an operation to solve. Explain your reasoning. Then solve the problem. Write your answer in simplest form. (Example 4)

10. If Juliana and Brody hiked both of the trails listed in the table, how far did they hike?

_____

Trail	Length (mi)
Woodland Park	$3\frac{2}{3}$
Mill Creek Way	$2\frac{5}{6}$

11. The length of Kasey's garden is $4\frac{5}{8}$ feet. Find the width of Kasey's garden if it is $2\frac{7}{8}$ feet shorter than the length.

_____

12. Karen wakes up at 6:00 A.M. It takes her $1\frac{1}{4}$ hours to shower, get dressed, and comb her hair. It takes her $\frac{1}{2}$ hour to eat breakfast, brush her teeth, and make her bed. At what time will she be ready for school? _____

Add or subtract. Write in simplest form.

13. $-3\frac{1}{4} + \left(-1\frac{3}{4}\right) =$ _____

14. $\dfrac{3\frac{1}{2}}{5} + \dfrac{4\frac{2}{3}}{2} =$ _____

15. $6\frac{1}{3} + 1\frac{2}{3} + 5\frac{5}{9} =$ _____

16. $3\frac{1}{4} + 2\frac{5}{6} - 4\frac{1}{3} =$ _____

 H.O.T. Problems Higher Order Thinking

17. **MP Model with Mathematics** Write a real-world problem that could be represented by the expression $5\frac{1}{2} - 3\frac{7}{8}$. Then solve your problem.

_____

_____

_____

_____

18. **MP Persevere with Problems** A string is cut in half. One of the halves is thrown away. One fifth of the remaining half is cut away and the piece left is 8 feet long. How long was the string initially? Justify your answer.

_____

_____

_____

19. **MP Model with Mathematics** Using three mixed numbers as side lengths, draw an equilateral triangle with a perimeter of $8\frac{1}{4}$ feet.

Show your work.

Extra Practice

Add or subtract. Write in simplest form.

20. $6\frac{1}{4} - 2\frac{3}{4} = 3\frac{1}{2}$

$$6\frac{1}{4} - 2\frac{3}{4} = 5\frac{5}{4} - 2\frac{3}{4}$$
$$= 3\frac{2}{4}$$
$$= 3\frac{1}{2}$$

21. $8\frac{3}{8} + 10\frac{1}{3} =$ _____

22. $13 - 5\frac{5}{6} =$ _____

23. $3\frac{2}{7} + 4\frac{3}{7} =$ _____

24. $4\frac{3}{10} - 1\frac{3}{4} =$ _____

25. $12\frac{1}{2} - 6\frac{5}{8} =$ _____

MP Justify Conclusions Choose an operation to solve. Explain your reasoning. Then solve the problem. Write your answer in simplest form.

26. The length of Alana's hair was $9\frac{3}{4}$ inches. After her haircut, the length was $6\frac{1}{2}$ inches. How many inches did she have cut?

_____

_____

27. Emeril used a total of $7\frac{1}{4}$ cups of flour to make three pastries. He used $2\frac{1}{4}$ cups of flour for the first and $2\frac{1}{3}$ cups for the second. How much flour did Emeril use for the third pastry?

_____

_____

28. Margarite made the jewelry shown. If the necklace is $10\frac{5}{8}$ inches longer than the bracelet, how long is the necklace?

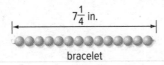

$7\frac{1}{4}$ in.

bracelet

necklace

_____

29. Find the perimeter of the figure. Write your answer in simplest form.

_____

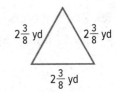

$2\frac{3}{8}$ yd $2\frac{3}{8}$ yd

$2\frac{3}{8}$ yd

30. Suppose you want to place a shelf that is $30\frac{1}{3}$ inches long in the center of a wall that is $45\frac{3}{4}$ inches wide. About how far from each edge of the wall should you place the shelf? _____

31. A recipe for snack mix calls for $4\frac{3}{4}$ cups of cereal. The amount of peanuts needed is $1\frac{2}{3}$ cups less than the amount of cereal needed. Complete each box below to make a true statement.

The recipe calls for ⬚ cups of peanuts. A total of

⬚ cups of peanuts and cereal are needed in all.

32. Maria practiced the piano for $2\frac{1}{2}$ hours last week and $1\frac{3}{4}$ hours this week. Use the bar diagram sections to construct a bar diagram that represents how many hours Maria practiced in the past 2 weeks.

⬚

⬚

How many hours did Maria practice the piano in the past 2 weeks?

⬚

Spiral Review

Round each mixed number to its nearest whole number. Then estimate each product.

33. $5\frac{1}{4} \times 7\frac{2}{3} \approx$ ⬚ $\times$ ⬚ $\approx$ ⬚

34. $1\frac{1}{11} \times 8\frac{14}{15} \approx$ ⬚ $\times$ ⬚ $\approx$ ⬚

35. Zoe's average running speed is about $6\frac{4}{5}$ miles per hour. Suppose Zoe runs for $1\frac{3}{4}$ hours. About how far will she have run? Explain.

_____

_____

Case #1 Science Experiment

Casey drops a ball from a height of 12 feet. It hits the ground and bounces up half as high as it fell. This is true for each successive bounce.

What is the height the ball reaches after the fourth bounce?

Understand *What are the facts?*

Casey dropped the ball from a height of 12 feet. It bounces up half as high for each successive bounce.

Plan *What is your strategy to solve this problem?*

Draw a diagram to show the height of the ball after each bounce.

Solve *How can you apply the strategy?*

The ball reaches a height of _____ foot after the fourth bounce.

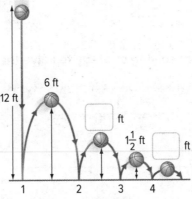

12 ft   6 ft   ____ ft $1\frac{1}{2}$ ft   ____ ft

1   2   3   4

Check *Does the answer make sense?*

Use division to check. $12 \div 2 = 6$, $6 \div 2 = 3$, $3 \div 2 = 1.5$, $1.5 \div 2 = 0.75$.

Analyze the Strategy

MP Be Precise If the ball is dropped from 12 feet and bounces up $\frac{2}{3}$ as high on each successive bounce, what is the height of the fourth bounce?

Case #2 Travel

Mr. Garcia has driven 60 miles, which is $\frac{2}{3}$ of the way to his sister's house.

How much farther does he have to drive to get to his sister's house?

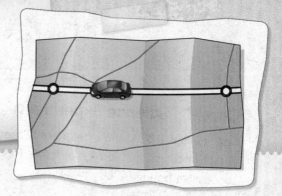

 Understand

Read the problem. What are you being asked to find?

I need to find _____.

What information do you know?

Mr. Garcia has driven _____ of the way to his sister's house. This is

equal to _____.

Is there any information that you do *not* need to know?

I do not need to know _____.

Plan

Choose a problem-solving strategy.

I will use the _____ strategy.

Solve

Use your problem-solving strategy to solve the problem.

Use the bar diagram that represents the distance to his sister's house.

Fill in two of the sections to represent $\frac{2}{3}$.

```
|------- 60 miles -------|
 _____
|      |      |       |
|_____|_____|_____|
```

☐ of the 3 parts = 60.

Each part is ☐ miles. The

distance to his sister's house

is 60 + ☐ = ☐.

So, Mr. Garcia has _____ miles left to drive.

Check

Use information from the problem to check your answer.

_____

**Work with a small group to solve the following cases.
Show your work on a separate piece of paper.**

Collaborate

Case #3 Fractions

Marta ate a quarter of a whole pie. Edwin ate $\frac{1}{4}$ of what was left.
Cristina then ate $\frac{1}{3}$ of what was left.

What fraction of the pie remains?

Case #4 Games

Eight members of a chess club are having a tournament. In the first round,
every player will play a chess game against every other player.

How many games will be in the first round of the tournament?

Case #5 Distance

Alejandro and Pedro are riding their bikes to school. After 1 mile,
they are $\frac{5}{8}$ of the way there.

How much farther do they have to go?

Case #6 Seats

The number of seats in the first row of a concert hall is 6. The second
row has 9 seats, the third row has 12 seats, and the fourth row has
15 seats.

How many seats will be in the eighth row?

Use any strategy!

Mid-Chapter Check

Vocabulary Check

1. Define *rational number*. Give some examples of rational numbers written in different forms.

_____

_____

_____

2. Fill in the blank in the sentence below with the correct term.

Repeating decimals can be represented using _____.

Skills Check and Problem Solving

Add or subtract. Write in simplest form.

3. $\frac{5}{8} + \frac{3}{8} =$ _____

4. $-\frac{1}{9} + \frac{2}{9} =$ _____

5. $-\frac{11}{15} - \frac{1}{15} =$ _____

6. $2\frac{5}{9} + 1\frac{2}{3} =$ _____

7. $8\frac{3}{4} - 2\frac{5}{12} =$ _____

8. $5\frac{1}{6} - 1\frac{1}{3} =$ _____

9. The table at the right shows the fraction of each state that is water. Order the states from least to greatest fraction of water.

_____

10. The maximum height of an Asian elephant is 9.8 feet. What mixed number represents this height? _____

11. **MP Persevere with Problems** The table shows the weight of a newborn infant for its first year. During which three-month period was the infant's weight gain the greatest? _____

What Part is Water?	
Alaska	$\frac{3}{41}$
Michigan	$\frac{40}{97}$
Wisconsin	$\frac{1}{6}$

Month	Weight (lb)
0	$7\frac{1}{4}$
3	$12\frac{1}{2}$
6	$16\frac{5}{8}$
9	$19\frac{4}{5}$
12	$23\frac{3}{20}$

Multiply Fractions

Lunch There are 12 students at the lunch table. Two thirds of the students ordered a hamburger for lunch. One half of those students that ordered a hamburger put cheese on it.

 Essential Question

WHAT happens when you add, subtract, multiply, and divide fractions?

 Virginia Standards
7.2

Step 1	Draw an X through the students that did not order a hamburger.

Step 2	Draw a C on the students that ordered cheese on their hamburger.

Didn't I order cheese with that?

1. What fraction of the students at the lunch table ordered a cheeseburger? Write in simplest form. _____

2. What is $\frac{1}{2}$ of $\frac{2}{3}$? Write in simplest form. _____

3. Write your own word problem that involves fractions that can be solved using a diagram like the one above.

_____

_____

_____

 Which **MP Mathematical Process Goals** did you use? Shade the circle(s) that applies.

① Mathematical Problem Solving

② Mathematical Communication

③ Mathematical Reasoning

④ Mathematical Connections

⑤ Mathematical Representations

Multiply Fractions

Words To multiply fractions, multiply the numerators and multiply the denominators.

Examples Numbers

$$\frac{1}{2} \times \frac{2}{3} = \frac{1 \times 2}{2 \times 3} \text{ or } \frac{2}{6}$$

Algebra

$$\frac{a}{b} \cdot \frac{c}{d} = \frac{a \cdot c}{b \cdot d} \text{ or } \frac{ac}{bd}, \text{ where } b, d \neq 0$$

When multiplying two fractions, write the product in simplest form. The numerator and denominator of either fraction may have common factors. If this is the case, you can simplify before multiplying.

Examples

Multiply. Write in simplest form.

1. $\frac{1}{2} \times \frac{1}{3}$

$\frac{1}{2} \times \frac{1}{3} = \frac{1 \times 1}{2 \times 3}$ ← Multiply the numerators.
                                     ← Multiply the denominators.

$= \frac{1}{6}$ Simplify.

2. $2 \times \left(-\frac{3}{4}\right)$

$2 \times \left(-\frac{3}{4}\right) = \frac{2}{1} \times \left(\frac{-3}{4}\right)$ Write 2 as $\frac{2}{1}$ and $-\frac{3}{4}$ as $\frac{-3}{4}$.

$= \frac{2 \times (-3)}{1 \times 4}$ ← Multiply the numerators.
                          ← Multiply the denominators.

$= \frac{-6}{4}$ or $-1\frac{1}{2}$ Simplify.

3. $\frac{2}{7} \times \left(-\frac{3}{8}\right)$

$\frac{2}{7} \times \left(-\frac{3}{8}\right) = \frac{\overset{1}{\cancel{2}}}{7} \times \left(-\frac{3}{\underset{4}{\cancel{8}}}\right)$ Divide 2 and 8 by their GCF, 2.

$= \frac{1 \times (-3)}{7 \times 4}$ or $-\frac{3}{28}$ Multiply.

> **Got it?** Do these problems to find out.

Multiply. Write in simplest form.

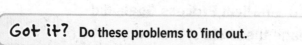

a. $\frac{3}{5} \times \frac{1}{2}$ b. $\frac{2}{3} \times (-4)$ c. $-\frac{1}{3} \times \left(-\frac{3}{7}\right)$

Work Zone

GCF

In Example 3, GCF stands for the greatest of the common factors of two or more numbers.

Example: The GCF of 8 and 2 is 2.

a. _____

b. _____

c. _____

Multiply Mixed Numbers

When multiplying by a mixed number, you can rename the mixed number as an improper fraction. You can also multiply mixed numbers using the Distributive Property and mental math.

Example

4. Find $\frac{1}{2} \times 4\frac{2}{5}$. Write in simplest form.

Estimate $\frac{1}{2} \times 4 = 2$

Method 1 | **Rename the mixed number.**

$$\frac{1}{2} \times 4\frac{2}{5} = \frac{1}{\overset{1}{\cancel{2}}} \times \frac{\overset{11}{\cancel{22}}}{5}$$ Rename $4\frac{2}{5}$ as an improper fraction, $\frac{22}{5}$.
Divide 2 and 22 by their GCF, 2.

$$= \frac{1 \times 11}{1 \times 5}$$ Multiply.

$$= \frac{11}{5}$$ Simplify.

$$= 2\frac{1}{5}$$ Simplify.

Method 2 | **Use mental math.**

The mixed number $4\frac{2}{5}$ is equal to $4 + \frac{2}{5}$.

So, $\frac{1}{2} \times 4\frac{2}{5} = \frac{1}{2}\left(4 + \frac{2}{5}\right)$. Use the Distributive Property to multiply, then add mentally.

$$\frac{1}{2}\left(4 + \frac{2}{5}\right) = 2 + \frac{1}{5}$$ Think Half of 4 is 2 and half of 2 fifths is 1 fifth.

$$= 2\frac{1}{5}$$ Rewrite the sum as a mixed number.

Check for Reasonableness $2\frac{1}{5} \approx 2$ ✔

So, $\frac{1}{2} \times 4\frac{2}{5} = 2\frac{1}{5}$.

Using either method, the answer is $2\frac{1}{5}$.

> ### Simplifying
> If you forget to simplify before multiplying, you can always simplify the final answer. However, it is usually easier to simplify before multiplying.

Got it? Do these problems to find out.

Multiply. Write in simplest form.

d. $\frac{1}{4} \times 8\frac{4}{9}$ **e.** $5\frac{1}{3} \times 3$ **f.** $-1\frac{7}{8} \times \left(-2\frac{2}{5}\right)$

d. _____

e. _____

f. _____

Show your work.

Example

5. Humans sleep about $\frac{1}{3}$ of each day. Let each year equal $365\frac{1}{4}$ days. Determine the number of days in a year the average human sleeps.

Find $\frac{1}{3} \times 365\frac{1}{4}$.

Estimate $\frac{1}{3} \times 360 = 120$

$\frac{1}{3} \times 365\frac{1}{4} = \frac{1}{3} \times \frac{1,461}{4}$ Rename the mixed number as an improper fraction.

$= \frac{1}{\overset{\scriptstyle 1}{3}} \times \frac{\overset{\scriptstyle 487}{1,461}}{4}$ Divide 3 and 1,461 by their GCF, 3.

$= \frac{487}{4}$ or $121\frac{3}{4}$ Multiply. Then rename as a mixed number.

Check for Reasonableness $121\frac{3}{4} \approx 120$ ✔

The average human sleeps $121\frac{3}{4}$ days each year.

Guided Practice

Multiply. Write in simplest form. (Examples 1–4)

1. $\frac{2}{3} \times \frac{1}{3} =$ _____

 Show your work.

2. $-\frac{1}{4} \times \left(-\frac{8}{9}\right) =$ _____

3. $2\frac{1}{4} \times \frac{2}{3} =$ _____

4. **STEM** The weight of an object on Mars is about $\frac{2}{5}$ its weight on Earth. How much would an $80\frac{1}{2}$-pound dog weigh on Mars? (Example 5) _____

5. **ⓔ Building on the Essential Question** How is the process of multiplying fractions different from the process of adding fractions?

_____

_____

_____

Rate Yourself!

How well do you understand multiplying fractions? Circle the image that applies.

Clear   Somewhat Clear   Not So Clear

For more help, go online to access a Personal Tutor.

FOLDABLES Time to update your Foldable!

Independent Practice

Go online for Step-by-Step Solutions

Multiply. Write in simplest form. (Examples 1–4)

1. $\frac{3}{4} \times \frac{1}{8} =$ _____

2. $\frac{2}{5} \times \frac{2}{3} =$ _____

3. $-9 \times \frac{1}{2} =$ _____

Show your work.

4. $-\frac{1}{5} \times \left(-\frac{5}{6}\right) =$ _____

5. $\frac{2}{3} \times \frac{1}{4} =$ _____

6. $-\frac{1}{12} \times \frac{2}{5} =$ _____

7. $\frac{2}{5} \times \frac{15}{16} =$ _____

8. $\frac{4}{7} \times \frac{7}{8} =$ _____

9. $\left(-1\frac{1}{2}\right) \times \frac{2}{3} =$ _____

10. The width of a vegetable garden is $\frac{1}{3}$ times its length. If the length of the garden is $7\frac{3}{4}$ feet, what is the width in simplest form? (Example 5)

_____

11. One evening, $\frac{2}{3}$ of the students in Rick's class watched television. Of those students, $\frac{3}{8}$ watched a reality show. Of the students that watched the show, $\frac{1}{4}$ of them recorded the show. What fraction of the students in Rick's class watched and recorded a reality TV show?

_____

Write each numerical expression. Then evaluate the expression.

12. one half of negative five eighths

13. one third of eleven sixteenths

14. **MP** **Model with Mathematics** Refer to the graphic novel frame below.

a. The height of the closet is 96 inches, and Aisha would like to have 4 rows of cube organizers. What is the most the height of each cube organizer can be?

b. Aisha would like to stack 3 shoe boxes on top of each other at the bottom of the closet. The height of each shoe box is $4\frac{1}{2}$ inches. What is the total height of the 3 boxes?

H.O.T. Problems Higher Order Thinking

15. **MP** **Model with Mathematics** Write a real-world problem that involves finding the product of $\frac{3}{4}$ and $\frac{1}{8}$.

16. **MP** **Persevere with Problems** Two positive improper fractions are multiplied. Is the product *sometimes*, *always*, or *never* less than 1? Explain.

17. **MP** **Reason Inductively** Find two fractions that satisify each of the following.
a. each greater than $\frac{2}{5}$ with a product less than $\frac{2}{5}$

b. each greater than $\frac{1}{2}$ with a product greater than $\frac{1}{2}$

Extra Practice

Multiply. Write in simplest form.

18. $\frac{4}{5} \times (-6) =$ ___$-4\frac{4}{5}$___

$$\frac{4}{5} \times (-6) = \frac{4}{5} \times \left(-\frac{6}{1}\right)$$

$$= \frac{4 \times (-6)}{5 \times 1}$$

$$= \frac{-24}{5} \text{ or } -4\frac{4}{5}$$

Homework Help →

19. $-\frac{4}{9} \times \left(-\frac{1}{4}\right) =$ _____

20. $3\frac{1}{3} \times \left(-\frac{1}{5}\right) =$ _____

21. $\frac{1}{3} \times \frac{3}{4} =$ _____

22. $\frac{4}{9} \times \left(-\frac{1}{8}\right) =$ _____

23. $\frac{5}{6} \times 2\frac{3}{5} =$ _____

24. Each DVD storage case is about $\frac{1}{5}$ inch thick What will be the height in simplest form of 12 cases sold together?

_____

25. Mark left $\frac{3}{8}$ of a pizza in the refrigerator. On Friday, he ate $\frac{1}{2}$ of what was left of the pizza. What fraction of the entire pizza did he eat on Friday?

_____

Multiply. Write in simplest form.

26. $\left(\frac{1}{4}\right)^2 =$ _____

27. $\left(-\frac{2}{3}\right)^3 =$ _____

28. $\frac{1\frac{1}{3}}{\frac{1}{4}} \times \frac{\frac{2}{5}}{\frac{1}{2}} =$ _____

29. **MP** **Justify Conclusions** Alano wants to make one and a half batches of the pasta salad recipe shown at the right. How much of each ingredient will Alano need? Explain how you solved the problem.

_____

_____

_____

Pasta Salad Recipe	
Ingredient	**Amount**
Broccoli	$1\frac{1}{4}$ c
Cooked pasta	$3\frac{3}{4}$ c
Salad dressing	$\frac{2}{3}$ c
Cheese	$1\frac{1}{3}$ c

30. Philip rode his bicycle at $9\frac{1}{2}$ miles per hour. If he rode for $\frac{3}{4}$ of an hour, how many miles in simplest form did

he cover? _____

31. Of the dolls in Marjorie's doll collection, $\frac{2}{5}$ have red hair. Of these, $\frac{1}{4}$ have green eyes, $\frac{2}{3}$ have blue eyes, and $\frac{1}{12}$ have brown eyes. Determine if each statement is true or false.

   a. $\frac{1}{10}$ of Marjorie's doll collection has red hair and green eyes.   ☐ True   ☐ False

   b. $\frac{4}{15}$ of Marjorie's doll collection has red hair and blue eyes.   ☐ True   ☐ False

   c. $\frac{29}{60}$ of Marjorie's doll collection has red hair and brown eyes.   ☐ True   ☐ False

32. The table shows the number of teaspoons of vanilla needed to make different batches of cookies.

Select one box from each row to describe how to find the number of teaspoons of vanilla needed to make n batches of cookies.

Batches	1	2	3	4	5	n
Vanilla (tsp)	$\frac{1}{4}$	$\frac{1}{2}$	$\frac{3}{4}$	1	$1\frac{1}{4}$	

Row 1 | Subtract | Add | Multiply | Divide |

Row 2 | 4 | n | $\frac{1}{4}$ |

Row 3 | to | by | from |

Row 4 | 4 | n | $\frac{1}{4}$ |

How many teaspoons of vanilla are needed to make $6\frac{1}{2}$ batches of cookies?

☐

Spiral Review

For each multiplication sentence, write two related division sentences.

33. $3 \times 4 = 12$

_____

_____

34. $\frac{1}{6} \times \frac{1}{3} = \frac{1}{18}$

_____

_____

35. $2\frac{2}{5} \times 4\frac{1}{2} = 10\frac{4}{5}$

_____

_____

36. $5\frac{5}{8} \times 1\frac{1}{5} = 6\frac{3}{4}$

_____

_____

Convert Between Systems

Virginia Standards
7.3

 ## Real-World Link

 Watch ▶

Essential Question

WHAT happens when you add, subtract, multiply, and divide fractions?

5K Race To raise money for a health organization, the Matthews family is participating in a 5K race. A 5K race is 5 kilometers.

1. How many meters long is the race?

    5 kilometers = [_____] meters

2. One mile is approximately 1.6 kilometers. About how many miles is the race?

    5 kilometers ≈ [_____] miles

3. A kilometer is a unit of length in the metric measurement system. A mile is a measure of length in the customary measurement system. Write the following units of length under the correct measurement system.

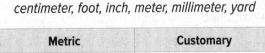
centimeter, foot, inch, meter, millimeter, yard

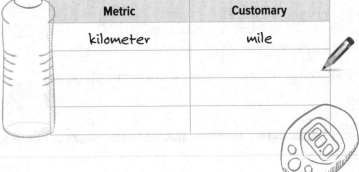

Metric	Customary
kilometer	mile

Which **MP** **Mathematical Process Goals** did you use? Shade the circle(s) that applies.

① Mathematical Problem Solving
② Mathematical Communication
③ Mathematical Reasoning
④ Mathematical Connections
⑤ Mathematical Representations

Convert Between Measurement Systems

You can multiply by fractions to convert between customary and metric units. The table below lists common customary and metric relationships.

Customary and Metric Relationships			
Type of Measure	Customary	$\longrightarrow$	Metric
Length	1 inch (in.)	$\approx$	2.54 centimeters (cm)
	1 foot (ft)	$\approx$	0.30 meter (m)
	1 yard (yd)	$\approx$	0.91 meter (m)
	1 mile (mi)	$\approx$	1.61 kilometers (km)
Weight/Mass	1 pound (lb)	$\approx$	453.6 grams (g)
	1 pound (lb)	$\approx$	0.4536 kilogram (kg)
	1 ton (T)	$\approx$	907.2 kilograms (kg)
Capacity	1 cup (c)	$\approx$	236.59 milliliters (mL)
	1 pint (pt)	$\approx$	473.18 milliliters (mL)
	1 quart (qt)	$\approx$	946.35 milliliters (mL)
	1 gallon (gal)	$\approx$	3.79 liters (L)

Examples

Tutor

1. **Convert 17.22 inches to centimeters. Round to the nearest hundredth if necessary.**

Since 2.54 centimeters $\approx$ 1 inch, multiply by $\frac{2.54 \text{ cm}}{1 \text{ in.}}$.

$17.22 \approx 17.22 \text{ in.} \cdot \frac{2.54 \text{ cm}}{1 \text{ in.}}$ Multiply by $\frac{2.54 \text{ cm}}{1 \text{ in.}}$. Divide out common units.

$\approx 43.7388 \text{ cm}$ Simplify.

So, 17.22 inches is approximately 43.74 centimeters.

2. **Convert 5 kilometers to miles. Round to the nearest hundredth if necessary.**

Since 1 mile $\approx$ 1.61 kilometers, multiply by $\frac{1 \text{ mi}}{1.61 \text{ km}}$.

$5 \text{ km} \approx 5 \text{ km} \cdot \frac{1 \text{ mi}}{1.61 \text{ km}}$ Multiply by $\frac{1 \text{ mi}}{1.61 \text{ km}}$. Divide out common units.

$\approx \frac{5 \text{ mi}}{1.61}$ or 3.11 mi   Simplify.

So, 5 kilometers is approximately 3.11 miles.

Got it? Do these problems to find out.

Complete. Round to the nearest hundredth if necessary.

a. 6 yd $\approx$ ▉ m   **b.** 1.6 cm $\approx$ ▉ in.   **c.** 17 m $\approx$ ▉ yd

Show your work.

a. _____

b. _____

c. _____

Examples

3. **Convert 828.5 milliliters to cups. Round to the nearest hundredth if necessary.**

Since 1 cup ≈ 236.59 milliliters, multiply by $\dfrac{1\,c}{236.59\,mL}$.

$828.5\ mL \approx 828.5\ \cancel{mL} \cdot \dfrac{1\,c}{236.59\ \cancel{mL}}$ 　　Multiply by $\dfrac{1\,c}{236.59\,mL}$ and divide out common units.

$\approx \dfrac{828.5\,c}{236.59}$ or 3.50 c 　　Simplify.

So, 828.5 milliliters is approximately 3.50 cups.

Dimensional Analysis

Recall that dimensional analysis is the process of including units of measurement when you compute.

---

4. **Convert 3.4 quarts to milliliters. Round to the nearest hundredth if necessary.**

Since 946.35 milliliters ≈ 1 quart, multiply by $\dfrac{946.35\,mL}{1\,qt}$.

$3.4\ qt \approx 3.4\ \cancel{qt} \cdot \dfrac{946.35\ mL}{1\ \cancel{qt}}$ 　　Multiply by $\dfrac{946.35}{1\,qt}$. Divide out common units.

$\approx 3{,}217.59\ mL$ 　　Simplify.

So, 3.4 quarts is approximately 3,217.59 milliliters.

---

5. **Convert 4.25 kilograms to pounds. Round to the nearest hundredth if necessary.**

Since 1 pound ≈ 0.4536 kilogram, multiply by $\dfrac{1\,lb}{0.4536\,kg}$.

$4.25\ kg \approx 4.25\ \cancel{kg} \cdot \dfrac{1\ lb}{0.4536\ \cancel{kg}}$ 　　Multiply by $\dfrac{1\,lb}{0.4536\,kg}$. Divide out common units.

$\approx \dfrac{4.25\,lb}{0.4536}$ or 9.37 lb 　　Simplify.

So, 4.25 kilograms is approximately 9.37 pounds.

d. _____

> **Got it?** Do these problems to find out.

e. _____

Complete. Round to the nearest hundredth if necessary.

   d. 7.44 c ≈ ■ mL

f. _____

   e. 22.09 lb ≈ ■ kg

   f. 35.85 L ≈ ■ gal

 Example

6. An Olympic-size swimming pool is 50 meters long. About how many feet long is the pool?

Since 1 foot ≈ 0.30 meter, use the ratio $\frac{1\,\text{ft}}{0.30\,\text{m}}$.

$50\,\text{m} \approx 50\,\text{m} \cdot \dfrac{1\,\text{ft}}{0.30\,\text{m}}$ \qquad Multiply by $\frac{1\,\text{ft}}{0.30\,\text{m}}$.

$\approx 50\,\cancel{\text{m}} \cdot \dfrac{1\,\text{ft}}{0.30\,\cancel{\text{m}}}$ \qquad Divide out common units, leaving the desired unit, feet.

$\approx \dfrac{50\,\text{ft}}{0.30}$ or $166.67\,\text{ft}$ \qquad Divide.

An Olympic-size swimming pool is about 166.67 feet long.

Guided Practice

Check ✓

Complete. Round to the nearest hundredth if necessary. (Examples 1–5)

1. 3.7 yd ≈ _____ m

2. 11.07 pt ≈ _____ mL

3. 650 lb ≈ _____ kg

Show your work.

4. About how many feet does a team of athletes run in a 1,600-meter relay race? (Example 6) _____

5. Raheem bought 3 pounds of bananas. About how many kilograms did he buy? (Example 6) _____

6. Ⓠ **Building on the Essential Question** How can you use dimensional analysis to convert between measurement systems?

_____

_____

_____

_____

Rate Yourself!

Are you ready to move on?
Shade the section that applies.

YES (?) NO

For more help, go online to access a Personal Tutor.

Tutor

Independent Practice

Go online for Step-by-Step Solutions

Complete. Round to the nearest hundredth if necessary. (Examples 1–5)

1. 5 in. ≈ _____ cm

2. 2 qt ≈ _____ mL

3 58.14 kg ≈ _____ lb

Show your work.

4. 4 L ≈ _____ gal

5. 10 mL ≈ _____ c

6. 63.5 T ≈ _____ kg

7. 4.725 m ≈ _____ ft

8. 3 T ≈ _____ kg

9. 680.4 g ≈ _____ lb

10. A notebook computer has a mass of 2.25 kilograms. About how many pounds does the notebook weigh? (Example 6)

_____

11. A glass bottle holds 3.75 cups of water. About how many milliliters of water can the bottle hold? (Example 6)

_____

12. A Cabbage Palmetto has a height of 80 feet. What is the approximate height of the tree in meters? (Example 6)

_____

MP Persevere with Problems Determine the greater amount for each situation.

 13 Which box is greater, a 1.5-pound box of raisins or a 650-gram box of raisins?

14. Which is greater a 2.75-gallon container of juice or a 12-liter container of juice?

🔥 H.O.T. Problems Higher Order Thinking

15. MP Reason Inductively One gram of water has a volume of 1 milliliter. What is the volume of the water if it has a mass of 1 kilogram?

16. MP Persevere with Problems The distance from Earth to the Sun is approximately 93 million miles. About how many gigameters is this? Round to the nearest hundredth. *(Hint: In 1 gigameter there are about 621,118.01 miles.)*

MP Be Precise Order each set of measures from greatest to least.

17. 1.2 cm, 0.6 in., 0.031 m, 0.1 ft

18. 2 lb, 891 g, 1 kg, 0.02 T

19. $1\frac{1}{4}$ c, 0.4 L, 950 mL, 0.7 gal

20. 4.5 ft, 48 in., 1.3 m, 120 cm

21. MP Model with Mathematics Convert $2\frac{1}{8}$ inches and $2\frac{5}{8}$ inches to centimeters. Round to the nearest tenth. Then draw a segment whose length is between those two measures.

Extra Practice

Complete. Round to the nearest hundredth if necessary.

22. 15 cm ≈ __5.91__ in.

$$15 \text{ cm} \approx 15 \text{ cm} \cdot \frac{1 \text{ in.}}{2.54 \text{ cm}}$$

 Homework Help ➡

$$\approx 15 \text{ cm} \cdot \frac{1 \text{ in.}}{2.54 \text{ cm}}$$

$$\approx \frac{15 \text{ in.}}{2.54} \approx 5.91 \text{ in.}$$

23. 350 lb ≈ __158.76__ kg

$$350 \text{ lb} \approx 350 \text{ lb} \cdot \frac{0.4536 \text{ kg}}{1 \text{ lb}}$$

$$\approx 350 \text{ lb} \cdot \frac{0.4536 \text{ kg}}{1 \text{ lb}}$$

$$\approx 158.76 \text{ kg}$$

24. 17 mi ≈ _____ km

25. 32 gal ≈ _____ L

26. 50 mL ≈ _____ fl oz

27. 19 kg ≈ _____ lb

28. The Willis Tower has a height of 1,451 feet. What is the estimated height of the building in meters? _____

29. Which is greater, a bottle containing 64 fluid ounces or a bottle containing 2 liters of water? _____

30. **MP Use Math Tools** A bakery uses 900 grams of peaches in a cobbler. About how many pounds of peaches does the bakery use in a cobbler?

_____

Determine which quantity is greater.

31. 3 gal, 10 L _____

32. 14 oz, 0.4 kg _____

33. 4 mi, 6.2 km _____

34. Velocity is a rate usually expressed in feet per second or meters per second. How can the units help you calculate velocity using the distance a car traveled and the time recorded? _____

_____

35. The diagram shows the length of a fork from the cafeteria. Which measurements are approximately equal to the length of the fork? Select all that apply.

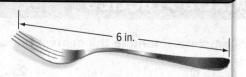
6 in.

☐ 15.2 cm   ☐ 0.152 m   ☐ 152 cm   ☐ 1.52 m

36. The masses of 4 different animals from a zoo are shown in the table. Convert each measure to pounds. Then sort the animals from least to greatest weight.

Animal	Mass (kg)
Brown Bear	272.16
Giraffe	1,134.0
Lion	226.8
Rhinoceros	1,587.6

	Animal	Weight (lb)
Least		
Greatest		

How many pounds greater is the heaviest animal than the lightest animal?

Explain how you can use units to be sure you are multiplying by the correct fraction when converting between measurement systems. Give an example.

Spiral Review

Convert. Round to the nearest tenth if necessary.

37. 17 ft = _____ yd

38. 82 in. = _____ ft

39. 3 mi = _____ ft

40. A skyscraper is 0.484 kilometer tall. What is the height of the skyscraper in meters? _____

Divide Fractions

 ## Real-World Link

Oranges Deandre has three oranges and each orange is divided evenly into fourths. Complete the steps below to find $3 \div \frac{1}{4}$.

Step 1 Draw three oranges. The first one is drawn for you.

Step 2 Imagine you cut each orange into fourths. Draw the slices for each orange.

So $3 \div \frac{1}{4} = 12$. Deandre will have ☐ orange slices.

1. Find $3 \div \frac{1}{2}$. Use a diagram. _____

2. What is true about $3 \div \frac{1}{2}$ and 3×2? _____

 Essential Question

WHAT happens when you add, subtract, multiply, and divide fractions?

 Virginia Standards
7.2

Which **MP** **Mathematical Process Goals** did you use? Shade the circle(s) that applies.

① Mathematical Problem Solving
② Mathematical Communication
③ Mathematical Reasoning
④ Mathematical Connections
⑤ Mathematical Representations

(Watch button top right)

Key Concept

Divide Fractions

Words   To divide by a fraction, multiply by its multiplicative inverse, or reciprocal.

Examples

Numbers

$$\frac{7}{8} \div \frac{3}{4} = \frac{7}{8} \cdot \frac{4}{3}$$

Algebra

$$\frac{a}{b} \div \frac{c}{d} = \frac{a}{b} \cdot \frac{d}{c}, \text{ where } b, c, d \neq 0$$

Dividing 3 by $\frac{1}{4}$ is the same as multiplying 3 by the reciprocal of $\frac{1}{4}$, which is 4.

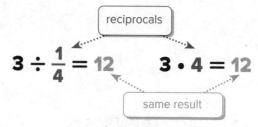

reciprocals

$$3 \div \frac{1}{4} = 12 \qquad 3 \cdot 4 = 12$$

same result

Is this pattern true for any division expression?

Consider $\frac{7}{8} \div \frac{3}{4}$, which can be rewritten as $\dfrac{\frac{7}{8}}{\frac{3}{4}}$.

$$\frac{\frac{7}{8}}{\frac{3}{4}} = \frac{\frac{7}{8} \times \frac{4}{3}}{\frac{3}{4} \times \frac{4}{3}}$$

Multiply the numerator and denominator by the reciprocal of $\frac{3}{4}$, which is $\frac{4}{3}$.

$$= \frac{\frac{7}{8} \times \frac{4}{3}}{1} \qquad \frac{3}{4} \times \frac{4}{3} = 1$$

$$= \frac{7}{8} \times \frac{4}{3}$$

So, $\frac{7}{8} \div \frac{3}{4} = \frac{7}{8} \times \frac{4}{3}$. The pattern is true in this case.

Examples

Tutor

1. Find $\frac{1}{3} \div 5$.

$$\frac{1}{3} \div 5 = \frac{1}{3} \div \frac{5}{1}$$ A whole number can be written as a fraction over 1.

$$= \frac{1}{3} \times \frac{1}{5}$$ Multiply by the reciprocal of $\frac{5}{1}$, which is $\frac{1}{5}$.

$$= \frac{1}{15}$$ Multiply.

Work Zone

STOP and Reflect

What is the reciprocal of $\frac{2}{3}$? of 15? of $-\frac{4}{9}$? Write your answers below.

---

2. Find $\frac{3}{4} \div \left(-\frac{1}{2}\right)$. Write in simplest form.

Estimate $1 \div \left(-\frac{1}{2}\right) = \boxed{}$

$\frac{3}{4} \div \left(-\frac{1}{2}\right) = \frac{3}{4} \cdot \left(-\frac{2}{1}\right)$ Multiply by the reciprocal of $-\frac{1}{2}$, which is $-\frac{2}{1}$.

$= \frac{3}{\overset{\displaystyle 4}{\underset{2}{}}} \cdot \left(-\frac{\overset{1}{2}}{1}\right)$ Divide 4 and 2 by their GCF, 2.

$= -\frac{3}{2}$ or $-1\frac{1}{2}$ Multiply.

Check for Reasonableness $-1\frac{1}{2} \approx -2$ ✔

Got it? Do these problems to find out.

Divide. Write in simplest form.

   a. $\frac{3}{4} \div \frac{1}{4}$ b. $-\frac{4}{5} \div \frac{8}{9}$ c. $-\frac{5}{6} \div \left(-\frac{2}{3}\right)$

Divide Mixed Numbers

To divide by a mixed number, first rename the mixed number as a fraction greater than one. Then multiply the first fraction by the reciprocal, or multiplicative inverse, of the second fraction.

Example

Tutor

3. Find $\frac{2}{3} \div 3\frac{1}{3}$. Write in simplest form.

$\frac{2}{3} \div 3\frac{1}{3} = \frac{2}{3} \div \frac{10}{3}$ Rename $3\frac{1}{3}$ a fraction greater than one.

$= \frac{2}{3} \cdot \frac{3}{10}$ Multiply by the reciprocal of $\frac{10}{3}$, which is $\frac{3}{10}$.

$= \frac{\overset{1}{2}}{3} \cdot \frac{\overset{1}{3}}{\underset{5}{10}}$ Divide out common factors.

$= \frac{1}{5}$ Multiply.

Got it? Do these problems to find out.

Divide. Write in simplest form.

   d. $5 \div 1\frac{1}{3}$ e. $-\frac{3}{4} \div 1\frac{1}{2}$ f. $2\frac{1}{3} \div 5$

Show your work.

a. _____

b. _____

c. _____

d. _____

e. _____

f. _____

Lesson 9 Divide Fractions **261**

 Watch | Tutor

4. The side pieces of a butterfly house are $8\frac{1}{4}$ inches long. How many side pieces can be cut from a board measuring $49\frac{1}{2}$ inches long?

To find how many side pieces can be cut, divide $49\frac{1}{2}$ by $8\frac{1}{4}$.

Estimate Use compatible numbers. $48 \div 8 = 6$

$$49\frac{1}{2} \div 8\frac{1}{4} = \frac{99}{2} \div \frac{33}{4}$$ Rename the mixed numbers as fractions greater than one.

$$= \frac{99}{2} \cdot \frac{4}{33}$$ Multiply by the reciprocal of $\frac{33}{4}$, which is $\frac{4}{33}$.

$$= \frac{\overset{3}{\cancel{99}}}{\underset{1}{\cancel{2}}} \cdot \frac{\overset{2}{\cancel{4}}}{\underset{1}{\cancel{33}}}$$ Divide out common factors.

$$= \frac{6}{1} \text{ or } 6$$ Multiply.

So, 6 side pieces can be cut.

Check for Reasonableness Compare to the estimate. $6 = 6$ ✓

 Check

Guided Practice

Divide. Write in simplest form. (Examples 1 – 3)

1. $\frac{1}{8} \div \frac{1}{3} =$ _____

2. $-3 \div \left(-\frac{6}{7}\right) =$ _____

3. $-\frac{7}{8} \div \frac{3}{4} =$ _____

 Show your work.

4. On Saturday, Lindsay walked $3\frac{1}{2}$ miles in $1\frac{2}{5}$ hours. What was her walking pace in miles per hour? Write in simplest form. (Example 4) _____

5. 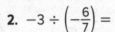 **Bulding on the Essential Question** How is dividing fractions related to multiplying? _____

_____

_____

Rate Yourself!

Are you ready to move on? Shade the section that applies.

I have a few questions.

I'm ready to move on.

I have a lot of questions.

For more help, go online to access a Personal Tutor. Tutor

FOLDABLES Time to update your Foldable!

Name _____ My Homework _____

Divide. Write in simplest form. (Examples 1 – 3)

1. $\dfrac{3}{8} \div \dfrac{6}{7} =$ _____

2. $-\dfrac{2}{3} \div \left(-\dfrac{1}{2}\right) =$ _____

3. $\dfrac{1}{2} \div 7\dfrac{1}{2} =$ _____

4. $6 \div \left(-\dfrac{1}{2}\right) =$ _____

5. $-\dfrac{4}{9} \div (-2) =$ _____

6. $\dfrac{2}{3} \div 2\dfrac{1}{2} =$ _____

7. Cheryl is organizing her movie collection. If each movie case is
$\dfrac{3}{4}$ inch wide, how many movies can fit on a shelf $5\dfrac{1}{4}$ feet wide? (Example 4)

_____

8. Use the table to solve. Write your answers in simplest form.

   a. How many times as heavy is the Golden Eagle as the Red-Tailed Hawk? _____

   b. How many times as heavy is the Golden Eagle as the Northern Bald Eagle? _____

Bird	Maximun Weight (lb)
Golden Eagle	$13\dfrac{9}{10}$
Northern Bald Eagle	$9\dfrac{9}{10}$
Red-Tailed Hawk	$3\dfrac{1}{2}$

9. **MP Model with Mathematics** Draw a model of the verbal expression below and then evaluate the expression. Explain how the model shows the division process.

   one half divided by two fifths _____

show your work.

_____

_____

_____

_____

10. **Multiple Representations** Jorge recorded the distance that five of his friends live from his house in the table shown.

    a. **Numbers** Tye lives about how many times farther away than Jamal?

    b. **Algebra** The mean is the sum of the data divided by the number of items in the data set. Write and solve an equation to find the mean number of miles that Jorge's friends live from his house. Write your answer in simplest form.

    c. **Model** Draw a bar diagram that can be used to find how many more miles Lon travels than Lucia to get to Jorge's house.

Student	Miles
Lucia	$5\frac{1}{2}$
Lon	$8\frac{2}{3}$
Sam	$12\frac{5}{6}$
Jamal	$2\frac{7}{9}$
Tye	$17\frac{13}{18}$

11. Tara bought a dozen folders. She took $\frac{1}{3}$ of the dozen and then divided the remaining folders equally among her four friends. What fraction of the dozen did each of her four friends receive? How many folders was this per person?

🔥 H.O.T. Problems

12. **Find the Error** Blake is finding $\frac{4}{5} \div \frac{6}{7}$. Find his mistake and correct it.

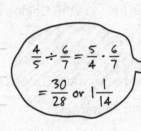

13. **Persevere with Problems** If $\frac{5}{6}$ is divided by a certain fraction $\frac{a}{b}$, the result is $\frac{1}{4}$. What is the fraction $\frac{a}{b}$? _____

14. **Reason Inductively** So far, the Rabun family has traveled 30 miles in $\frac{1}{2}$ hour. If it is currently 3:00 P.M. and their destination is 75 miles away from them, at what time will the Rabun family reach their destination? Explain how you solved the problem

Extra Practice

Divide. Write in simplest form.

15. $\frac{5}{9} \div \frac{5}{6} = \frac{2}{3}$

$$\frac{5}{9} \div \frac{5}{6} = \frac{5}{9} \times \frac{6}{5}$$

$$= \frac{\overset{1}{\cancel{5}}}{\underset{3}{\cancel{9}}} \times \frac{\overset{2}{\cancel{6}}}{\underset{1}{\cancel{5}}}$$

$$= \frac{1 \times 2}{3 \times 1}$$

$$= \frac{2}{3}$$

Homework Help

16. $-5\frac{2}{7} \div \left(-2\frac{1}{7}\right) =$ _____

17. $-5\frac{1}{5} \div \frac{2}{3} =$ _____

18. Vinh bought $4\frac{1}{2}$ gallons of ice cream to serve. If a pint is $\frac{1}{8}$ of a gallon, how many pint-sized servings can be made? _____

19. William has $8\frac{1}{4}$ cups of fruit juice. If he divides the juice into $\frac{3}{4}$-cup servings, how many servings will he have? _____

20. **MP** **Justify Conclusions** So far, a storm has traveled 35 miles in $\frac{1}{2}$ hour. If it is currently 5:00 P.M. and the storm is 105 miles away from you, at what time will the storm reach you? Explain how you solved the problem.

_____

_____

_____

21. Find $\dfrac{1\frac{2}{3}}{9} \div \dfrac{1\frac{1}{9}}{3}$. Write in simplest form. _____

22. **MP** **Use Math Tools** Write the letter of each statement below in the section of any operation to which the statement applies.

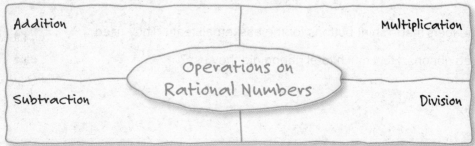

A Use a common denominator.

B Multiply by the multiplicative inverse.

C Write the result in simplest form.

23. Tracy has $94\frac{1}{4}$ inches of string that she uses for making bracelets. She uses $7\frac{1}{4}$ inches of string to make each bracelet. How many bracelets can Tracy make?

24. A grocery store offers 4 different size boxes of peanuts as shown below.

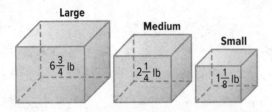

Write large, medium, or small in each box to make a true statement.

The [   ] box is 3 times larger than the [   ] box.

The [   ] box is 6 times larger than the [   ] box.

The [   ] box is 2 times larger than the [   ] box.

Spiral Review

Add or subtract. Write in simplest form.

25. $\frac{1}{5} + \frac{1}{4} =$ _____

26. $\frac{1}{3} - \frac{1}{6} =$ _____

27. $\frac{4}{9} + \frac{2}{7} =$ _____

28. $\frac{11}{15} - \frac{3}{20} =$ _____

29. The cheerleaders made spirit buttons for the basketball team. They used blue and red ribbons. How much total ribbon did they use?

Ribbon	
Blue	**Red**
$\frac{3}{8}$ ft	$\frac{3}{8}$ ft

30. How much longer is a $2\frac{1}{2}$-inch-long piece of string than a $\frac{2}{5}$-inch-long piece of string? _____

21ST CENTURY CAREER
in Fashion Design

Fashion Designer

Do you enjoy reading fashion magazines, keeping up with the latest trends, and creating your own unique sense of style? You might want to consider a career in fashion design. Fashion designers create new designs for clothing, accessories, and shoes. In addition to being creative and knowledgeable about current fashion trends, fashion designers need to be able to take accurate measurements and calculate fit by adding, subtracting, and dividing measurements.

Is This the Career for You?

Are you interested in a career as a fashion designer? Take some of the following courses in high school.

◆ Algebra
◆ Art
◆ Digital Design
◆ Geometry

Find out how math relates to a career in Fashion Design.

^{MP} A Flair for Fashion!

Use the information in the table to solve each problem. Write in simplest form.

1. For size 8, does Dress Style A or B require more fabric? Explain. _____

2. How many yards of fabric are needed to make Style A in sizes 8 and 14? _____

3. Estimate how many yards of fabric are needed to make Style B in each of the sizes shown. Then find the actual amount of fabric. _____

4. For Style B, how much more fabric is required for size 14 than for size 12? _____

5. A designer has half the amount of fabric needed to make Style A in size 10. How much fabric does she have? _____

6. A bolt has $12\frac{1}{8}$ yards of fabric left on it. How many dresses in Style B size 12 could be made? How much fabric is left over?

Amount of Fabric Needed (yards)				
Dress Style	Size 8	Size 10	Size 12	Size 14
A	$3\frac{3}{8}$	$3\frac{1}{2}$	$3\frac{3}{4}$	$3\frac{7}{8}$
B	$3\frac{1}{4}$	$3\frac{1}{2}$	$3\frac{7}{8}$	4

^{MP} Career Project

It's time to update your career portfolio! Use blogs and webpages of fashion designers to answer some of these questions: Where did they go to school? What was their first job? What do they say is the most difficult part about being a fashion designer? What inspires them to create their designs? What advice do they have for new designers?

_____

_____

_____

Suppose you are an employer hiring a fashion designer. What questions would you ask a potential employee?

- _____

- _____

Vocabulary Check

Unscramble each of the clue words. After unscrambling each of the terms, use the numbered letters to find a vocabulary term that relates to all of the other terms.

RAB TONNOTIA
☐☐☐ ☐☐☐☐☐☐☐☐
　　1　　　　　　7

TAMTINRINGE
☐☐☐☐☐☐☐☐☐☐☐
　　　　　　3

GIEPEATNR
☐☐☐☐☐☐☐☐☐
　　　　4

KIEL STAFCOIRN
☐☐☐☐☐ ☐☐☐☐☐☐☐☐
　　　　　　　　　5

LUKIEN
☐☐☐☐☐☐
　6　8

NOMMOC NIOAREOMNDT
☐☐☐☐☐☐ ☐☐☐☐☐☐☐☐☐☐☐
　　　　　　　　　　2

☐☐☐☐☐☐☐☐
1　2　3　4　5　6　7　8

Complete each sentence using one of the unscrambled words above.

1. The process of using a line over the repeating digits of a decimal is called _____.

2. Fractions with different denominators are called _____ fractions.

3. The least common multiple of the denominators is called the least _____.

4. The decimal form of a fraction is a(n) _____ decimal.

5. A _____ decimal is a decimal in which the repeating digit is zero.

6. Fractions with the same denominator are called _____.

Use Your FOLDABLES

Use your Foldable to help review the chapter.

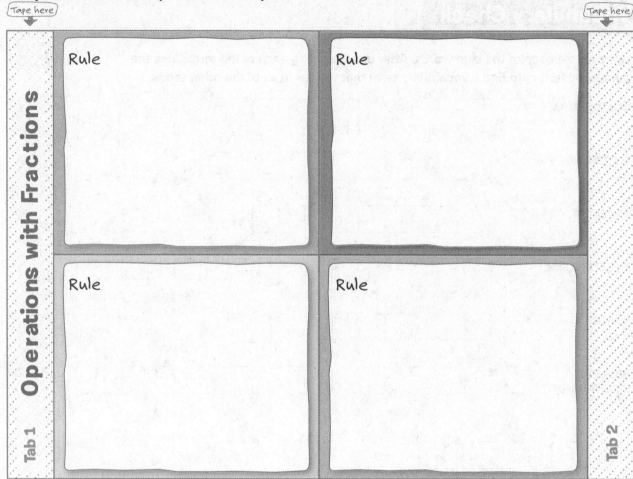

Tape here

Tape here

Operations with Fractions

Tab 1

Rule

Rule

Rule

Rule

Tab 2

Got it?

Circle the correct term or number to complete each sentence.

1. $\frac{1}{5}$ and $\left(\frac{1}{3}, \frac{3}{5}\right)$ are like fractions.

2. To add like fractions, add the (numerators, denominators).

3. To add unlike fractions, rename the fractions using the least common (numerator, denominator).

4. The reciprocal of $\frac{1}{3}$ is $(-3, 3)$.

5. To divide by a fraction, (multiply, divide) by its reciprocal.

6. The least common denominator of $\frac{1}{5}$ and $\frac{1}{10}$ is (10, 50).

Managing Money

Tamiko has recently started managing her own finances. She tracks her debts and income, as well as any gifts that she receives from her family members. Some of her recent transactions are listed below.

Transaction	Amount ($)
Borrowed money from a friend	43.75
Received a gift from Dad	50.00
Spent money on lunches	62.50
Received allowance	20.00

Write your answers on another piece of paper. Show all of your work to receive full credit.

Part A

What rational number represents the net result of the transactions shown in the table? Explain what your answer represents.

Part B

The following week, Tamiko receives a check for $109.60 for working at a local fast food restaurant and a small bonus check for $34.15. Determine the net result of her transactions using the result from Part A. She wants to save $\frac{3}{5}$ of this amount. How much will she save?

Part C

The next month, Tamiko develops a budget for her income. One-fourth of her income is budgeted for car insurance, $\frac{1}{10}$ of her income is budgeted for gasoline, $\frac{2}{5}$ of her income is budgeted for savings, and the remainder is budgeted for spending money. She earns $234.80 for working at the fast food restaurant, $64 for baby sitting, and $20 in allowance. According to her budget, how much of her total monthly income is allotted for spending money?

Reflect

Use what you learned about operations with rational numbers to complete the graphic organizer. Describe a process to perform each operation.

Add

Subtract

Essential Question

WHAT happens when you add, subtract, multiply, and divide fractions?

Multiply

Divide

Answer the Essential Question. WHAT happens when you add, subtract, multipy, and divide fractions?

_____

_____

Chapter 4
Expressions

HOW can you use numbers and symbols to represent mathematical ideas?

 Virginia Standards
7.1a, b, d; 7.11

 Math in the Real World

Meerkats live in burrows. Because meerkats have sharp claws, they are able to dig at a rate of 1 foot per second.

Suppose a meerkat digs for 3 seconds. Cross out the expression that does not represent the underground distance dug by the meerkat.

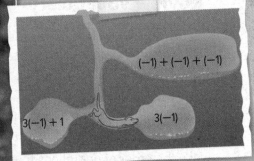

$(-1) + (-1) + (-1)$

$3(-1) + 1$

$3(-1)$

 FOLDABLES®
Study Organizer

1 Cut out the Foldable in the back of the book.

2 Place your Foldable on page 378.

3 Use the Foldable throughout this chapter to help you learn about percents.

Vocabulary

Additive Identity Property	Distributive Property	perfect cube
algebra	equivalent expressions	perfect square
algebraic expression	exponent	power
arithmetic sequence	factor	property
Associative Property	factored form	radical sign
base	linear expression	scientific notation
coefficient	monomial	sequence
Commutative Property	Multiplicative Identity	square root
counterexample	Property	term
cube root	Multiplicative Property	variable
define a variable	of Zero	

Review Vocabulary

Order of Operations The order of operations is a four-step process used to evaluate numerical expressions.

1. Evaluate the expressions inside grouping symbols.
2. Evaluate all powers.
3. Multiply and divide in order from left to right.
4. Add and subtract in order form left to right.

Use the order of operations to evaluate $3 + 5^2(4 + 4)$. Write each step in the organizer below.

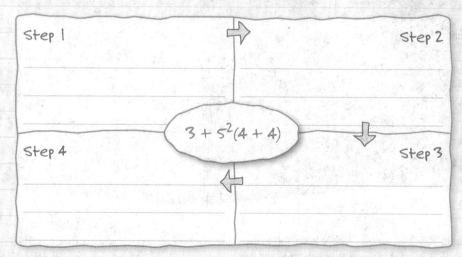

Read each statement. Decide whether you agree (A) or disagree (D). Place a checkmark in the appropriate column and then justify your reasoning.

	Expressions		
Statement	A	D	Why?
A power expresses a product of repeated factors.			
Scientific notation is when a number is written as the product of a factor and an integer power of 10.			
Squares of integers are called perfect squares.			
A property is an example that shows that a conjecture is false.			
When you use the Distributive Property to combine like terms, you are simplifying the expression.			
Equivalent expressions have the same value.			

When Will You Use This?

Here are a few examples of how expressions are used in the real world.

Activity 1 Do you or your parents have a texting plan? If so, how much does it cost per text or per month? Ask your parents to help you research different texting plans. Then compare and contrast each plan.

_____

_____

Activity 2 Go online at **connectED.mcgraw-hill.com** to read the graphic novel *Too Many Texts*. How many text messages are

included in Dario's texting plan? _____

Hiroshi, Caitlyn, and Dario in

Too Many Texts

Oh, NO! What's THIS going to cost me?

Your plan:
250 text messages
= $5.00

Messages sent to date:

275

Are You Ready?

Try the Quick Check below.
Or, take the Online Readiness Quiz.

 Check ✓

Quick Review

Example 1

Evaluate 2^5.

$$2^5 = 2 \cdot 2 \cdot 2 \cdot 2 \cdot 2$$
$$= 32$$

Example 2

Write $3 \cdot 3 \cdot 3 \cdot 3 \cdot 3 \cdot 3 \cdot 3$ in exponential form.

3 is the base. It is used as a factor 7 times. So, the exponent is 7.

$$3 \cdot 3 \cdot 3 \cdot 3 \cdot 3 \cdot 3 \cdot 3 = 3^7$$

Example 3

Find $4(-2)$.

$4(-2) = -8$ The integers have different signs. The product is negative.

Example 4

Find $-5(-8)$.

$-5(-8) = 40$ The integers have the same signs. The product is positive.

Quick Check

Exponents Evaluate each expression.

1. $2^4 = $ _____

2. $3^3 = $ _____

3. $4^2 = $ _____

 Show your work.

4. Write $4 \cdot 4 \cdot 4 \cdot 4$ in exponential form. _____

Integer Operations Multiply.

5. $5(-10) = $ _____

6. $-9(-4) = $ _____

7. $-5^2 = $ _____

 How Did You Do?

Which problems did you answer correctly in the Quick Check?
Shade those exercise numbers below.

① ② ③ ④ ⑤ ⑥ ⑦

Algebraic Expressions

Vocabulary Start-Up

A **variable** is a symbol that represents an unknown quantity. An **algebraic expression**, such as $n + 2$, is an expression that contains variables, numbers, and at least one operation.

$$\boxed{\text{Variable}} \cdots\!\!\rightarrow\ n + 2$$

Write each of the following phrases in the correct section of the Venn diagram: *contains an operation, has variables and numbers, has only numbers.*

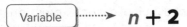

Characteristics of Expressions

numerical expression   algebraic expression

Essential Question

HOW can you use numbers and symbols to represent mathematical ideas?

Vocabulary

variable
algebraic expression
algebra
coefficient
define a variable

 Virginia Standards
7.11

Real-World Link

The expression $(F - 32) \times \frac{5}{9}$ can be used to convert a temperature from Fahrenheit to Celsius. In this algebraic expression, the variable _____ represents the temperature in degrees Fahrenheit.

Brrr...!

Which MP Mathematical Process Goals did you use? Shade the circle(s) that applies.

① Mathematical Problem Solving   ④ Mathematical Connections

② Mathematical Communication   ⑤ Mathematical Representations

③ Mathematical Reasoning

Evaluate an Algebraic Expression

The branch of mathematics that involves expressions with variables is called **algebra**. In algebra, the multiplication sign is often omitted.

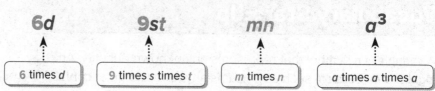

6d	9st	mn	a^3
6 times d	9 times s times t	m times n	a times a times a

The numerical factor of a multiplication expression that contains a variable is called a **coefficient**. So, 6 is the coefficient of 6d.

Expressions like $\frac{y}{2}$ can be written as $y \div 2$ or $y \times \frac{1}{2}$.

Order of Operations

1. Evaluate the expressions inside grouping symbols.
2. Evaluate all powers.
3. Multiply and divide in order from left to right.
4. Add and subtract in order from left to right.

Examples

Watch | Tutor

1. Evaluate $2(n + 3)$ if $n = -4$.

$$2(n + 3) = 2(-4 + 3) \quad \text{Replace } n \text{ with } -4.$$
$$= 2(-1) \quad \text{Evaluate inside the parentheses.}$$
$$= -2 \quad \text{Multiply.}$$

2. Evaluate $8w - 2v$ if $w = 5$ and $v = 3$.

$$8w - 2v = 8(5) - 2(3) \quad \text{Replace } w \text{ with 5 and } v \text{ with 3.}$$
$$= 40 - 6 \quad \text{Do all of the multiplication first.}$$
$$= 34 \quad \text{Subtract 6 from 40.}$$

3. Evaluate $4y^3 + 2$ if $y = 3$.

$$4y^3 + 2 = 4(3)^3 + 2 \quad \text{Replace } y \text{ with 3.}$$
$$= 4(27) + 2 \quad \text{Evaluate the power.}$$
$$= 110 \quad \text{Multiply, then add.}$$

Got It? Do these problems to find out.

Evaluate each expression if $c = 8$ and $d = -5$.

a. $c - 3$ **b.** $15 - c$ **c.** $3(c + d)$

d. $2c - 4d$ **e.** $d - c^2$ **f.** $2d^2 + 5d$

Show your work.

a. _____

b. _____

c. _____

d. _____

e. _____

f. _____

Example

Tutor

4. Athletic trainers use the formula $\dfrac{3(220-a)}{5}$, where a is a person's age, to find their minimum training heart rate. Find Latrina's minimum training heart rate if she is 15 years old.

Fractions
The fraction bar is a grouping symbol. Evaluate the expressions in the numerator and denominator separately before dividing.

$$\dfrac{3(220-a)}{5} = \dfrac{3(220-15)}{5}$$ Replace a with 15.

$$= \dfrac{3(205)}{5}$$ Subtract 15 from 220.

$$= \dfrac{615}{5}$$ Multiply 3 and 205.

$$= 123$$ Divide 615 by 5.

Latrina's minimum training heart rate is 123 beats per minute.

Got It? Do this problem to find out.

g. To find the area of a triangle, use the formula $\dfrac{bh}{2}$, where b is the base and h is the height. What is the area in square inches of a triangle with a height of 6 inches and base of 8 inches?

Show your work.

g. _____

Write Expressions

To translate a verbal phrase into an algebraic expression, the first step is to define a variable. When you **define a variable**, you choose a variable to represent an unknown quantity.

Examples

Tutor

5. Marisa wants to buy a DVD player that costs $150. She already saved $25 and plans to save an additional $10 each week. Write an expression that represents the total amount of money Marisa has saved after any number of weeks.

Words	savings of $25 plus ten dollars each week
Variable	Let w represent the number of weeks.
Expression	25 + 10 · w

$25 + 10w$ represents the total saved after any number of weeks.

6. Refer to Example 5. Will Marisa have saved enough money to buy the $150 DVD player in 11 weeks? Use the expression $25 + 10w$.

$$25 + 10w = 25 + 10(11) \quad \text{Replace } w \text{ with 11.}$$
$$= 25 + 110 \quad \text{Multiply.}$$
$$= 135 \quad \text{Add.}$$

Marisa will have saved $135 after 11 weeks. Since $135 < $150, Marisa will not have enough money to buy the DVD player.

Got It? Do this problem to find out.

Show your work.

h. _____

h. An MP3 player costs $70 and song downloads cost $0.85 each. Write an expression that represents the cost of the MP3 player and x number of downloaded songs. Then find the total cost if 20 songs are downloaded.

Guided Practice

Check ✓

Show your work.

Evaluate each expression if $m = 2$, $n = 6$, and $p = -4$. (Examples 1–4)

1. $3m + 4p$ _____

2. $n^2 + 5$ _____

3. $6p^3$ _____

4. A Web site charges $0.99 to download a game and a $12.49 membership fee. Write an expression that gives the total cost in dollars to download g games. Then find the cost of downloading 6 games. (Examples 5 and 6)

_____

5. @ **Building on the Essential Question** Tell whether the statement below is *sometimes*, *always*, or *never* true. Justify your reasoning.

The expressions $x - 3$ and $y - 3$ represent the same value.

_____

_____

Independent Practice

Go online for Step-by-Step Solutions eHelp

Evaluate each expression if $d = 8$, $e = 3$, $f = 4$, and $g = -1$. (Examples 1 – 3)

1. $2(d + 9)$ _____

 Show your work.

2. $\dfrac{d}{4}$ _____

3. $\dfrac{ef}{4}$ _____

4. $4f + d$ _____

5. $\dfrac{5d - 25}{5}$ _____

6. $d^2 + 7$ _____

7. $\dfrac{d - 4}{2}$ _____

8. $10(e + 7)$ _____

9. $\dfrac{2g}{2}$ _____

10. The expression $5n + 2$ can be used to find the total cost in dollars of bowling where n is the number of games bowled and 2 represents the cost of shoe rental. How much will it cost Vincent to bowl 3 games? (Example 4)

_____

11. **MP** **Reason Abstractly** A car rental company's fees are shown. Suppose you rent a car using Option 2. Write an expression that gives the total cost in dollars for driving m miles. Then find the cost for driving 150 miles. (Examples 5 and 6)

_____

Car Rental Prices	
Option 1	**Option 2**
$19.99 per day	$50 fee
$0.17 per mi	$0.17 per mi

12. Refer to Exercise 11. Suppose you rent a car using Option 1. Write an expression that gives the total cost in dollars to rent a car for d days and m miles. Then find the cost for renting a car for 2 days and driving 70 miles. (Examples 5 and 6)

_____

Evaluate each expression if $x = 3.2$, $y = 6.1$, and $z = 0.2$.

13. $x + y - z$ _____

14. $14.6 - (x + y + z)$ _____

15. $xz + y^2$ _____

 H.O.T. Problems Higher Order Thinking

16. **MP Reason Abstractly** Write an algebraic expression with the variable x that has a value of 3 when evaluated.

_____

17. **MP Model with Mathematics** Write a real-world problem that can be represented by the expression $5x + 10$.

_____

_____

_____

18. **MP Persevere with Problems** To find the total number of diagonals for any given polygon, you can use the expression $\frac{n(n-3)}{2}$, where n is the number of sides of the polygon.

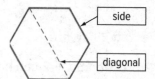

a. Determine the minimum value that n could be. _____

b. Make a table of four possible values of n. Then complete the table by evaluating the expression for each value of n.

c. Check by drawing the diagonals of a pentagon and counting the diagonals.

n	value

19. **MP Persevere with Problems** Franco constructed the objects below using toothpicks.

Figure 1

Figure 2

Figure 3

Write two different rules that relate the figure number to the number of toothpicks in each figure.

_____

Extra Practice

Evaluate each expression if $d = 8$, $e = 3$, $f = 4$, and $g = -1$.

20. $10 - e$ 7

$10 - e$

$10 - 3 = 7$

Homework Help →

21. $\dfrac{16}{f}$ 4

$\dfrac{16}{f}$

$\dfrac{16}{4} = 4$

22. $4e^2$ _____

23. $8g - f$ _____

24. $\dfrac{(5 + g)^2}{2}$ _____

25. $e^2 - 4$ _____

26. The expression $\dfrac{w}{30}$, where w is a person's weight in pounds, is used to find the approximate number of quarts of blood in the person's body. How many quarts of blood does a 120-pound person have?

_____

27. **MP Model with Mathematics** Refer to the graphic novel frame below. Let n represent the number of text messages. Evaluate the expression

$0.15(n - 250) + 5$ to find the cost of 275 text messages. _____

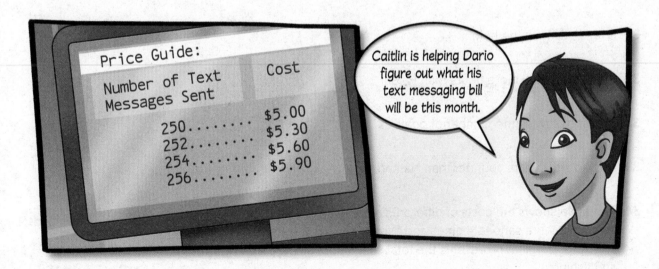

Power Up! Test Practice

28. Tonya has x quarters, y dimes, and z nickels in her pocket. Select the appropriate operations to complete the expression that represents the total amount of change Tonya has in her pocket.

×	÷
+	−

($0.25 ☐ x) ☐ ($0.1 ☐ y) ☐ ($0.05 ☐ z)

Evaluate the expression for $x = 3$, $y = 5$, and $z = 2$. What does this value represent?

☐

29. The prices of magazines and books at the school book fair are shown in the table. Determine if each statement is true or false.

School Book Fair Prices	
Item	**Cost**
Magazines	$4.95
Paperback books	$7.95

  a. The expression $7.95b + 4.95m$ represents the cost of buying b books and m magazines. ☐ True ☐ False

  b. The expression $12.90(b + m)$ represents the cost of buying b books and m magazines. ☐ True ☐ False

  c. The total cost of buying 3 books and 4 magazines is $43.65. ☐ True ☐ False

Spiral Review

Define a variable and write each phrase as an algebraic expression.

30. 8 feet less than the height _____

31. Sarah worked 8 more hours than Paida. _____

32. Kumar has twice the number of goals as Jacob. _____

33. Addison is 3 years younger than Nathan. _____

34. The table shows the costs of different camping activities. Over the summer, Maura canoed 4 times and fished 3 times. Write and evaluate an expression that represents the total cost Maura spent canoeing and fishing.

Camping Activity Costs	
Activity	**Cost**
Canoeing	$8
Fishing	$5

Vocabulary Start-Up

A **sequence** is an ordered list of numbers. Each number in a sequence is called a **term**. In an **arithmetic sequence**, each term is found by adding the same number to the previous term.

Complete the graphic organizer below.

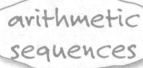

arithmetic sequences

Numbers

Continue each sequence.

1, 3, 5, 7, ☐ , ...

1, 1.5, 2, ☐ , ☐ , ☐ , ...

Words

Describe each sequence.

Add ☐ to the previous term.

Essential Question

HOW can you use numbers and symbols to represent mathematical ideas?

Vocabulary

sequence
term
arithmetic sequence

Real-World Link

Horseback Riding The number of students who went on each horseback riding trip is shown. Do the numbers represent the terms of an arithmetic sequence? Explain.

Trip	1	2	3	4	5
Number of Students	15	16	18	21	25

Which **MP** **Mathematical Process Goals** did you use? Shade the circle(s) that applies.

① Mathematical Problem Solving   ④ Mathematical Connections

② Mathematical Communication   ⑤ Mathematical Representations

③ Mathematical Reasoning

Describe and Extend Sequences

In an arithmetic sequence, the terms can be whole numbers, fractions, or decimals.

Examples

Tutor

1. Describe the relationship between the terms in the arithmetic sequence 8, 13, 18, 23, ... Then write the next three terms in the sequence.

$$8, \quad 13, \quad 18, \quad 23, ...$$
$$+5 \quad +5 \quad +5$$

Each term is found by adding 5 to the previous term.

Continue the pattern to find the next three terms.

$$23 + 5 = 28 \qquad 28 + 5 = 33 \qquad 33 + 5 = 38$$

The next three terms are 28, 33, and 38.

2. Describe the relationship between the terms in the arithmetic sequence 0.4, 0.6, 0.8, 1.0, ... Then write the next three terms in the sequence.

$$0.4, \quad 0.6, \quad 0.8, \quad 1.0, ...$$
$$+0.2 \quad +0.2 \quad +0.2$$

Each term is found by adding 0.2 to the previous term.

Continue the pattern to find the next three terms.

$$1.0 + 0.2 = 1.2 \qquad 1.2 + 0.2 = 1.4 \qquad 1.4 + 0.2 = 1.6$$

The next three terms are 1.2, 1.4, and 1.6.

Got It? Do these problems to find out.

Describe the relationship between the terms in each arithmetic sequence. Then write the next three terms in the sequence.

a. 0, 13, 26, 39, ...   b. 4, 7, 10, 13, ...

c. 1.0, 1.3, 1.6, 1.9, ...   d. 2.5, 3.0, 3.5, 4.0, ...

Show your work.

a. _____

b. _____

c. _____

d. _____

Write an Algebraic Expression

In a sequence, each term has a specific position within the sequence. Consider the sequence 2, 4, 6, 8,...

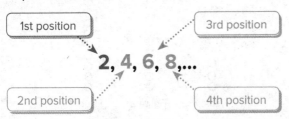

Notice that as the position number increases by 1, the value of the term increases by 2.

Position	Operation	Value of Term
1	$1 \cdot 2 = 2$	2
2	$2 \cdot 2 = 4$	4
3	$3 \cdot 2 = 6$	6
4	$4 \cdot 2 = 8$	8

+1 on positions, +2 on values of term

You can also write an algebraic expression to represent the relationship between any term in a sequence and its position in the sequence. In this case, if n represents the position in the sequence, the value of the term is $2n$.

Arithmetic Sequences

When looking for a pattern between the position number and each term in the sequence, it is often helpful to make a table.

Example

  Tutor

3. The greeting cards that Meredith makes are sold in boxes at a gift store. The first week, the store sold 5 boxes. Each week, the store sells five more boxes. The pattern continues. What algebraic expression can be used to find the total number of boxes sold at the end of the 100th week? What is the total?

Position	Operation	Value of Term
1	$1 \cdot 5$	5
2	$2 \cdot 5$	10
3	$3 \cdot 5$	15
n	$n \cdot 5$	$5n$

Each term is 5 times its position. So, the expression is $5n$.

$5n$ Write the expression.

$5(100) = 500$ Replace n with 100.

At the end of 100 weeks, 500 boxes will have been sold.

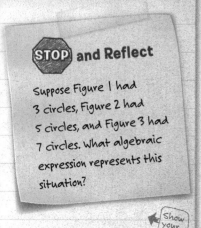

STOP and Reflect

Suppose Figure 1 had 3 circles, Figure 2 had 5 circles, and Figure 3 had 7 circles. What algebraic expression represents this situation?

Show your work.

e. If the pattern continues, what algebraic expression can be used to find the number of circles used in any figure? How many circles will be in the 50th figure?

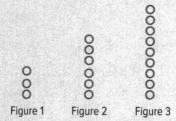

Figure 1   Figure 2   Figure 3

e. _____

Guided Practice

Check ✓

Describe the relationship between the terms in each arithmetic sequence. Then write the next three terms in each sequence. (Examples 1 and 2)

Show your work.

1. 0, 9, 18, 27, ...

2. 4, 9, 14, 19, ...

3. 1, 1.1, 1.2, 1.3, ...

4. Hannah has a doll collection. The table shows the total number of dolls in her collection for three years. Suppose this pattern continues. Write an algebraic expression to find the number of dolls in her collection after n years. How many dolls will Hannah have after 25 years? (Example 3)

Year	Number of Dolls
1	6
2	12
3	18

5. **Building on the Essential Question** Explain why the following sequence is considered an arithmetic sequence.

5, 9, 13, 17, 21,...

Rate Yourself!

How confident are you about sequences? Check the box that applies.

For more help, go online to access a Personal Tutor.

Tutor

Independent Practice

Go online for Step-by-Step Solutions

Describe the relationship between the terms in each arithmetic sequence. Then write the next three terms in each sequence. (Examples 1 and 2)

1. 0, 7, 14, 21, ...

 Show your work.

_____

_____

2. 1, 7, 13, 19, ...

_____

_____

3 26, 34, 42, 50, ...

_____

_____

4. 0.1, 0.4, 0.7, 1.0, ...

_____

_____

5. 2.4, 3.2, 4.0, 4.8, ...

_____

_____

6. 2.0, 3.1, 4.2, 5.3, ...

_____

_____

7 Refer to the table shown. If the pattern continues, what algebraic expression can be used to find the plant's height for any month? What will be the plant's height at 12 months? (Example 3)

_____

Month	Height (in.)
1	3
2	6
3	9

8. **MP** **Model with Mathematics** Explain how the number of text messages Dario sent and the cost form an arithmetic sequence. Then write an expression to find Dario's text messaging bill if he sends *n* text messages over 250.

_____

_____

9. **MP Multiple Representations** Kendra is stacking boxes of tissues for a store display. She stacks 3 boxes in the first minute, 6 boxes by the end of the second minute, and 9 boxes by the end of the third minute. Suppose the pattern continues for parts **a–d**.

a. **Table** Make a table of values for 1, 2, 3, 4, and 5 minutes.

b. **Symbols** Write an expression to find the *n*th term in the sequence.

c. **Graph** Graph the table of values from part **a** on the coordinate plane. Let *x* represent the number of minutes and *y* represent the number of boxes. Then describe the graph.

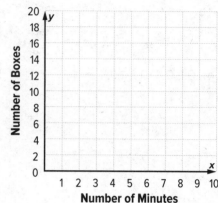

d. **Numbers** How many boxes will be displayed after 45 minutes?

🔥 H.O.T. Problems Higher Order Thinking

10. **MP Justify Conclusions** Write five terms of an arithmetic sequence and describe the rule for finding the terms.

MP Persevere with Problems Not all sequences are arithmetic. But, there is still a pattern. Describe the relationship between the terms in each sequence. Then write the next three terms in the sequence.

11. 1, 2, 4, 7, 11, ...

12. 0, 2, 6, 12, 20, ...

13. **MP Persevere with Problems** Use an arithmetic sequence to find the number of multiples of 6 between 41 and 523. Justify your reasoning.

Extra Practice

Describe the relationship between the terms in each arithmetic sequence. Then write the next three terms in each sequence.

14. 19, 31, 43, 55, ...

12 is added to the previous term; 67, 79, 91

15. 6, 16, 26, 36, ...

10 is added to the previous term; 46, 56, 66

16. 33, 38, 43, 48, ...

_____

ework
elp

17. 4.5, 6.0, 7.5, 9.0, ...

_____

_____

18. 1.2, 3.2, 5.2, 7.2, ...

_____

_____

19. 4.6, 8.6, 12.6, 16.6, ...

_____

_____

20. 18, 33, 48, 63, ...

_____

_____

21. 20, 45, 70, 95, ...

_____

_____

22. 38, 61, 84, 107, ...

_____

_____

23. **MP** **Reason Abstractly**   Refer to the figures for parts **a** and **b.**

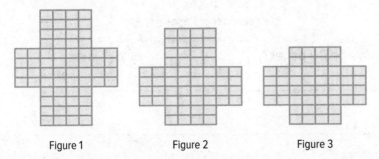

Figure 1   Figure 2   Figure 3

a. Describe the relationship between the figures and the number of

rectangles shown. _____

b. If the pattern continues, how many rectangles will be in the next

2 figures? _____

The terms of an arithmetic sequence can be related by subtraction. Write the next three terms of each sequence.

24. 32, 27, 22, 17, ...

_____

25. 45, 42, 39, 36, ...

_____

26. 10.5, 10, 9.5, 9, ...

_____

27. The table shows the first 5 terms of a sequence. Determine if each statement is true or false.

Position	1	2	3	4	5	n
Value of Term	2	5	10	17	26	■

  a. The expression $n^2 + 1$ can be used to find the nth term of the sequence.   ☐ True   ☐ False

  b. The 8th term of the sequence is 65.   ☐ True   ☐ False

  c. The table represents an arithmetic sequence.   ☐ True   ☐ False

28. Katie is putting photos in an album. She puts five pictures on the first page. Each page after that contains five pictures. Suppose the pattern continues. Complete the table of values for 1, 2, 3, 4, and 5 pages. Then graph the table of values on the coordinate plane. Let x represent the number of pages and y represent the total number of photos.

Number of Pages	Total Photos
1	
2	
3	
4	
5	

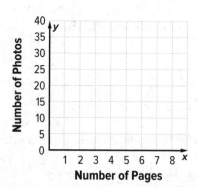

How many photos will Katie have on 20 pages? ☐

Spiral Review

Evaluate.

29. $1^4 =$ _____

30. $3^3 =$ _____

31. $8^2 =$ _____

32. $10^4 =$ _____

33. $5^1 =$ _____

34. $7^5 =$ _____

35. Jayden goes to the batting cage. He purchases three tokens and rents a helmet. If he spends a total of $6.50, how much is each token?

Batting Cage Prices	
Tokens	■
Helmet Rental	$2

_____

Inquiry HOW can geometric figures be used to model numerical patterns?

A fencing company uses 4 planks of wood for one section of fencing, 7 planks for two sections, and 10 planks of wood for three sections. The fence sections are represented using the toothpicks shown. Determine how many planks would be used to create 5 sections of fencing.

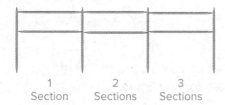

1	2	3
Section	Sections	Sections

Hands-On Activity

Step 1 Find a pattern in the table. Then fill in the number of planks that would be in 4 and 5 sections of fencing.

Number of Sections	Number of Planks
1	4
2	7
3	10
4	
5	

Step 2 Check your work by using toothpicks to show 5 fence sections. Draw the result in the space below.

So, there will be [   ] planks in 5 sections of fencing.

Investigate

Work with a partner. Complete the table. You can use toothpicks to continue each pattern if needed.

1.

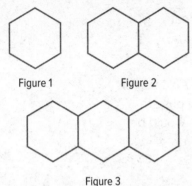

Figure 1   Figure 2

Figure 3

Figure Number	Number of Toothpicks
1	6
2	11
3	16
4	
5	

2. Refer to Exercise 1. Write an expression that could be used to find the number of toothpicks that would be needed for any figure.

_____

3. Use your expression from Exercise 2 to find the number of toothpicks that would be needed to create Figure 10. Explain.

_____

_____

Create

On Your Own

4. **MP Reason Abstractly** Refer to the activity. Write an expression that could be used to find the number of planks in any number of sections.

_____

5. **MP Justify Conclusions** Use the expression in Exercise 4 to find the number of planks that would be needed to create 10 sections of fencing. Explain.

_____

_____

6. **Inquiry** HOW can geometric figures be used to model numerical patterns?

_____

_____

_____

Properties of Operations

Real-World Link

Driving Miss Ricardo drives up and down her street to complete different errands. Some of the places on her street are shown below. The number of blocks between the places are also shown.

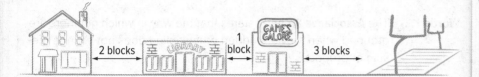

2 blocks | 1 block | 3 blocks

1. Suppose Miss Ricardo drives from home to the game store and back. Write an expression for each distance.

   from home to
   the game store: _____

   from the game
   store to home: _____

2. Circle the property that is illustrated in Exercise 1.

   Commutative   Associative

3. On Monday, Miss Ricardo drives from home, stops at the library, and then drives to the football field. On Tuesday, she drives from home, stops at the game store, and then drives to the football field. Write an expression for each distance.

   Monday: _____   Tuesday: _____

4. Circle the property that is illustrated in Exercise 3.

   Commutative   Associative

Essential Question

HOW can you use numbers and symbols to represent mathematical ideas?

Vocabulary

Commutative Property
Associative Property
property
Additive Identity Property
Multiplicative Identity Property
Multiplicative Property of Zero
counterexample

Which MP Mathematical Process Goals did you use? Shade the circle(s) that applies.

① Mathematical Problem Solving
② Mathematical Communication
③ Mathematical Reasoning
④ Mathematical Connections
⑤ Mathematical Representations

Properties of Operations

Watch

Words	The **Commutative Property** states that the order in which numbers are added or multiplied does not change the sum or product.

	Addition	Multiplication
Symbols	$a + b = b + a$	$a \cdot b = b \cdot a$
Examples	$6 + 1 = 1 + 6$	$7 \cdot 3 = 3 \cdot 7$

Words	The **Associative Property** states that the way in which numbers are grouped when they are added or multiplied does not change the sum or product.

	Addition	Multiplication
Symbols	$a + (b + c) = (a + b) + c$	$a \cdot (b \cdot c) = (a \cdot b) \cdot c$
Examples	$2 + (3 + 8) = (2 + 3) + 8$	$3 \cdot (4 \cdot 5) = (3 \cdot 4) \cdot 5$

A **property** is a statement that is true for any number. The following properties are also true for any numbers.

Property	Words	Symbols	Examples
Additive Identity	When 0 is added to any number, the sum is the number.	$a + 0 = a$ $0 + a = a$	$9 + 0 = 9$ $0 + 9 = 9$
Multiplicative Identity	When any number is multiplied by 1, the product is the number.	$a \cdot 1 = a$ $1 \cdot a = a$	$5 \cdot 1 = 5$ $1 \cdot 5 = 5$
Multiplicative Property of Zero	When any number is multiplied by 0, the product is 0.	$a \cdot 0 = 0$ $0 \cdot a = 0$	$8 \cdot 0 = 0$ $0 \cdot 8 = 0$

Example

Tutor

1. **Name the property shown by the statement $2 \cdot (5 \cdot n) = (2 \cdot 5) \cdot n$.**

The order of the numbers and variable did not change, but their grouping did. This is the Associative Property of Multiplication.

Got It? **Do these problems to find out.**

a. $42 + x + y = 42 + y + x$ **b.** $3x + 0 = 3x$

a. _____

b. _____

Show your work.

You may wonder if any of the properties apply to subtraction or division. If you can find a **counterexample**, an example that shows that a conjecture is false, the property does not apply.

Example

2. **State whether the following conjecture is *true* or *false*. If *false*, provide a counterexample.**

   Division of whole numbers is commutative.

   Write two division expressions using the Commutative Property.

   $15 \div 3 \overset{?}{=} 3 \div 15$ State the conjecture.

   $5 \neq \dfrac{1}{5}$ Divide.

   The conjecture is false. We found a counterexample. That is, $15 \div 3 \neq 3 \div 15$. So, division is *not* commutative.

Got It? Do this problem to find out.

c. The difference of two different whole numbers is always less than both of the two numbers.

Show your work.

c. _____

Example

3. **Alana wants to buy a sweater that costs $38, sunglasses that costs $14, a pair of jeans that costs $22, and a T-shirt that costs $16. Use mental math to find the total cost before tax.**

   Write an expression for the total cost. You can rearrange the numbers using the properties of math. Look for sums that are multiples of ten.

   $38 + 14 + 22 + 16$

   $= 38 + 22 + 14 + 16$ Commutative Property of Addition

   $= (38 + 22) + (14 + 16)$ Associative Property of Addition

   $= 60 + 30$ Add.

   $= 90$ Simplify.

   The total cost of the items is $90.

Got It? Do this problem to find out.

Show your work.

d. Lance made four phone calls from his cell phone today. The calls lasted 4.7, 9.4, 2.3, and 10.6 minutes. Use mental math to find the total amount of time he spent on the phone.

d. _____

Examples

Simplify each expression. Justify each step.

4. $(7 + g) + 5$

$(7 + g) + 5 = (g + 7) + 5$	Commutative Property of Addition
$= g + (7 + 5)$	Associative Property of Addition
$= g + 12$	Simplify.

5. $(m \cdot 11) \cdot m$

$(m \cdot 11) \cdot m = (11 \cdot m) \cdot m$	Commutative Property of Multiplication
$= 11 \cdot (m \cdot m)$	Associative Property of Multiplication
$= 11m^2$	Simplify.

Show your work.

Got It? Do this problem to find out.

e. _____

e. $4 \cdot (3c \cdot 2)$

Guided Practice

Check ✓

Name the property shown by each statement. (Example 1)

1. $3m \cdot 0 \cdot 5m = 0$ _____

2. $7c + 0 = 7c$ _____

3. State whether the following conjecture is *true* or *false*. If *false*, provide a counterexample. (Example 2)

Subtraction of whole numbers is associative.

_____

4. Simplify $9c + (8 + 3c)$. Justify each step. (Examples 3–5)

_____

_____

_____

5. 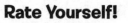 **Building on the Essential Question** Explain the difference between the Commutative and Associative

Properties. _____

_____

_____

Rate Yourself!

Are you ready to move on? Shade the section that applies.

YES ? NO

For more help, go online to access a Personal Tutor.

Tutor

Independent Practice

Go online for Step-by-Step Solutions

Name the property shown by each statement. (Example 1)

1. $a + (b + 12) = (b + 12) + a$

_____

2. $(5 + x) + 0 = 5 + x$

_____

3. $16 + (c + 17) = (16 + c) + 17$

_____

4. $d \cdot e \cdot 0 = 0$

_____

5. **MP Use a Counterexample** State whether the conjecture is *true* or *false*. If *false*, provide a counterexample. (Example 2)

Division of whole numbers is associative.

_____

6. Darien ordered a soda for $2.75, a sandwich for $8.50, and a dessert for $3.85. Sales tax was $1.15. Use mental math to

find the total amount of the bill. Explain. (Example 3) _____

_____

_____

Simplify each expression. Justify each step. (Examples 4 and 5)

7. $15 + (12 + 8a)$

_____

_____

_____

_____

8. $(5n \cdot 9) \cdot 2n$

_____

_____

_____

_____

9. $3x \cdot (7 \cdot x)$

_____

_____

_____

_____

_____

10. $(4m \cdot 2) \cdot 5m$

_____

_____

_____

_____

_____

11. Simplify the expression $(7 + 47 + 3)[5 \cdot (2 \cdot 3)]$. Use properties to justify each step.

12. 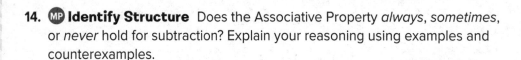 **Model with Mathematics** Write about something you do every day that is commutative. Then write about another situation that is not commutative.

13. **Find the Error** Blake is simplifying $4 \cdot (5 \cdot m)$. Find his mistake and correct it.

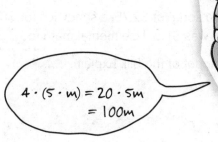

$$4 \cdot (5 \cdot m) = 20 \cdot 5m$$
$$= 100m$$

14. **Identify Structure** Does the Associative Property *always*, *sometimes*, or *never* hold for subtraction? Explain your reasoning using examples and counterexamples.

15. **Persevere with Problems** If you take any two whole numbers and add them together, the sum is always a whole number. This is the Closure Property for Addition. The set of whole numbers is *closed* under addition.

a. Is the set of whole numbers closed under subtraction? If not, give a counterexample.

b. Suppose you had a very small set of numbers that contained only 0 and 1. Would this set be closed under addition? If not, give a counterexample.

Extra Practice

Name the property shown by each statement.

16. $9(ab) = (9a)b$

Associative (×)

17. $y \cdot 7 = 7y$

_____

18. $1 \times c = c$

_____

19. $5 + (a + 8) = (5 + a) + 8$

_____

20. State whether the conjecture is *true* or *false*. If *false*, provide a counterexample.

Subtraction of whole numbers is commutative.

_____

21. 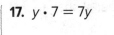 **Use Math Tools** The times for each leg of a relay for four runners are shown. Use mental math to find the total time for the relay team. Explain.

_____

_____

Runner	Time (s)
Jamal	12.4
Kenneth	11.8
Bryce	11.2
Jorge	12.6

Simplify each expression. Justify each step.

22. $(22 + 19b) + 7$

_____

_____

23. $18 + (5 + 6m)$

_____

_____

24. $11s(4)$

_____

_____

25. $10y(7)$

_____

_____

26. $(9 + 31 + 5)[(7 \cdot 5) \cdot 4]$

_____

_____

_____

27. The table shows the cost of different items at a bakery. Yolanda buys 2 doughnuts, a muffin, and 2 cookies. Which of the following expressions represents the total cost? Select all that apply.

☐ $2(2.29) + 2(2.21) + 2.50$

☐ $2(2.29) + 2.50 + 2(2.21)$

☐ $2(2.29 + 2.21 + 2.50)$

☐ $2.50 + 2(2.21 + 2.29)$

Item	Cost ($)
Cookie	2.21
Doughnut	2.29
Muffin	2.50
Roll	1.15

28. Determine if the two expressions in each pair are equivalent. If they are equivalent, select the property that is illustrated.

Commutative Property

Identity Property

Associative Property

Multiplicative Property of Zero

	Equivalent?	Property
$9 \cdot 4 \div 20 = 9 \cdot 20 \div 4$		
$3b \cdot 0 \cdot c = 0$		
$35 + 2m + n = 35 + n + 2m$		
$12t \cdot 3v + 0 = 12t \cdot 3v$		

Spiral Review

Evaluate each expression if $a = 6$, $b = 15$, and $c = 9$.

29. $a + 2b$ _____

30. $c^2 - 5$ _____

31. $10 + a^3$ _____

32. $8c - 9 + 25$ _____

33. $14 + 8b \div 2$ _____

34. $3^3 \div (3a)$ _____

35. A package of pencils costs $1.25. A new eraser costs $0.45. Write an expression to find the total cost of 3 packages of pencils and 2 erasers. Then find the total cost.

_____

The Distributive Property

 ## Real-World Link

School Supplies Jordan buys three notebooks that cost $5 each. He also buys three packages of pens for $6 each.

Essential Question

HOW can you use numbers and symbols to represent mathematical ideas?

Vocab

Vocabulary

Distributive Property
equivalent expressions

1. Write an expression that shows the cost of three notebooks added to the cost of three packages of pens.

   $\boxed{} \cdot 5 + \boxed{} \cdot 6$

2. Write an expression that shows three times the cost of one notebook and one package of pens.

   $\boxed{} \left(\boxed{} + \boxed{} \right)$

3. Evaluate both expressions. What do you notice?

4. Suppose Jordan buys five notebooks that cost $3 each and five packages of pens that cost $1 each. Circle the expressions that represent Jordan's purchases.

   $5 \cdot 3 + 5 \cdot 1$ $5 \cdot 3 \cdot 5 \cdot 1$ $5(3 + 1)$

5. Suppose Jordan buys two rulers that cost $1 each and two folders that cost $1.50 each. Circle the expressions that represent Jordan's purchases.

   $2 + 1 + 2 + 1.50$ $2(1 + 1.50)$ $2 \cdot 1 + 2 \cdot 1.50$

 Which **MP** **Mathematical Process Goals** did you use? Shade the circle(s) that applies.

① Mathematical Problem Solving   ④ Mathematical Connections

② Mathematical Communication   ⑤ Mathematical Representations

③ Mathematical Reasoning

Use the Distributive Property

Watch Tools

Work Zone

Words The **Distributive Property** states that to multiply a sum or difference by a number, multiply each term inside the parentheses by the number outside the parentheses.

Symbols $a(b + c) = ab + ac$ $a(b - c) = ab - ac$

Examples $4(6 + 2) = 4 \cdot 6 + 4 \cdot 2$ $3(7 - 5) = 3 \cdot 7 - 3 \cdot 5$

You can model the Distributive Property with algebraic expressions using algebra tiles. The expression $2(x + 2)$ is modeled below.

Model $x + 2$ using algebra tiles.

Double the amount of tiles to represent $2(x + 2)$.

Rearrange the tiles by grouping together the ones with the same shapes.

$$2(x + 2) = 2(x) + 2(2) \quad \text{Distributive Property}$$
$$= 2x + 4 \quad \text{Multiply.}$$

The expressions $2(x + 2)$ and $2x + 4$ are **equivalent expressions**. No matter what x is, these expressions have the same value.

Example

Tutor

Show your work.

1. Use the Distributive Property to evaluate $8(-9 + 4)$.

$$8(-9 + 4) = 8(-9) + 8(4) \quad \text{Expand using the Distributive Property.}$$
$$= -72 + 32 \text{ or } -40 \quad \text{Multiply. Then add.}$$

Got It? Do these problems to find out.

a. _____

b. _____

c. _____

a. $5(-9 + 11)$ **b.** $7(10 - 5)$ **c.** $(12 - 8)9$

Examples

Use the Distributive Property to rewrite each expression.

2. $4(x + 7)$

$$4(x + 7) = 4(x) + 4(7) \qquad \text{Expand using the Distributive Property.}$$
$$= 4x + 28 \qquad \text{Simplify.}$$

3. $6(p - 5)$

$$6(p - 5) = 6[p + (-5)] \qquad \text{Rewrite } p - 5 \text{ as } p + (-5).$$
$$= 6(p) + 6(-5) \qquad \text{Expand using the Distributive Property.}$$
$$= 6p + (-30) \qquad \text{Simplify.}$$
$$= 6p - 30 \qquad \text{Definition of subtraction}$$

4. $-2(x - 8)$

$$-2(x - 8) = -2[x + (-8)] \qquad \text{Rewrite } x - 8 \text{ as } x + (-8).$$
$$= -2(x) + -2(-8) \qquad \text{Expand using the Distributive Property.}$$
$$= -2x + 16 \qquad \text{Simplify.}$$

5. $5(-3x + 7y)$

$$5(-3x + 7y) = 5(-3x) + 5(7y) \qquad \text{Expand using the Distributive Property.}$$
$$= -15x + 35y \qquad \text{Simplify.}$$

6. $\frac{1}{3}(x - 6)$

$$\frac{1}{3}(x - 6) = \frac{1}{3}[x + (-6)] \qquad \text{Rewrite } x - 6 \text{ as } x + (-6).$$
$$= \frac{1}{3}(x) + \left(\frac{1}{3}(-6)\right) \qquad \text{Expand using the Distributive Property.}$$
$$= \frac{1}{3}x + (-2) \qquad \text{Simplify.}$$
$$= \frac{1}{3}x - 2 \qquad \text{Definition of subtraction}$$

Got It? Do these problems to find out.

d. $6(a + 4)$ **e.** $(m + 3n)8$

f. $-3(y - 10)$ **g.** $\frac{1}{2}(w - 4)$

d. _____

e. _____

f. _____

g. _____

Example

7. Mr. Ito needs to buy batting helmets for the baseball team. The helmets he plans to buy are $19.95 each. Find the total cost if Mr. Ito needs to buy 9 batting helmets for the team.

Rename $19.95 as $20.00 − $0.05. Then use the Distributive Property to find the total cost mentally.

$9(\$20.00 − \$0.05) = 9(\$20.00) − 9(\$0.05)$ Distributive Property.

$\qquad\qquad\qquad\quad = \$180 − \$0.45$ Multiply.

$\qquad\qquad\qquad\quad = \$179.55$ Subtract.

The total cost of the helmets is $179.55.

Show your work.

Got It? Do this problem to find out.

h. _____

h. A sports club rents dirt bikes for $37.50 each. Find the total cost for the club to rent 20 bikes. Justify your answer by using the Distributive Property.

Guided Practice

Use the Distributive Property to evaluate or rewrite each expression. (Examples 1–6)

1. $(8 + 11)(−3) = $ _____

2. $−5(2x + 4y) = $ _____

3. $\frac{1}{5}(g − 10) = $ _____

 Show your work.

4. A housefly can fly about 6.4 feet per second. At this rate, how far can it fly in 25 seconds? Justify your answer by using the Distributive Property. (Example 7)

_____

5. **Building on the Essential Question** Describe how the formula to find the perimeter of a rectangle is an application of the Distributive Property. _____

_____

_____

_____

Rate Yourself!

How confident are you about the Distributive Property? Check the box that applies.

For more help, go online to access a Personal Tutor.

Independent Practice

Go online for Step-by-Step Solutions

Use the Distributive Property to evaluate each expression. (Example 1)

1. $3(5 + 6) =$ _____

2. $(6 + 4)(-12) =$ _____

3 $-6(9 - 4) =$ _____

4. $5(-6 + 4) =$ _____

5. $4(8 - 7) =$ _____

6. $(5 - 7)(-3) =$ _____

MP Identify Structure **Use the Distributive Property to rewrite each expression.** (Examples 2–6)

7. $3(-4x + 8) =$ _____

8. $4(x - 6y) =$ _____

9. $6(5 - q) =$ _____

10. $\frac{1}{2}(c - 8) =$ _____

11. $-3(5 - b) =$ _____

12. $(d + 2)(-7) =$ _____

13 Amelia bought roast beef for $6.85 per pound. Find the total cost if Amelia bought 4 pounds of roast beef. Justify your answer by using the Distributive Property. (Example 7)

14. The table shows the different prices of items at a movie theater.

  a. Suppose Mina and two of her friends go to the movies. Write an expression that could be used to find the total cost for them to go to the movies and buy one of each item.

  _____

  b. What is the total cost for all three people?

  _____

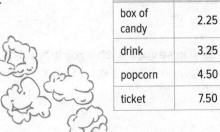

Movie Theater Prices	
Item	Cost ($)
box of candy	2.25
drink	3.25
popcorn	4.50
ticket	7.50

MP **Use Math Tools** Find each product mentally. Justify your answer.

15. $9 \cdot 35 = $ _____

16. $8 \cdot 28 = $ _____

17. $112 \cdot 6 = $ _____

18. $85 \cdot 8 = $ _____

19. $4 \cdot 122 = $ _____

20. $12 \cdot 64 = $ _____

🔥 H.O.T. Problems Higher Order Thinking

21. **MP** **Reason Abstractly** Write an expression that when using the Distributive Property can be simplified to $12a + 18b - 6c$.

_____

22. **MP** **Identify Structure** Use the Distributive Property to rewrite the expression $7bx + 7by$ as an equivalent expression.

_____

23. **MP** **Persevere with Problems** Use the Distributive Property to write an equivalent expression for the expression $(a + b)(2 + y)$.

_____

24. **MP** **Find the Error** Julia is using the Distributive Property to simplify $3(x + 2)$. Find her mistake and correct it.

$$3(x + 2) = 3x + 2$$

_____

_____

25. **MP** **Persevere with Problems** Is $3 + (x \cdot y) = (3 + x) \cdot (3 + y)$ a true statement? If so, explain your reasoning. If not, give a counterexample.

_____

_____

Extra Practice

Use the Distributive Property to evaluate each expression.

26. $(3 + 6)(-8) = $ -72

$3 \cdot (-8) + 6\,(-8) =$

$-24 + (-48) = -72$

Homework Help

27. $4(11 - 5) = $ _____

28. $(12 - 4)(-5)$ _____

Use the Distributive Property to rewrite each expression.

29. $-8(a + b) = $ _____

30. $(2b + 8)5 = $ _____

31. $(p + 7)(-2) = $ _____

32. **MP Justify Conclusions** Theresa is planning on making a fleece blanket for her nephew. She learns that the fabric she wants to use is $7.99 per yard. Find the total cost of 4 yards of fabric. Justify your answer by using the Distributive Property.

_____

_____

33. You are ordering T-shirts with your school's mascot printed on them. Each T-shirt costs $4.75. The printer charges a setup fee of $30 and $2.50 to print each shirt. Write two expressions to represent the total cost of printing n T-shirts.

_____

_____

Use the Distributive Property to rewrite each expression.

34. $0.5x(y - z)$

$ = $ _____

35. $-6a(2b + 5c)$

$ = $ _____

36. $-4m(3n - 6p)$

$ = $ _____

37. $3(2y + 4z)$

$ = $ _____

38. $-2(3a - 2b)$

$ = $ _____

39. $-6(12p - 8n)$

$ = $ _____

40. Write two equivalent expressions for the area of the figure.

_____

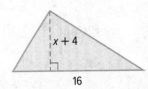

$x + 4$

16

41. A group of 3 seniors, 3 adults, and 3 children bought tickets to the aquarium.

Type of Ticket	Cost ($)
Adult	18.95
Senior	14.95
Child	9.95

Fill in the boxes to model the total amount spent with an expression.

$$\boxed{} \times (\boxed{} + \boxed{} + \boxed{})$$

How much did the group spend on tickets altogether? How does applying the Distributive Property make it easier to find this amount?

42. Celeste is going to summer camp. The table shows the cost of items she will need to purchase with the camp logo. She needs to buy four of each item.

Item	Cost ($)
T-shirt	8.00
Shorts	4.50
Socks	2.25

Which of the following expressions represents the total cost of the items? Select all that apply.

☐ $4(14.75)$

☐ $4(8.00) + 4.50 + 2.25$

☐ $4(8) + 4(4.50) + 4(2.25)$

☐ $4(8.00 + 4.50 + 2.25)$

Spiral Review

Evaluate each expression if $x = 9$ and $y = 3$.

43. $x + y - 58$ _____

44. $y^3 + x^3$ _____

45. $y^4 - 128 =$ _____

46. In the expression below, identify the coefficient and the variable.

$$4x + 450$$

coefficient: _____   variable: _____

Case #1 Mountain Biking

Hoshi wants to purchase a membership to a bike park.
The cost depends on the number of people on the membership.
It costs $55 for 5 people, $65 for 6 people, and $75 for 7 people.

Find the cost of a membership that includes 8 people.

Understand *What are the facts?*

The cost of a membership depends on the number
of people included on the membership.

Plan *What is your strategy to solve this problem?*

Make a table that shows the number of people and the cost.

Solve *How can you apply the strategy?*

Make a table. Find the cost for 8 people.

Number of People (p)	Cost
5	$55
6	$65
7	$75
8	

+10
+10
+10

So, the cost for 8 people is ⬚.

Check *Does the answer make sense?*

The expression $10p + 5$ can be used to represent the situation.

Since $10(8) + 5 = 85$, the solution is reasonable.

Analyze the Strategy

MP Justify Conclusions Hoshi wants to purchase a membership for four people.
Explain how the table would change and then solve.

Case #2 Financial Literacy

Latoya is saving money to buy a saxophone. After 1 month, she has $75. After 2 months, she has $120. After 3 months, she has $165. She plans to keep saving at the same rate.

How long will it take Latoya to save enough money to buy a saxophone that costs $300?

Understand

Read the problem. What are you being asked to find?

I need to find _____

_____.

Underline key words and values. What information do you know?

After 1 month, Latoya has [ ]. After 2 months, she has [ ].

After 3 months, she has [ ]. She continues to save at the same rate.

Is there any information that you do *not* need to know?

I do not need to know _____

Plan

Choose a problem-solving strategy.

I will use the _____ strategy.

Solve

Use your problem-solving strategy to solve the problem.

Months	1	2	3	4	5	6
Amount Saved ($)	75	120	165			

+45 +45 +45 +45 +45

Latoya will have $300 saved in _____.

Check

Use information from the problem to check your answer.

_____

_____

Work with a small group to solve the following cases.
Show your work on a separate piece of paper.

Case #3 Carnivals

For a carnival game, containers are arranged in a triangular display. The top row has 1 container. The second row has 2 containers. The third row has 3 containers. The pattern continues until the bottom row, which has 10 containers.

A contestant knocks down 29 containers on the first throw. How many containers remain?

Case #4 Budget

Tamara earns $2,050 each month. She spends 65% of the amount she earns. The rest of the money is equally divided and deposited into two separate accounts.

How many months until Tamara has deposited more than $2,500 in one of her accounts?

Case #5 Toothpicks

Write an expression that can be used to find the number of toothpicks needed to make any figure. Then find the number of toothpicks needed to make the eighth figure.

Figure 1   Figure 2   Figure 3

Use any strategy!

Case #6 Diving

A diver descends to −15 feet after 1 minute, −30 feet after 2 minutes, and −45 feet after 3 minutes.

If the diver keeps descending at this rate, what is their position after 12 minutes?

Mid-Chapter Check

Vocabulary Check

1. Fill in the blank in the sentence below with the correct term.

A _____ is a symbol that represents an unknown quantity.

2. Define *arithmetic sequence*. Then provide an example.

Skills Check and Problem Solving

Describe the relationship between the terms in each arithmetic sequence. Then write the next three terms in each sequence.

3. 5, 8, 11, 14, ...

4. 4, 11, 18, 25, ...

5. 5.8, 10.8, 15.8, 20.8, ...

Use the Distributive Property to rewrite each expression.

6. $4(x + 9) =$ _____

7. $2(x + 5) =$ _____

8. $3(-2x + 4) =$ _____

9. **MP Identify Structure** What property is shown by the statement $8x + 0 = 8x$?

10. **MP Persevere with Problems** A coach bought some baseball bats and five baseball gloves. Let *b* represent the number of bats. Write an expression that can be used to find the total cost of the bats and gloves. Then find the total cost if he bought three bats.

$35

$48

Add Linear Expressions

Real-World Link

Homework Luke has 20 math problems and 11 science questions for homework. Cameron has 23 math problems and 10 science questions for homework.

1. The expression below represents the types of exercises that Luke has for homework.

   20 math problems + 11 science questions

   Complete the expression that represents the types of exercises that Cameron has for homework.

   [ ] math problems + [ ] science questions

2. Write an expression for the total number of math problems and science questions for both boys.

   [ ] math problems + [ ] science questions

3. Suppose Luke has x math problems and 5 science questions for homework and Cameron has x math problems and 6 science questions. The algebra tiles below represent the total number of math problems and science questions for both boys. Write an expression in simplest form that represents the algebra tiles.

Expression: _____

Essential Question

HOW can you use numbers and symbols to represent mathematical ideas?

Vocabulary

linear expression
constant
like term
simplest form

Which **MP** **Mathematical Process Goals** did you use? Shade the circle(s) that applies.

① Mathematical Problem Solving
② Mathematical Communication
③ Mathematical Reasoning
④ Mathematical Connections
⑤ Mathematical Representations

Add Linear Expressions

A **linear expression** is an algebraic expression in which the variable is raised to the first power and variable are not multiplied or divided. The table below gives some examples of expressions that are linear and some examples of expressions that are not linear.

Linear Expressions	Nonlinear Expressions
$5x$	$5mn$
$3x + 2$	$3x^3 + 2$
$x - 7$	$x^4 - 7$

You can add linear expression with or without models. Sometimes you will need to use zero pairs.

Examples

Tutor

Add.

1. $(2x + 3) + (x + 4)$

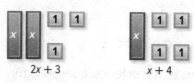
$2x + 3$ $x + 4$

Model each linear expression.

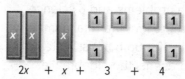
$2x \ + \ x \ + \ 3 \ + \ 4$

Combine like tiles and write a linear expression for the combined tiles.

So, $(2x + 3) + (x + 4) = 3x + 7$.

2. $(2x - 1) + (x - 5)$

$(2x - 1) + (x - 5) = [2x + (-1)] + [x + (-5)]$ Definition of subtraction

$$2x + (-1)$$
$$\underline{+ \ x + (-5)}$$ Arrange like terms in columns.
$$3x + (-6)$$ Add.

So, $(2x - 1) + (x - 5) = 3x + (-6)$ or $3x - 6$.

Show your work.

a. _____

b. _____

Got It? Do these problems to find out.

a. $(3x + 5) + (2x + 3)$ **b.** $(2x - 4) + (3x - 7)$

3. Find $(2x - 3) + (-x + 4)$. Use models if needed.

Model each linear expression.

$2x \quad + \quad (-3)$

$-x \quad + \quad 4$

  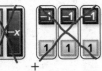

Combine like tiles. Then remove all zero pairs and write a linear expression for the remaining tiles.

$x \quad + \quad 1$

So, $(2x - 3) + (-x + 4) = x + 1$.

4. Find $2(x + 3) + (3x + 1)$.

$2(x + 3) + (3x + 1) = (\mathbf{2} \cdot x + \mathbf{2} \cdot 3) + (3x + 1)$ Use the Distributive Property.

$= (2x + 6) + (3x + 1)$ Simplify.

$$
\begin{array}{r}
2x + 6 \\
+\ 3x + 1 \\
\hline
5x + 7
\end{array}
$$

Arrange like terms in columns.

Add.

So, $2(x + 3) + (3x + 1) = 5x + 7$.

5. Find $5(x - 4) + (2x - 7)$.

$5(x - 4) + (2x - 7) = (\mathbf{5} \cdot x - \mathbf{5} \cdot 4) + (2x - 7)$ Use the Distributive Property.

$= (5x - 20) + (2x - 7)$ Simplify.

$$
\begin{array}{r}
5x - 20 \\
+\ 2x -\ 7 \\
\hline
7x - 27
\end{array}
$$

Arrange like terms in columns.

Add.

So, $5(x - 4) + (2x - 7) = 7x - 27$.

Show your work.

c. _____

d. _____

e. _____

f. _____

Got It? Do these problems to find out.

Add. Use models if needed.

c. $(x - 1) + (2x + 3)$

d. $(x - 4) + (-2x + 1)$

e. $6(x + 7) + (x + 3)$

f. $(12x + 19) + 2(x - 10)$

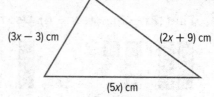

Example

6. Write a linear expression in simplest form to represent the perimeter of the triangle. Find the perimeter if the value of x is 5 centimeters.

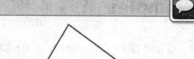

$(3x - 3)$ cm $(2x + 9)$ cm

$(5x)$ cm

Properties

The Commutative Property allows the terms of the expression to be reordered.

Write a linear expression for the perimeter of the triangle.

$(3x - 3) + (2x + 9) + (5x)$	Write each expression.
$(3x + 2x + 5x) + (-3 + 9)$	Rearrange to combine like terms.
$10x + 6$	Add.

Find the perimeter.

$10x + 6 = 10(5) + 6$ or 56 Replace x with 5. Simplify.

So, the perimeter of the triangle is 56 centimeters.

Show your work.

Got It? Do this problem to find out.

g. A rectangle has side lengths $(x + 4)$ feet and $(2x - 2)$ feet. Write a linear expression in simplest form to represent the perimeter. Find the perimeter if the value of x is 7 feet.

g. _____

Guided Practice

Check

Add. Use models if needed. (Examples 1–5)

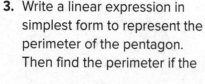
Show your work.

1. $(2x + 3) + (x + 1) =$ _____

2. $10(x - 2) + (6x - 6) =$ _____

3. Write a linear expression in simplest form to represent the perimeter of the pentagon. Then find the perimeter if the value of x is 3 yards. (Example 6)

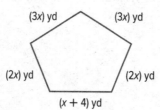

$(3x)$ yd $(3x)$ yd

$(2x)$ yd $(2x)$ yd

$(x + 4)$ yd

_____

Rate Yourself!

How confident are you about adding linear expressions? Check the box that applies.

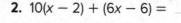

4. **Building on the Essential Question** Explain how adding linear expressions is similar to simplifying expressions.

_____

_____

For more help, go online to access a Personal Tutor.

FOLDABLES Time to update your Foldable!

Independent Practice

Go online for Step-by-Step Solutions

Add. Use models if needed. (Examples 1–5)

1. $(4x + 8) + (7x + 3) =$ _____

2. $(-3x + 7) + (-6x + 9) =$ _____

Show your work.

3 $(x - 10) + (3x - 6) =$ _____

4. $(-3x - 7) + (4x + 7) =$ _____

5. $2(x + 14) + (2x - 14) =$ _____

6. $(11x - 8) + 7(x - 1) =$ _____

7. Write a linear expression in simplest form to represent the perimeter of the triangle at the right. Then find the perimeter if the value of x is 10 millimeters. (Example 6)

_____

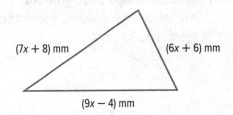

$(7x + 8)$ mm $(6x + 6)$ mm

$(9x - 4)$ mm

8. A rectangle has side lengths $(2x - 5)$ meters and $(2x + 6)$ meters. Write a linear expression in simplest form to represent the perimeter. Find the perimeter if the value of x is 12 meters. (Example 6)

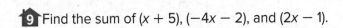

9 Find the sum of $(x + 5)$, $(-4x - 2)$, and $(2x - 1)$.

_____

Add.

10. $(-3.5x + 1.7) + (9.1x - 0.3) =$ _____

11. $(0.5x + 15) + (8.2x - 16.6) =$ _____

12. **MP Reason Abstractly** The table shows the breakdown of the points scored in last week's basketball game.

	1st Quarter Field Goal Points	2nd Quarter Field Goal Points	3rd Quarter Field Goal Points	4th Quarter Field Goal Points	Total Free Throw Points
Panthers	$2x - 6$	$x + 2$	$2x$	$x - 6$	9

a. Write a linear expression in simplest form to represent the total field goal points scored in the first two quarters.

_____

b. Write a linear expression in simplest form to represent the total points scored in the game.

_____

H.O.T. Problems Higher Order Thinking

13. **MP Reason Inductively** Write two linear expressions with a sum of $-5x + 4$.

_____

_____

14. **MP Construct an Argument** Will the sum of two linear expressions, each with an x-term, *always*, *sometimes*, or *never* have an x-term? Explain your reasoning.

_____

_____

_____

15. **MP Persevere with Problems** An integer can be represented by x. The next integer can then be represented as $(x + 1)$. Write a linear expression that represents the sum of any two consecutive integers. Show that the sum of any two consecutive integers is always odd.

_____

_____

_____

16. **MP Reason Inductively** Explain how algebra tiles represent like terms and zero pairs.

_____

_____

_____

Extra Practice

Add. Use models if needed.

17. $(-x + 10) + (-3x + 6) =$ ___$-4x + 16$___

$$-x + 10$$
$$\underline{(+)\ -3x + 6}$$
$$-4x + 16$$

18. $(-4x + 3) + (-2x + 8) =$ _____

19. $(-6x + 5) + (4x - 7) =$ _____

20. $(-4x + 5) + (15x - 3) =$ _____

21. $(-5x + 4) + -1(x - 1) =$ _____

22. $17(2x - 5) + (-x + 4) =$ _____

23. Write a linear expression in simplest form to represent the perimeter of the trapezoid at the right. Then find the

perimeter if the value of x is 7 yards. _____

(7x + 3) yd

(6x + 3) yd   (6x + 3) yd

(5x) yd

24. **MP Reason Abstractly** The table shows the points earned by a contestant in four rounds on a game show.

Round 1	Round 2	Round 3	Round 4
2x + 40	5x + 12	100	6x − 10

a. Write a linear expression in simplest form to represent the total points earned by the contestant in rounds 1 and 2.

_____

b. Write a linear expression in simplest form to represent the total points earned in all four rounds.

_____

Show your work.

c. If the value of x is 8, what is the total points earned in all four rounds?

_____

25. Karina makes x dollars per hour working at the grocery store. She makes y dollars per hour working at the library. One week she worked 9 hours at the grocery store and 12 hours at the library. Determine if each statement is true or false.

   a. The expression $21x$ represents Karina's earnings from the library.   ☐ True   ☐ False

   b. The expression $9y$ represents Karina's earnings from the grocery store.   ☐ True   ☐ False

   c. The expression $9x + 12y$ represents Karina's total earnings for the week.   ☐ True   ☐ False

26. A triangle has the side lengths represented by the expressions shown in the figure. Select the appropriate numbers and expressions to complete the model representing the perimeter of the triangle.

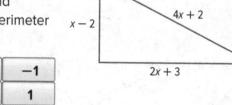

$$\boxed{} + \boxed{}$$
$$\boxed{} + \boxed{}$$
$$\boxed{} + \boxed{} + \boxed{}$$
$$\overline{}$$
$$\boxed{} + \boxed{} + \boxed{}$$

x	-1
$2x$	1
$4x$	2
$5x$	3
$7x$	7
-2	

Spiral Review

Use the Distributive Property to evaluate each expression.

27. $7(9 - 4) =$ _____

28. $(9 + 2)6 =$ _____

29. $5(9 + 8) =$ _____

30. The number of students in each of the seventh grade homerooms that volunteer in the office are shown in the table. Use mental math to find the total number of students who volunteered. Explain.

_____

_____

Office Volunteers	
Homeroom	Number of Students
A	6
B	5
C	4
D	8

Subtract Linear Expressions

Real-World Link

Watch

Dog Sledding The Iditarod is a dog sledding race over 1,150 miles across Alaska. The table shows two winning times.

Iditarod				
	Days	**Hours**	**Minutes**	**Seconds**
Race 1	9	11	46	48
Race 2	9	5	8	41

1. What is the difference in hours, minutes, and seconds between the two races?

   ☐ h ☐ min ☐ s

2. Explain how you could find the difference in times between any two races, given the days, hours, minutes, and seconds.

   _____

   _____

3. Describe another situation in which finding the difference involves subtracting like units.

   _____

   _____

   _____

Essential Question

HOW can you use numbers and symbols to represent mathematical ideas?

Which **MP Mathematical Process Goals** did you use? Shade the circle(s) that applies.

① Mathematical Problem Solving

② Mathematical Communication

③ Mathematical Reasoning

④ Mathematical Connections

⑤ Mathematical Representations

Subtract Linear Expressions

When subtracting linear expressions, subtract like terms. Use zero pairs if needed.

Examples

Tools Tutor

Subtract. Use models if needed.

1. $(6x + 3) - (2x + 2)$

6x   +   3

Model the linear expression $6x + 3$.

4x   +   1

To subtract $2x + 2$, remove two x-tiles and two 1-tiles. Then write the linear expression for the remaining tiles.

There are four x-tiles and one 1-tile remaining.

So, $(6x + 3) - (2x + 2) = 4x + 1$.

. . . .

2. $(2x - 3) - (x - 2)$

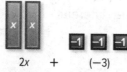

2x   +   (−3)

Model the linear expression $2x - 3$.

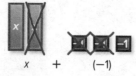

x   +   (−1)

To subtract $x - 2$, remove one x-tile and two −1-tiles. Then write the linear expression for the remaining tiles.

There is one x-tile and one −1-tile remaining.

So, $(2x - 3) - (x - 2) = x - 1$.

Show your work

Got It? Do these problems to find out.

a. $(5x - 9) - (2x - 7)$ b. $(6x - 10) - (2x - 8)$

a. _____

b. _____

Example

Tutor

3. Find $(-2x - 4) - (2x)$. Use models if needed.

$-2x \quad + \quad (-4)$

Model the linear expression $-2x - 4$.

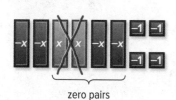

zero pairs

Since there are no positive x-tiles to remove, add two zero pairs of x-tiles. Remove two positive x-tiles.

So, $(-2x - 4) - (2x) = -4x - 4$.

Got It? Do these problems to find out.

c. $(3x - 2) - (5x - 4)$

d. $(4x - 4) - (-2x + 2)$

Show your work.

c. _____

d. _____

Use the Additive Inverse to Subtract

When subtracting integers, you add the opposite, or the additive inverse. The same process is used when subtracting linear expressions.

Examples

Tutor

4. Find $(6x + 5) - (3x + 1)$.

$$\begin{array}{r} 6x + 5 \\ (+)\ -3x - 1 \\ \hline 3x + 4 \end{array}$$

Arrange like terms in columns.
The additive inverse of $3x + 1$ is $(-3x - 1)$.

Additive Inverse
The additive inverse is found by multiplying the linear expression by -1.

5. Find $(-4x - 7) - (-5x - 2)$.

$$\begin{array}{r} -4x - 7 \\ (+)\ 5x + 2 \\ \hline x - 5 \end{array}$$

Arrange like terms in columns.
The additive inverse of $(-5x - 2)$ is $(5x + 2)$.

Got It? Do these problems to find out.

e. $(4x - 3) - (2x + 7)$

f. $(5x - 4) - (2x + 3)$

e. _____

f. _____

 Example

6. A hat store tracks the sale of college and professional team hats for *m* months. The number of college hats sold is represented by (6*m* + 3). The number of professional hats sold is represented by (5*m* − 2). Write an expression to show how many more college hats were sold than professional hats. Then evaluate the expression if *m* equals 10.

Find (6*m* + 3) − (5*m* − 2).

$$6m + 3$$
$$\underline{(+) -5m + 2}$$
$$m + 5$$

Arrange like terms in columns.

The additive inverse of 5*m* − 2 is (−5*m* + 2).

Evaluate the expression if *m* = 10.

$m + 5 = \mathbf{10} + 5$ Substitute 10 for *m*.

$\quad\quad = 15$ Simplify.

So, 15 more college team hats were sold.

Check

Guided Practice

Subtract. Use models if needed. (Examples 1–5)

1. $(2x + 4) − (−x + 5) = $ _____

2. $(6x + 9) − (7x − 1) = $ _____

Show your work.

3. The number of runs scored by the home team at a baseball game is represented by (*x* + 7). The number of runs scored by the visiting team is represented by (3*x* − 7). Write an expression to find how many more runs the home team scored than the visiting team. Then evaluate the expression if the value of *x* is 6. (Example 6)

_____

_____

4. **Building on the Essential Question** How can you use the additive inverse to help you subtract linear expressions?

_____

_____

_____

Rate Yourself!

How well do you understand subtracting linear expressions? Circle the image that applies.

Clear   Somewhat   Not So
                Clear   Clear

For more help, go online to access a Personal Tutor.

Tutor

FOLDABLES Time to update your Foldable!

Independent Practice

Go online for Step-by-Step Solutions

eHelp

Subtract. Use models if needed. (Examples 1–5)

1. $(9x + 5) - (4x + 3) =$ _____

2. $(-x + 3) - (x - 5) =$ _____

Show your work.

3. $(3x + 4) - (x + 2) =$ _____

4. $(7x + 5) - (3x + 2) =$ _____

5. $(9x - 8) - (x + 4) =$ _____

6. $(9x - 12) - (5x - 7) =$ _____

7. **MP** **Reason Abstractly** The number of customers in a store on the first day is represented by $(6x - 3)$. The number of customers on the second day is represented by $(x - 1)$. Write an expression to find how many more customers visited the store on the first day. Then evaluate the expression if x is equal to 50. (Example 6)

_____

_____

8. The perimeter of the garden shown is $(6x + 2)$ units. Find the length of the missing side.

_____

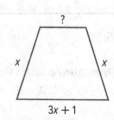

9. The cost for shipping a package that weighs x pounds from Boise to Los Angeles is shown at the right. How much more does Shipping Central charge than Globe Delivery?

_____

Company	Cost ($)
Shipping Central	$3x + 3.50$
Globe Delivery	$2x + 2.99$

10. Find the difference in the given lengths of the polygons. _____

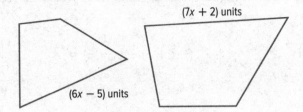

(7x + 2) units

(6x − 5) units

🔥 **H.O.T. Problems** Higher Order Thinking

11. (MP) **Find the Error** Theresa is finding $(5x + 3) - (2x + 1)$. Find her mistake and correct it.

$$(5x + 3) - (2x + 1)$$
$$= 5x + 3 - 2x + 1$$
$$= 5x - 2x + 3 + 1$$
$$= 3x + 4$$

12. (MP) **Reason Inductively** Name two linear expressions whose difference is $5x - 4$.

13. (MP) **Persevere with Problems** One linear expression is subtracted from a second linear expression and the difference is $x - 5$. What is the difference when the second linear expression is subtracted from the first? _____

14. (MP) **Persevere with Problems** Suppose A and B represent linear expressions. If $A + B = 2x - 2$ and $A - B = 4x - 8$, find A and B.

15. (MP) **Reason Inductively** Explain how you can apply the rule for subtracting integers to linear expressions.

Extra Practice

Subtract. Use models if needed.

16. $(-3x - 2) - (7x + 9) = \underline{-10x - 11}$

$$\begin{array}{r} -3x - 2 \\ (+)\ -7x - 9 \\ \hline -10x - 11 \end{array}$$

 Homework Help

17. $(-2x - 1) - (x - 7) = \underline{\hspace{2cm}}$

18. $(9x + 5) - (6x - 8) = \underline{\hspace{2cm}}$

19. $(-8x + 1) - (8x - 1) = \underline{\hspace{2cm}}$

20. $(4x + 10) - (-3x + 5) = \underline{\hspace{2cm}}$

21. $(-6x - 11) - (-2x - 4) = \underline{\hspace{2cm}}$

22. **MP** **Reason Abstractly** The number of questions on a math test is represented $(3x + 1)$. The number of questions on a spelling test is represented by $(x + 12)$. Write an expression to find how many more questions were on the math test. Then evaluate the expression if the value of x is 8.

_____

Subtract.

23. $(5.7x - 0.8) - (4.9x - 1.4) = \underline{\hspace{2cm}}$

24. $\left(-\dfrac{5}{6}x + 5\dfrac{1}{2}\right) - \left(\dfrac{2}{3}x + 4\right) = \underline{\hspace{2cm}}$

25. $2(x + 1) - 3x = \underline{\hspace{2cm}}$

26. $5(x - 3) - x = \underline{\hspace{2cm}}$

Power Up! Test Practice

27. The costs for a large pizza and each topping for two pizzerias are shown in the table.

Pizzeria	Cost per Pizza ($)	Cost per Topping ($)
Mario's Pizza	10	1.25
Pizza Palace	12	1.50

Select the appropriate values to complete the model to show how much more a pizza with t toppings costs at Pizza Palace than at Mario's Pizza.

0.25	2.75	1.25	1.50
2	10	12	22

$$\boxed{} + \boxed{}\, t - (\boxed{} + \boxed{}\, t) = \boxed{} + \boxed{}\, t$$

28. Mei wants to frame a picture. The picture is $(12x + 4)$ units long, and the frame is $(7x + 1)$ units long. Determine if each statement is true or false.

a. The picture is longer than the frame.   ☐ True   ☐ False

b. The frame is longer than the picture.   ☐ True   ☐ False

c. Mei will have to trim $(5x + 3)$ units from the picture to fit it in the frame.   ☐ True   ☐ False

Spiral Review

29. Camilla wants to attach a string of lights to the edges of her patio for a party. She does not want the string to go across the edge with the steps. Write a linear expression that represents the length of string in feet she will need. Then find the length if $x = 3$.

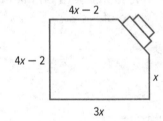

_____

Evaluate each expression if $x = \frac{1}{2}$ and $y = \frac{3}{4}$.

30. xy _____

31. $x - y$ _____

32. $x + y$ _____

33. x^3 _____

34. $3y + 2x$ _____

35. $x \div y$ _____

Inquiry HOW do models help you factor linear expressions?

Max has enough 1 inch square glass tiles to create a rectangular piece of mosaic art that has an area of 24 square inches. Some of the possible dimensions of the rectangle are listed in the table. Write the two missing possible dimensions.

Each of the dimensions listed are factors of 24. Sometimes, you know the product and are asked to find the factors. This process is called *factoring*.

Length (in.)	Width (in.)
24	1
3	8

Hands-On Activity 1

Tools

Use algebra tiles to factor 2x + 6.

Step 1 Model the expression 2x + 6.

Step 2 Arrange the tiles into a rectangle with equal rows and columns. The total area of the tiles represents the product. Its length and width represent the factors.

The rectangle has a width of two 1-tiles and a length of one x-tile and three 1-tiles.

So, $2x + 6 = 2(x + \boxed{})$.

Hands-On Activity 2

Use algebra tiles to factor $2x - 8$.

Step 1   Model the expression $2x - 8$.

Step 2   Arrange the tiles into a rectangle with equal rows and columns.

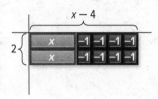

The rectangle has a width of two 1-tiles and a length of one x-tile and four -1-tiles.

So, $2x - 8 = $ _____.

Hands-On Activity 3

Use algebra tiles to factor $3x - 6$.

Step 1   Draw the tiles that represent the expression $3x - 6$.

Step 2   Redraw the tiles into a rectangle with equal rows and columns.

The rectangle has a width of _____ 1-tiles and a

length of one x-tile and _____ -1-tiles.

So, $3x - 6 = $ _____.

Work with a partner. Factor each expression by arranging the appropriate algebra tiles into equal rows and columns. Draw the finished product.

1. $4x + 6 =$ _____

Show your work.

2. $5x + 10 =$ _____

3. $3x + 12 =$ _____

4. $4x - 10 =$ _____

5. $3x - 9 =$ _____

6. $2x - 4 =$ _____

7. $4x + 2 =$ _____

8. $5x - 5 =$ _____

Work with a partner to complete the table. Use algebra tiles if needed.

	Original Expression	Factored Expression	Distributive Property
	$2x + 8$	$2(x + 4)$	$2(x) + 2(4) = 2x + 8$
9.	$4x - 8$	$4(x - \boxed{})$	$4(x) - 4(2) = 4x - 8$
10.	$6x + 2$	$2(\boxed{}x + 1)$	$2(3x) + 2(1) =$
11.	$2x - 10$		$2(x) - 2(5) =$
12.	$8x + 6$		

13. **MP Reason Inductively** How is factoring related to using the Distributive Property?

_____

_____

14. **MP Construct an Argument** Is the expression $2x - 2$ equivalent to the expression $2(x - 2)$? Explain.

_____

_____

_____

Create
On Your Own

15. **MP Justify Conclusions** Explain how you could use algebra tiles to factor $5x + 15$.

_____

_____

_____

16. **Inquiry** HOW do models help you factor linear expressions?

_____

_____

_____

Factor Linear Expressions

Real-World Link

Tools

Yard Sale A rectangular yard is being separated into four equal-size sections for different items at a yard sale. The area of the yard is $(8x + 12)$ square meters.

Housewares

Toys

Clothing

Books

1. How can you find the area of each section of the yard sale?

_____

_____

2. What is the area of each section? Explain your answer.

_____

_____

_____

3. The algebra tiles represent the area of the entire yard sale. Fill in the length and width. Write an expression that represents the area in terms of the length and width of the model. _____

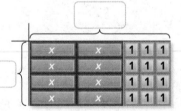

Which **MP** Mathematical Process Goals did you use? Shade the circle(s) that applies.

① Mathematical Problem Solving

② Mathematical Communication

③ Mathematical Reasoning

④ Mathematical Connections

⑤ Mathematical Representations

Essential Question

HOW can you use numbers and symbols to represent mathematical ideas?

Vocabulary

monomial

factor

factored form

Find the GCF of Monomials

A **monomial** is a number, a variable, or a product of a number and one or more variables.

Monomials	Not Monomials
25, x, 40x	$x + 4$, 40x + 120

To **factor** a number means to write it as a product of its factors. A monomial can be factored using the same method you would use to factor a number.

The greatest common factor (GCF) of two monomials is the greatest monomial that is a factor of both.

Examples

Find the GCF of each pair of monomials.

1. 4x, 12x

$4x = 2 \cdot 2 \cdot x$ — Write the prime factorization of 4x and 12x.

$12x = 2 \cdot 2 \cdot 3 \cdot x$ — Circle the common factors.

The GCF of 4x and 12x is 2 · 2 · x or 4x.

STOP and Reflect

Which of the following is not a factor of 22x? Circle your response.

4   2   11 x

2. 18a, 20ab

$18a = 2 \cdot 3 \cdot 3 \cdot a$ — Write the prime factorization of 18a and 20ab.

$20ab = 2 \cdot 2 \cdot 5 \cdot a \cdot b$ — Circle the common factors.

The GCF of 18a and 20ab is 2 · a or 2a.

3. 12cd, 36cd

$12cd = 2 \cdot 2 \cdot 3 \cdot c \cdot d$ — Write the prime factorization of 12cd and 36cd.

$36cd = 2 \cdot 2 \cdot 3 \cdot 3 \cdot c \cdot d$ — Circle the common factors.

The GCF of 12cd and 36cd is 2 · 2 · 3 · c · d or 12cd.

Show your work.

Got It? Do these problems to find out.

Find the GCF of each pair of monomials.

a. 12, 28c b. 25x, 15xy c. 42mn, 14mn

a. _____

b. _____

c. _____

Factor Linear Expressions

You can use the Distributive Property and the work backward strategy to express a linear expression as a product of its factors. A linear expression is in **factored form** when it is expressed as the product of its factors.

$$8x + 4y = 4(2x) + 4(y)$$ The GCF of $8x$ and $4y$ is 4.

$$= 4(2x + y)$$ Distributive Property

Examples

Tutor

4. Factor $3x + 9$.

> **Method 1**   Use a model.

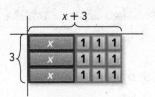

Arrange three x-tiles and nine 1-tiles into equal rows and columns. The rectangle has a width of three 1-tiles, or 3, and a length of one x-tile and three 1-tiles, or $x + 3$.

> **Method 2**   Use the GCF.

$3x = 3 \cdot x$ Write the prime factorization of $3x$ and 9.

$9 = 3 \cdot 3$ Circle the common factors.

The GCF of $3x$ and 9 is 3. Write each term as a product of the GCF and its remaining factors.

$3x + 9 = \mathbf{3}(x) + \mathbf{3}(3)$

      $= \mathbf{3}(x + 3)$ Distributive Property

So, $3x + 9 = 3(x + 3)$.

> **Factoring Expressions**
>
> To check your factored answers, multiply your factors out. You should get your original expression as a result.

5. Factor $12x + 7y$.

Find the GCF of $12x$ and $7y$.

$12x = 2 \cdot 2 \cdot 3 \cdot x$

$7y = 1 \cdot 7 \cdot y$

There are no common factors, so $12x + 7y$ *cannot be factored.*

> **Got It?** Do these problems to find out.

Factor each expression. If the expression cannot be factored, write *cannot be factored*. Use algebra tiles if needed.

   d. $4x - 28$ **e.** $3x + 33y$ **f.** $4x + 35$

Show your work.

d. _____

e. _____

f. _____

 ## Example

Tutor

6. The drawing of a garden at the right has a total area of (15x + 18) square feet. Find possible dimensions of the garden.

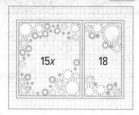

Factor 15x + 18.

$15x = \widehat{3 \cdot 5} \cdot x$ Write the prime factorization of 15x and 18.

$18 = 2 \cdot 3 \cdot 3$ Circle the common factors.

The GCF of 15x and 18 is 3. Write each term as a product of the GCF and its remaining factors.

$15x + 18 = \mathbf{3}(5x) + \mathbf{3}(6)$

$= \mathbf{3}(5x + 6)$ Distributive Property

So, the possible dimensions are 3 feet by (5x + 6) feet.

Guided Practice

Check ✓

Find the GCF of each pair of monomials. (Examples 1–3)

1. 32x, 18 _____

Show your work.

2. 27s, 54st _____

3. 18cd, 30cd _____

Factor each expression. If the expression cannot be factored, write cannot be factored. Use algebra tiles if needed. (Examples 4 and 5)

4. 36x + 24 _____

5. 4x + 9 _____

6. 14x − 16y _____

7. Mr. Phen's monthly income can be represented by the expression 25x + 120 where x is the number of hours worked. Factor the expression 25x + 120. (Example 6)

_____

8. ⓔ **Building on the Essential Question** Explain how the GCF is used to factor an expression. Use the term *Distributive Property* in your response.

_____

_____

_____

Rate Yourself!

Are you ready to move on? Shade the section that applies.

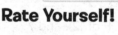

YES   ?   NO

For more help, go online to access a Personal Tutor.

Tutor

FOLDABLES Time to update your Foldable!

Independent Practice

Go online for Step-by-Step Solutions

Find the GCF of each pair of monomials. (Examples 1–3)

1. 24, 48m _____

2. 32a, 48b _____

3 36k, 144km _____

Show your work.

Factor each expression. If the expression cannot be *factored*, write *cannot be factored*. Use algebra tiles if needed. (Examples 4 and 5)

4. 3x + 6 _____

5. 2x − 15 _____

6. 12x + 30y _____

7 The area of a rectangular dance floor is (4x − 8) square units. Factor 4x − 8 to find possible dimensions of the dance floor. (Example 6)

_____

8. The area of a rectangular porch is (9x + 18) square units. Factor 9x + 18 to find possible dimensions of the porch. (Example 6)

_____

9. Six friends visited a museum to see the new holograms exhibit. The group paid for admission to the museum and $12 for parking. The total cost of the visit can be represented by the expression $6x + $12. What expression would represent the cost of the visit for one person?

_____

10. The diagram represents a flower border that is 3 feet wide surrounding a rectangular sitting area. Write an expression in factored form that represents the area of the flower border.

_____

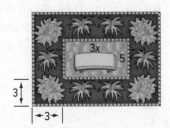

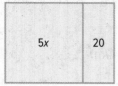

Reason Abstractly Write an expression in factored form to represent the total area of each rectangle.

11.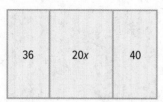

| 5x | 20 |

_____

12.

| 7 | 49x |

_____

13.

| 36 | 20x | 40 |

_____

14.

| 18 |
| 6x |
| 12 |

_____

H.O.T. Problems Higher Order Thinking

15. **Reason Inductively** Write two monomials whose greatest common factor is 4m.

_____

_____

16. **Find the Error** Jamar is factoring $90x - 15$. Find his mistake and correct it.

$$90x - 15 = 15(6x)$$
$$= 9$$

17. **Persevere with Problems** The area of a rectangle is found using the formula $A = \ell w$, where ℓ is the length and w is the width of the rectangle. Write an expression in factored form that represents the area of the shaded region at the right.

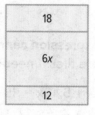

6x

2 4

3y

_____

Extra Practice

Find the GCF of each pair of monomials.

18. 63*p*, 84   21

$63p = 3 \cdot 3 \cdot 7 \cdot p$

$84 = 2 \cdot 2 \cdot 3 \cdot 7$

Homework Help The GCF of 63*p* and 84
is 3 • 7 or 21.

19. 30*rs*, 42*rs*   6*rs*

$30rs = 2 \cdot 3 \cdot 5 \cdot r \cdot s$

$42rs = 2 \cdot 3 \cdot 7 \cdot r \cdot s$

The GCF of 30*rs* and 42*rs*
is 2 • 3 • *r* • *s* or 6*rs*.

20. 60*jk*, 45*jkm* _____

21. 40*x*, 60*x* _____

22. 54*gh*, 72*g* _____

23. 100*xy*, 75*xyz* _____

Factor each expression. If the expression cannot be factored, write *cannot be factored*. **Use algebra tiles if needed.**

24. 5*x* + 5 _____

25. 18*x* + 6 _____

26. 4*x* − 7 _____

27. 10*x* − 35 _____

28. 32*x* + 24*y* _____

29. 30*x* − 40 _____

30. James has $120 in his savings account and plans to save $*x* each month for 6 months. The expression $6*x* + $120 represents the total amount in the account after 6 months. Factor the expression 6*x* + 120.

_____

31. A square scrapbooking page has a perimeter of (8*x* + 20) inches. What is the length of one side of the scrapbooking page?

_____

Copy and Solve **Write an expression in factored form that is equivalent to the given expression. Show your work on a separate piece of paper.**

32. $\frac{1}{2}x + 4$

33. $\frac{2}{3}x + 6$

34. $\frac{3}{4}x - 24$

35. $\frac{5}{6}x - 30$

36. $\frac{2}{5}x + 16$

37. $\frac{3}{8}x + 18$

38. Select the correct terms to fill in the Venn diagram to show the factors of 12 and 18x.

1	9
2	12
3	18
4	x
6	

Factors of 12   Factors of 18x

What is the GCF of 12 and 18x? Explain how the Venn diagram helped you find the GCF.

39. Which pairs of monomials have a GCF of 4a? Select all that apply.

☐ 8a, 18a   ☐ 16a, 8b   ☐ 16ab, 12a   ☐ 28a, 20a

Spiral Review

Use the Distributive Property to rewrite each expression.

40. 4(x + 1) = _____

41. 3(a + 10) = _____

42. 7(2b + 5) = _____

43. The letters P, E, M, D, A, and S form PEMDAS. This is a mnemonic device that can be used to help you remember the order of operations. Each letter stands for something. Complete the organizer.

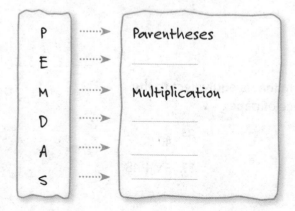

P ┈┈┈▶ Parentheses

E ┈┈┈▶ _____

M ┈┈┈▶ Multiplication

D ┈┈┈▶ _____

A ┈┈┈▶ _____

S ┈┈┈▶ _____

Powers and Exponents

Real-World Link

Savings Yogi decided to start saving money by putting a penny in his piggy bank, then doubling the amount he saves each week. Use the questions below to find how much money Yogi will save in 8 weeks.

1. Complete the table below to find the amount Yogi saved each week and the total amount in his piggy bank.

Week	0	1	2	3	4	5	6
Weekly Savings	1¢	2¢					
Total Savings	1¢	3¢					

2. How many 2s are multiplied to find his savings in Week 4? ☐

   Week 5? ☐

3. How much money will Yogi save in Week 8? _____

4. Continue the table to find when he will have enough to buy

   a pair of shoes for $80. _____

Week	7	8	9	10	11	12
Weekly Savings						
Total Savings						

 Essential Question

HOW can you use numbers and symbols to represent mathematical ideas?

 Vocabulary

power
base
exponent

Which ⓂⓅ **Mathematical Process Goals** did you use? Shade the circle(s) that applies.

① Mathematical Problem Solving

② Mathematical Communication

③ Mathematical Reasoning

④ Mathematical Connections

⑤ Mathematical Representations

Write and Evaluate Powers

A product of repeated factors can be expressed as a **power**, that is, using an exponent and a base.

The **base** is the common factor.

$$\overbrace{2 \cdot 2 \cdot 2 \cdot 2}^{\text{4 factors}} = 2^4$$

The **exponent** tells how many times the base is used as a factor.

Powers are read in a certain way.

Read and Write Powers		
Power	**Words**	**Factors**
3^1	3 to the first power	3
3^2	3 to the second power or 3 squared	$3 \cdot 3$
3^3	3 to the third power or 3 cubed	$3 \cdot 3 \cdot 3$
3^4	3 to the fourth power or 3 to the fourth	$3 \cdot 3 \cdot 3 \cdot 3$
$\vdots$	$\vdots$	$\vdots$
3^n	3 to the nth power or 3 to the nth	$\underbrace{3 \cdot 3 \cdot 3 \cdot \ldots \cdot 3}_{n \text{ factors}}$

Examples

Tutor

Write each expression using exponents.

1. $(-2) \cdot (-2) \cdot (-2) \cdot 3 \cdot 3 \cdot 3 \cdot 3$

The base -2 is a factor 3 times, and the base 3 is a factor 4 times.

$(-2) \cdot (-2) \cdot (-2) \cdot 3 \cdot 3 \cdot 3 \cdot 3 = (-2)^3 \cdot 3^4$

2. $a \cdot b \cdot b \cdot a \cdot b$

Use the properties of operations to rewrite and group like bases together. The base a is a factor 2 times, and the base b is a factor 3 times.

$a \cdot b \cdot b \cdot a \cdot b = a \cdot a \cdot b \cdot b \cdot b$
$\qquad\qquad\qquad = a^2 \cdot b^3$

> Show your work.

a. _____

b. _____

c. _____

Got it? Do these problems to find out.

a. $\dfrac{1}{2} \cdot \dfrac{1}{2} \cdot \dfrac{1}{2} \cdot \dfrac{1}{2}$ b. $4 \cdot 4 \cdot 4 \cdot 5 \cdot 5$ c. $m \cdot m \cdot n \cdot n \cdot m$

Example

Tutor

3. Evaluate $\left(-\dfrac{2}{3}\right)^4$.

$$\left(-\frac{2}{3}\right)^4 = \left(-\frac{2}{3}\right) \cdot \left(-\frac{2}{3}\right) \cdot \left(-\frac{2}{3}\right) \cdot \left(-\frac{2}{3}\right)$$
   Write the power as a product.

$$= \frac{16}{81}$$
   Multiply.

Evaluate
Remember that to evaluate an expression means to find its value.

Got it? Do these problems to find out.

d. 4^4 e. $(-2)^6$ f. $\left(\dfrac{1}{5}\right)^3$

Show your work.

d. _____

e. _____

f. _____

Example

Tutor

4. The deck of a skateboard has an area of about $2^5 \cdot 7$ square inches. What is the area of the skateboard deck?

$$2^5 \cdot 7 = 2 \cdot 2 \cdot 2 \cdot 2 \cdot 2 \cdot 7$$ Write the power as a product.

$$= (2 \cdot 2 \cdot 2 \cdot 2 \cdot 2) \cdot 7$$ Associative Property

$$= 32 \cdot 7 \text{ or } 224$$ Multiply.

The area of the skateboard deck is about 224 square inches.

Got it? Do this problem to find out.

g. A school basketball court has an area of $2^3 \cdot 3 \cdot 5^2 \cdot 7$ square feet. What is the area of a school basketball court?

g. _____

Examples

Tutor

Evaluate each expression if $a = 3$ and $b = 5$.

5. $a^2 + b^4$

$$a^2 + b^4 = 3^2 + 5^4$$ Replace a with 3 and b with 5.

$$= (3 \cdot 3) + (5 \cdot 5 \cdot 5 \cdot 5)$$ Write the powers as products.

$$= 9 + 625 \text{ or } 634$$ Add.

6. $(a - b)^2$

$$(a - b)^2 = (3 - 5)^2$$ Replace a with 3 and b with 5.

$$= (-2)^2$$ Perform operations in the parentheses first.

$$= (-2) \cdot (-2) \text{ or } 4$$ Write the powers as products. Then simplify.

h. _____

i. _____

j. _____

Got it? Do these problems to find out.

Show your work.

Evaluate each expression if $c = -4$ and $d = 9$.

h. $c^3 + d^2$ **i.** $(c + d)^3$ **j.** $d^3 - (c^2 - 2)$

Guided Practice

Check ✓

Write each expression using exponents. (Examples 1 and 2)

1. $(-11)(-11)(-11) =$ _____

2. $2 \cdot 2 \cdot 2 \cdot 3 \cdot 3 \cdot 3 =$ _____

3. $r \cdot s \cdot r \cdot r \cdot s \cdot s \cdot r \cdot r =$ _____

Evaluate each expression. (Example 3)

4. $2^6 =$ _____

5. $(-4)^4 =$ _____

6. $\left(\frac{1}{7}\right)^3 =$ _____

7. The table shows the average weights of some endangered mammals. What is the weight of each animal? (Example 4)

_____

Animal	Weight (lb)
Black bear	$2 \cdot 5^2 \cdot 7$
Key deer	$3 \cdot 5^2$
Panther	$2^3 \cdot 3 \cdot 5$

Evaluate each expression if $x = 2$ and $y = 10$. (Examples 5 and 6)

8. $x^2 + y^4 =$ _____

9. $(x^2 + y)^3 =$ _____

10. 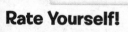 **Building on the Essential Question** How can I write repeated multiplication using powers? _____

_____

_____

_____

Rate Yourself!

Are you ready to move on? Shade the section that applies.

YES   ?   NO

For more help, go online to access a Personal Tutor.

Tutor

Independent Practice

Go online for Step-by-Step Solutions eHelp

Write each expression using exponents. (Examples 1 and 2)

1. $(-5)(-5)(-5)(-5) =$ _____

2. $3 \cdot 3 \cdot 5 \cdot q \cdot q \cdot q =$ _____

3. $m \cdot m \cdot m \cdot m \cdot m =$ _____

Evaluate each expression. (Example 3)

4. $(-9)^4 =$ _____

5. $\left(\dfrac{1}{3}\right)^4 =$ _____

6. $\left(\dfrac{5}{7}\right)^3 =$ _____

7. In the United States, nearly $8 \cdot 10^9$ text messages are sent every month. About how many text messages is this?

(Example 4) _____

_____

8. Interstate 70 stretches almost $2^3 \cdot 5^2 \cdot 11$ miles across the United States. About how many miles long is Interstate 70?

(Example 4) _____

Evaluate each expression. (Examples 5 and 6)

9. $g^5 - h^3$ if $g = 2$ and $h = 7$ _____

10. $c^2 + d^3$, if $c = 8$ and $d = -3$ _____

11. $a^2 \cdot b^6$ if $a = \dfrac{1}{2}$ and $b = 2$ _____

12. $(r - s)^3 + r^2$ if $r = -3$ and $s = -4$ _____

13. **⏺ Model with Mathematics** Refer to the graphic novel frame below for Exercises a–d.

The metric system is based on powers of 10. For example, one kilometer is equal to 1,000 meters or 10^3 meters. Write each measurement in meters as a power of 10.

a. hectometer (100 meters) _____

b. megameter (1,000,000 meters) _____

c. gigameter (1,000,000,000 meters) _____

d. petameter (1,000,000,000,000,000 meters) _____

🔥 H.O.T. Problems Higher Order Thinking

14. **⏺ Identify Structure** Write an expression with an exponent that has a value between 0 and 1. _____

15. **⏺ Identify Repeated Reasoning** Describe the following pattern: $3^4 = 81, 3^3 = 27, 3^2 = 9, 3^1 = 3$. Then use a similar pattern to predict the value of 2^{-1}. _____

16. **⏺ Reason Abstractly** Simplify the expressions below to develop a rule for multiplying powers with the same base.

$2^2 \cdot 2^3 = 32$ or $2^{\square}$ $3 \cdot 3^2 = 27$ or $3^{\square}$

$4^3 \cdot 4 = 256$ or $4^{\square}$ $x^2 \cdot x^3 = x^{\square}$

Extra Practice

17. Write $3 \cdot p \cdot p \cdot p \cdot 3 \cdot 3$ using exponents.

$\underline{3^3 \cdot p^3}$

$3 \cdot p \cdot p \cdot p \cdot 3 \cdot 3 = 3 \cdot 3 \cdot 3 \cdot p \cdot p \cdot p$

$\qquad\qquad\quad = 3^3 \cdot p^3$

Homework Help

18. Evaluate $x^3 + y^4$ if $x = -3$ and $y = 4$.

$\underline{229}$

$x^3 + y^4 = (-3)^3 + 4^4$

$\qquad\quad = (-3) \cdot (-3) \cdot (-3) + 4 \cdot 4 \cdot 4 \cdot 4$

$\qquad\quad = (-27) + 256$

$\qquad\quad = 229$

Write each expression using exponents.

19. $\left(-\dfrac{5}{6}\right)\left(-\dfrac{5}{6}\right)\left(-\dfrac{5}{6}\right) = $ _____

20. $s \cdot (7) \cdot s \cdot (7) \cdot (7) = $ _____

21. $4 \cdot b \cdot b \cdot 4 \cdot b \cdot b = $ _____

Evaluate each expression.

22. $k^4 \cdot m$, if $k = 3$ and $m = \dfrac{5}{6}$

23. $(c^3 + d^4)^2 - (c + d)^3$, if $c = -1$ and $d = 2$

Fill in each $\bigcirc$ with $<$, $>$, or $=$ to make a true statement.

24. $(6 - 2)^2 + 3 \cdot 4 \bigcirc 5^2$

25. $5 + 7^2 + 3^3 \bigcirc 3^4$

26. $\left(\dfrac{1}{2}\right)^4 \bigcirc \left(\dfrac{1}{4}\right)^2$

27. **MP** **Multiple Representations** A square has a side length of s inches.

a. **Tables** Copy and complete the table showing the side length, perimeter, and area of the square on a separate piece of paper.

b. **Graphs** On a separate piece of grid paper, graph the ordered pairs (side length, perimeter) and (side length, area) on the same coordinate plane. Then connect the points for each set.

c. **Words** On a separate sheet of paper, compare and contrast the graphs of the perimeter and area of the square. Which graph is a line?

Side Length (in.)	Perimeter (in.)	Area (in²)
1	4	1
2		
3		
4		
5		
⋮		
10		

28. Hard drive storage capacity is measured in bytes using the metric system. The metric system is based on powers of 10. For example, 1 kilobyte is equal to 1,000 bytes or 103 bytes. The table shows some common units of storage capacity. Select the correct power of 10 to complete the table.

Unit	Number of Bytes
megabyte	1,000,000
terabyte	1,000,000,000,000
gigabyte	1,000,000,000

Unit	Power of 10
megabyte	
terabyte	
gigabyte	

| 10^3 | 10^6 | 10^9 | 10^{12} | 10^{15} |

29. A cube has the dimensions shown below.

6 in.

What is the volume of the cube expressed as a power?

Spiral Review

30. The table below shows the number of ants in an ant farm on different days. The number of ants doubles every ten days.

Day	51	61	71
Number of Ants	320	640	1,280

a. How many ants were in the farm on Day 1? _____

b. How many ants will be in the farm on Day 91? _____

Add.

31. $-12 + (-19) =$ _____

32. $-8 + (-11) =$ _____

33. $-5 + 6 =$ _____

Negative Exponents

 Real-World Link

 Essential Question

HOW can you use numbers and symbols to represent mathematical ideas?

 Virginia Standards
7.1a

Insects The table shows the approximate wing beats per minute for certain insects.

Insect	Wing Beats per Minute
house fly	10,000
small butterfly	100

1. Write a ratio in simplest form that compares the number of wing beats for a butterfly to a housefly.

$$\frac{}{}$$

2. Write the ratio as a fraction with an exponent in the denominator and as a decimal.

$$\frac{}{} ; \boxed{}$$

3. Complete the 1st 4 rows of the table showing the exponential and standard forms of power of 10.

4. What operation is performed when you move down the table?

5. What happens to the exponent?

6. Extend the table to include the next three entries.

Exponential Form	Standard Form
10^3	
$10^{\boxed{}}$	100
10^1	
10^0	

Which **MP Mathematical Process Goals** did you use? Shade the circle(s) that applies.

① Mathematical Problem Solving
② Mathematical Communication
③ Mathematical Reasoning
④ Mathematical Connections
⑤ Mathematical Representations

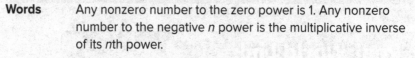

Key Concept: Zero and Negative Exponents

Words Any nonzero number to the zero power is 1. Any nonzero number to the negative *n* power is the multiplicative inverse of its *n*th power.

Examples

Numbers

$5^0 = 1$

$7^{-3} = \frac{1}{7} \cdot \frac{1}{7} \cdot \frac{1}{7}$ or $\frac{1}{7^3}$

Algebra

$x^0 = 1, x \neq 0$

$x^{-n} = \frac{1}{x^n}, x \neq 0$

Work Zone

Negative Exponents
Remember that 6^{-3} is equal to $\frac{1}{6^3}$, not -216 or -18.

You can use exponents to represent very small numbers.

Negative powers are the result of repeated division.

Examples

Show your work.

Write each expression using a positive exponent.

1. 6^{-3}

$6^{-3} = \frac{1}{6^3}$ Definition of negative exponent

2. a^{-5}

$a^{-5} = \frac{1}{a^5}$ Definition of negative exponent

Got it? Do these problems to find out.

a. 7^{-2}

b. b^{-4}

c. 5^0

d. m^{-3}

Examples

Write each fraction as an expression using a negative exponent other than −1.

3. $\frac{1}{5^2}$

$\frac{1}{5^2} = 5^{-2}$ Definition of negative exponent

4. $\frac{1}{36}$

$\frac{1}{36} = \frac{1}{6^2}$ Definition of exponent

$= 6^{-2}$ Definition of negative exponent

Got it? Do these problems to find out.

e. $\frac{1}{8^3}$

f. $\frac{1}{4}$

g. $\frac{1}{c^5}$

h. $\frac{1}{27}$

a. _____

b. _____

c. _____

d. _____

e. _____

f. _____

g. _____

h. _____

Example

Tutor

5. **STEM** One human hair is about 0.001 inch in diameter. Write the decimal as a power of 10.

$$0.001 = \frac{1}{1,000}$$ Write the decimal as a fraction.

$$= \frac{1}{10^3}$$ $1,000 = 10^3$

$$= 10^{-3}$$ Definition of negative exponent

A human hair is 10^{-3} inch thick.

Got it? Do this problem to find out.

   i. **STEM** A water molecule is about 0.0000000001 meter long. Write the decimal as a power of 10.

Multiply and Divide with Negative Exponents

The Product of Powers and the Quotient of Powers rules can be used to multiply and divide powers with negative exponents.

Examples

Tutor

Simplify each expression.

6. $5^3 \cdot 5^{-5}$

$$5^3 \cdot 5^{-5} = 5^{3 + (-5)}$$ Product of Powers

$$= 5^{-2}$$ Simplify.

$$= \frac{1}{5^2} \text{ or } \frac{1}{25}$$ Write using positive exponents. Simplify.

7. $\dfrac{w^{-1}}{w^{-4}}$

$$\frac{w^{-1}}{w^{-4}} = w^{-1 - (-4)}$$ Quotient of Powers

$$= w^{(-1) + 4} \text{ or } w^3$$ Subtract the exponents.

Got it? Do these problems to find out.

   j. $3^{-8} \cdot 3^2$ **k.** $\dfrac{11^2}{11^4}$

   l. $n^9 \cdot n^{-4}$ **m.** $\dfrac{b^{-4}}{b^{-7}}$

STOP and Reflect

Explain below the difference between the expressions $(-4)^2$ and 4^{-2}.

i. _____

Show your work.

j. _____

k. _____

l. _____

m. _____

Guided Practice

Write each expression using a positive exponent. (Examples 1 and 2)

Show your work.

1. $2^{-4} =$ _____

2. $10^{-5} =$ _____

3. $a^{-4} =$ _____

4. $g^{-7} =$ _____

Write each fraction as an expression using a negative exponent other than −1.

(Examples 3 and 4)

5. $\dfrac{1}{3^4} =$ _____

6. $\dfrac{1}{m^5} =$ _____

7. $\dfrac{1}{16} =$ _____

8. $\dfrac{1}{10,000} =$ _____

9. An American green tree frog tadpole is about 0.00001 kilometer in length when it hatches. Write this decimal as a power of 10.

(Example 5) _____

Simplify. (Examples 6 and 7)

10. $3^{-3} \cdot 3^{-2} =$ _____

11. $r^{-7} \cdot r^3 =$ _____

12. $\dfrac{p^{-2}}{p^{-12}} =$ _____

13. **Building on the Essential Question** How are negative exponents and positive exponents related?

_____

_____

_____

_____

_____

Independent Practice

Go online for Step-by-Step Solutions

eHelp

Write each expression using a positive exponent. (Examples 1 and 2)

1. $7^{-10} =$ _____

2. $(-10)^{-6} =$ _____

3. $g^{-7} =$ _____

4. $w^{-13} =$ _____

Write each fraction as an expression using a negative exponent other than −1.

(Examples 3 and 4)

5. $\frac{1}{12^4} =$ _____

6. $\frac{1}{(-5)^7} =$ _____

7. $\frac{1}{125} =$ _____

8. $\frac{1}{1,024} =$ _____

9. The table shows different metric measurements. Write each decimal

as a power of 10. (Example 5) _____

Measurement	Value
Decimeter	0.1
Centimeter	0.01
Millimeter	0.001
Micrometer	0.000001

10. **STEM** An atom is a small unit of matter. A small atom measures about 0.0000000001 meter. Write the decimal as a power of 10.

(Example 5)

_____

Simplify. (Examples 6 and 7)

11. $2^{-3} \cdot 2^{-4} =$ _____

12. $10^{-4} \times 10^7 =$ _____

13. $y^{-1} \cdot y^4 =$ _____

14. $(3a)(a^{-3}) =$ _____

15. $\frac{3^{-1}}{3^{-5}} =$ _____

16. $\frac{a^{-4}}{a^{-6}} =$ _____

17. $\frac{y^{-6}}{y^{-10}} =$ _____

18. $\frac{z^{-4}}{z^{-8}} =$ _____

19 STEM The mass of a molecule of penicillin is 10^{-18} kilogram and the mass of a molecule of insulin is 10^{-23} kilogram. How many times greater is the mass of a molecule of penicillin than the mass of a molecule of insulin?

_____

20. (MP) **Justify Conclusions** A common flea that is 2^{-4} inch long can jump about 2^3 inches high. About how many times its body size can a flea jump? Explain your reasoning.

_____

H.O.T. Problems Higher Order Thinking

21. (MP) **Identify Structure** Without evaluating, order 11^{-3}, 11^2, and 11^0 from least to greatest. Explain your reasoning.

_____

_____

22. (MP) **Identify Structure** Write an expression with a negative exponent that has a value between 0 and $\frac{1}{2}$.

_____

_____

23. (MP) **Persevere with Problems** Select several fractions between 0 and 1. Find the value of each fraction after it is raised to the -1 power. Explain the relationship between the -1 power and the original fraction.

_____

_____

_____

24. (MP) **Reason Abstractly** For each power, write an equivalent multiplication expression with two factors. The first factor should have a positive exponent and the second factor should have a negative exponent.

a. $10^4 = $ _____

b. $8^2 = $ _____

c. $x^7 = $ _____

Extra Practice

25. Write 3^{-5} using positive exponents. $\frac{1}{3^5}$

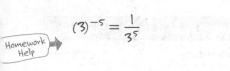

$$(3)^{-5} = \frac{1}{3^5}$$

26. Simplify $(4^{-4})(4^2)$. $\frac{1}{16}$

$$(4^{-4})(4^2) = 4^{-4+2}$$
$$= 4^{-2}$$
$$= \frac{1}{4^2} \text{ or } \frac{1}{16}$$

Write each expression using a positive exponent.

27. $6^{-8} =$ _____

28. $10^{-10} =$ _____

29. $s^{-9} =$ _____

30. $t^{-11} =$ _____

Simplify.

31. $z^2 \cdot z^{-3} =$ _____

32. $10^{-1} \times 10^3 =$ _____

33. $\frac{b^{-7}}{b^5} =$ _____

34. $\frac{x^4}{x^{-2}} =$ _____

35. $2^{-4} =$ _____

36. $(-5)^{-4} =$ _____

37. $(-10)^{-4} =$ _____

38. $(0.5)^{-4} =$ _____

MP Persevere with Problems Find the missing exponent.

39. $\frac{17^{\bullet}}{17^4} = 17^8$ _____

40. $\frac{k^6}{k^{\bullet}} = k^2$ _____

41. $\frac{p^{-1}}{p^{\bullet}} = p^{10}$ _____

42. The diameter of the average human cell is about 4^{-4} inch. Which of the following expressions are equivalent to this diameter? Select all that apply.

☐ $\frac{1}{4^4}$ in   ☐ $-\frac{1}{4^4}$ in.   ☐ $\frac{1}{256}$ in.   ☐ 0.00390625 in.

43. The table shows the values of different measurements in the metric system.

Select the correct answer to write each measurement as a power of 10.

Measurement	Power of 10
micrometer	
millimeter	
nanometer	
picometer	

10^{-12}	10^{-5}
10^{-9}	10^{-3}
10^{-6}	10^{-2}

Measurement	Value
micrometer	0.000001 m
millimeter	0.001 m
nanometer	0.000000001 m
picometer	0.000000000001 m

Spiral Review

Evaluate.

44. $10^2 =$ _____

45. $10^3 =$ _____

46. $10^6 =$ _____

47. $10^5 =$ _____

Find each missing value.

48. $0.003 \times$ _____ $= 3$

49. $0.079 \times$ _____ $= 7.9$

50. $0.00041 \times$ _____ $= 4.1$

51. $987 \div$ _____ $= 9.87$

52. $3,400 \div$ _____ $= 3.4$

53. $7,450 \div$ _____ $= 745$

Scientific Notation

Lesson 10

Real-World Link

Electronics A single sided, single layer DVD has a storage capacity of 4.7 gigabytes. One gigabyte is equal to 10^9 bytes.

1. Write a multiplication expression that represents how many bytes can be stored on the DVD. _____

2. Complete the table below.

Expression	Product	Expression	Product
$4.7 \times 10^1 = 4.7 \times 10$	47	$4.7 \times 10^{-1} = 4.7 \times \frac{1}{10}$	0.47
$4.7 \times 10^2 = 4.7 \times 100$		$4.7 \times 10^{-2} = 4.7 \times \frac{1}{100}$	
$4.7 \times 10^3 = 4.7 \times 1{,}000$		$4.7 \times 10^{-3} = 4.7 \times \frac{1}{1000}$	
$4.7 \times 10^4 = 4.7 \times$ _____		$4.7 \times 10^{-4} = 4.7 \times$ _____	

3. If 4.7 is multiplied by a positive power of 10, what relationship exists between the decimal point's new position and the exponent?

_____

_____

4. When 4.7 is multiplied by a negative power of 10, how does the new position of the decimal point relate to the negative exponent? _____

_____

Essential Question

HOW can you use numbers and symbols to represent mathematical ideas?

Vocab

Vocabulary

scientific notation

Virginia Standards
7.1b

Which **MP** **Mathematical Process Goals** did you use? Shade the circle(s) that applies.

① Mathematical Problem Solving
② Mathematical Communication
③ Mathematical Reasoning
④ Mathematical Connections
⑤ Mathematical Representations

Scientific Notation

Words **Scientific notation** is when a number is written as the product of a factor and an integer power of 10. When the number is positive the factor must be greater than or equal to 1 and less than 10.

Symbols $a \times 10^n$, where $1 \le a < 10$ and n is an integer

Example $425{,}000{,}000 = 4.25 \times 10^8$

Use these rules to express a number in scientific notation.

- If the number is greater than or equal to 1, the power of ten is positive.
- If the number is between 0 and 1, the power of ten is negative.

Work Zone

Powers of Ten

Multiplying a factor by a positive power of 10 moves the decimal point right. Multiplying a factor by a negative power of 10 moves the decimal point left.

Examples

Write each number in standard form.

1. 5.34×10^4

$5.34 \times 10^4 = 53{,}400.$

2. 3.27×10^{-3}

$3.27 \times 10^{-3} = 0.00327$

Got it? Do these problems to find out.

Show your work.

a. 7.42×10^5 b. 6.1×10^{-2} c. 3.714×10^2

a. _____

b. _____

c. _____

Examples

Write each number in scientific notation.

3. 3,725,000

$$3{,}725{,}000 = 3.725 \times 1{,}000{,}000$$
$$= 3.725 \times 10^6$$

The decimal point moves 6 places.

Since $3{,}725{,}000 > 1$, the exponent is positive.

4. 0.000316

$$0.000316 = 3.16 \times 0.0001$$
$$= 3.16 \times 10^{-4}$$

The decimal point moves 4 places.

Since $0 < 0.000316 < 1$, the exponent is negative.

Got it? Do these problems to find out.

d. 14,140,000   e. 0.00876   f. 0.114

Example

5. Refer to the table at the right. Order the countries according to the amount of money visitors spent in the United States from greatest to least.

Dollars Spent by International Visitors in the U.S	
Country	**Dollars Spent**
Canada	1.03×10^7
India	1.83×10^6
Mexico	7.15×10^6
United Kingdom	1.06×10^7

Canada and United Kingdom   Mexico and India

Step 1 $\begin{Bmatrix} 1.06 \times 10^7 \\ 1.03 \times 10^7 \end{Bmatrix} > \begin{Bmatrix} 7.15 \times 10^6 \\ 1.83 \times 10^6 \end{Bmatrix}$ ← Group the numbers by their power of 10.

Step 2 $1.06 > 1.03$ $7.15 > 1.83$ ← Order the decimals.

United Kingdom Canada   Mexico India

Got it? Do this problem to find out.

g. Some of the top U.S. cities visited by overseas travelers are shown in the table. Order the cities according to the number of visitors from least to greatest.

U.S. City	Number of Visitors
Boston	7.21×10^5
Las Vegas	1.3×10^6
Los Angeles	2.2×10^6
Metro D.C. area	9.01×10^5

g. _____

Example

6. **STEM** If you could walk at a rate of 2 meters per second, it would take you 1.92×10^8 seconds to walk to the moon. Is it more appropriate to report this time as 1.92×10^8 seconds or 6.09 years? Explain your reasoning.

The measure 6.09 years is more appropriate. The number 1.92×10^8 seconds is very large so choosing a larger unit of measure is more meaningful.

Got it? Do this problem to find out.

h. _____

h. **STEM** In an ocean, the sea floor moved 475 kilometers over 65 million years. Is it more appropriate to report this rate as 7.31×10^{-5} kilometer per year or 7.31 centimeters per year? Explain your reasoning.

Guided Practice

Check ✓

Write each number in standard form. (Examples 1 and 2)

1. $9.931 \times 10^5 =$ _____

2. $6.02 \times 10^{-4} =$ _____

Show your work.

Write each number in scientific notation. (Examples 3 and 4)

3. $8{,}785{,}000{,}000 =$ _____

4. $0.524 =$ _____

5. The table lists the total value of music shipments for four years. List the years from least to greatest dollar amount.
(Example 5)

_____

_____

Year	Music Shipments ($)
1	1.22×10^{10}
2	1.12×10^{10}
3	7.15×10^6
4	1.06×10^7

6. **STEM** A plant cell has a diameter of 1.3×10^{-8} kilometer. Is it more appropriate to report the diameter of a plant cell as 1.3×10^{-8} kilometer or 1.3×10^{-2} millimeter? Explain your reasoning. (Example 6)

_____

_____

7. **Building on the Essential Question** How is scientific notation useful in the real world?

_____

_____

_____

_____

Rate Yourself!

☐ I understand how to write numbers in scientific notation.

▶▶ Great! You're ready to move on!

☐ I still have some questions about how to write numbers in scientific notation.

⫘ No Problem! Go online to access a Personal Tutor.

Tutor

Write each number in standard form. (Examples 1 and 2)

1. $3.16 \times 10^3 =$ _____

2. $1.1 \times 10^{-4} =$ _____

3. $2.52 \times 10^{-5} =$ _____

 Show your work.

Write each number in scientific notation. (Examples 3 and 4)

4. $43{,}000 =$ _____

5. $0.0072 =$ _____

6. $0.0000901 =$ _____

7 The areas of the world's oceans are listed in the table. Order the oceans according to their area from least to greatest. (Example 5)

_____

_____

World's Oceans	
Ocean	Area (mi^2)
Atlantic	2.96×10^7
Arctic	5.43×10^6
Indian	2.65×10^7
Pacific	6×10^7
Southern	7.85×10^6

8. The space shuttle can travel about 8×10^5 centimeters per second. Is it more appropriate to report this rate as 8×10^5 centimeters per second or 8 kilometers per second? Explain. (Example 6)

_____

_____

9. The inside diameter of a certain size of ring is 1.732×10^{-2} meter. Is it more appropriate to report the ring diameter as 1.732×10^{-2} meter or 17.32 millimeters? Explain. (Example 6)

_____

_____

Fill in each ◯ **with <, >, or = to make a true statement.**

10. $678{,}000$ ◯ 6.78×10^6

11 6.25×10^3 ◯ 6.3×10^3

12. **MP Model with Mathematics** Refer to the graphic novel frame below for Exercises a–c.

a. Find Jacob's and Sarah's heights in nanometers.

b. Write each height using scientific notation.

c. Give an example of something that would be appropriately measured by nanometers.

H.O.T. Problems Higher Order Thinking

13. **MP Justify Conclusions** Determine whether 1.2×10^5 or 1.2×10^6 is closer to one million. Explain.

14. **MP Persevere with Problems** Compute and express each value in scientific notation.

a. $\dfrac{(130,000)(0.0057)}{0.0004} = $

b. $\dfrac{(90,000)(0.0016)}{(200,000)(30,000)(0.00012)} = $

15. **MP Model with Mathematics** Write two numbers in scientific notation with values between 100 and 1,000. Then write an inequality that shows the relationship between your two numbers.

Extra Practice

16. Write 7.113×10^7 in standard form.

71,130,000

$7.113 \times 10^7 = 7113\underset{\smile\smile\smile\smile\smile}{0000.}$ The decimal
point moves
7 places right.

Homework
Help

17. Write 0.00000707 in scientific notation.

7.07×10^{-6}

$0.00000707 = 7.07 \times 0.000001$
$\qquad\qquad\;\; = 7.07 \times 10^{-6}$

The decimal point moves 6 places.
Since $0 < 0.00000707 < 1$,
the exponent is negative.

Write each number in standard form.

18. $2.08 \times 10^2 =$ _____

19. $7.8 \times 10^{-3} =$ _____

20. $8.73 \times 10^{-4} =$ _____

Write each number in scientific notation.

21. $6,700 =$ _____

22. $52,300,000 =$ _____

23. $0.037 =$ _____

24. **STEM** The table shows the mass in grams of one atom of each of several elements. List the elements in order from the least mass to greatest mass per atom.

Element	Mass per Atom
Carbon	1.995×10^{-23} g
Gold	3.272×10^{-22} g
Hydrogen	1.674×10^{-24} g
Oxygen	2.658×10^{-23} g
Silver	1.792×10^{-22} g

MP Identify Structure Arrange each set of numbers in increasing order.

25. $216,000,000,\ 2.2 \times 10^3,\ 3.1 \times 10^7,\ 310,000$

_____

26. $4.56 \times 10^{-2},\ 4.56 \times 10^3,\ 4.56 \times 10^2,\ 4.56 \times 10^{-3}$

_____

27. The thermosphere layer of the atmosphere is between 90,000 and 110,000 meters above sea level. Which of the following elevations are in the thermosphere? Select yes or no.

a. 9.8×10^{-4} ☐ Yes ☐ No

b. 1.04×10^{5} ☐ Yes ☐ No

c. 9.72×10^{4} ☐ Yes ☐ No

d. 1.45×10^{5} ☐ Yes ☐ No

28. The attendance for four Major League baseball teams for a recent year is shown below.

Sort the teams from least to greatest attendance.

Team	Attendance
Los Angeles Angels	3.06×10^{6}
Miami Marlins	22.2×10^{5}
Pittsburgh Pirates	20.9×10^{5}
St. Louis Cardinals	3.26×10^{6}

	Team	Attendance
Least		
Greatest		

Which team had the greatest attendance? ☐

Spiral Review

Find each sum or difference.

29. $9.7 + 0.532 =$ _____

30. $4.39 - 0.035 =$ _____

31. $679 - 1.4 =$ _____

Vocabulary Start-Up

A **square root** of a number is one of its two equal factors. Numbers such as 1, 4, 9, 16, and 25 are called **perfect squares** because they are squares of integers.

Complete the graphic organizer.

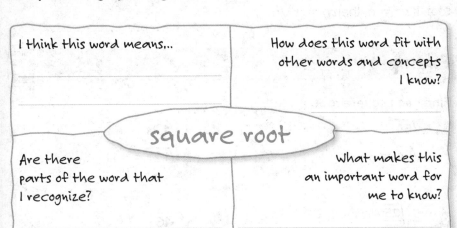

I think this word means...

_____

_____

How does this word fit with other words and concepts I know?

square root

Are there parts of the word that I recognize?

What makes this an important word for me to know?

What is the relationship between squaring a number and finding the

square root? _____

 Real-World Link

The square base of the Great Pyramid of Giza covers almost 562,500 square feet. How could you determine the length of each side of the base?

_____

 Which **MP** **Mathematical Process Goals** did you use? Shade the circle(s) that applies.

① Mathematical Problem Solving

② Mathematical Communication

③ Mathematical Reasoning

④ Mathematical Connections

⑤ Mathematical Representations

 Essential Question

HOW can you use numbers and symbols to represent mathematical ideas?

 Vocabulary

square root
perfect square
radical sign
cube root
perfect cube

 Virginia Standards
7.1d

Square Root

Words	A square root of a number is one of its two equal factors.
Symbols	If $x^2 = y$, then x is a square root of y.
Example	$5^2 = 25$ so 5 is a square root of 25.

Every positive number has *both* a positive and negative square root. In most real-world situations, only the positive or *principal* square root is considered. A **radical sign**, $\sqrt{}$, is used to indicate the principal square root. If $n^2 = a$, then $n = \pm\sqrt{a}$.

Examples

Tutor

Find each square root.

1. $\sqrt{64}$

$\sqrt{64} = 8$ Find the positive square root of 64; $8^2 = 64$.

2. $\pm\sqrt{1.21}$

$\pm\sqrt{1.21} = \pm 1.1$ Find both square roots of 1.21; $1.1^2 = 1.21$.

Show your work.

3. $-\sqrt{\dfrac{25}{36}}$

$-\sqrt{\dfrac{25}{36}} = -\dfrac{5}{6}$ Find the negative square root of $\dfrac{25}{36}$; $\left(\dfrac{5}{6}\right)^2 = \dfrac{25}{36}$.

4. $\sqrt{-16}$

There is no real square root because no number times itself is equal to -16.

Got it? Do these problems to find out.

a. $\sqrt{\dfrac{9}{16}}$ **b.** $\pm\sqrt{0.81}$ **c.** $-\sqrt{49}$ **d.** $\sqrt{-100}$

Example

Tutor

5. Solve $t^2 = 169$. Check your solution(s).

$t^2 = 169$ Write the equation.

$t = \pm\sqrt{169}$ Definition of square root

$t = 13$ and -13 **Check** $13 \cdot 13 = 169$ and $(-13)(-13) = 169$ ✓

Got it? Do these problems to find out.

e. $289 = a^2$ **f.** $m^2 = 0.09$ **g.** $y^2 = \dfrac{4}{25}$

Cube Roots

Words A **cube root** of a number is one of its three equal factors.

Symbols If $x^3 = y$, then x is the cube root of y.

Numbers such as 8, 27, and 64 are **perfect cubes** because they are the cubes of integers.

$8 = 2 \cdot 2 \cdot 2$ or 2^3 $27 = 3 \cdot 3 \cdot 3$ or 3^3 $64 = 4 \cdot 4 \cdot 4$ or 4^3

The symbol $\sqrt[3]{}$ is used to indicate a cube root of a number.

If $n^3 = a$, then $n = \sqrt[3]{a}$. You can use this relationship to solve equations that involve cubes.

Examples

Find each cube root.

6. $\sqrt[3]{125}$

$\sqrt[3]{125} = 5$ $5^3 = 5 \cdot 5 \cdot 5$ or 125

7. $\sqrt[3]{-27}$

$\sqrt[3]{-27} = -3$ $(-3)^3 = (-3) \cdot (-3) \cdot (-3)$ or -27

> **Cube Roots**
> While $\sqrt{-16}$ is not a real number, $\sqrt[3]{-27}$ is a real number. $-3 \cdot -3 \cdot -3 = -27$

Got it? Do these problems to find out.

h. $\sqrt[3]{729}$ i. $\sqrt[3]{-64}$ j. $\sqrt[3]{1,000}$

Show your work.

h. _____

i. _____

j. _____

Example

8. Dylan has a planter in the shape of a cube that holds 8 cubic feet of potting soil. Solve the equation $8 = s^3$ to find the side length s of the container.

$8 = s^3$ Write the equation.

$\sqrt[3]{8} = s$ Take the cube root of each side.

$2 = s$ Definition of cube root

So, each side of the container is 2 feet.

Check $(2)^3 = 8$ ✓

Got it? Do this problem to find out.

k. _____

k. An aquarium in the shape of a cube that will hold 25 gallons of water has a volume of 3.375 cubic feet. Solve $s^3 = 3.375$ to find the length of one side of the aquarium.

Guided Practice

Find each square root. (Examples 1–4)

1. $\sqrt{9} =$ _____

Show your work.

2. $\sqrt{\dfrac{4}{9}} =$ _____

3. $\sqrt{144} =$ _____

Solve each equation. Check your solution(s). (Example 5)

4. $p^2 = 36$ _____

5. $t^2 = \dfrac{1}{9}$ _____

6. $6.25 = r^2$ _____

Find each cube root. (Examples 6 and 7)

7. $\sqrt[3]{216} =$ _____

8. $\sqrt[3]{-125} =$ _____

9. $\sqrt[3]{-8} =$ _____

10. A cube-shaped packing box can hold 729 cubic inches of packing material. Solve $729 = s^3$ to find the length of one side of the box. (Example 8) _____

11. **Building on the Essential Question** Why would I need to use square roots and cube roots?

_____

_____

_____

_____

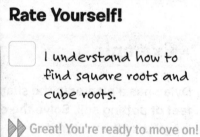

Rate Yourself!

☐ I understand how to find square roots and cube roots.

▶▶ Great! You're ready to move on!

☐ I still have some questions about finding square roots and cube roots.

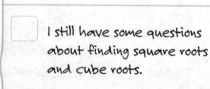
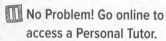
No Problem! Go online to access a Personal Tutor. Tutor

Independent Practice

 eHelp
Go online for Step-by-Step Solutions

Find each square root. (Examples 1–4)

1. $\sqrt{16} =$ _____

 Show your work.

2. $\sqrt{361} =$ _____

3. $\sqrt{-36} =$ _____

4. $\pm\sqrt{\dfrac{9}{49}} =$ _____

5. $-\sqrt{2.56} =$ _____

6. $\sqrt{121} =$ _____

Solve each equation. Check your solution(s). (Example 5)

7. $v^2 = 81$ _____

8. $w^2 = \dfrac{36}{100}$ _____

9. $0.0169 = c^2$ _____

Find each cube root. (Examples 6 and 7)

10. $\sqrt[3]{1,728} =$ _____

11. $\sqrt[3]{-0.125} =$ _____

12. $\sqrt[3]{\dfrac{27}{125}} =$ _____

13. A group of 169 students needs to be seated in a square formation for a yearbook photo. Solve the equation $169 = s^2$ to find how many students should be in each row. (Example 8) _____

14. Chloe wants to build a storage container in the shape of a cube to hold 15.625 cubic meters of hay for her horse. Solve the equation $15.625 = s^3$ to find the length of one side of the container. (Example 8)

_____

MP Persevere with Problems Given the area of each square, find the perimeter.

15.

```
Area =
121 square
inches
```
_____

16.

```
Area =
25 square
feet
```
_____

17.

```
Area =
36 square
meters
```
_____

H.O.T. Problems Higher Order Thinking

MP Persevere with Problems Find each value.

18. $\left(\sqrt{36}\right)^2 =$ _____

19. $\left(\sqrt{\dfrac{25}{81}}\right)^2 =$ _____

20. $\left(\sqrt{199}\right)^2 =$ _____

21. $\left(\sqrt{x}\right)^2 =$ _____

22. MP Reason Abstractly Based on your solutions to Exercises 18–21, write a rule that could be used to simplify the square of any square root of a number.

_____

_____

23. MP Reason Inductively Explain why $\sqrt{-4}$ is not a real number, but $\sqrt[3]{-8}$ is.

_____

_____

24. MP Reason Inductively Describe the difference between an exact value and an approximation when finding square roots of numbers that are not perfect squares. Give an example of each.

_____

_____

_____

Extra Practice

Find each square root.

25. $-\sqrt{81} = \underline{-9}$

homework Help → $9 \cdot 9 = 81$

So, $-\sqrt{81} = -9$.

26. $\sqrt{225} = $ _____

27. $\sqrt{196} = $ _____

28. $\pm\sqrt{1.44} = $ _____

Find each cube root.

29. $\sqrt[3]{-216} = $ _____

30. $\sqrt[3]{-512} = $ _____

31. $\sqrt[3]{-1,000} = $ _____

32. $\sqrt[3]{-343} = $ _____

Solve each equation. Check your solution(s).

33. $b^2 = 100$

34. $\frac{9}{64} = c^2$

35. $a^2 = 1.21$

36. $\frac{1}{8} = z^3$

37. $1.331 = c^3$

38. $m^3 = 8,000$

39. $\sqrt{x} = 5$

40. $\sqrt{y} = 20$

41. $\sqrt{z} = 10.5$

42. **MP Persevere with Problems** A concert crew needs to set up some chairs on the floor level. The chairs are to be placed in a square pattern consisting of four square sections. If one of the square sections holds 900 chairs, how many chairs will there be along each length of the larger square? _____

43. Mr. Freeman has a square cornfield. Which of the following could be the area of the cornfield if the sides are measured in whole numbers? Select all that apply.

☐ 164,000 ft^2 ☐ 156,816 ft^2 ☐ 174,724 ft^2 ☐ 215,908 ft^2

44. The area of each square in the figures below is 81 square units. Select the perimeter of each figure.

88 units	99 units
90 units	108 units
94 units	117 units

Do any of the figures have the same perimeter? If so, explain why.

Spiral Review

Evaluate each expression.

45. $13^3 =$ _____

46. $25^2 =$ _____

47. $15^3 =$ _____

48. $34^2 =$ _____

49. $5 \cdot \sqrt{121} =$ _____

50. $-6 \cdot \sqrt{36} =$ _____

51. $10 \cdot \sqrt[3]{8} =$ _____

52. $-4 \cdot \sqrt{144} =$ _____

21ST CENTURY CAREER
in Animal Conservation

Shark Scientist

Are you fascinated by sharks, especially those that are found around the coasts of the United States? If so, you should consider a career as a shark scientist. Shark scientists use satellite-tracking devices, called tags, to study and track the movements of sharks. By analyzing the data transmitted by the tags, scientists are able to learn more about the biology and ecology of sharks. Their research is helpful in protecting shark populations around the world.

College
& Career
R E A D I N E S S

Is This the Career for You?

Are you interested in a career as a shark scientist? Take some of the following courses in high school.

◆ Algebra
◆ Calculus
◆ Physics
◆ Statistics

Find out how math relates to a career in Animal Conservation.

MP Tag, You're It!

The *fork length* of a shark is the length from the tip of the snout to the fork of the tail. Use the information on the note cards to solve each problem.

1. Write an expression to represent the total length of a hammerhead shark that has a fork length of *f* feet. _____

2. Use the expression from Exercise 1 to find the total length of a hammerhead shark that has a fork length of 11.6 feet. _____

3. Write an expression to represent the average fork length of a tiger shark, given the average fork length s of a sandbar shark. _____

4. Use the expression from Exercise 3 to find the average fork length of a tiger shark if the average fork length of a sandbar shark is 129 centimeters. _____

5. Write an expression to find the average fork length of a white shark with a total length of *t* centimeters. _____

6. The total length of a white shark is 204 centimeters. Use the expression in Exercise 5 to find the approximate fork length of the white shark. _____

Tiger Shark

A study found that the average fork length of a tiger shark is 55 centimeters less than twice the average fork length of a sandbar shark.

Hammerhead Shark

The total length of a hammerhead shark is about 1.3 times the fork length.

White Shark

The fork length of a white shark is about 5.74 centimeters less than 0.94 times the total length *t*.

MP Career Project

It's time to update your career portfolio! Describe the skills that would be necessary for a shark scientist to possess. Determine whether this type of career would be a good fit for you.

List several challenges associated with this career.

- _____
- _____
- _____
- _____
- _____

Vocabulary Check

In the puzzle below, write a vocabulary term for each clue.

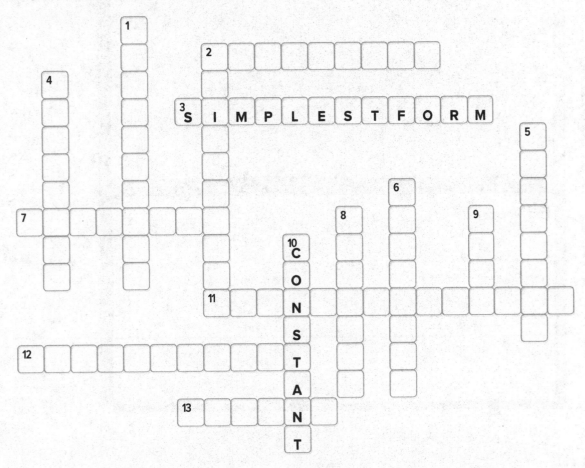

The completed crossword shows 3 Across as SIMPLEST FORM, and 10 Down as CONSTANT.

Across

2. a type of expression that contains a variable or variables

3. an algebraic expression that has no like terms and no parentheses is in this form (two words)

7. an ordered list of numbers

11. an example showing a statement is not true

12. the numerical factor of a multiplication expression

13. what is done to a variable to represent an unknown quantity

Down

1. expressions like 4(3 + 2) and 4(3) + 4(2)

2. a sequence in which each term is found by adding the same number

4. this tells how many times the base is used as a factor

5. a letter or symbol

6. a statement that is true for any number or variable

8. a branch of mathematics that uses variables

9. a number in a sequence

10. a term that contains a number only

Use Your FOLDABLES

Use your Foldable to help review the chapter.

Tape here

Linear Expressions

Explanation

Explanation

Got it?

Draw a line to match each expression with its equivalent expression.

1. $3 + 1$

2. $4(2 - x)$

3. $3x - 2 - x + 6$

4. 4^3

5. $3x + 21$

a. $8 - 4x$

b. $4 \times 4 \times 4$

c. $3(x + 7)$

d. $1 + 3$

e. $2x + 4$

Movie Time

The Townsends, a family of five, are going to the local movie theater. The family consists of two adults and three children. Mr. Townsend wants to calculate the cost of the night out. He looks up the admission prices online.

Admission:

Adults — $10.50

Children — $6.50

All shows before 6 P.M. $\frac{1}{2}$ price

Before leaving, Mr. Townsend decides that he will get some items at the theater concession stand, a large drink for each person and a large tub of popcorn for everyone to share. He will not know the prices of the items at the concession stand until they arrive.

Write your answers on another piece of paper. Show all of your work to receive full credit.

Part A
Write an expression that represents the cost of the admission prices and the concession stand items based on the available information. Let *d* represent the cost for a large drink and let *p* represent the cost of the popcorn. The initial expression must include parentheses. Then simplify the expression by using the Distributive Property and combining like terms.

Part B
Two children from next door join the Townsends. The neighbor children have movie passes and have already eaten, so Mr. Townsend will only need to pay for two more large drinks. At the concession stand, one of the children gives Mr. Townsend a five dollar bill to help pay for the drinks. Write an expression that represents the cost of the drinks for the neighbor children and includes the money given to Mr. Townsend.

Part C
While at the concession stand, Mr. Townsend sees that the large tub of popcorn is $7.50, and large drinks are $6 each. Using your answers from Part A and Part B, write an expression that represents the total cost. Then substitute the values for the popcorn and drinks in your expression. What is the total cost for the evening?

Reflect

Use what you learned about algebraic expressions to complete the graphic organizer. Then answer the chapter's Essential Question below.

When do you use a variable?

Essential Question

HOW can you use numbers and symbols to represent mathematical ideas?

How do you know which operation symbol to use?

Answer the Essential Question. HOW can you use numbers and symbols to represent mathematical ideas?

The eGlossary contains words and definitions in the following 13 languages:

Arabic	Cantonese	Hmong	Spanish	Urdu
Bengali	English	Korean	Tagalog	Vietnamese
Brazilian Portuguese	Haitian Creole	Russian		

English	Español

Aa

absolute value   The distance between a number and zero on a number line.

valor absoluto   Distancia entre un número y cero en la recta numérica.

accuracy   The degree of closeness of a measurement to the true value.

exactitud   Cercanía de una medida a su valor verdadero.

acute angle   An angle with a measure greater than 0° and less than 90°.

ángulo agudo   Ángulo que mide más de 0° y menos de 90°.

acute triangle   A triangle having three acute angles.

triángulo acutángulo   Triángulo con tres ángulos agudos.

Addition Property of Equality   If you add the same number to each side of an equation, the two sides remain equal.

propiedad de adición de la igualdad   Si sumas el mismo número a ambos lados de una ecuación, los dos lados permanecen iguales.

Additive Identity Property   The sum of any number and zero is the number.

propiedad de identidad de la suma   La suma de cualquier número y cero es el mismo número.

additive inverse   Two integers that are opposites. The sum of an integer and its additive inverse is zero.

inverso aditivo   Dos enteros opuestos.

adjacent angles   Angles that share a common vertex, a common side, and do not overlap. In the figure, the adjacent angles are ∠5 and ∠6.

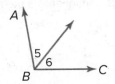

ángulos adyacentes   Ángulos que comparten un vértice, un lado común y no se traslapan. En la figura, los ángulos adyacentes son ∠5 y ∠6.

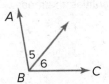

algebraic expression A combination of variables, numbers, and at least one operation.

algebra A branch of mathematics that involves expressions with variables.

alternate exterior angles Exterior angles that lie on opposite sides of the transversal. In the figure, transversal *t* intersects lines ℓ and *m*. $\angle 1$ and $\angle 7$, and $\angle 2$ and $\angle 8$ are alternate exterior angles. If line ℓ and *m* are parallel, then these pairs of angles are congruent.

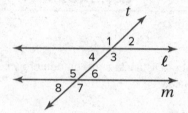

analyze To use observations to describe and compare data.

angle of rotation The degree measure of the angle through which a figure is rotated.

angle Two rays with a common endpoint form an angle. The rays and vertex are used to name the angle.

$\angle ABC$, $\angle CBA$, or $\angle B$

arc One of two parts of a circle separated by a central angle.

arithmetic sequence A sequence in which the difference between any two consecutive terms is the same.

Associative Property The way in which three numbers are grouped when they are added or multiplied does not change their sum or product.

average The sum of two or more quantities divided by the number of quantities; the mean.

expresión algebraica Una combinación de variables, números y por lo menos una operación.

álgebra Rama de las matemáticas que trata de las expresiones con variables.

ángulos alternos externos Ángulos externos que se encuentran en lados opuestos de la transversal. En la figura, la transversal *t* interseca las rectas ℓ y *m*. $\angle 1$ y $\angle 7$, y $\angle 2$ y $\angle 8$ son ángulos alternos externos. Si las rectas ℓ y *m* son paralelas, entonces estos ángulos son pares de ángulos congruentes.

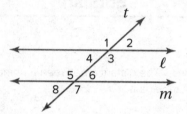

analizar Usar observaciones para describir y comparar datos.

ángulo de rotación Medida en grados del ángulo sobre el cual se rota una figura.

ángulo Dos rayos con un extremo común forman un ángulo. Los rayos y el vértice se usan para nombrar el ángulo.

$\angle ABC$, $\angle CBA$ o $\angle B$

arco Una de dos partes de un círculo separadas por un ángulo central.

sucesión aritmética Sucesión en la cual la diferencia entre dos términos consecutivos es constante.

propiedad asociativa La forma en que se agrupan tres números al sumarlos o multiplicarlos no altera su suma o producto.

promedio La suma de dos o más cantidades dividida entre el número de cantidades; la media.

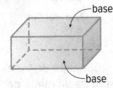

bar notation In repeating decimals, the line or bar placed over the digits that repeat. For example, $2.\overline{63}$ indicates that the digits 63 repeat.

notación de barra Línea o barra que se coloca sobre los dígitos que se repiten en decimales periódicos. Por ejemplo, $2.\overline{63}$ indica que los dígitos 63 se repiten.

base Any side of a parallelogram.

base Cualquier lado de un paralelogramo.

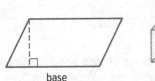

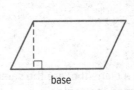

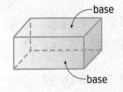

biased sample A sample drawn in such a way that one or more parts of the population are favored over others.

muestra sesgada Muestra en que se favorece una o más partes de una población.

bivariate data Data with two variables, or pairs of numerical observations.

datos bivariantes Datos con dos variables, o pares de observaciones numéricas.

box plot A method of visually displaying a distribution of data values by using the median, quartiles, and extremes of the data set. A box shows the middle 50% of the data.

diagrama de caja Un método de mostrar visualmente una distribución de valores usando la mediana, cuartiles y extremos del conjunto de datos. Una caja muestra el 50% del medio de los datos.

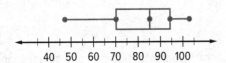

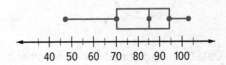

center of dilation The center point from which dilations are performed.

centro de la homotecia Punto fijo en torno al cual se realizan las homotecias.

center of rotation A fixed point around which shapes move in a circular motion to a new position.

centro de rotación Punto fijo alrededor del cual se giran las figuras en movimiento circular alrededor de un punto fijo.

center The point from which all points on circle are the same distance.

centro El punto desde el cual todos los puntos en una circunferencia están a la misma distancia.

central angle An angle that intersects a circle in two points and has its vertex at the center of the circle.

ángulo central Ángulo que interseca un círculo en dos puntos y cuyo vértice es el centro del círculo.

chord A segment with endpoints that are on a circle.

cuerda Segmento cuyos extremos están sobre un círculo.

circle graph   A graph that shows data as parts of a whole. In a circle graph, the percents add up to 100.

Area of Oceans

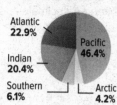

gráfica circular   Gráfica que muestra los datos como partes de un todo. En una gráfica circular los porcentajes suman 100.

Área de superficie de los océanos

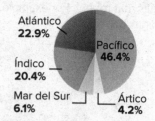

circle   The set of all points in a plane that are the same distance from a given point called the center.

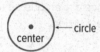

círculo   Conjunto de todos los puntos en un plano que equidistan de un punto dado llamado centro.

circumference   The distance around a circle.

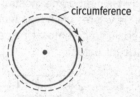

circunferencia   Distancia en torno a un círculo.

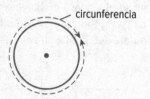

cluster   Data that are grouped closely together.

agrupamiento   Conjunto de datos que se agrupan.

coefficient   The numerical factor of a term that contains a variable.

coeficiente   Factor numérico de un término que contiene una variable.

common denominator   A common multiple of the denominators of two or more fractions. 24 is a common denominator for $\frac{1}{3}$, $\frac{5}{8}$, and $\frac{3}{4}$ because 24 is the LCM of 3, 8, and 4.

común denominador   El múltiplo común de los denominadores de dos o más fracciones. 24 es un denominador común para $\frac{1}{3}$, $\frac{5}{8}$ y $\frac{3}{4}$ porque 24 es el mcm de 3, 8 y 4.

common difference   The difference between any two consecutive terms in an arithmetic sequence.

diferencia común   La diferencia entre cualquier par de términos consecutivos en una sucesión aritmética.

Commutative Property   The order in which numbers are added or multiplied does not change the sum or product.

propiedad commutativa   La forma en que se suman o multiplican dos números no altera su suma o producto.

compatible numbers   Numbers that are easy to use to perform computations mentally.

números compatibles   Números que son fáciles de usar para realizar computations mentales.

complementary angles   Two angles are complementary if the sum of their measures is 90°.

∠1 and ∠2 are complementary angles.

ángulos complementarios   Dos ángulos son complementarios si la suma de sus medidas es 90°.

∠1 y ∠2 son complementarios.

complementary events The events of one outcome happening and that outcome not happening. The sum of the probabilities of an event and its complement is 1 or 100%. In symbols, $P(A) + P(not\ A) = 1$.

complex fraction A fraction $\frac{A}{B}$ where A or B are fractions and B does not equal zero.

composite figure A figure made of triangles, quadrilaterals, semicircles, and other two-dimensional figures.

composite solid An object made up of more than one type of solid.

composition of transformations The resulting transformation when a transformation is applied to a figure and then another transformation is applied to its image.

compound event An event consisting of two or more simple events.

compound interest Interest paid on the initial principal and on interest earned in the past.

cone A three-dimensional figure with one circlular base connected by a curved surface to a single vertex.

congruent angles Angles that have the same measure.

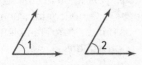

∠1 and ∠2 are congruent angles.

eventos complementarios Los eventos de un resultado que ocurre y ese resultado que no ocurre. La suma de las probabilidades de un evento y su complemento es 1 ó 100. En símbolos $P(A) + P(no\ A) = 1$.

fracción compleja Una fracción $\frac{A}{B}$ en la cual A o B son fracciones y B no es igual a cero.

figura compuesta Figura formada por triángulos, cuadriláteros, semicírculos y otras figuras bidimensionales.

sólido complejo Cuerpo compuesto de más de un tipo de sólido.

composición de transformaciones Transformación que resulta cuando se aplica una transformación a una figura y luego se le aplica otra transformación a su imagen.

evento compuesto Un evento que consiste en dos o más eventos simples.

interés compuesto Interés que se paga por el capital inicial y sobre el interés ganado en el pasado.

cono Una figura tridimensional con una circlular base conectada por una superficie curva para un solo vértice.

ángulos congruentes Ángulos que tienen la misma medida.

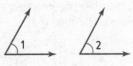

∠1 y ∠2 son congruentes.

congruent figures Figures that have the same size and same shape and corresponding sides and angles with equal measure.

figuras congruentes Figuras que tienen el mismo tamaño y la misma forma y los lados y los ángulos correspondientes tienen igual medida.

congruent segments Sides with the same length.

segmentos congruentes Lados con la misma longitud.

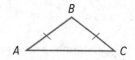

Side $\overline{AB}$ is congruent to side $\overline{BC}$.

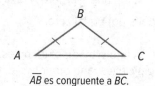

$\overline{AB}$ es congruente a $\overline{BC}$.

congruent Having the same measure; if one image can be obtained by another by a sequence of rotations, reflections, or translations.

congruente Que tienen la misma medida; si una imagen puede obtenerse de otra por una secuencia de rotaciones, reflexiones o traslaciones.

constant of proportionality A constant ratio or unit rate of two variable quantities. It is also called the constant of variation.

constante de proporcionalidad Una razón constante o tasa por unidad de dos cantidades variables. También se llama constante de variación.

constant of variation The constant ratio in a direct variation. It is also called the constant of proportionality.

constante de variación Una razón constante o tasa por unidad de dos cantidades variables. También se llama constante de proporcionalidad.

constant rate of change The rate of change between any two points in a linear relationship is the same or *constant*.

tasa constante de cambio La tasa de cambio entre dos puntos cualesquiera en una relación lineal permanece igual o *constante*.

constant A term that does not contain a variable.

constante Término que no contiene ninguna variable.

continuous data Data that take on any real number value. It can be determined by considering what numbers are reasonable as part of the domain.

datos continuos Datos que asumen cualquier valor numérico real. Se pueden determinar al considerar qué números son razonables como parte del dominio.

convenience sample A sample which includes members of the population that are easily accessed.

muestra de conveniencia Muestra que incluye miembros de una población fácilmente accesibles.

converse The converse of a theorem is formed when the parts of the theorem are reversed. The converse of the Pythagorean Theorem can be used to test whether a triangle is a right triangle. If the sides of the triangle have lengths a, b, and c, such that $c^2 = a^2 + b^2$, then the triangle is a right triangle.

recíproco El recíproco de un teorema se forma cuando se invierten las partes del teorema. El recíproco del teorema de Pitágoras puede usarse para averiguar si un triángulo es un triángulo rectángulo. Si las longitudes de los lados de un triángulo son a, b y c, tales que $c^2 = a^2 + b^2$, entonces el triángulo es un triángulo rectángulo.

coordinate plane A plane in which a horizontal number line and a vertical number line intersect at their zero points. Also called a coordinate grid.

plano de coordenadas Plano en el cual se han trazado dos rectas numéricas, una horizontal y una vertical, que se intersecan en sus puntos cero. También conocido como sistema de coordenadas.

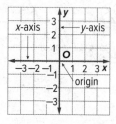

coplanar   Lines or points that lie in the same plane.

corresponding angles   Angles that are in the same position on two parallel lines in relation to a transversal.

corresponding parts   Parts of congruent or similar figures that match.

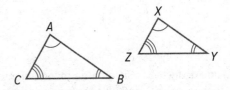

corresponding sides   The sides of similar figures that are in the same relative position.

counterexample   A specific case which proves a statement false.

cross product   The product of the numerator of one ratio and the denominator of the other ratio. The cross products of any proportion are equal.

cross section   The cross section of a solid and a plane.

cube root   One of three equal factors of a number. If $a^3 = b$, then a is the cube root of b. The cube root of 64 is 4 since $4^3 = 64$.

cubed   The product in which a number is a factor three times. Two cubed is 8 because $2 \times 2 \times 2 = 8$.

cubic units   Used to measure volume. Tells the number of cubes of a given size it will take to fill a three-dimensional figure.

3 cubic units

cylinder   A three-dimensional figure with two parallel congruent circular bases connected by a curved surface.

coplanar   Líneas o puntos situados en el mismo plano.

ángulos correspondientes   Ángulos que están en la misma posición sobre dos rectas paralelas en relación con la transversal.

partes correspondientes   Partes de figuras congruentes o semejantes que coinciden.

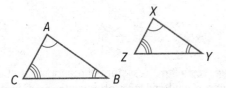

lados correspondientes   Lados de figuras semejantes que estan en la misma posición.

contraejemplo   Caso específico que demuestra la falsedad de un enunciado.

producto cruzado   Producto del numerador de una razón por el denominador de la otra razón. Los productos cruzados de cualquier proporción son iguales.

sección transversal   Intersección de un sólido con un plano.

raíz cúbica   Uno de tres factores iguales de un número. Si $a^3 = b$, entonces a es la raíz cúbica de b. La raíz cúbica de 64 es 4, dado que $4^3 = 64$.

al cubo   El producto de un número por sí mismo, tres veces. Dos al cubo es 8 porque $2 \times 2 \times 2 = 8$.

unidades cúbicas   Se usan para medir el volumen. Indican el número de cubos de cierto tamaño que se necesitan para llenar una figura tridimensional.

3 unidades cúbicas

cilindro   Una figura tridimensional con dos paralelas congruentes circulares bases conectados por una superficie curva.

Dd

data Information, often numerical, which is gathered for statistical purposes.

datos Información, con frecuencia numérica, que se recoge con fines estadísticos.

decagon A polygon having ten sides.

decágono Un polígono con diez lados.

deductive reasoning A system of reasoning that uses facts, rules, definitions, or properties to reach logical conclusions.

razonamiento deductivo Sistema de razonamiento que emplea hechos, reglas, definiciones o propiedades para obtener conclusions lógicas.

defining a variable Choosing a variable and a quantity for the variable to represent in an expression or equation.

definir una variable El elegir una variable y una cantidad que esté representada por la variable en una expresión o en una ecuacion.

degree A unit used to measure temperature and angles.

grado Unidad que se usa para medir la temperatura y los àngulos.

dependent events Two or more events in which the outcome of one event affects the outcome of the other event(s).

eventos dependientes Dos o más eventos en que el resultado de un evento afecta el resultado de otro u otros eventos.

dependent variable The variable in a relation with a value that depends on the value of the independent variable.

variable dependiente La variable en una relación cuyo valor depende del valor de la variable independiente.

derived unit A unit that is derived from a measurement system base unit, such as length, mass, or time.

unidad derivada Unidad derivada de una unidad básica de un sistema de medidas como por ejemplo, la longitud, la masa o el tiempo.

diagonal A line segment whose endpoints are vertices that are neither adjacent nor on the same face.

diagonal Segmento de recta cuyos extremos son vértices que no son ni adyacentes ni yacen en la misma cara.

diameter The distance across a circle through its center.

diámetro Segmento que pasa por el centro de un círculo y lo divide en dos partes iguales.

diameter

diámetro

dilation A transformation that enlarges or reduces a figure by a scale factor.

homotecia Transformación que produce la ampliación o reducción de una imagen por un factor de escala.

dimensional analysis The process of including units of measurement when you compute.

análisis dimensional Proceso que incluye las unidades de medida al hacer cálculos.

direct variation A relationship between two variable quantities with a constant ratio.

variación directa Relación entre las cantidades de dos variables que tienen una tasa constante.

discount The amount by which the regular price of an item is reduced.

descuento Cantidad que se le rebaja al precio regular de un artículo.

discrete data Data with space between possible data values. Graphs are represented by dots.

datos discretos Datos con espacios entre posibles valores de datos. Las gráficas están representadas por puntos.

disjoint events Events that cannot happen at the same time.

eventos disjuntos Eventos que no pueden ocurrir al mismo tiempo.

Distance Formula The distance d between two points with coordinates (x_1, y_1) and (x_2, y_2) is given by the formula

$$d = \sqrt{(x_1 - x_2)^2 + (y_1 - y_2)^2}.$$

fórmula de la distancia La distancia d entre dos puntos con coordenadas (x_1, y_1) and (x_2, y_2) viene dada por la fórmula

$$d = \sqrt{(x_1 - x_2)^2 + (y_1 - y_2)^2}.$$

distribution A way to show the arrangement of data values.

distribución Una manera de mostrar la agrupación de valores.

Distributive Property To multiply a sum by a number, multiply each addend of the sum by the number outside the parentheses. For any numbers a, b, and c, $a(b + c) = ab + ac$ and $a(b - c) = ab - ac$.

Example: $2(5 + 3) = (2 \times 5) + (2 \times 3)$ and $2(5 - 3) = (2 \times 5) - (2 \times 3$

propiedad distributiva Para multiplicar una suma por un número, multiplíquese cada sumando de la suma por el número que está fuera del paréntesis. Sean cuales fuere los números a, b, y c, $a(b + c) = ab + ac$ y $a(b - c) = ab - ac$.

Ejemplo: $2(5 + 3) = (2 \cdot 5) + (2 \cdot 3)$ y $2(5 - 3) = (2 \cdot 5) - (2 \cdot 3)$

Division Property of Equality If you divide each side of an equation by the same nonzero number, the two sides remain equal.

propiedad de igualdad de la división Si divides ambos lados de una ecuación entre el mismo número no nulo, los lados permanecen iguales.

Division Property of Inequality When you divide each side of an inequality by a negative number, the inequality symbol must be reversed for the inequality to remain true.

propiedad de desigualdad en la división Cuando se divide cada lado de una desigualdad entre un número negativo, el símbolo de desigualdad debe invertirse para que la desigualdad siga siendo verdadera.

domain The set of input values for a function or a set of x-coordinates in a relation.

dominio El conjunto de valores de entrada para una función o un conjunto de coordenadas x en una relaciòn.

dot plot A diagram that shows the frequency of data on a number line. Also known as a line plot.

doble diagrama de caja Dos diagramas de caja sobre la misma recta numérica.

double dot plot A method of visually displaying a distribution of two sets of data values where each value is shown as a dot above a number line.

doble diagrama de puntos Un método de mostrar visualmente una distribución de dos conjuntos de valores donde cada valor se muestra como un punto arriba de una recta numérica.

Ee

edge The line segment where two faces of a polyhedron intersect.

enlargement An image larger than the original.

equals sign A symbol of equality, =.

equation A mathematical sentence showing two expressions are equal. An equation contains an equals sign, =.

equation A mathematical sentence that contains an equals sign, =, stating that two quantities are equal.

equiangular A polygon in which all angles are congruent.

equilateral triangle A triangle having three congruent sides.

equilateral In a polygon, all of the sides are congruent.

equivalent equations Two or more equations with the same solution.

equivalent expressions Expressions that have the same value regardless of the value(s) of the variable(s).

equivalent ratios Ratios that express the same relationship between two quantities.

evaluate To find the value of an algebraic expression by replacing variables with numbers.

event An outcome is a possible result.

arista El segmento de línea donde se cruzan dos caras de un poliedro.

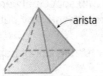

ampliación Imagen más grande que la original.

signo de igualdad Símbolo que indica igualdad, =.

ecuación Enunciado matemático que muestra que dos expresiones son iguales. Una ecuación contiene el signo de igualdad, =.

ecuación Enunciado matemático que contiene el signo de igualdad = indicando que dos cantidades son iguales.

equiangular Polígono en el cual todos los ángulos son congruentes.

triángulo equilátero Triángulo con tres lados congruentes.

equilátero En un polígono, todos los lados son congruentes.

ecuaciones equivalentes Dos o más ecuaciones con la misma solución.

expresiones equivalentes Expresiones que poseen el mismo valor, sin importar los valores de la(s) variable(s).

razones equivalentes Razones que expresan la misma relación entre dos cantidades.

evaluar Calcular el valor de una expresión sustituyendo las variables por número.

evento Un resultado posible.

experimental probability   An estimated probability based on the relative frequency of positive outcomes occurring during an experiment. It is based on what *actually* occurred during such an experiment.

exponential form   Numbers written with exponents.

exponential function   A nonlinear function in which the base is a constant and the exponent is an independent variable.

exponent   In a power, the number that tells how many times the base is used as a factor. In 5^3, the exponent is 3. That is, $5^3 = 5 \times 5 \times 5$.

exterior angles   The four outer angles formed by two lines cut by a transversal.

probabilidad experimental   Probabilidad estimada que se basa en la frecuencia relativa de los resultados positivos que ocurren durante un experimento. Se basa en lo que *en realidad* ocurre durante dicho experimento.

forma exponencial   Números escritos usando exponentes.

función exponencial   Función no lineal en la cual la base es una constante y el exponente es una variable independiente.

exponente   En una potencia, el número que indica las veces que la base se usa como factor. En 5^3, el exponente es 3. Es decir, $5^3 = 5 \times 5 \times 5$.

ángulo externo   Los cuatro ángulos exteriores que se forman cuando una transversal corta dos rectas.

face   A flat surface of a polyhedron.

cara   Una superficie plana de un poliedro.

factor the expression   The process of writing numeric or algebraic expressions as a product of their factors.

factored form   An expression expressed as the product of its factors.

factors   Two or more numbers that are multiplied together to form a product.

factor   To write a number as a product of its factors.

fair game   A game where each player has an equally likely chance of winning.

first quartile   For a data set with median *M*, the first quartile is the median of the data values less than *M*.

five-number summary   A way of characterizing a set of data that includes the minimum, first quartile, median, third quartile, and the maximum.

formal proof   A two-column proof containing statements and reasons.

factorizar la expresión   El proceso de escribir expresiones numéricas o algebraicas como el producto de sus factores.

forma factorizada   Una expresión expresada como el producto de sus factores.

factores   Dos o más números que se multiplican entre sí para formar un producto.

factorizar   Escribir un número como el producto de sus factores.

juego justo   Juego donde cada jugador tiene igual posibilidad de ganar.

primer cuartil   Para un conjunto de datos con la mediana *M*, el primer cuartil es la mediana de los valores menores que *M*.

resumen de los cinco números   Una manera de caracterizar un conjunto de datos que incluye el mínimo, el primer cuartil, la mediana, el tercer cuartil y el máximo.

demonstración formal   Demonstración endos columnas contiene enunciados y razonamientos.

formula   An equation that shows the relationship among certain quantities.

fórmula   Ecuación que muestra la relación entre ciertas cantidades.

fraction   A number that represents part of a whole or part of a set. $\frac{1}{2}, \frac{1}{3}, \frac{1}{4}, \frac{3}{4}$

fracción   Número que representa parte de un todo o parte de un conjunto. $\frac{1}{2}, \frac{1}{3}, \frac{1}{4}, \frac{3}{4}$

frequency distribution   How many pieces of data are in each interval.

distribución de frecuencias   Cantidad de datos asociada con cada intervalo.

frequency table   A table that shows the number of pieces of data that fall within the given intervals.

tabla de frecuencias   Tabla que muestra el número de datos en cada intervalo.

function rule   An expression that describes the relationship between each input and output.

regla de funciones   Expresión que describe la relación entre cada valor de entrada y de salida.

function table   A table organizing the input, rule, output, domain, rule, and range of a function.

tabla de funciones   Tabla que organiza la entrada, regla, salida, dominio, regla y rango de una función.

function   A relation in which each member of the domain (input value) is paired with exactly one member of the range (output value).

función   Relación en la cual a cada elemento del dominio (valor de entrada) le corresponde exactamente un único elemento del rango (valor de salida).

Fundamental Counting Principle   Uses multiplication of the number of ways each event in an experiment can occur to find the number of possible outcomes in a sample space.

principio fundamental de contar   Método que usa la multiplicación del número de maneras en que cada evento puede ocurrir en un experimento, para calcular el número de resultados posibles en un espacio muestral.

Gg

gap   An empty space or interval in a set of data.

laguna   Espacio o intervalo vacío en un conjunto de datos.

geometric sequence   A sequence in which each term after the first is found by multiplying the previous term by a constant.

sucesión geométrica   Sucesión en la cual cada término después del primero se determina multiplicando el término anterior por una constante.

gram   A unit of mass in the metric system equivalent to 0.001 kilogram. The amount of matter an object can hold.

gramo   Unidad de masa en el sistema métrico que equivale a 0.001 de kilogramo. La cantidad de materia que puede contener un objeto.

graph   The process of placing a point on a number line or on a coordinate plane at its proper location.

graficar   Proceso de dibujar o trazar un punto en una recta numérica o en un plano de coordenadas en su ubicación correcta.

gratuity   Also known as a tip. It is a small amount of money in return for a service.

gratificación   También conocida como propina. Es una cantidad pequeña de dinero en retribución por un servicio.

Greatest Common Factor (GCF)   The greatest of the common factors of two or more numbers. The greatest common factor of 12, 18, and 30 is 6.

máximo común divisor (MCD)   El mayor de los factores comunes de dos o más números. El máximo común divisor de 12, 18 y 30 es 6.

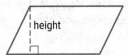

Hh

half-plane The part of the coordinate plane on one side of the boundary.

semiplano Parte del plano de coordenadas en un lado de la frontera.

height The shortest distance from the base of a parallelogram to its opposite side.

altura La distancia más corta desde la base de un paralelogramo hasta su lado opuesto.

hemisphere One of two congruent halves of a sphere.

hemisferio Una de dos mitades congruentes de una esfera.

heptagon A polygon having seven sides.

heptágono Polígono con siete lados.

hexagon A polygon having six sides.

hexágono Polígono con seis lados.

histogram A type of bar graph used to display numerical data that have been organized into equal intervals.

histograma Tipo de gráfica de barras que se usa para exhibir datos que se han organizado en intervalos iguales.

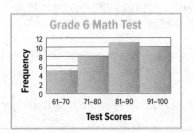

hypotenuse The side opposite the right angle in a right triangle.

hipotenusa El lado opuesto al ángulo recto de un triángulo rectángulo.

Ii

Identity Properties Properties that state that the sum of any number and 0 equals the number and that the product of any number and 1 equals the number.

propiedades de identidad Propiedades que establecen que la suma de cualquier número y 0 es igual al número y que el producto de cualquier número y 1 es igual al número.

Identity Property of Zero   The sum of an addend and zero is the addend. Example: $5 + 0 = 5$

propiedad de identidad del cero   La suma de un sumando y cero es igual al sumando. Ejemplo: $5 + 0 = 5$

identity   An equation that is true for every value for the variable.

identidad   Ecuación que es verdad para cada valor de la variable.

image   The resulting figure after a transformation.

imagen   Figura que resulta después de una transformación.

independent events   Two or more events in which the outcome of one event does not affect the outcome of the other event(s).

eventos independientes   Dos o más eventos en los cuales el resultado de uno de ellos no afecta el resultado de los otros eventos.

independent variable   The variable in a function with a value that is subject to choice.

variable independiente   Variable en una función cuyo valor está sujeto a elección.

Indirect measurement   Finding a measurement using similar figures to find the length, width, or height of objects that are too difficult to measure directly.

medición indirectia   Hallar una medicion usando figuras semejantes para calcular el largo, ancho o altura de objetos que son dificiles de medir directamente.

inductive reasoning   Reasoning that uses a number of specific examples to arrive at a plausible generalization or prediction. Conclusions arrived at by inductive reasoning lack the logical certainty of those arrived at by deductive reasoning.

razonamiento inductivo   Razonamiento que usa varios ejemplos especificos para lograr una generalización o una predicción plausible. Las conclusiones obtenidas por razonamiento inductivo carecen de la certeza lógica de aquellas obtenidas por razonamiento deductivo.

inequality   A mathematical sentence that uses $<$, $>$, $\neq$, $\leq$, or $\geq$, comparing two unequal quantities.

desigualdad   Enunciado matemático que utiliza $<$, $>$, $\neq$, $\leq$, o $\geq$, comparaciòn de dos cantidades desiguales.

informal proof   A paragraph proof.

demostración informal   Demonstración en forma de párrafo.

inscribed angle   An angle that has its vertex on the circle. Its sides contain chords of the circle.

ángulo inscrito   Ángulo cuyo vértice está en el círculo y cuyos lados contienen cuerdas del círculo.

integer   Any number from the set {... -4, -3, -2, -1, 0, 1, 2, 3, 4 ...} where ... means *continues without end.*

entero   Cualquier número del conjunto {... -4, -3, -2, -1, 0, 1, 2, 3, 4 ...} donde ... significa que *continúa sin fin.*

interest   The amount of money paid or earned for the use of money.

interés   Cantidad que se cobra o se paga por el uso del dinero.

interior angle   An angle inside a polygon or the four inside angles formed by two lines cut by a transversal.

ángulo interno   Ángulo dentro de un polígono o los cuatro àngulos interiores formados por dos lineas cortadas por una transversal.

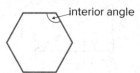
interior angle

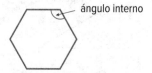
ángulo interno

interquartile range   A measure of variation in a set of numerical data, the interquartile range is the distance between the first and third quartiles of the data set.

rango intercuartil   El rango intercuartil, una medida de la variación en un conjunto de datos numéricos, es la distancia entre el primer y el tercer cuartil del conjunto de datos.

intersecting lines *Line*s that meet or cross at a common *point*.

interval The difference between successive values on a scale.

inverse operations Pairs of operations that undo each other. Addition and subtraction are inverse operations. Multiplication and division are inverse operations.

inverse variation A relationship where the product of *x* and *y* is a constant *k*. As *x* increases in value, *y* decreases in value, or as *y* decreases in value, *x* increases in value.

irrational number A number that cannot be expressed as the quotient $\frac{a}{b}$, where *a* and *b* are integers and $b \neq 0$.

isosceles triangle A triangle having at least two congruent sides.

rectas secantes *Rectas* que se intersectan o se cruzan en un *punto* común.

intervalo La diferencia entre valores sucesivos de una escala.

peraciones inversas Pares de operaciones que se anulan mutuamente. La adición y la sustracción son operaciones inversas. La multiplicación y la división son operaciones inversas.

variación inversa Relación en la cual el producto de *x* y *y* es una constante *k*. A medida que aumenta el valor de *x*, disminuye el valor de *y* o a medida que disminuye el valor de *y*, aumenta el valor de *x*.

números irracionales Número que no se puede expresar como el cociente $\frac{a}{b}$, donde *a* y *b* son enteros y $b \neq 0$.

triángulo isósceles Triángulo que tiene por lo menos dos lados congruentes.

Kk

kilogram The base unit of mass in the metric system. One kilogram equals 1,000 grams.

kilogramo Unidad básica de masa del sistema métrico. Un kilogramo equivale a 1,000 gramos.

Ll

lateral area The sum of the areas of the lateral faces of a solid.

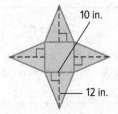

10 in.

12 in.

lateral area $= 4\left(\frac{1}{2} \times 10 \times 12\right) = 240$ square inches

lateral face Any flat surface that is not a base.

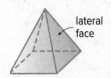

lateral face

área lateral La suma de las áreas de las caras laterales de un sólido.

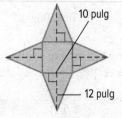

10 pulg

12 pulg

área lateral $= 4\left(\frac{1}{2} \times 10 \times 12\right) = 240$ pulgadas cuadradas

cara lateral Cualquier superficie plana que no es la base.

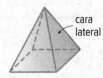

cara lateral

lateral surface area The sum of the areas of all of the lateral faces of a solid.

área de superficie lateral Suma de las áreas de todas las caras de un sólido.

least common denominator (LCD) The least common multiple of the denominators of two or more fractions. You can use the LCD to compare fractions.

mínimo común denominador (mcd) El menor de los múltiplos de los denominadores de dos o más fracciones. Puedes usar el mínimo común denominador para comparar fracciones.

least common multiple (LCM) The smallest whole number greater than 0 that is a common multiple of each of two or more numbers. The LCM of 2 and 3 is 6.

mínimo común múltiplo (mcm) El menor número entero, mayor que 0, múltiplo común de dos o más números. El mcm de 2 y 3 es 6.

leaves The digits of the least place value of data in a stem-and-leaf plot.

hoja En un diagrama de tallo y hojas, los dígitos del menor valor de posición.

legs The two sides of a right triangle that form the right angle.

catetos Los dos lados de un triángulo rectángulo que forman el ángulo recto.

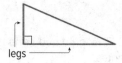

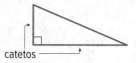

like fractions Fractions that have the same denominators.

fracciones semejantes Fracciones que tienen el mismo denominador.

like terms Terms that contain the same variables raised to the same power. Example: 5x and 6x are like terms.

términos semejante Términos que contienen las mismas variables elevadas a la misma potencia. Ejemplo: 5x y 6x son *términos semejante*.

line graph A type of statistical graph using lines to show how values change over a period of time.

gráfica lineal Tipo de gráfica estadística que usa segmentos de recta para mostrar cómo cambian los valores durante un período de tiempo.

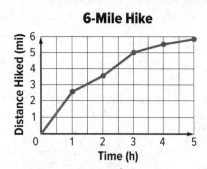

line of best fit A line that is very close to most of the data points in a scatter plot.

recta de mejor ajuste Recta que más se acerca a la mayoría de puntos de los datos en un diagrama de dispersión.

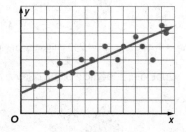

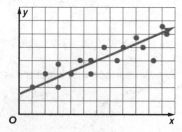

line of reflection   The line over which a figure is reflected.

line of symmetry   A line that divides a figure into two halves that are reflections of each other.

line of symmetry

line plot   A diagram that shows the frequency of data on a number line. Also known as a dot plot.

line segment   A part of a *line* that connects two points.

line symmetry   A figure has line symmetry if a line can be drawn so that one half of the figure is a mirror image of the other half.

linear equation   An equation with a graph that is a straight line.

linear expression   An algebraic expression in which the variable is raised to the first power, and variables are not multiplied nor divided.

linear function   A function in which the graph of the solution forms a straight line.

linear relationship   A relationship for which the graph is a straight line.

linear   To fall in a straight line.

line   A set of *points* that form a straight path that goes on forever in opposite directions.

literal equation   An equation or formula that has more than one variable.

liter   The base unit of capacity in the metric system. The amount of dry or liquid material an object can hold.

línea de reflexión   Línea a través de la cual se refleja una figura.

eje de simetría   Recta que divide una figura en dos mitades especulares.

eje de simetría

esquema lineal   Diagrama que muestra la frecuencia de los datos sobre una recta numérica.

segmento de recta   Parte de una *recta* que conecta dos puntos.

simetría lineal   Una figura tiene simetría lineal si se puede trazar una recta de manera que una mitad de la figura sea una imagen especular de la otra mitad.

ecuación lineal   Ecuación cuya gráfica es una recta.

expresión lineal   Expresión algebraica en la cual la variable se eleva a la primera potencia.

función lineal   Función en la que la gráfica de la solución forma una línea recta.

relación lineal   Una relación para la cual la gráfica es una línea recta.

lineal   Que cae en una línea recta.

recta   Conjunto de *puntos* que forman una trayectoria recta sin fin en direcciones oputestas.

ecuación literal   Ecuación o fórmula con más de una variable.

litro   Unidad básica de capacidad del sistema métrico. La cantidad de materia líquida o sólida que puede contener un objeto.

Mm

markdown   An amount by which the regular price of an item is reduced.

rebaja   Una cantidad por la cual el precio regular de un artículo se reduce.

markup   The amount the price of an item is increased above the price the store paid for the item.

margen de utilidad   Cantidad de aumento en el precio de un artículo por encima del precio que paga la tienda por dicho artículo.

mean absolute deviation   The average of the absolute values of differences between the mean and each value in a data set.

desviación media absoluta   El promedio de los valores absolutos de diferencias entre el medio y cada valor de un conjunto de datos.

mean   The sum of the data divided by the number of items in the set.

media   La suma de datos dividida entre el número total de artículos.

measures of center   Numbers that are used to describe the center of a set of data. These measures include the mean, median, and mode.

medidas del centro   Numéros que se usan para describir el centro de un conjunto de datos. Estas medidas incluyen la media, la mediana y la moda.

measures of variation   A measure used to describe the distribution of data.

medidas de variación   Medida usada para describir la distribución de los datos.

median   A measure of center in a set of numerical data. The median of a list of values is the value appearing at the center of a sorted version of the list—or the mean of the two central values, if the list contains an even number of values.

mediana   Una medida del centro en un conjunto de datos numéricos. La mediana de una lista de valores es el valor que aparece en el centro de una versión ordenada de la lista, o la media de los dos valores centrales si la lista contiene un número par de valores.

meter   The base unit of length in the metric system.

metro   Unidad fundamental de longitud del sistema métrico.

metric system   A decimal system of measures. The prefixes commonly used in this system are kilo-, centi-, and milli-.

sistema métrico   Sistema decimal de medidas. Los prefijos más comunes son kilo-, centi- y mili-.

mode   The number or numbers that appear most often in a set of data. If there are two or more numbers that occur most often, all of them are modes.

moda   El número o números que aparece con más frecuencia en un conjunto de datos. Si hay dos o más números que ocurren con más frecuencia, todosellos son modas.

monomial   A number, a variable, or a product of a number and one or more variables.

monomio   Un número, una variable o el producto de un número por una o más variables.

Multiplication Property of Equality   If you multiply each side of an equation by the same nonzero number, the two sides remain equal.

propiedad de multiplicación de la igualdad   Si multiplicas ambos lados de una ecuación por el mismo número no nulo, lo lados permanecen iguales.

Multiplication Property of Inequality   When you multiply each side of an inequality by a negative number, the inequality symbol must be reversed for the inequality to remain true.

propiedad de desigualdad en la multiplicación   Cuando se multiplica cada lado de una desigualdad por un número negativo, el símbolo de desigualdad debe invertirse para que la desigualdad siga siendo verdadera.

Multiplicative Identity Property   The product of any number and one is the number.

propiedad de identidad de la multiplicación   El producto de cualquier número y uno es el mismo número.

multiplicative inverses Two numbers with a product of 1. For example, the multiplicative inverse of $\frac{2}{3}$ is $\frac{3}{2}$.

inversos multiplicativo Dos números cuyo producto es 1. El inverso multiplicativo de $\frac{2}{3}$ es $\frac{3}{2}$.

Multiplicative Property of Zero The product of any number and zero is zero.

propiedad del cero en la multiplicación El producto de cualquier número y cero es cero.

Nn

negative exponent Any nonzero number to the negative *n* power. It is the multiplicative inverse of its *n*th power.

exponente negativo Cualquier número que no sea cero a la potencia negative de *n*. Es el inverso multiplicativo de su *enésimo* potencia.

negative integer An integer that is less than zero. Negative integers are written with a — sign.

entero negativo Número menor que cero. Se escriben con el signo —.

net A two-dimensional pattern of a three-dimensional figure.

red Patrón bidimensional de una figura tridimensional.

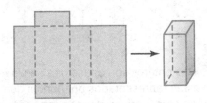

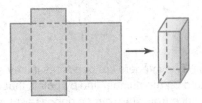

nonagon A polygon having nine sides.

enágono Polígono que tiene nueve lados.

nonlinear function A function whose rate of change is not constant. The graph of a nonlinear function is not a straight line.

función no lineal Función cuya tasa de cambio no es constante. La gráfica de una función no lineal no es una recta.

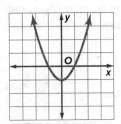

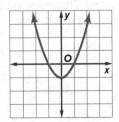

nonproportional The relationship between two ratios with a rate or ratio that is not constant.

no proporcional Relación entre dos razones cuya tasa o razón no es constante.

null set The empty set.

conjunto nulo El conjunto vacío.

numerical expression A combination of numbers and operations.

expresión numérica Una combinación de números y operaciones.

obtuse angle   Any angle that measures greater than 90° but less than 180°.

ángulo obtuso   Cualquier ángulo que mide más de 90° pero menos de 180°.

obtuse triangle   A triangle having one obtuse angle.

triángulo obtusángulo   Triángulo que tiene un ángulo obtuso.

octagon   A polygon having eight sides.

octágono   Polígono que tiene ocho lados.

opposites   Two integers are opposites if they are represented on the number line by points that are the same distance from zero, but on opposite sides of zero. The sum of two opposites is zero.

opuestos   Dos enteros son opuestos si, en la recta numérica, están representados por puntos que equidistan de cero, pero en direcciones opuestas. La suma de dos opuestos es cero.

order of operations   The rules to follow when more than one operation is used in a numerical expression.

orden de las operaciones   Reglas a seguir cuando se usa más de una operación en una expresión numérica.

ordered pair   A pair of numbers used to locate a point in the coordinate plane. The ordered pair is written in this form: (*x*-coordinate, *y*-coordinate).

par ordenado   Par de números que se utiliza para ubicar un punto en un plano de coordenadas. Se escribe de la siguiente forma: (coordenada *x*, coordenada *y*).

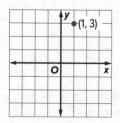

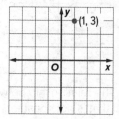

origin   The point of intersection of the *x*-axis and *y*-axis in a coordinate plane. The origin as at (0,0)

origen   Punto en que el eje *x* y el eje *y* se intersecan en un plano de coordenadas. El origen como en (0,0)

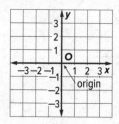

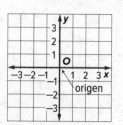

outcome Any one of the possible results of an action. For example, 4 is an outcome when a number cube is rolled.

outlier A data value that is either much *greater* or much *less* than the median.

resultado Cualquiera de los resultados posibles de una acción. Por ejemplo, 4 puede ser un resultado al lanzar un cubo numerado.

valor atípico Valor de los datos que es mucho *mayor* o mucho *menor* que la mediana.

---

paragraph proof A paragraph that explains why a statement or conjecture is true.

prueba por párrafo Párrafo que explica por qué es verdadero un enunciado o una conjetura.

parallel lines Lines in the same plane that never intersect or cross. The symbol ‖ means parallel.

rectas paralelas Rectas que yacen en un mismo plano y que no se intersecan. El símbolo ‖ significa paralela a.

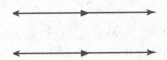

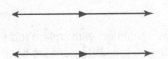

parallelogram A quadrilateral with opposite sides parallel and opposite sides congruent.

paralelogramo Cuadrilátero cuyos lados opuestos son paralelos y congruentes.

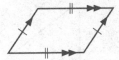

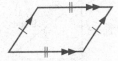

parallel Lines that never intersect no matter how far they extend.

paralelo Rectas que nunca se intersecan sea cual sea su extensión.

peak The most frequently occurring value in a line plot.

pico El valor que ocurre con más frecuencia en un diagrama de puntos.

pentagon A polygon having five sides.

pentágono Polígono que tiene cinco lados.

percent equation An equivalent form of a percent proportion in which the percent is written as a decimal. part = percent · whole

ecuación porcentual Ecuación que describe la relación entre la parte, el todo y el por ciento. parte = por ciento · todo

percent error A ratio that compares the inaccuracy of an estimate (amount of error) to the actual amount.

porcentaje de error Una razón que compara la inexactitud de una estimación (cantidad del error) con la cantidad real.

percent of change A ratio that compares the change in quantity to the original amount.

$$\text{percent of change} = \frac{\text{amount of change}}{\text{original amount}}$$

porcentaje de cambio Razón que compara el cambio en una cantidad a la cantidad original.

$$\text{procentaje de cambio} = \frac{\text{cantidad de cambio}}{\text{cantidad original}}$$

percent of decrease   A negative percent of change.

porcentaje de disminución   Porcentaje de cambio negativo.

percent of increase   A positive percent of change.

porcentaje de aumento   Porcentaje de cambio positivo.

percent proportion   One ratio or fraction that compares part of a quantity to the whole quantity. The other ratio is the equivalent percent written as a fraction with a denominator of 100.

$$\frac{\text{part}}{\text{whole}} = \frac{\text{percent}}{100}$$

proporción porcentual   Razón o fracción que compara parte de una cantidad a toda la cantidad. La otra razón es el porcentaje equivalente escrito como fracción con 100 de denominador.

$$\frac{\text{parte}}{\text{todo}} = \frac{\text{porcentaje}}{100}$$

percent   A ratio that compares a number to 100.

por ciento   Razón en que se compara un número a 100.

perfect cube   A rational number whose cube root is a whole number. 27 is a perfect cube because its cube root is 3.

cubo perfecto   Número racional cuya raíz cúbica es un número entero. 27 es un cubo perfecto porque su raíz cúbica es 3.

perfect squares   Numbers with square roots that are whole numbers. 25 is a perfect square because the square root of 25 is 5.

cuadrados perfectos   Números cuya raíz cuadrada es un número entero. 25 es un cuadrado perfecto porque la raíz cuadrada de 25 es 5.

perimeter   The distance around a figure.

perímetro   La distancia alrededor de una figura.

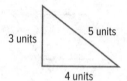

$$P = 3 + 4 + 5 = 12 \text{ units}$$

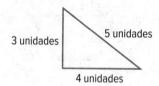

$$P = 3 + 4 + 5 = 12 \text{ unidades}$$

permutation   An arrangement, or listing, of objects in which order is important.

permutación   Arreglo o lista de objetos en la cual el orden es importante.

perpendicular lines   Two lines that intersect to form right angles.

rectas perpendiculares   Dos rectas que se intersecan formando ángulos rectos.

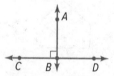

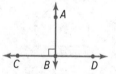

pi   The ratio of the circumference of a circle to its diameter. The Greek letter π represents this number. The value of pi is always 3.1415926... .

pi   Razón de la circunferencia de un círculo al diámetro del mismo. La letra griega π representa este número. El valor de pi es siempre 3.1415926... .

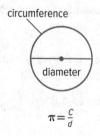

$$\pi = \frac{c}{d}$$

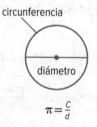

$$\pi = \frac{c}{d}$$

plane   A two-dimensional flat surface that extends in all directions.

plano   Superficie bidimensional que se extiende en todas direcciones.

point-slope form   An equation of the form $y - y_1 = m(x - x_1)$, where m is the slope and (x_1, y_1) is a given point on a nonvertical line.

forma punto-pendiente   Ecuación de la forma $y - y_1 = m(x - x_1)$ donde m es la pendiente y $(x_1 - y_1)$ es un punto dado de una recta no vertical.

point   An exact location in space that is represented by a dot.

punto   Ubicación exacta en el espacio que se representa con un marca puntual.

polygon   A simple, closed figure formed by three or more line segments.

polígono   Figura simple y cerrada formada por tres o más segmentos de recta.

polyhedron   A three-dimensional figure with faces that are polygons.

poliedro   Una figura tridimensional con caras que son polígonos.

population   The entire group of items or individuals from which the samples under consideration are taken.

población   El grupo total de individuos o de artículos del cual se toman las muestras bajo estudio.

positive integer   A number that is greater than zero. It can be written with or without a + sign.

entero positivo   Número que es mayor que cero y se puede escribir con o sin el signo +.

powers   Numbers expressed using exponents. The power 3_2 is read *three to the second power,* or *three squared.*

potencias   Números que se expresan usando exponentes. La potencia 3_2 se lee *tres a la segunda potencia* o *tres al cuadrado.*

precision   The ability of a measurement to be consistently reproduced.

precisión   Capacidad de una medida a ser reproducida consistentemente.

preimage   The original figure before a transformation.

preimagen   Figura original antes de una transformación.

principal   The amount of money invested or borrowed.

capital   Cantidad de dinero que se invierte o que se toma prestada.

prism   A three-dimensional figure with at least three rectangular lateral faces and top and bottom faces parallel.

prisma   Figura tridimensional que tiene por lo menos tres caras laterales rectangulares y caras paralelas superior e inferior.

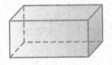

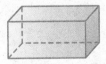

probability model A model used to assign probabilities to outcomes of a chance process by examining the nature of the process.

modelo de probabilidad Un modelo usado para asignar probabilidades a resultados de un proceso aleatorio examinando la naturaleza del proceso.

probability The chance that some event will happen. It is the ratio of the number of favorable outcomes to the number of possible outcomes.

probabilidad La posibilidad de que suceda un evento. Es la razón del número de resultados favorables al número de resultados posibles.

proof A logical argument in which each statement that is made is supported by a statement that is accepted as true.

prueba Argumento lógico en el cual cada enunciado hecho se respalda con un enunciado que se acepta como verdadero.

properties Statements that are true for any number or variable.

propiedades Enunciados que son verdaderos para cualquier número o variable.

property A statement that is true for any numbers.

propiedad Enunciado que se cumple para cualquier número.

proportional The relationship between two ratios with a constant rate or ratio.

proporcional Relación entre dos razones con una tasa o razón constante.

proportion An equation stating that two ratios or rates are equivalent.

proporción Ecuación que indica que dos razones o tasas son equivalentes.

pyramid A polyhedron with one base that is a polygon and three or more triangular faces that meet at a common vertex.

pirámide Un poliedro con una base que es un polígono y tres o más caras triangulares que se encuentran en un vértice común.

Pythagorean Theorem In a right triangle, the square of the length of the hypotenuse c is equal to the sum of the squares of the lengths of the legs a and b.
$a^2 + b^2 = c^2$

Teorema de Pitágoras En un triángulo rectángulo, el cuadrado de la longitud de la hipotenusa es igual a la suma de los cuadrados de las longitudes de los catetos.
$a^2 + b^2 = c^2$

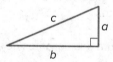

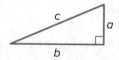

Qq

quadrants The four sections of the coordinate plane separated by the x-axis and y-axis.

cuadrantes Las cuatro secciones del plano de coordenadas separadas por el eje x y el eje y.

quadratic function A function in which the greatest power of the variable is 2.

función cuadrática Función en la cual la potencia mayor de la variable es 2.

quadrilateral A closed figure having four sides and four angles.

cuadrilátero Figura cerrada que tiene cuatro lados y cuatro ángulos.

qualitative graph A graph used to represent situations that do not necessarily have numerical values.

gráfica cualitativa Gráfica que se usa para representar situaciones que no tienen valores numéricos necesariamente.

quantitative data Data that can be given a numerical value.

datos cualitativos Datos que se pueden dar un valor numérico.

quartile A value that divides the data set into four equal parts.

cuartil Valor que divide el conjunto de datos en cuatro partes iguales.

Rr

radical sign The symbol used to indicate a nonnegative square root, $\sqrt{\ }$

signo radical Símbolo que se usa para indicar una raíz cuadrada no negativa, $\sqrt{\ }$.

radius The distance from the center of a circle to any point on the circle.

radio Distancia desde el centro de un círculo hasta cualquier punto del mismo.

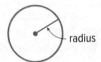

radius

radio

random Outcomes occur at random if each outcome occurs by chance. For example, rolling a number on a number cube occurs at random.

azar Los resultados ocurren aleatoriamente si cada resultado ocurre por casualidad. Por ejemplo, sacar un número en un cubo numerado ocurre al azar.

range The difference between the greatest number (maximum) and the least number (minimum) in a set of data The set of y coordinates in a relation.

rango La diferencia entre el número mayor (máximo) y el número menor (mínimo) en un conjunto de datos. El conjunto de coordenadas y en una relaciòn.

rate of change A rate that describes how one quantity changes in relation to another. A rate of change is usually expressed as a unit rate.

tasa de cambio Tasa que describe cómo cambia una cantidad con respecto a otra. Por lo general, se expresa como tasa unitaria.

rate A ratio comparing two quantities with different kinds of units.

tasa Razón que compara dos cantidades que tienen diferentes tipos de unidades.

ratio table A table with columns filled with pairs of numbers that have the same ratio.

tabla de razones Tabla cuyas columnas contienen pares de números que tienen una misma razón.

rational numbers The set of numbers that can be written in the form $\frac{a}{b}$, where a and b are integers and $b \neq 0$. All integers, fractions, mixed numbers, and percents are rational numbers.

Examples: $1 = \frac{1}{1}, \frac{2}{9}, -2.3 = -2\frac{3}{10}$

números racionales Conjunto de números que puede escribirse en la forma $\frac{a}{b}$, donde a y b son números enteros y $b \neq 0$. Todos los enteros, fracciones, nùmeros mixtos y porcentajes son números racionales.

Ejemplos: $1 = \frac{1}{1}, \frac{2}{9}, -2.3 = -2\frac{3}{10}$

ratio   A comparison of two quantities by division. The ratio of 2 to 3 can be stated as 2 out of 3, 2 to 3, 2 : 3, or $\frac{2}{3}$.

razón   Comparación de dos cantidades mediante división. La razón de 2 a 3 puede escribirse como 2 de cada 3, 2 a 3, 2 : 3, 2 : 3, or $\frac{2}{3}$.

ray   A line that has one endpoint and goes on forever in only one direction.

rayo   Recta con un extremo y la cual se extiende infinitamente en una sola dirección.

real numbers   A set made up of rational and irrational numbers.

números reales   Conjunto de números racionales e irracionales.

reciprocals   The multiplicative inverse of a number. Any two numbers that have a product of 1. Since $\frac{5}{6} \times \frac{6}{5} = 1$, $\frac{5}{6}$ and $\frac{6}{5}$ are reciprocals.

recíproco   El inverso multiplicativo de un nùmero. Cualquier par de números cuyo producto es 1. Como $\frac{5}{6} \times \frac{6}{5} = 1$, $\frac{5}{6}$ y $\frac{6}{5}$ son recíprocos.

rectangle   A parallelogram having four right angles.

rectángulo   Paralelogramo con cuatro ángulos rectos.

rectangular prism   A prism that has two parallel congruent bases that are rectangles.

prisma rectangular   Un prisma con dos bases paralelas congruentes que son rectángulos.

reduction   An image smaller than the original.

reducción   Imagen más pequeña que la original.

reflection   The mirror image produced by flipping a figure over a line. Also called a flip.

reflexión   Transformación en la cual una figura se voltea sobre una recta. También se conoce como simetría de espejo. Tambièn se llama flip.

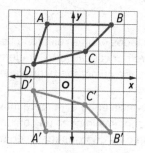

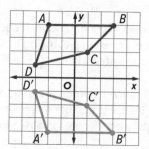

regular polygon   A polygon that has all sides congruent and all angles congruent.

polígono regular   Polígono con todos los lados y todos los ángulos congruentes.

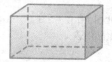

regular pyramid   A pyramid whose base is a regular polygon and in which the segment from the vertex to the center of the base is the altitude.

pirámide regular   Pirámide cuya base es un polígono regular y en la cual el segmento desde el vértice hasta el centro de la base es la altura.

relation   Any set of ordered pairs.

relación   Cualquier conjunto de pares ordenados.

relative frequency   The ratio of the number of experimental successes to the total number of experimental attempts.

frecuencia relativa   Razón del número de éxitos experimentales al número total de intentos experimentales.

remote interior angles   The angles of a triangle that are not adjacent to a given exterior angle.

ángulos internos no adyacentes   Ángulos de un triángulo que no son adya centes a un ángulo exterior dado.

repeating decimal   Decimal form of a rational number.

decimal periódico   Forma decimal de un número racional.

rhombus   A parallelogram having four congruent sides.

rombo   Paralelogramo que tiene cuatro lados congruentes.

right angle   An angle that measures exactly 90°.

ángulo recto   Ángulo que mide exactamente 90°.

right triangle   A triangle having one right angle.

triángulo rectángulo   Triángulo que tiene un ángulo recto.

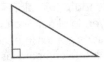

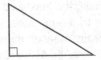

rise   The vertical change between any two points on a line.

elevación   El cambio vertical entre cualquier par de puntos en una recta.

rotational symmetry   A type of symmetry a figure has if it can be rotated less than 360° about its center and still look like the original.

simetría rotacional   Tipo de simetría que tiene una figura si se puede girar menos que 360° en torno al centro y aún sigue viéndose como la figura original.

rotation   A transformation in which a figure is turned about a fixed point.

rotación   Transformación en la cual una figura se gira alrededor de un punto fijo.

run   The horizontal change between any two points on a line.

carrera   El cambio horizontal entre cualquier par de puntos en una recta.

Ss

sales tax   An additional amount of money charged on certain goods and services.

impuesto sobre las ventas   Cantidad de dinero adicional que se cobra por ciertos artículos y servicios.

sample space   The set of all possible outcomes of a probability experiment.

espacio muestral   Conjunto de todos los resultados posibles de un experimento probabilístico.

sample   A randomly selected group chosen for the purpose of collecting data.

muestra   Grupo escogido al azar o aleatoriamente que se usa con el propósito de recoger datos.

scale drawing   A drawing that is used to represent objects that are too large or too small to be drawn at actual size.

dibujo a escala   Dibujo que se usa para representar objetos que son demasiado grandes o demasiado pequeños como para dibujarlos de tamaño natural.

scale factor   The ratio of the lengths of two corresponding sides of two similar polygons.

factor de escala   La razón de las longitudes de dos lados correspondientes de dos polígonos semejantes.

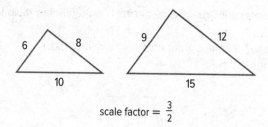

scale factor = $\frac{3}{2}$

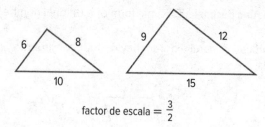

factor de escala = $\frac{3}{2}$

scale model   A model used to represent objects that are too large or too small to be built at actual size.

modelo a escala   Réplica de un objeto real, el cual es demasiado grande o demasiado pequeño como para construirlo de tamaño natural.

scalene triangle   A triangle having no congruent sides.

triángulo escaleno   Triángulo sin lados congruentes.

scale   The set of all possible values of a given measurement, including the least and greatest numbers in the set, separated by the intervals used. Gives the ration that compares the measurements of a drawing or model to the measurement s of the real object.

escala   Conjunto de todos los valores posibles de una medida dada, incluyendo el número menor y el mayor del conjunto, separados por los intervalos usados. Proporciona la ración que compara las mediciones de un dibujo o modelo con la medida s del objeto real.

scaling   To multiply or divide two related quantities by the same number.

homotecia   Multiplicar o dividir dos cantidades relacionadas entre un mismo número.

scatter plot   A graph that shows the relationship between a data set with two variables graphed as ordered pairs on a coordinate plane.

diagrama de dispersión   Gráfica que muestra la relación entre un conjunto de datos con dos variables graficadas como pares ordenados en un plano de coordenadas.

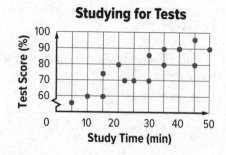

scientific notation   A compact way of writing numbers with absolute values that are very large or very small. In scientific notation, 5,500 is 5.5×10^3

notación científica   Manera abreviada de escribir números con valores absolutos que son muy grandes o muy pequeños. En notación científica, 5,500 es 5.5×10^3.

selling price   The amount the customer pays for an item.

precio de venta   Cantidad de dinero que paga un consumidor por un artículo.

semicircle Half of a circle. The formula for the area of a semicircle is $A = \frac{1}{2}\pi r^2$. The arc measuring 180°

sequence A list of numbers in a specific order, such as 0, 1, 2, 3, or 2, 4, 6, 8.

similar figures Figures that have the same shape but not necessarily the same size.

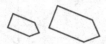

similar polygons Polygons that have the same shape.

similar solids Solids with the same shape. Their corresponding linear measures are proportional, but not necessarily the same size.

similar If one image can be obtained from another by a sequence of transformations and dilations.

simple event One outcome or a collection of outcomes.

simple interest The amount paid or earned for the use of money. The formula for simple interest is $I = prt$.

simple random sample An unbiased sample where each item or person in the population is as likely to be chosen as any other.

simplest form An algebraic expression that has no like terms and no parentheses.

simplify To perform all possible operations in an expression.

simulation An experiment that is designed to model the action in a given situation.

skew lines Lines that do not intersect and are not coplanar.

slant height The altitude or height of each lateral face of a pyramid.

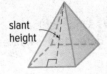

slant height

semicírculo Medio círculo La fórmula para el área de un semicírculo es $A = \frac{1}{2}\pi r^2$. El arco que mide 180°.

sucesión Lista de números en un orden específico como, por ejemplo, 0, 1, 2, 3 ó 2, 4, 6, 8.

figuras semejantes Figuras que tienen la misma forma, pero no necesariamente el mismo tamaño.

polígonos semejantes Polígonos con la misma forma.

sólidos semejantes Sólidos con la misma forma. Sus medidas lineales correspondientes son proporcionales, pero no necesariamente del mismo tamaño.

similar Si una imagen puede obtenerse de otra mediante una secuencia de transformaciones y dilataciones.

eventos simples Un resultado o una colección de resultados.

interés simple Cantidad que se paga o que se gana por el uso del dinero. La fórmula para calcular el interés simple es $I = prt$.

muestra aleatoria simple Muestra de una población que tiene la misma probabilidad de escogerse que cualquier otra.

forma reducida Expresión algebraica que carece de términos semejantes y de paréntesis.

simplificar Realizar todas las operaciones posibles en una expresión.

simulacro Un experimento diseñado para modelar la acción en una situación dada.

rectas alabeadas Rectas que no se intersecan y que no son coplanares.

altura oblicua La longitud de la altura de cada cara lateral de una pirámide.

altura oblicua

slope-intercept form   An equation written in the form $y = mx + b$, where m is the slope and b is the y-intercept.

forma pendiente intersección   Ecuación de la forma $y = mx + b$, donde m es la pendiente y b es la intersección y.

slope   The rate of change between any two points on a line. The ratio of the rise, or vertical change, to the run, or horizontal change. The slope tells you how steep the line is.

pendiente   Razón de cambio entre cualquier par de puntos en una recta. La razón de la altura, o cambio vertical, a la carrera, o cambio horizontal. La pendiente te dice lo empinado que está la línea.

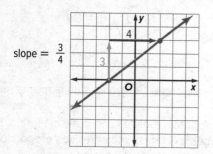

$$\text{slope} = \frac{3}{4}$$

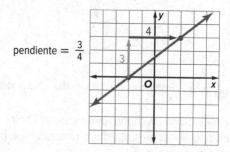

$$\text{pendiente} = \frac{3}{4}$$

solid   A three-dimensional figure formed by intersecting planes.

sólido   Figura tridimensional formada por planos que se intersecan.

solution   The value of a variable that makes an equation true. The solution of $12 = x + 7$ is 5.

solución   Valor de la variable de una ecuación que hace verdadera la ecuación. La solución de $12 = x + 7$ es 5.

solve   To replace a variable with a value that results in a true sentence.

resolver   Reemplazar una variable con un valor que resulte en un enunciado verdadero.

sphere   The set of all points in space that are a given distance from a given point called the center.

esfera   Conjunto de todos los puntos en el espacio que están a una distancia dada de un punto dado llamado centro.

square root   One of the two equal factors of a number. If $a^2 = b$, then a is the square root of b. A square root of 144 is 12 since $12^2 = 144$.

raíz cuadrada   Uno de dos factores iguales de un número. Si $a^2 = b$, la a es la raíz cuadrada de b. Una raíz cuadrada de 144 es 12 porque $12^2 = 144$.

squared   The product of a number and itself. 36 is the square of 6.

raíz cuadrada   El producto de un número por sí mismo. 36 es el cuadrado de 6.

square   A parallelogram having four right angles and four congruent sides.

cuadrado   Paralelogramo con cuatro ángulos rectos y cuatro lados congruentes.

standard deviation   A measure of variation that describes how the data deviates from the mean of the data.

desviación estándar   Una medida de variación que describe cómo los datos se desvía de la media de los datos.

standard form   An equation written, without exponents, in the form $Ax + By = C$.

forma estándar   Una ecuación, sin exponentes, escrita en la forma $Ax + By = C$.

statistical question   A question that anticipates and accounts for a variety of answers.

statistics   The study of collecting, organizing, and interpreting data.

stem-and-leaf plot   A system where data are organized from least to greatest. The digits of the least place value usually form the leaves, and the next place-value digits form the stems.

Stem	Leaf
1	2 4 5
2	1 2 3 3 9
3	0 4 6 7
4	

4 | 7 = 47

stems   The digits of the greatest place value of data in a stem-and-leaf plot.

straight angle   An angle that measures exactly 180°.

substitution   An algebraic model that can be used to find the exact solution of a system of equations.

Subtraction Property of Equality   If you subtract the same number from each side of an equation, the two sides remain equal.

Subtraction Property of Inequality   If you subtract the same number from each side of an inequality, the inequality remains true.

supplementary angles   Two angles are supplementary if the sum of their measures is 180°.

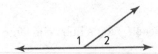

∠1 and ∠2 are supplementary angles.

surface area   The sum of the areas of all the surfaces (faces) of a three-dimensional figure.
S.A. = 2ℓh + 2ℓw + 2hw

S.A. = 2(7 × 3) + 2(7 × 5) + 2(3 × 5)
= 142 square feet

cuestión estadística   Una pregunta que se anticipa y da cuenta de una variedad de respuestas.

estadística   Estudio que consiste en recopilar, organizar e interpretar datos.

diagrama de tallo y hojas   Sistema donde los datos se organizan de menor a mayor. Por lo general, los dígitos de los valores de posición menores forman las hojas y los valores de posición más altos forman los tallos.

Tallo	Hojas
1	2 4 5
2	1 2 3 3 9
3	0 4 6 7
4	

4 | 7 = 47

tallo   Los dígitos del mayor valor de posición de los datos en un diagrama de tallo y hojas.

ángulo llano   Ángulo que mide exactamente 180°.

sustitución   Modelo algebraico que se puede usar para calcular la solución exacta de un sistema de ecuaciones.

propiedad de sustracción de la igualdad   Si restas el mismo número de ambos lados de una ecuación, los dos lados permanecen iguales.

propiedad de desigualdad en la resta   Si se resta el mismo número a cada lado de una desigualdad, la desigualdad sigue siendo verdadera.

ángulos suplementarios   Dos ángulos son suplementarios si la suma de sus medidas es 180°.

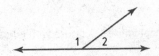

∠1 y ∠2 son ángulos suplementarios.

área de superficie   La suma de las áreas de todas las superficies (caras) de una figura tridimensional.
S.A. = 2ℓh + 2ℓw + 2hw

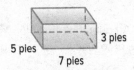

S.A. = 2(7 × 3) + 2(7 × 5) + 2(3 × 5)
= 142 pies cuadrados

survey A question or set of questions designed to collect data about a specific group of people, or population.

encuesta Pregunta o conjunto de preguntas diseñadas para recoger datos sobre un grupo específico de personas o población.

symmetric distribution Data that are evenly distributed.

distribución simétrica Datos que están distribuidos.

symmetric A description of the shape of a distribution in which the left side of the distribution looks like the right side.

simétrico Una descripción de la forma de una distribución en la que el lado izquierdo de la distribución se parece el lado derecho.

system of equations A set of two or more equations with the same variables.

sistema de ecuaciones Sistema de ecuaciones con las mismas variables.

systematic random sample A sample where the items or people are selected according to a specific time or item interval.

muestra aleatoria sistemática Muestra en que los elementos o personas se eligen según un intervalo de tiempo o elemento específico.

Tt

terminating decimal A decimal is called terminating if its repeating digit is 0.

decimal finito Un decimal se llama finito si el dígito que se repite es 0.

term A number, variable, or a product or quotient of numbers and variables separated by a plus or minus signs.

término Un número, una variable, o un producto o cociente de números y variables separados por un signo más o menos.

theorem A statement or conjecture that can be proven.

teorema Un enunciado o conjetura que puede probarse.

theoretical probability The ratio of the number of ways an event can occur to the number of possible outcomes. It is based on what *should* happen when conducting a probability experiment.

probabilidad teórica Razón del número de maneras en que puede ocurrir un evento al número de resultados posibles. Se basa en lo que *debería* pasar cuando se conduce un experimento probabilístico.

third quartile For a data set with median M, the third quartile is the median of the data values greater than M.

tercer cuartil Para un conjunto de datos con la mediana M, el tercer cuartil es la mediana de los valores mayores que M.

three-dimensional figure A figure with length, width, and height.

figura tridimensional Figura que tiene largo, ancho y alto.

tip Also known as a gratuity, it is a small amount of money in return for a service.

propina También conocida como gratificación; es una cantidad pequeña de dinero en recompensa por un servicio.

total surface area The sum of the areas of the surfaces of a solid.

área de superficie total La suma del área de las superficies de un sólido.

transformation An operation that maps a geometric figure, preimage, onto a new figure, image.

transformación Operación que convierte una figura geométrica, la pre-imagen, en una figura nueva, la imagen.

translation A transformation that slides a figure from one position to another without turning.

traslación Transformación en la cual una figura se desliza de una posición a otra sin hacerla girar.

transversal   The third line formed when two parallel lines are intersected.

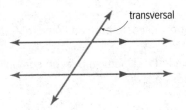

transversal

transversal   Tercera recta que se forma cuando se intersecan dos rectas paralelas.

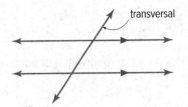

transversal

trapezoid   A quadrilateral with one pair of parallel sides.

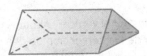

trapecio   Cuadrilátero con un único par de lados paralelos.

tree diagram   A diagram used to show the total number of possible outcomes in a probability experiment.

diagrama de árbol   Diagrama que se usa para mostrar el número total de resultados posibles en un experimento de probabilidad.

triangle   A figure formed by three line segments that intersect only at their endpoints.

triángulo   Figura formada por tres segmentos de recta que se intersecan sólo en sus extremos.

triangular prism   A prism that has two parallel congruent bases that are triangles.

prisma triangular   Un prisma que tiene dos bases congruentes paralelas que triángulos.

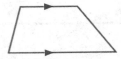

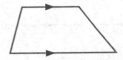

two-column proof   A formal proof that contains statements and reasons organized in two columns. Each step is called a statement, and the properties that justify each step are called reasons.

demostración de dos columnas   Demonstración formal que contiene enunciados y razones organizadas en dos columnas. Cada paso se llama enunciado y las propiedades que lo justifican son las razones.

two-step equation   An equation having two different operations.

ecuación de dos pasos   Ecuación que contiene dos operaciones distintas.

two-step inequality   An inequality than contains two operations.

desigualdad de dos pasos   Desigualdad que contiene dos operaciones.

two-way table   A table that shows data that pertain to two different categories.

tabla de doble entrada   Una tabla que muestra datos que pertenecen a dos categorías diferentes.

Uu

unbiased sample   A sample that is selected so that it is representative of the entire population.

muestra no sesgada   Muestra que se selecciona de modo que sea representativa de la población entera.

unfair game   A game where there is not a chance of each player being equally likely to win.

juego injusto   Juego donde cada jugador no tiene la misma posibilidad de ganar.

uniform probability model   A probability model which assigns equal probability to all outcomes.

modelo de probabilidad uniforme   Un modelo de probabilidad que asigna igual probabilidad a todos los resultados.

unit price   The cost per unit.

precio unitario   El costo por cada unidad.

unit rate/ratio   A rate or ratio with a denominator of 1.

tasa/razón unitaria   Una tasa o razón con un denominador de 1.

univariate data   Data with one variable.

datos univariante   Datos con una variable.

unlike fractions   Fractions with different denominators.

fracciones con distinto denominador   Fracciones cuyos denominadores son diferentes.

variable   A symbol, usually a letter, used to represent a number in mathematical expressions or sentences.

variable   Símbolo, por lo general una letra, que se usa para representar un número en expresiones o enunciados matemáticos.

vertex   A vertex of an angle is the common endpoint of the rays forming the angle.

vértice   El vértice de un ángulo es el extremo común de los rayos que lo forman.

vertical angles   Opposite angles formed by the intersection of two lines. Vertical angles are congruent. In the figure, the vertical angles are $\angle 1$ and $\angle 3$, and $\angle 2$ and $\angle 4$.

ángulos opuestos por el vértice   Ángulos congruentes que se forman de la intersección de dos rectas. En la figura, los ángulos opuestos por el vértice son $\angle 1$ y $\angle 3$, y $\angle 2$ y $\angle 4$.

visual overlap   A visual demonstration that compares the centers of two distributions with their variation, or spread.

superposición visual   Una demostración visual que compara los centros de dos distribuciones con su variación, o magnitud.

volume   The measure of the space occupied by a solid. Standard measures are cubic units such as in^3 or ft^3.

volumen   Medida del espacio que ocupa un sólido. Las medidas estándares son las unidades cúbicas, como $pulg^3$ o $pies^3$.

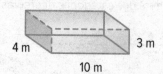

$V = 10 \times 4 \times 3 = 120$ cubic meters

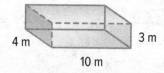

$V = 10 \times 4 \times 3 = 120$ metros cúbicos

voluntary response sample   A sample which involves only those who want to participate in the sampling.

muestra de respuesta voluntaria   Muestra que involucra sólo aquellos que quieren participar en el muestreo.

x-axis The horizontal line of the two perpendicular number lines in a coordinate plane.

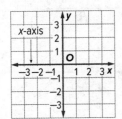

eje x La recta horizontal de las dos rectas numéricas perpendiculares en un plano de coordenadas.

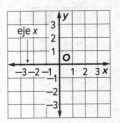

x-coordinate The first number of an ordered pair. It corresponds to a number on the x-axis.

coordenada x El primer número de un par ordenado. Corresponde a un número en el eje x.

x-intercept The x-coordinate of the point where the line crosses the x-axis.

intersección x La coordenada x del punto donde cruza la gráfica el eje x.

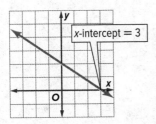

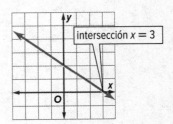

y-axis The vertical line of the two perpendicular number lines in a coordinate plane.

eje y La recta vertical de las dos rectas numéricas perpendiculares en un plano de coordenadas.

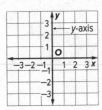

y-coordinate The second number of an ordered pair. The y-coordinate corresponds to a number on the y-axis.

coordenada y El segundo número de un par ordenado, el cual corresponde a un número en el eje y.

y-intercept The *y*-coordinate of the point where the line crosses the *y*-axis.

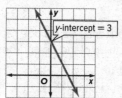

y-intercept = 3

intersección y La coordenada *y* del punto donde cruza la gráfica el eje *y*.

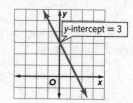

y-intercept = 3

Zz

zero pair The result when one positive counter is paired with one negative counter. The value of a zero pair is 0.

par nulo Resultado de hacer coordinar una ficha positiva con una negativa. El valor de un par nulo es 0.

Chapter 1 Ratios and Proportional Reasoning

Page 4   Chapter 1   Are You Ready?

1. $\frac{2}{15}$ **3.** $\frac{1}{51}$ **5.** No; $\frac{12}{20} = \frac{3}{5}$, $\frac{15}{30} = \frac{1}{2}$

Pages 11–12   Lesson 1-1   Independent Practice

1. 60 mi/h   **3** 3.5 m/s   **5.** Sample answer: about $0.50 per pair   **7.** 510 words   **9** a. 20.04 mi/h   **b.** about 1.5 h
13. Sometimes; a ratio that compares two measurements with different units is a rate, such as $\frac{2 \text{ miles}}{10 \text{ minutes}}$.   **15.** $6.40; Sample answer: The unit rate for the 96-oz container is $0.05 per ounce. So, 128 ounces would cost $0.05 × 128 or $6.40.

Pages 13–14   Lesson 1-1   Extra Practice

17. 203.75 Calories per serving   **19.** 32 mi/gal
21. $108.75 ÷ 15 = $7.25, $7.25 × 18 = $130.50

23.

	Hours Worked	Amount Earned ($)	Earnings per hour ($)	Highest Hourly Rate?
Caleb	5	36.25	7.25	
Jeremy	7.5	65.25	8.70	✔
Rosa	8	54.00	6.75	
Maria	4.25	34.00	8.00	

25. $\frac{2}{7}$ **27.** $\frac{2}{3}$

Pages 19–20   Lesson 1-2   Independent Practice

1. $1\frac{1}{2}$ **3** $\frac{4}{27}$ **5.** $\frac{2}{25}$ **7** $6 per yard   **9.** $\frac{5}{6}$ page per minute   **11.** $\frac{39}{250}$ **13.** $\frac{11}{200}$ **15.** Sample answer: If one of the numbers in the ratio is a fraction, then the ratio can be a complex fraction.   **17.** $\frac{1}{2}$ **19.** $12\frac{1}{2}$ mph

Pages 21–22   Lesson 1-2   Extra Practice

21. 20   **23.** 2   **25.** $\frac{3}{2}$ or $1\frac{1}{2}$ **27.** 3,000 square feet per hour
29. $\frac{31}{400}$ **31.** Sample answer: Set $1\frac{1}{4}$ over 100. Write $1\frac{1}{4}$ as an improper fraction. Then divide the numerator by the denominator.

33.

	Rider	Speed (mph)
Slowest	Julio	$8\frac{1}{6}$
	Elena	$9\frac{1}{9}$
	Kevin	$12\frac{2}{5}$
Fastest	Lorena	$14\frac{1}{4}$

35. 10,000   **37.** 100   **39.** 1,000

Pages 27–28   Lesson 1-3   Independent Practice

1 115 mi/h   **3** 322,000 m/h   **5.** 6.1 mi/h
7. 7,200 Mb/h   **9.** 500 ft/min; Sample answer: All of the other rates are equal to 60 miles per hour.   **11.** 461.5 yd/h

Pages 29–30   Lesson 1-3   Extra Practice

13. 1,760   **15.** 66   **17.** 35.2   **19a.** 6.45 ft/s
19b. 2,280 times   **19c.** 0.11 mi   **19d.** 900,000 times
21.

Animal	Top Speed (mph)
Cheetah	70
Elk	45
Lion	50
Quarter Horse	55

cheetah
23. yes; Since the unit rates are the same, $\frac{1 \text{ poster}}{3 \text{ students}}$, the rates are equivalent.

Pages 35–36   Lesson 1-4   Independent Practice

1

Time (days)	1	2	3	4
Water (L)	225	450	675	900

Yes; the time to water ratios are all equal to $\frac{1}{225}$.
3. The table for Desmond's Time shows a proportional relationship. The ratio between the time and the number of laps is always 73.

5 a. yes; Sample answer:

Side Length (units)	1	2	3	4
Perimeter (units)	4	8	12	16

The side length to perimeter ratio for side lengths of 1, 2, 3, and 4 units is $\frac{1}{4}$, $\frac{2}{8}$ or $\frac{1}{4}$, $\frac{3}{12}$ or $\frac{1}{4}$, $\frac{4}{16}$ or $\frac{1}{4}$. Since these ratios are all equal to $\frac{1}{4}$, the measure of the side length of a square is proportional to the square's perimeter.
b. no; Sample answer:

Side Length (units)	1	2	3	4
Area (units²)	1	4	9	16

The side length to area ratio for side lengths of 1, 2, 3, and 4 units is $\frac{1}{1}$ or 1, $\frac{2}{4}$ or $\frac{1}{2}$, $\frac{3}{9}$ or $\frac{1}{3}$, $\frac{4}{16}$ or $\frac{1}{4}$. Since these ratios are not equal, the measure of the side length of a square is not proportional to the square's area.   **7.** It is not proportional because the ratio of laps to time is not consistent; $\frac{4}{1} \neq \frac{6}{2} \neq \frac{8}{3} \neq \frac{10}{4}$.   **9.** Sample answer: At Beautiful Bouquet, there are always 2 red flowers for every 8 pink flowers in a bouquet. At

All Occasions Flowers, there are always 3 more pink flowers than red flowers in a bouquet. The bouquet for Beautiful Bouquet is a proportional relationship, while the bouquet for All Occasions Flowers is nonproportional.

Pages 37–38 Lesson 1-4 Extra Practice

11.

Degrees Celsius	0	10	20	30
Degrees Fahrenheit	32	50	68	86

No; the degrees Celsius to degrees Fahrenheit ratios are not all equal. **13a.** No; the fee to ride tickets ratios are not equal.
13b. no; Sample answer: The fee increase is inconsistent. The table shows an increase of $4.50 from 5 to 10 tickets, an increase of $4 from 10 to 15 tickets, and an increase of $2.50 from 15 to 20 tickets. **15a.** yes **15b.** no **15c.** no **17.** 20
19. 12 **21.** 3

Page 41 Problem-Solving Investigation The Four-Step Plan

Case 3. $360 **Case 5.** Add 2 to the first term, 3 to the second, 4 to the third, and so on; 15, 21, 28.

Pages 47–48 Lesson 1-5 Independent Practice

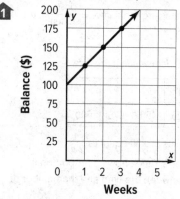

not proportional; The graph does not pass through the origin.
3 Plant B; The graph is a straight line through the origin.
5. proportional; Sample answer: The ordered pairs would be (0, 0), (1, 35), (2, 70). This would be a straight line through origin.

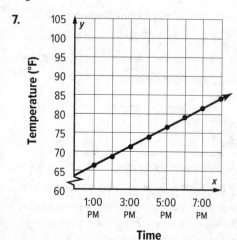

7.

not proportional; The graph does not pass through the origin.

Pages 49–50 Lesson 1-5 Extra Practice

9.

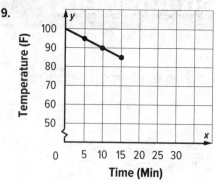

not proportional; The graph does not pass through the origin.
11.

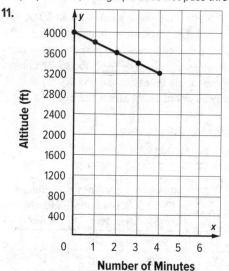

not proportional; The graph does not pass through the origin. **13a.** Yes **13b.** No **13c.** Yes **15.** $\frac{2}{3}$ **17.** $\frac{1}{3}$

Pages 57–58 Lesson 1-6 Independent Practice

1 40 **3.** 3.5 **5.** $\frac{2}{5} = \frac{x}{20}$; 8 ounces **7** $c = 0.50p$; $4.00
9. $\frac{360}{3} = \frac{n}{7}$; 840 visitors **11.** 256 c; Sample answer: The ratio of cups of mix to cups of water is 1:8, which means that the proportion $\frac{1}{8} = \frac{32}{x}$ is true and can be solved. **13.** 18
15. Sample answer: The product of the length and width is constant. The length is not proportional to the width. The proportions are not equal.

Pages 59–60 Lesson 1-6 Extra Practice

17. 7.2 **19.** $\frac{6}{7} = \frac{c}{40}$; about 34 patients **21.** $s = 45w$; $360
23. 11.25 c **25.** No; sample answer: $\frac{12.50}{1} \neq \frac{20}{2} \neq \frac{27.50}{3} \neq \frac{35}{4}$
27. 20 mi/gal

Pages 67–68 Lesson 1-7 Independent Practice

1 6 m per s **3** $9 per shirt; Sample answer: The point (0, 0) represents 0 T-shirts purchased and 0 dollars spent. The point (1, 9) represents 9 dollars spent for 1 T-shirt.
5. 10 inches per hour

7. Sample answer:

Feet	Inches
3	18
6	36
9	54
12	72

9. $x = 8, y = 16, z = 24$

Pages 69–70   Lesson 1-7   Extra Practice

11. $0.03 per minute   **13.** Josh; sample answer: The unit rate for Ramona is $9 per hour. The unit rate for Josh is $10 per hour.   **15.** 195 mi

17.

Input	Add 4	Output
1	1 + 4	5
2	2 + 4	6
3	3 + 4	7
4	4 + 4	8

19.

Input	Multiply by 2	Output
1	1 × 2	2
2	2 × 2	4
3	3 × 2	6
4	4 × 2	8

Pages 75–76   Lesson 1-8   Independent Practice

1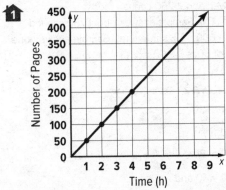

$\frac{50}{1}$ or 50; Adriano read 50 pages every hour.

3 **a.** It shows that car A travels 120 miles in 2 hours.
b. It shows that car B travels 67.5 miles in 1.5 hours.   **c.** the speed of each car at that point   **d.** the average speed of the car   **e.** Car A; the slope is steeper.   **5.** Marisol found $\frac{\text{run}}{\text{rise}}$. Her answer should be $\frac{3}{2}$.   **7.** no; Sample answer: the slope of $\overline{AB}$ is $\frac{0-1}{1-5}$ or $\frac{1}{4}$ and the slope of $\overline{BC}$ is $\frac{3-0}{3-1}$ or $\frac{3}{2}$. If the points were on the same line, the slopes would be equal.

Pages 77–78   Lesson 1-8   Extra Practice

9.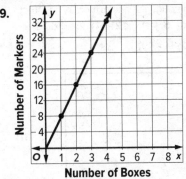

$\frac{8}{1}$; So, there are 8 markers in every box.

11.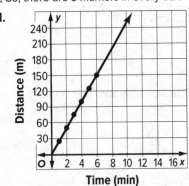

13.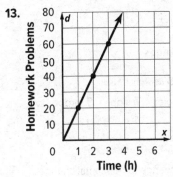

15. 12   **17.** No; sample answer: $\frac{3.50}{1} \neq \frac{4.50}{2}$ **19.** Yes; sample answer: $\frac{7.50}{1} = \frac{15}{2} = \frac{22.5}{3} = \frac{30}{4}$

Pages 83–84   Lesson 1-9   Independent Practice

1 30 lb per bag

3.

Time (h)	1	2	3	4
Charge ($)	75	100	125	150

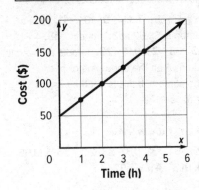

No; sample answer: $\frac{75}{1} \neq \frac{100}{2}$; Because there is no constant ratio and the line does not go through the origin, there is no direct variation. **5** no **7.** no **9.** $y = \frac{7}{4}x$; 21 **11.** $y = \frac{1}{4}x$; 28
13. Sample answer: 9; $5\frac{1}{2}$; 36; 22
15.

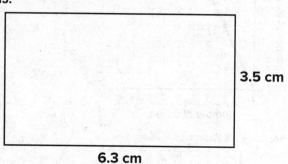

3.5 cm

6.3 cm

19.6 cm

17. 7 c **19.** yes; 0.2 **21a.** No **21b.** Yes **21c.** Yes
21d. No
23.

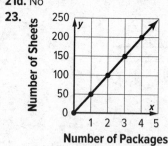

Number of Sheets (y-axis): 0, 50, 100, 150, 200, 250
Number of Packages (x-axis): 1, 2, 3, 4, 5

1. rate **3.** ordered **5.** complex **7.** slope **9.** proportion
11. Dimensional

1. denominator **3.** vertical change to horizontal change

Chapter 2 Percents

1. 48 **3.** $70 **5.** 72.5% **7.** 92%

1. 120.9 **3.** $147.20 **5** 17.5 **7.** 1.3 **9.** 30.1 **11.** $7.19 at Pirate Bay, $4.46 at Funtopia, $9.62 at Zoomland **13.** 4
15 0.61 **17.** 520 **19.** 158 **21.** 0.14 **23.** Sample answer: It is easiest to use a fraction when the denominator of the fraction is a factor of the number. If this is not the case, a decimal may be easier to use.

25. 45.9 **27.** 14.7 **29.** $54 **31.** 0.3 **33.** 2.3 **35.** $19.95
37. 92 customers **39.** 91.8 **41.** 133.92

1. Sample answer: 35
$$\frac{1}{2} \cdot 70 = 35$$
$$0.1 \cdot 70 = 7 \text{ and}$$
$$5 \cdot 7 = 35$$
3 Sample answer: 18
$$\frac{1}{5} \cdot 90 = 18$$
$$0.1 \cdot 90 = 9 \text{ and}$$
$$2 \cdot 9 = 18$$
5. Sample answer: 168
$$\frac{7}{10} \cdot 240 = 168$$
$$0.1 \cdot 240 = 24 \text{ and}$$
$$7 \cdot 24 = 168$$
7. Sample answer: 720
$$(2 \cdot 320) + \left(\frac{1}{4} \cdot 320\right) = 720$$
9. Sample answer: 2
$$0.01 \cdot 500 = 5 \text{ and}$$
$$\frac{2}{5} \cdot 5 = 2$$
11 Sample answer: about 96 mi; $0.01 \cdot 12,000 = 120$ and
$\frac{4}{5} \cdot 120 = 96$
13. Sample answer: 6
$$\frac{2}{3} \cdot 9 = 6$$
15. Sample answer: 24
$$\frac{1}{10} \cdot 240 = 24$$
17a. Sample answer: about 260 canned foods;
$200 + 0.3 \cdot 200$ **17b.** Sample answer: about 780 canned foods; $600 + 0.3 \cdot 600$ **19.** sometimes; Sample answer: one estimate for 37% of 60 is $\frac{2}{5} \cdot 60 = 24$.

21. Sample answer: 135
23. Sample answer: 90
$$\frac{9}{10} \cdot 100 = 90$$
$$0.1 \cdot 100 = 10 \text{ and}$$
$$9 \cdot 10 = 90$$
25. Sample answer: 0.7
$$0.01 \cdot 70 = 0.7$$
27. Sample answer: about 12 muscles; $\frac{3}{10} \cdot 40 = 12$
29a. Sample answer: 420; $\frac{7}{10} \cdot 600 = 420$ **29b.** Greater; both the number of passes and the percent were rounded up.
29c. Tony Romo; sample answer: 64% of 520 must be greater than 64% of 325. **31a.** Yes **31b.** Yes **31c.** No **33.** 300
35. $\frac{1}{4}$

1. 25% **3** 75 **5.** 36% **7.** $68 **9.** 80 **11** 0.2%
13a. about 3.41% **13b.** about 24,795.62 km **13c.** about 6,378.16 km **15.** 20% of 500, 20% of 100, 5% of 100; If the

percent is the same but the base is greater, then the part is greater. If the base is the same but the percent is greater, then the part is greater.

Pages 125–126   Lesson 2-3   Extra Practice

17. 45   **19.** 20   **21.** 20%   **23.** 8 pencils; $\frac{2}{b} = \frac{25}{100}$
25. 120%   **27.** 60%   **29.** $\frac{1}{3}$ **31.** $\frac{1}{21}$ **33.** $\frac{2}{5}$

Pages 131–132   Lesson 2-4   Independent Practice

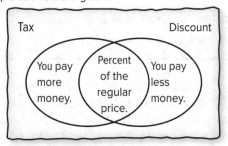

1 75 = n · 150; 50%   **3.** $p = 0.65 \cdot 98$; 63.7   **5.** $p = 0.24 \cdot$
25; 6   **7.** 50 books   **9** a. 37%   b. 31%   **11.** $p = 0.004 \cdot 82.1$;
0.3   **13.** 230 = $n \cdot 200$; 115%   **15.** Sample answer: If the
percent is less than 100%, then the part is less than the whole; if
the percent equals 100%, then the part equals the whole; if the
percent is greater than 100%, then the part is greater than the
whole.   **17.** Sample answer: It may be easier if the percent and
the base are known because after writing the percent as a
decimal or fraction, the only step is to multiply. When using the
percent proportion, you must first find the cross products and
then divide.

Pages 133–134   Lesson 2-4   Extra Practice

19. 26 = $n \times 96$; 27.1%   **21.** 30 = $n \cdot 64$; 46.9%
23. 84 = 0.75 · w; 112   **25.** 64 = 0.8 · w; 80
27. $p = 0.0002 \cdot 5,000$; 1   **29.** $14.80   **31.** <   **33.** <

Page 137   Problem-Solving Investigation   Determine Reasonable Answers

Case 3. no; Sample answer: 48% − 24% = 24% and 24% of 140
is about 35   **Case 5.** 15 + b = 0.5(36 + b); 6 boys; 42 students

Pages 145–146   Lesson 2-5   Independent Practice

1. 20%; increase   **3** 25%; decrease   **5.** 41%; decrease
7 28%   **9.** 38%; decrease   **11a.** 100%   **11b.** 300%
13. about 4.2%   **15.** He did not write a ratio comparing the
change to the original amount. It should have had a
denominator of $52 and the percent of change would be
about 140%.

Pages 147–148   Lesson 2-5   Extra Practice

17. 50%; decrease   **19.** 33%; increase   **21a.** about 3.8%;
increase   **21b.** about 2.9%; decrease   **23.** 25%
25. Monica; 2%   **27.** 3.75   **29.** $75.14

Pages 153–154   Lesson 2-6   Independent Practice

1. $69.60   **3** $1,605   **5** $35.79   **7.** $334.80   **9.** $10.29
11. 7%   **13.** $54, $64.80; The percent of gratuity is 20%. All of
the other pairs have a gratuity of 15%.   **15.** false; Sample
answer: An item costs $25 and you want to mark it up 125%.
Multiply $25 by 125% or 1.25. The new price is $25 + $31.25
or $56.25

Pages 155–156   Lesson 2-6   Extra Practice

17. $14.95   **19.** $44.85   **21.** $14.88   **23.** He should have
added the markup to the cost. $40 + $12 = $52   **25.** printer
paper, file cabinet   **27.** 57.85   **29.** $50

Pages 161–162   Lesson 2-7   Independent Practice

1. $51.20   **3** $6.35   **5** $4.50   **7a.** $28.76, $25.29,
$28.87   **7b.** Funtopia   **9.** $9.00
11. Sample answers are given.

Tax   Discount

You pay more money. | Percent of the regular price. | You pay less money.

13. $25

Pages 163–164   Lesson 2-7   Extra Practice

15. $102.29   **17.** $169.15   **19.** Mr. Chang; $22.50 < $23.99
21. washing machine, dryer, chest freezer   **23.** 29%; increase
25. 35%; decrease

Pages 169–170   Lesson 2-8   Independent Practice

1. $38.40   **3.** $5.80   **5** $1,417.50   **7.** $75.78   **9** a. 5%
b. Yes; he would have $5,208.   **11.** Sample answer: If the rate
is increased by 1%, then the interest earned is $60 more. If the
time is increased by 1 year, then the interest earned is $36
more.   **13.** Investment A; Sample answer: Investment A has a
balance of $2,850 after 30 years and Investment B has a
balance of $2,512.50 after 15 years.

Pages 171–172   Lesson 2-8   Extra Practice

15. $6.25   **17.** $123.75   **19.** $45.31   **21.** $14.06   **23a.** True
23b. False   **23c.** True
25–27.

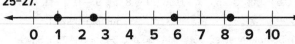

Page 177   Chapter Review   Vocabulary Check

Down
1. increase   **3.** markdown   **5.** selling   **7.** discount
9. sales tax
Across
11. interest

Page 178   Chapter Review   Key Concept Check

1. 300   **3.** 18   **5.** 12

Chapter 3 Rational Numbers

Page 184 Chapter 3 Are You Ready?

1. $\frac{2}{3}$ **3.** $\frac{8}{11}$

5–7.

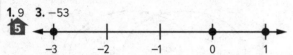

Pages 189–190 Lesson 3-1 Independent Practice

1. 9 **3.** −53

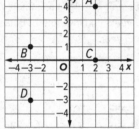

7. 10 **9** 8 **11.** −7 **13.** $299.97; |−200| + |−40| + |−60| = 200 + 40 + 60 = 300 **15.** always; It is true if A and B are both positive or if A or B is negative, and if both A and B are negative. **17a.** Always; the absolute value of a number and its opposite are equal. **17b.** Sometimes; the expressions are equal when $x = 0$. **17c.** Sometimes; the expressions are equal when $x = 0$.

Pages 191–192 Lesson 3-1 Extra Practice

19. 12

21.

23. 11 **25.** 25 **27.** 5 **29a.** True **29b.** True **29c.** True **29d.** False **31.** (−2, 4); II **33.** (−3, −1); III

35–37.

Pages 199–200 Lesson 3-2 Independent Practice

1. 0.5 **3** 0.125 **5.** −0.66 **7.** 5.875 **9.** −0.$\overline{8}$ **11.** −0.$\overline{72}$ **13.** −$\frac{1}{5}$ **15.** $5\frac{24}{25}$ **17** $10\frac{1}{2}$ cm **19.** Sample answer: $\frac{3}{5}$ **21.** Sample answer: $3\frac{1}{7} \approx 3.14286$ and $3\frac{10}{71} \approx 3.14085$; Since 3.1415926... is between $3\frac{1}{7}$ and $3\frac{10}{71}$, Archimedes was correct. **23.** Sample answer: Jason was building a cabin. He cut a board to the length of $8\frac{7}{16}$ feet long.

Pages 201–202 Lesson 3-2 Extra Practice

25. −7.05 **27.** 5.$\overline{3}$ **29.** −$\frac{9}{10}$ **31.** $2\frac{33}{50}$ **33.** $\frac{22}{3}$ **35.** 2.3 hours **37.** $12\frac{1}{20}; \frac{241}{20}; 12\frac{5}{100}$ **39.** 0.1

41–43.

Pages 207–208 Lesson 3-3 Independent Practice

1. >

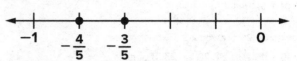

3. > **5** first quiz **7.** −$\frac{5}{8}$, −0.62, −0.615 **9** < **11.** Yes; $69\frac{1}{8} < 69\frac{6}{8}$. **13.** Sample answer: $\frac{63}{32}$ is closest to 2 because the difference of $\frac{63}{32}$ and 2 is the least. **15.** Sample answer: The lengths of four birds are 0.375 foot, $\frac{5}{8}$ foot, 0.4 foot, and $\frac{2}{3}$ feet. List the lengths from least to greatest.; 0.375, 0.4, $\frac{5}{8}, \frac{2}{3}$

Pages 209–210 Lesson 3-3 Extra Practice

17. =

19. > **21.** 7.5%, 7.49, $7\frac{49}{50}$ **23a.** Masked Shrew **23b.** Eastern Chipmunk **23c.** European Mole, Eastern Chipmunk, Spiny Pocket Mouse, Masked Shrew **25a.** True **25b.** False **25c.** True **27.** > **29.** > **31.** >

Pages 219–220 Lesson 3-4 Independent Practice

1. $1\frac{4}{7}$ **3.** −$\frac{2}{3}$ **5** −$1\frac{1}{2}$ **7** $\frac{3}{14}$ **9a.** $\frac{33}{100}$ **9b.** $\frac{67}{100}$ **9c.** $\frac{41}{100}$ **11.** Sample answer: $\frac{11}{18}$ and $\frac{5}{18}; \frac{11}{18} - \frac{5}{18} = \frac{6}{18}$, which simplifies to $\frac{1}{3}$. **13.** always; Sample answer: $\frac{5}{12} - \left(-\frac{1}{12}\right) = \frac{5}{12} + \frac{1}{12}$ or $\frac{6}{12}$ **15.** $15\frac{1}{2}$; Sample answer; $3\frac{3}{8} + 3\frac{3}{8} + 4\frac{3}{8} + 4\frac{3}{8} = 14\frac{12}{8}$ or $15\frac{1}{2}$

Pages 221–222 Lesson 3-4 Extra Practice

17. −$1\frac{2}{3}$ **19.** $\frac{1}{4}$ **21.** $\frac{1}{9}$ **23.** $1\frac{47}{100}$ **25.** $\frac{1}{2}$ c **27.** $1\frac{3}{8}$ or 1.375 pizzas **29.** > **31.** < **33.** 6 **35.** 30 **37.** pizza

Pages 227–228 Lesson 3-5 Independent Practice

1 $\frac{13}{24}$ **3.** $1\frac{2}{5}$ **5.** $\frac{4}{9}$ **7.** −$\frac{26}{45}$ **9.** $1\frac{11}{18}$ **11** subtraction; Sample answer: To find how much time remained, subtract $\left(\frac{1}{6} + \frac{1}{4}\right)$ from $\frac{2}{3}; \frac{1}{4}$ h

13.

Homework	Fraction of Time	
	Pepita	Francisco
Math	$\frac{1}{6}$	$\frac{1}{2}$
English	$\frac{2}{3}$	$\frac{1}{8}$
Science	$\frac{1}{6}$	$\frac{3}{8}$

15. Sample answer: Let $\frac{1}{a}$ and $\frac{1}{b}$ represent the unit fractions, where a and b are not zero. Multiply the first numerator by b and the second numerator by a. Write the product over the denominator ab. Write in simplest form. **17.** $\frac{5}{12}$; Sample answer: $\frac{1}{6}$ of the bucket will be filled with one faucet, while another $\frac{1}{4}$ of the bucket will be filled by the other faucet. Add these fractions to find the sum.

Pages 229–230   Lesson 3-5   Extra Practice

19. $\frac{19}{30}$ **21.** $\frac{11}{20}$ **23.** $-\frac{13}{24}$ **25.** subtraction; Sample answer: To find how much more turkey Makalaya bought, subtract $\frac{1}{4}$ from $\frac{5}{8}$; $\frac{3}{8}$ lb **27.** Theresa did not rename the fractions using the LCD. $\frac{5}{20} + \frac{12}{20} = \frac{17}{20}$ **29a.** False **29b.** True **29c.** True **31.** $4\frac{2}{3}$ **33.** $2\frac{4}{9}$ **35.** $2\frac{7}{8}$

Pages 235–236   Lesson 3-6   Independent Practice

1. $9\frac{5}{9}$ **3.** $8\frac{3}{5}$ **5** $7\frac{5}{12}$ **7.** $4\frac{14}{15}$ **9.** $4\frac{1}{3}$ **11** Subtraction; the width is shorter than the length; $1\frac{3}{4}$ ft **13.** -5 **15.** $13\frac{5}{9}$ **17.** Sample answer: A board with a length of $3\frac{7}{8}$ ft needs to be cut from a $5\frac{1}{2}$-foot existing board. How much wood will be left after the cut is made?; $1\frac{5}{8}$ ft **19.** Sample answer:

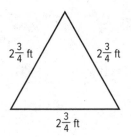

$2\frac{3}{4}$ ft $2\frac{3}{4}$ ft $2\frac{3}{4}$ ft

Pages 237–238   Lesson 3-6   Extra Practice

21. $18\frac{17}{24}$ **23.** $7\frac{5}{7}$ **25.** $5\frac{7}{8}$ **27.** Subtraction twice; the amount of flour is less than the original amount; $2\frac{2}{3}$ c **29.** $7\frac{1}{8}$ yd **31.** $3\frac{1}{12}$; $7\frac{5}{6}$ **33.** 5; 8; 40 **35.** 14 mi; Sample answer: $6\frac{4}{5} \approx 7$ and $1\frac{3}{4} \approx 2$; $7 \times 2 = 14$

Page 241   Problem-Solving Investigation   Draw a Diagram

Case 3. $\frac{3}{8}$ **Case 5.** $\frac{3}{5}$ mi

Pages 247–248   Lesson 3-7   Independent Practice

1. $\frac{3}{32}$ **3.** $-4\frac{1}{2}$ **5.** $\frac{1}{6}$ **7** $\frac{3}{8}$ **9.** -1 **11** $\frac{1}{16}$ **13.** $\frac{1}{3} \times \left(\frac{11}{16}\right) = \frac{11}{48}$ **15.** Sample answer: Three fourths of the students at Walnut Middle School were on the honor roll. Of that group, only $\frac{1}{8}$ of them received all As. What fraction of the students received all As? **17a.** Sample answer: $\frac{1}{2} \times \frac{2}{3} = \frac{2}{6}$ or $\frac{1}{3}$ **17b.** Sample answer: $\frac{3}{4} \times \frac{4}{5} = \frac{12}{20}$ or $\frac{3}{5}$

Pages 249–250   Lesson 3-7   Extra Practice

19. $\frac{1}{9}$ **21.** $\frac{1}{4}$ **23.** $2\frac{1}{6}$ **25.** $\frac{3}{16}$ **27.** $-\frac{8}{27}$ **29.** broccoli: $1\frac{7}{8}$ c, pasta: $5\frac{5}{8}$ c, salad dressing: 1 c, cheese: 2 c; Multiply each amount by $1\frac{1}{2}$. **31a.** True **31b.** True **31c.** False **33.** $12 \div 4 = 3$; $12 \div 3 = 4$ **35.** $10\frac{4}{5} \div 4\frac{1}{2} = 2\frac{2}{5}$; $10\frac{4}{5} \div 2\frac{2}{5} = 4\frac{1}{2}$

Pages 255–256   Lesson 3-8   Independent Practice

1. 12.7 **3** 128.17 **5.** 0.04 **7.** 15.75 **9.** 1.5 **11.** 887.21 mL **13** 1.5 lb **15.** 1,000 mL or 1 L **17.** 0.031 m, 0.1 ft, 0.6 in., 1.2 cm **19.** 0.7 gal, 950 mL, 0.4 L, $1\frac{1}{4}$ c **21.** 5.4 cm; 6.7 cm

Pages 257–258   Lesson 3-8   Extra Practice

23. 158.76 **25.** 121.28 **27.** 41.89 **29.** 2 L **31.** 3 gal **33.** 4 mi **35.** 15.2 cm; 0.152 m **37.** 5.7 **39.** 15,840

Pages 263–264   Lesson 3-9   Independent Practice

1. $\frac{7}{16}$ **3** $\frac{1}{15}$ **5.** $\frac{2}{9}$ **7** 84 movies **9.** $1\frac{1}{4}$

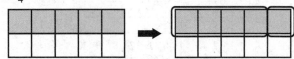

Sample answer: The model on the left shows that one half of a rectangle with ten sections is five sections. Two fifths of ten sections is four sections. The model on the right shows the five sections divided into $1\frac{1}{4}$ groups of four sections **11.** $\frac{1}{6}$ of a dozen; 2 folders **13.** $\frac{10}{3}$

Pages 265–266   Lesson 3-9   Extra Practice

15. $\frac{2}{3}$ **17.** $-7\frac{4}{5}$ **19.** 11 servings **21.** $\frac{1}{2}$ **23.** 13 bracelets **25.** $\frac{9}{20}$ **27.** $\frac{46}{63}$ **29.** $\frac{3}{4}$ ft

Page 269   Chapter Review   Vocabulary Check

1. bar notation **3.** common denominator **5.** terminating

Page 270   Chapter Review   Key Concept Check

1. $\frac{3}{5}$ **3.** denominator **5.** multiply

Chapter 4 Expressions

Page 276   Chapter 4   Are You Ready?

1. 16 **3.** 16 **5.** -50 **7.** -25

Pages 281–282   Lesson 4-1   Independent Practice

1. 34 **3** 3 **5.** 3 **7.** 2 **9.** -1 **11** $50 + 0.17m$; $75.50 **13.** 9.1 **15.** 37.85 **17.** Sample answer: The fee to rent a bicycle is $10 plus $5 for each hour. The expression $5x + 10$ represents the total cost for renting a bicycle for x hours. **19.** Sample answer: $2n + 4$; $2(n + 2)$

Pages 283–284 Lesson 4-1 Extra Practice

21. 4 **23.** −12 **25.** 5 **27.** $8.75 **29a.** True **29b.** False
29c. True **31.** Let p = the number of hours Paida worked;
$p + 8$ **33.** Let n = Nathan's age; $n − 3$

Pages 289–290 Lesson 4-2 Independent Practice

1. 7 is added to the previous term; 28, 35, 42 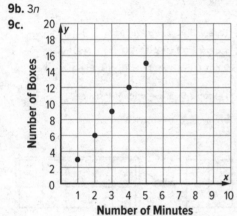 8 is added
to the previous term; 58, 66, 74 **5.** 0.8 is added to the
previous term; 5.6, 6.4, 7.2 **7.** $3n$; 36 in.

9a.

x	1	2	3	4	5
y	3	6	9	12	15

9b. $3n$

9c.

Sample answer: The number of boxes increases by 3 each
minute. The points appear to fall in a straight line passing
through the origin. **9d.** 135 boxes **11.** + 1, + 2, + 3, + 4, ...;
16, 22, 29 **13.** 81; Sample answer: The multiples of 6 from 41
to 523 can be represented by the sequence 42, 48, 54, ...
522. The expression $6n + 36$ represents this sequence. When
$n = 81$, the value of the expression is 522. So, the 81st term
of the sequence is 522. There are 81 multiples of 6 between
41 and 523.

Pages 291–292 Lesson 4-2 Extra Practice

15. 10 is added to the previous term; 46, 56, 66 **17.** 1.5 is
added to the previous term; 10.5, 12.0, 13.5 **19.** 4 is added to
the previous term; 20.6, 24.6, 28.6 **21.** 25 is added to the
previous term; 120, 145, 170 **23a.** Each figure is 8 less than
the previous figure. **23b.** 40, 32 **25.** 33, 30, 27 **27a.** True
27b. True **27c.** False **29.** 1 **31.** 64 **33.** 5 **35.** $1.50

Pages 299–300 Lesson 4-3 Independent Practice

1. Commutative (+) **3** Associative (+) **5.** false;
Sample answer: $(24 \div 4) \div 2 \neq 24 \div (4 \div 2)$
7. = (15 + 12) + 8a   Associative (+)
   = 27 + 8a   Simplify.

9 = $3x \cdot (x \cdot 7)$ Commutative (×)
   = $(3x \cdot x) \cdot 7$ Associative (×)
   = $3x^2 \cdot 7$ Simplify.
   = $3 \cdot 7 \cdot x^2$ Commutative (×)
   = $(3 \cdot 7) \cdot x^2$ Associative (×)
   = $21x^2$ Simplify.

11. [7 + (47 + 3)][5 · (2 · 3)], Associative (+); (7 + 50)[5 · (2 · 3)],
Simplify; 57[5 · (2 · 3)], Simplify; 57[(5 · 2) · 3], Associative (×);
57 · 10 · 3, Simplify; (57 · 10) · 3, Associative (×); 570 · 3,
Simplify; 1,710 **13.** Blake incorrectly multiplied both the 5
and m by 4. He should have used the Associative Property to
group the 5 and 4 together, simplify, and then multiply by m.
$4 \cdot (5 \cdot m) = 20m$ **15a.** no; Sample answer: $2 − 3 = −1$
and −1 is not a whole number **15b.** no; Sample answer:
$1 + 1 = 2$ and 2 is not a member of the set.

Pages 301–302 Lesson 4-3 Extra Practice

17. Commutative (×) **19.** Associative (+) **21.** 48 s; Sample
answer: 12.4 + 12.6 = 25 and 11.8 + 11.2 = 23, 25 + 23 = 48
23. = (18 + 5) + 6m   Associative (+)
   = 23 + 6m   Simplify.

25. = 10 · 7 · y   Commutative (×)
   = (10 · 7) · y   Associative (×)
   = 70y   Simplify.
27. 2(2.29) + 2(2.21) + 2.50; 2(2.29) + 2.50 + 2(2.21);
2.50 + 2(2.21 + 2.29) **29.** 36 **31.** 226 **33.** 74
35. $1.25(3) + $0.45(2); $4.65

Pages 307–308 Lesson 4-4 Independent Practice

1. 33 **3** −30 **5.** 4 **7.** $−12x + 24$ **9.** $30 − 6q$
11. $−15 + 3b$ **13** $27.40; 4($7.00 − $0.15) =
$4 · 7 − 4 · 0.15$
15. 315;
    $9(30 + 5) = 9(30) + 9(5)$
           $= 270 + 45$
17. 672;
    $(100 + 12)6 = 100(6) + 12(6)$
             $= 600 + 72$
19. 488;
    $4(120 + 2) = 4(120) + 4(2)$
           $= 480 + 8$
21. Sample answer: $6(2a + 3b − c)$ **23.** $2a + ay + 2b + by$
25. No; $3 + (4 \cdot 5) = 23$ but $(3 + 4) \cdot (3 + 5) = 56$

Pages 309–310 Lesson 4-4 Extra Practice

27. 24 **29.** $−8a − 8b$ **31.** $−2p − 14$ **33.** $n(4.75 + 2.50)$ +
30; $7.25n + 30$ **35.** $−12ab − 30ac$ **37.** $6y + 12z$
39. $−72p + 48n$ **41.** 3 × ($18.95 + $14.95 + $9.95); $131.55;
Sample answer: The ticket prices can be added first and then
the sum can be multiplied by 3. This requires fewer steps and
easier computations than multiplying each price by 3 and then
adding the resulting products. **43.** −46 **45.** −47

Page 313 Problem-Solving Investigation Make a Table

Case 3. 26 containers **Case 5.** $2n + 2$; 18 toothpicks

Pages 319–320 Lesson 4-5 Independent Practice

1. $11x + 11$ **3** $4x − 16$ **5.** $4x + 14$ **7.** $(22x + 10)$ mm;
230 mm **9** $−x + 2$ **11.** $8.7x − 1.6$ **13.** Sample answer:
$(10x + 2)$ and $(−15x + 2)$ **15.** $2x + 1$; The expression $2x + 1$
will always be odd when x is an integer because when an

integer is doubled, the result is always even. Adding one to the result will give an odd number.

Pages 321–322 Lesson 4-5 Extra Practice

17. $-4x + 16$ **19.** $-2x - 2$ **21.** $-6x + 5$ **23.** $(24x + 9)$ yd; 177 yd **25a.** False **25b.** False **25c.** True **27.** 35 **29.** 85

Pages 327–328 Lesson 4-6 Independent Practice

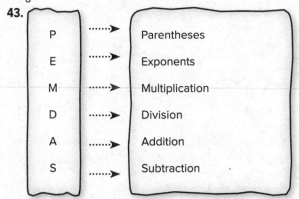 $5x + 2$ **3.** $2x + 2$ **5.** $8x - 12$ **7.** $5x - 2$; 248 customers **9.** $x + 0.51$ **11.** Sample answer: The additive inverse of $(2x + 1)$ is $(-2x - 1)$.

$(5x + 3) - (2x + 1) = (5x + 3) + (-2x - 1)$
$= 5x + 3 + (-2x) + (-1)$
$= 5x + (-2x) + 3 + (-1)$
$= 3x + 2$

13. $-x + 5$ **15.** Sample answer: The rule is to add the inverse when subtracting integers, and is applied to each term in the linear expression that is subtracted.

Pages 329–330 Lesson 4-6 Extra Practice

17. $-3x + 6$ **19.** $-16x + 2$ **21.** $-4x - 7$ **23.** $0.8x + 0.6$ **25.** $-x + 2$ **27.** $12 + 1.50t - (10 + 1.25t) = 2 + 0.25t$ **29.** $(12x - 4)$ ft; 32 ft **31.** $-\frac{1}{4}$ **33.** $\frac{1}{8}$ **35.** $\frac{2}{3}$

Pages 339–340 Lesson 4-7 Independent Practice

1. 24 **3** $36k$ **5.** cannot be factored **7** 4 units by $(x - 2)$ units **9.** $(x + 2)$ dollars **11.** $5(x + 4)$ units^2 **13.** $4(5x + 19)$ units^2 **15.** Sample answer: $20m$ and $12mn$ **17.** $6(4x - y)$

Pages 341–342 Lesson 4-7 Extra Practice

19. $6rs$ **21.** $20x$ **23.** $25xy$ **25.** $6(3x + 1)$ **27.** $5(2x - 7)$ **29.** $10(3x - 4)$ **31.** $(2x + 5)$ in. **33.** $\frac{2}{3}(x + 9)$ **35.** $\frac{5}{6}(x - 36)$ **37.** $\frac{3}{8}(x + 48)$ **39.** $16ab, 12a; 28a, 20a$ **41.** $3a + 30$

43.

P	·······➤	Parentheses
E	·······➤	Exponents
M	·······➤	Multiplication
D	·······➤	Division
A	·······➤	Addition
S	·······➤	Subtraction

Pages 347–348 Lesson 4-8 Independent Practice

1. $(-5)^4$ **3.** m^5 **5.** $\frac{1}{81}$ **7** 8,000,000,000 or 8 billion **9** -311 **11.** 16 **13a.** 10^2 **13b.** 10^6 **13c.** 10^9 **13d.** 10^{15} **15.** Sample answer: As the exponent decreases by 1, the simplified answer is divided by 3; $\frac{1}{2}$

Pages 349–350 Lesson 4-8 Extra Practice

17. $3^3 \cdot p^3$ **19.** $\left(-\frac{5}{6}\right)^3$ **21.** $4^2 \cdot b^4$ **23.** 224 **25.** =

27a.

Side Length (in.)	Perimeter (in.)	Area (in^2)
1	4	1
2	8	4
3	12	9
4	16	16
5	20	25
6	24	36
7	28	49
8	32	64
9	36	81
10	40	100

27b.

Perimeter and Area of a Square

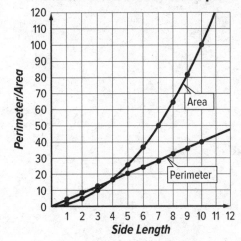

27c. Sample answer: The graph representing perimeter of a square is linear because each side length is multiplied by 4. The graph representing area of a square is nonlinear because each side length is squared and does not increase at a constant rate. **29.** 6^3 in^3 **31.** -31 **33.** 1

Pages 355–356 Lesson 4-9 Independent Practice

1. $\frac{1}{7^{10}}$ **3.** $\frac{1}{g^7}$ **5.** 12^{-4} **7.** 5^{-3} **9.** $10^{-1}, 10^{-2}, 10^{-3}, 10^{-6}$ **11.** $\frac{1}{128}$ **13** y^3 **15.** 81 **17.** y^4 **19** 10^5 or 100,000 times **21.** $11^{-3}, 11^0, 11^2$; Sample answer: The exponents in order from least to greatest are $-3, 0, 2$. **23.** Sample answer: $\left(\frac{1}{2}\right)^{-1} = 2, \left(\frac{34}{43}\right)^{-1} = \frac{43}{34}, \left(\frac{56}{65}\right)^{-1} = \left(\frac{65}{56}\right)$; When you raise a fraction to the -1 power, it is the same as finding the reciprocal of the fraction.

Pages 357–358 Lesson 4-9 Extra Practice

25. $\frac{1}{3^5}$ **27.** $\frac{1}{6^8}$ **29.** $\frac{1}{s^9}$ **31.** z^{-1} or $\frac{1}{z}$ **33.** b^{-12} or $\frac{1}{b^{12}}$ **35.** $\frac{1}{16}$ **37.** $\frac{1}{10,000}$ **39.** 12 **41.** -11 **43.** micrometer: 10^{-6}; millimeter: 10^{-3}; nanometer: 10^{-9}; picometer: 10^{-12} **45.** 1,000 **47.** 100,000 **49.** 100 **51.** 100 **53.** 10

Pages 363–364   Lesson 4-10   Independent Practice

1. 3,160   **3.** 0.0000252   **5.** 7.2×10^{-3} **7** Arctic, Southern, Indian, Atlantic, Pacific   **9.** 17.32 millimeters; the number is small so choosing a smaller unit of measure is more meaningful.   **11** $<$ **13.** 1.2×10^6; 1.2×10^5 is only 120,000, but 1.2×10^6 is just over one million.   **15.** Sample answer: 3.01×10^2, 5.01×10^2; $3.01 \times 10^2 < 5.01 \times 10^2$

Pages 365–366   Lesson 4-10   Extra Practice

17. 7.07×10^{-6} **19.** 0.0078   **21.** 6.7×10^3 **23.** 3.7×10^{-2} **25.** 2.2×10^3, 310,000, 3.1×10^7, 216,000,000   **27a.** No   **27b.** Yes   **27c.** Yes   **27d.** No   **29.** 10.232   **31.** 677.6   **33.** $50x^7$

Pages 371–372   Lesson 4-11   Independent Practice

1. 4   **3.** no real solution   **5** -1.6 **7.** ± 9 **9.** ± 0.13 **11.** -0.5 **13** 13 students   **15.** 44 in.   **17.** 24 m   **19.** $\frac{25}{81}$ **21.** x **23.** Sample answer: There are no two equal numbers that have a product of -4, but $(-2)(-2)(-2) = -8$.

Pages 373–374   Lesson 4-11   Extra Practice

25. -9 **27.** 14   **29.** -6 **31.** -10 **33.** ± 10 **35.** ± 1.1 **37.** 1.1   **39.** 25   **41.** 110.25   **43.** 156,816 ft^2, 174,724 ft^2 **45.** 2,197   **47.** 3,375   **49.** 55   **51.** 20   **53.** $64r^9 s^3$ units^3

Page 377   Chapter Review   Vocabulary Check

Across
7. sequence   **11.** counterexample
13. define
Down
1. exponent   **5.** variable   **9.** term

Page 378   Chapter Review   Key Concept Check

1. $1 + 3$ **3.** $2x - 4$ **5.** $3(x + 7)$

Index

Index

Index

Index

=

Name _____

Work Mats

WM2   **Centimeter Grid**

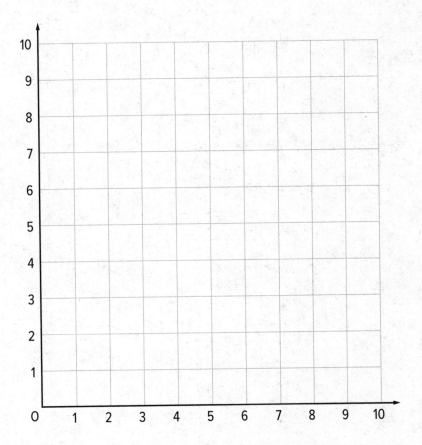

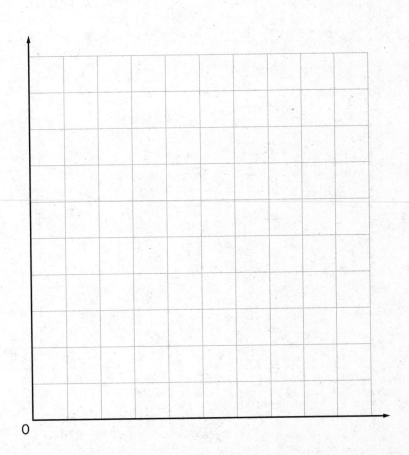

Work Mats

Name ______________________

0 1 2 3 4 5 6 7 8 9
−11 −10 −9 −8 −7 −6 −5 −4 −3 −2 −1 0 1 2 3 4 5 6 7 8 9 10 11

What Are Foldables and How Do I Create Them?

Foldables are three-dimensional graphic organizers that help you create study guides for each chapter in your book.

Step 1 Go to the back of your book to find the Foldable for the chapter you are currently studying. Follow the cutting and assembly instructions at the top of the page.

Step 2 Go to the Key Concept Check at the end of the chapter you are currently studying. Match up the tabs and attach your Foldable to this page. Dotted tabs show where to place your Foldable. Striped tabs indicate where to tape the Foldable.

Step 1

Step 2

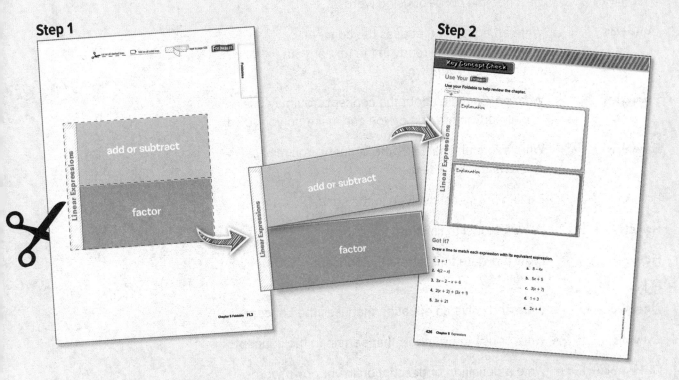

How Will I Know When to Use My Foldable?

When it's time to work on your Foldable, you will see a Foldables logo at the bottom of the **Rate Yourself!** box on the Guided Practice pages. This lets you know that it is time to update it with concepts from that lesson. Once you've completed your Foldable, use it to study for the chapter test.

Rate Yourself!

How well do you understand percent and proportions? Circle the image that applies.

Clear   Somewhat   No So
          Clear   Clear

For more help, go online to access a Personal Tutor.

Tutor

FOLDABLES Time to update your Foldable!

How Do I Complete My Foldable?

No two Foldables in your book will look alike. However, some will ask you to fill in similar information. Below are some of the instructions you'll see as you complete your Foldable. **HAVE FUN** learning math using Foldables!

Instructions and what they mean

Best Used to...	Complete the sentence explaining when the concept should be used.
Definition	Write a definition in your own words.
Description	Describe the concept using words.
Equation	Write an equation that uses the concept. You may use one already in the text or you can make up your own.
Example	Write an example about the concept. You may use one already in the text or you can make up your own.
Formulas	Write a formula that uses the concept. You may use one already in the text.
How do I...?	Explain the steps involved in the concept.
Models	Draw a model to illustrate the concept.
Picture	Draw a picture to illustrate the concept.
Solve Algebraically	Write and solve an equation that uses the concept.
Symbols	Write or use the symbols that pertain to the concept.
Write About It	Write a definition or description in your own words.
Words	Write the words that pertain to the concept.

Meet Foldables Author Dinah Zike

Dinah Zike is known for designing hands-on manipulatives that are used nationally and internationally by teachers and parents. Dinah is an explosion of energy and ideas. Her excitement and joy for learning inspires everyone she touches.

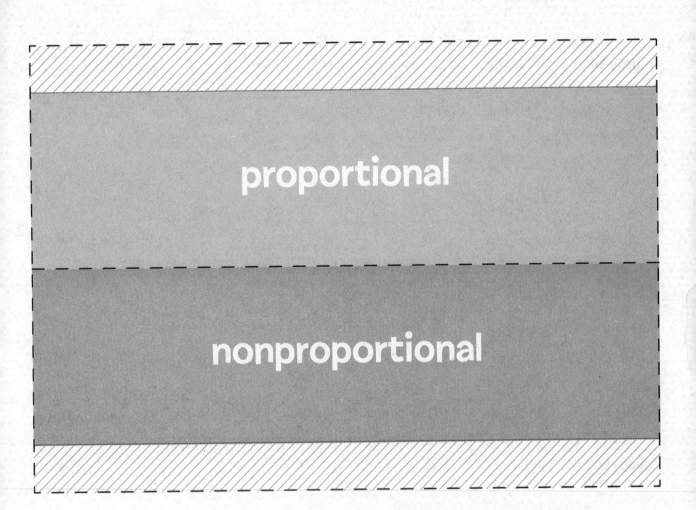

proportional

nonproportional

cut on all dashed lines | fold on all solid lines | tape to page 90

FOLDABLES®

page 90

Tab 1

Write About It

Write About It

page 90

Tab 2

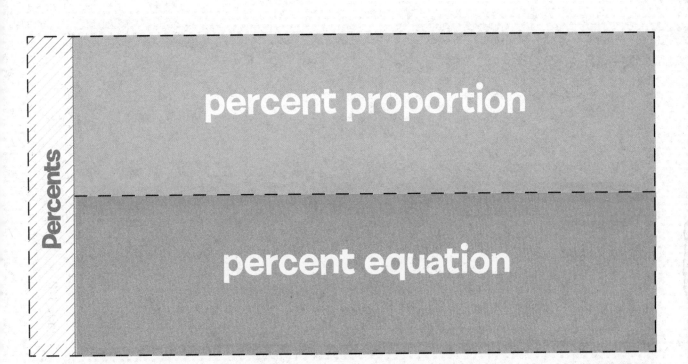

Percents

percent proportion

percent equation

cut on all dashed lines   fold on all solid lines   tape to page 178   **FOLDABLES**

Definition

Definition

page 178

Operations with Fractions

➕ or ➖ like fractions	➗ fractions
✖ fractions	➕ or ➖ unlike fractions

✂ cut on all dashed lines   ▭ fold on all solid lines   tape to page 270   **FOLDABLES**

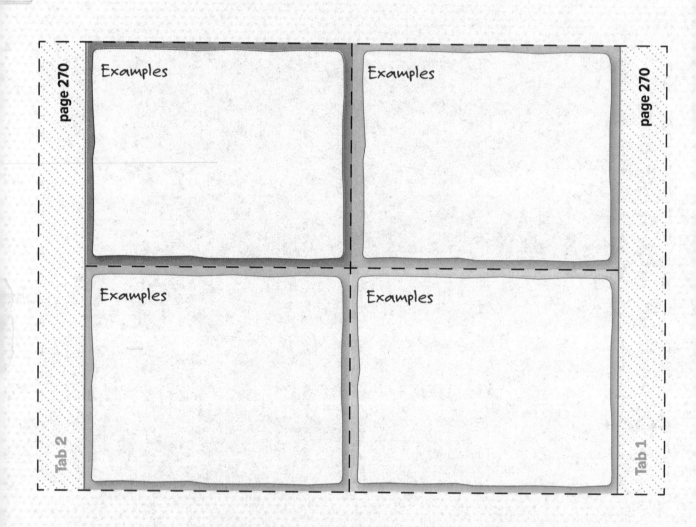

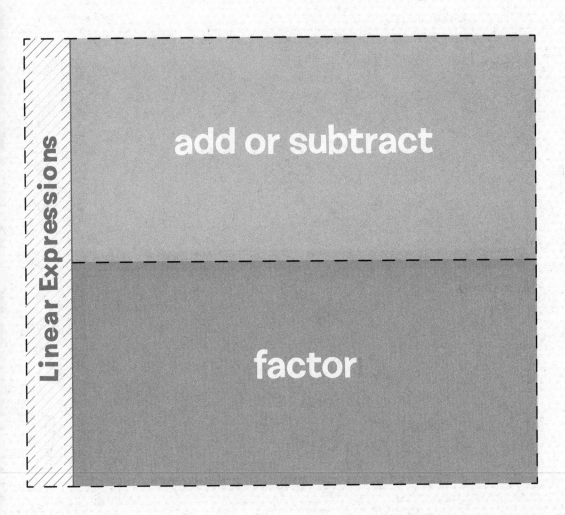

Linear Expressions

add or subtract

factor

Examples

Examples

page 378